Psychology, Spelling and Education

Multilingual Matters

Attitudes and Language
    COLIN BAKER
Breaking the Boundaries
    EUAN REID and HANS H. REICH (eds)
Child Language Disability: Volume I and II
    KAY MOGFORD-BEVAN and JANE SADLER (eds)
Critical Theory and Classroom Talk
    ROBERT YOUNG
Deaf-ability - Not Disability
    WENDY McCRACKEN and HILARY SUTHERLAND
Education for Work
    DAVID CORSON (ed.)
Education of Chinese Children in Britain:
A Comparative Study with the United States of America
    LORNITA YUEN-FAN WONG
Emerging Partnerships: Current Research in Language and Literacy
    DAVID WRAY (ed.)
Fluency and Accuracy
    HECTOR HAMMERLY
Language Acquisition: The Age Factor
    D.M. SINGLETON
Language Policy Across the Curriculum
    DAVID CORSON
Local Management of Schools
    GWEN WALLACE (ed.)
Managing Better Schools and Colleges
    PAMELA LOMAX (ed.)
Oral Language Across the Curriculum
    DAVID CORSON
Parents on Dyslexia
    S. van der STOEL (ed.)
Performance Indicators
    C.T. FITZ-GIBBON (ed.)
School to Work in Transition in Japan
    KAORI OKANO
Story as Vehicle
    EDIE GARVIE
Teacher Supply and Teacher Quality
    GERALD GRACE and MARTIN LAWN (eds)
The World in a Classroom
    V. EDWARDS and A. REDFERN

Please contact us for the latest book information:
Multilingual Matters Ltd,
Frankfurt Lodge, Clevedon Hall, Victoria Road,
Clevedon, Avon BS21 7SJ, England

Psychology, Spelling and Education

Edited by

Chris M. Sterling and Cliff Robson

MULTILINGUAL MATTERS LTD
Clevedon • Philadelphia • Adelaide

Library of Congress Cataloging in Publication Data

Psychology, Spelling and Education/Edited by Chris M. Sterling & Cliff Robson
p. cm.
Includes bibliographical references and index.
1. English language–Orthography and spelling–Congresses.
I. Sterling, Chris M., 1950- . II. Robson, Cliff.
LB1574.P79   1992
428.1–dc20

British Library Cataloguing in Publication Data

A CIP catalogue record for this book is available from the British Library.

ISBN 1-85359-166-1 (hbk)
ISBN 1-85359-165-3 (pbk)

Multilingual Matters Ltd

UK: Frankfurt Lodge, Clevedon Hall, Victoria Road, Clevedon, Avon BS21 7SJ.
USA: 1900 Frost Road, Suite 101, Bristol, PA 19007, USA.
Australia: P.O. Box 6025, 83 Gilles Street, Adelaide, SA 5000, Australia.

Copyright © 1992 Chris M. Sterling, Cliff Robson and the authors of individual chapters.

All rights reserved. No part of this work may be reproduced in any form or by any means without permission in writing from the publisher.

Typeset by Wayside Books, Clevedon.
Printed and bound in Great Britain by the Longdunn Press, Bristol.

Contents

Preface
Chris Sterling and Cliff Robson vii

Glossary ix

Introduction to the Psychology of Spelling
Chris Sterling 1

SECTION ONE: THE ENGLISH SPELLING SYSTEM 15

1 Teaching Literacy First, Traditional English Orthography Second
   Christopher Upward 18

2 An Orthography as a Theory of a Language
   Robert Veltman 30

SECTION TWO: SPELLING PROCESSES 43

3 Cognitive Theories of Spelling and Implications for Education
   Philip H. K. Seymour 50

4 Interactions Between Lexical and Assembled Spelling
   (In English, Italian and Welsh)
   Christopher Barry 71

5 On Recognising Misspelled Words
   Elaine Funnell 87

6 Methodological Issues in the Investigation of Spelling and Spelling
   Development
   H. M. Pattison and J. Collier 100

SECTION THREE: THE DEVELOPMENT OF SPELLING ABILITY 115

7 Spelling is Integral to Learning to Read
   Nick Ellis and Suzanne Cataldo 122

8 Alphabetic Spelling: Predicting Eventual Literacy Attainment
   Nata Kyrtsis Goulandris 143

9 'Invented' Spelling and Learning to Read
   Laura Huxford, Colin Terrell and Lynette Bradley 159

10 Developmental Differences in Phonological Spelling Strategies
   Emma Taylor and Margaret Martlew 168

SECTION FOUR: SPELLING PROBLEMS 181

11 Spelling and Speaking in Pre-lingual Deafness: Unexpected Evidence for Isolated 'Alphabetic' Spelling Skills
   Ruth Campbell, Vivian Burden and Helen Wright 185

12 Why are Some 'Normal' Readers Such Poor Spellers?
   Vivian Burden 200

SECTION FIVE: EDUCATIONAL PRACTICE 215

13 Towards Spelling Autonomy
   Margaret L. Peters 220

14 A Framework for Orthographic Assessment and Remediation
   Philip H. K. Seymour, Frances Bunce and Henryka M. Evans 224

15 Spelling Remediation for Dyslexic Children using the SelfSpell Programs
   Roderick I. Nicolson, Susan Pickering and Angela J. Fawcett 250

16 Phonological Spelling in Young Children and some Origins of Phonetically Plausible and Implausible Errors
   Chris Sterling and Julie Seed 268

CONCLUSIONS
Chris Sterling 282

INDEX 295

Preface

The chapters in this book are based on work presented by the authors at a conference on 'Psychology, Spelling and Education' at Newcastle Polytechnic on 9 July, 1990. The purpose of the conference was to bring together all those interested in spelling, especially researchers from linguistics, psychology, and education. In our experience, people from these different areas seem to be working in relative isolation from each other and it was hoped that the conference would go some way to remedying this unsatisfactory situation. There is clearly a long way to go before we reach the kind of cross-fertilisation of ideas we'd like to see and we hope that this volume continues what the conference began.

Chris Sterling
Cliff Robson
Newcastle Polytechnic
September 1991

Glossary

Alphabetic writing systems. Orthographies which represent each sound (phoneme) of the language with a different symbol (letter). English is substantially, but not wholly, alphabetic.

Digraphs. Graphemes, representing single phonemes, which consist of two-letter combinations, e.g. **CH, TH, OA**, etc. Note: **PR, CL**, etc. are not digraphs because each letter represents a different phoneme, /**p+r**/, /**k+l**/, etc.

Dyslexia. A disorder manifested by difficulty in learning to read despite conventional instructional, adequate intelligence and sociocultural opportunity. It is dependent upon fundamental cognitive disabilities which are frequently of constitutional origin (World Federation of Neurology, 1968).

Dysgraphia. Used in this text in a circumscribed way to mean an inability to spell.

Graphemes. Units in a writing system. In English they usually represent phonemes and are generally equivalent to letters (e.g. **B, P, A, E**) but sometimes consist of more than one letter (e.g. **SH, EE, TT, AI**).

Graphotactic Rules. Literally 'letter positioning' rules. Typical of many traditional spelling rules, e.g. 'I before E except after C'. Usually devised and understood in an arbitrary manner and learned by rote, without reference to the internal structure of the language the orthography represents. They are therefore 'spelling', rather than 'orthographical' rules but many of them can be orthographically explained, e.g. the rule preventing the occurrence of VV.

Homophones. Words which sound the same but which are spelled differently, e.g. *maid & made, herd & heard,* etc.

Hypermedia. A term first coined by Nelson in the 60s to refer to 'new forms of writing appearing on computer screens that will branch or perform at the reader's command. A hypertext is a non-sequential form of writing: only the computer display makes it practical'. Only recently has sufficient and affordable computer power become available to realise this dream, and within the last two years, fuelled by Atkinson's HyperCard™ environment on the Apple Macintosh, hypertext (the more logical term) and hypermedia applications and developments have burgeoned. Hypermedia refers to computer-based information resources which transcend the traditional sequential organisation of textbooks ('flat text') to provide a variety of links (usually hierarchical) to related information, thus encouraging 'browsing' where the reader can navigate through a large database naturally, just accessing the information directly relevant at that time.

Lexicon. Generally synonymous with dictionary. Usually used in this text to refer specifically to an individual's mental dictionary *or* vocabulary *or* words known to him/her. Psychologists often refer to an orthographic lexicon (mental dictionary of the written form of words) and a phonological lexicon (mental dictionary based on the sounds of words).

Logographic writing systems. Orthographies in which symbols represent whole words or meanings, e.g. Chinese.

Morphemes. The smallest meaning-bearing units in the composition of words. Commonly classified into free morphemes, which can occur on their own as words (e.g. *cat, walk, sad*) and bound morphemes, which can only occur in combinations (e.g. **PRE-, UN-, -S, -ED, -NESS**). Thus words sometimes consist of single, free, morphemes (e.g. *cat, walk, sad*), sometimes of combinations of free morphemes (e.g. *catwalk, bedroom, rainfall*) and sometimes of combinations of free and bound morphemes (*cat+s, walk+ed, sad+ness, un+appreciat+ive+ly*).

Morphophonemic writing systems. Orthographies, such as English, which represent morphemic as well as phonemic information, e.g. in English the spelling of the past tense morpheme is always **-ED** (ignoring exceptions such as *heard*) even though its sound varies. Contrast: *walked* ('walkt'), *hunted* ('huntid') and *called* ('calld').

Orthography. The writing system of a language, particularly the rules or principles underlying it. English orthography is substantially, but not wholly, alphabetic in that there is a general correspondence between the sounds (phonemes) and the letters of the alphabet. Orthographies include the symbols used, the rules for combining them to write words or sounds, rules of punctuation, rules of 'pointing' (e.g. accents in French) and conventions such as capitalisation and use of apostrophes. Orthographies which represent only sounds are sometimes referred to as 'shallow', while those which *also* represent other kinds of linguistic information, such as morphemes, are somtimes referred to as 'deep'.

Phonemes. The individual sounds of a language which combine to form the words of that language. Thought to be a product of perception rather than identifiable units in the acoustic signal. Written using the phonetic alphabet, which consists of a combination of conventional letters and special symbols between slashes, e.g. /kæt/ = *cat*; /ʃIp/ = *ship*; /laIt/ = *light*.

Phonetic features. The individual articulatory and acoustic elements which combine to form phonemes. Phonetic features have to do with characteristics of the vocal organs during speech. Characteristics such as the height of the tongue, the closure of the lips, the volume of the vocal cavity, the operation of the vocal cords, etc. Phonemes result from a combination of phonetic features and can be distinguished on the basis of the 'bundles' of phonetic features (e.g. voicing, nasality) of which they are composed. Unlike phonemes (which are largely perceptual) phonetic features are essentially physical.

Phonographic writing systems. Orthographies in which symbols represent only units of sound. These units may be phonemes (as in alphabetic systems) or may be larger 'chunks' such as syllables (as in syllabaries).

Phonology. The sound system of a language. The human vocal cords are capable of producing a huge number of sounds only some of which are used by a particular language. The set of sounds used by a given language and the rules governing their use constitute the phonology of that language.

Phonetics. A branch of linguistics which is concerned with the description, classification and transcription (using the phonetic alphabet) of *all* human speech sounds, e.g. phonetic analyses of many languages distinguish between consonant and vowel sounds, which are described in terms of how they are articulated, their acoustic signal, and how they are heard or perceived.

Addresses of Contributors

Dr Chris Barry, Department of Psychology, University of Wales College of Cardiff, Tower Building, Park Place, Cardiff CF1 3YG.

Ms Frances Bunce, Department of Psychology, The University, Dundee, DD1 4HN.

Dr Vivian Burden, 65C Main Street, Witchford, Ely CB6 5HG.

Professor Ruth Campbell, Department of Psychology, Goldsmiths' College, New Cross, London SE14 6NW.

Dr N. Ellis, Department of Psychology, University College of North Wales, Bangor, Gwynedd LL57 2DG.

Dr Elaine Funnell, Department of Psychology, Birkbeck College, Malet Street, London WC1E 7HX.

Nata Goulandris, National Hospitals College of Speech Sciences, BSc Department, Chandler House, 2 Wakefield Street, London WC1N 1PG.

Laura Huxford, Cheltenham & Gloucester College of Higher Education, P.O. Box 220, The Park Campus, Cheltenham, Gloucestershire GL50 2RH.

Dr Rod Nicholson, Department of Psychology, University of Sheffield, Sheffield S10 2TN.

Dr H. Pattison, Department of Human Sciences, Loughborough University, Leicestershire, LE11 3BX.

Dr Margaret Peters, Castle Lodge, 50 Church Street, Saffron Walden, Essex CB10 1JQ.

Dr Cliff Robson, Department of Education Studies, Newcastle Polytechnic, Coach Lane Campus, Benton, Newcastle upon Tyne NE7 7XA.

Professor Philip Seymour, Department of Psychology, University of Dundee, Scotland DD1 4HN.

Dr Chris Sterling, Department of Applied Social Science, Newcastle Polytechnic, Northumberland Building, Newcastle upon Tyne NE1 8ST.

Emma Taylor, MRC/ESRC Social & Applied Psychology, Department of Psychology, University of Sheffield, Sheffield S10 2TN.

Mr C. Upward, The Simplified Spelling Society, 61 Valentine Road, Birmingham B14 7AJ.

Dr Rob Veltman, School of European and Modern Language Studies, Eliot College, University of Kent, Canterbury CT2 7NS.

Introduction to the Psychology of Spelling

CHRIS STERLING

The purpose of this introductory chapter is to provide the reader with a brief review of major issues in the psychology of spelling. It is written principally for those who know little about the work of psychologists, and seeks to provide them with enough background knowledge to understand the various contributions that make up the rest of the book.

English Orthography

It is impossible to discuss any aspect of spelling without being drawn into a consideration of the English spelling system, a system notorious for its irregularities and idiosyncrasies. Explaining why people have problems with it is easier than explaining how they become proficient in its use and it is the drive to explain this latter ability that has been responsible for such progress as we have made. Those interested in why English spelling is the way it is are referred to a history by Scragg (1974), and a monograph by Albrow (1972) arguing that it really consists of three subsystems. For now, we simply describe some aspects of English spelling.

In a truly alphabetic orthography each sound of the language (phonemes such as /b/, /p/, /t/) is written using a particular letter (graphemes such as **B**, **P**, **T**). Each word, consisting of a string of phonemes (e.g. /g/ + /l/ + /æ/ + /d/) would therefore be spelt with a string of graphemes (**G** + **L** + **A** + **D**). Because of the strict one-to-one correspondence between phonemes and graphemes the spelling of any word would be completely predictable. Unfortunately, English is substantially, but not wholly, alphabetic.

Some sounds are spelt using combinations of letters or digraphs, a state of affairs necessitated by the fact that there are fewer letters than sounds:

/ʃ/ → **SH**; /θ/ → **TH**; /iː/ → **EE**. Furthermore, there are some sounds spelt not just by an ordinary digraph but by one that is split, the two parts being separated by a consonant: /eI/ → **A_E** (**GATE**); /əʊ/ → **O_E** (**BONE**); /aI/ → **I_E** (**TIME**). While certainly an increase in complexity over the notion of one-to-one correspondences, a system consisting of sounds spelt with digraphs would not, we suspect, be as notorious as English. Where then does the problem lie?

The real problem with English is that the relationships between sounds and spellings are too often ambiguous or idiosyncratic. Fortunately, in some cases the ambiguities are rule governed. For example, the spelling of /k/, at the beginning of words, is governed by the identity of the immediately following letter. Thus, it is generally spelt with a **C** if it precedes **A**, **O** or **U** (*cat, cot* and *cut*) but with a **K** before **E** or **I** (*keg* and *kit*). In other cases the spelling of a sound depends systematically on where in the word the sound occurs. Thus, for example, we find /eI/ being spelt **AY** at the end of words (e.g. *day, stay*) but as **AI** or **A_E** when it occurs in the middle (e.g. *raid, fade*). Unfortunately, in too many cases there is no obvious rule or regularity that enables the speller to predict which alternative should be used. The most numerous examples of this ambiguity are those words called homophones, which have the same sound but different spellings, e.g. **MAID/MADE, BEEN/BEAN**. Finally, while alternative spellings such as **EA** and **EE** do at least have the merit of occurring in large numbers of words, the notoriety that English spelling has achieved is probably most attributable to the so-called exception word, the spelling of which is both unprincipled and infrequent (e.g. **LAUGH, COLONEL**).

If English orthography is judged only by the degree to which it unambiguously spells the sounds of the language then it clearly leaves much to be desired. This is the position held by spelling reformers. A number of people, however, have argued that if we take other factors into account it becomes a more comprehensible and even 'near optimal' system (Chomsky & Halle, 1968). Thus, for example, spelling two words which sound the same (e.g. /meId/ in different ways (**MAID, MADE**) is argued to be a desirable state of affairs because the different spellings capture the important fact that, even though they sound the same, they are different words (*maid, made*) with different meanings. This example, the argument goes, is evidence that English orthography is *lexical* as well as phonological because it reflects differences in meaning as well as differences in sound. By a related argument English orthography is also *morphemic* because it preserves the identity of morphemes of the language across variations in their pronunciation. For example, even though, in a truly phonetic orthography, *fished, hunted,* and *played* might be spelt **FISHT, HUNTID** and **PLAYD**, the conventional spellings, **FISHED**, **HUNTED** and **PLAYED** are argued to be the more desirable because they spell the past tense morpheme -**ED** (which is the same in all cases) not its sound (which differs). Similarly, English spelling preserves the relationship between, say, *plastic* and *plasticity* by retaining the C, which would not happen if the spellings were phonetic, e.g. **PLASTIK** and **PLASTISITY**.

In general, research has dealt pragmatically with the complexities of English spelling by distinguishing between regular and irregular words, a distinction which has sufficed for most investigative purposes. Regular words are defined in general terms, to the effect that their spelling is predictable from the sound given a knowledge of sound–spelling correspondences and spelling rules, e.g. **BELL**, **SING**, **HARM**. Irregular words are defined by exclusion. They aren't regular, e.g. **WERE**, **SAID**, **HAVE**, **PEOPLE**. No one has tried to specify precisely the conditions a word has to fulfil before it can be called regular, and so investigators have proceeded on the basis of a rule-of-thumb and mutual agreement. Though seemingly a lax way of going about research, the distinction has been used in countless papers without too many disputes and with impressively consistent results.

Barry & Seymour (1988) have argued that the regular/irregular distinction should be replaced by the notion of *sound–spelling contingency*. Details and discussion of this will be found in their separate papers (respectively Chapters 4 and 3 this volume) and in the final chapter. For now, we present only the basic idea. The nub of sound–spelling contingency is the fact that many sounds can be spelt in different ways, with each spelling being found in a certain proportion of all words with that sound. Given a particular sound, each spelling of that sound has a certain contingency or probability. Thus, to use their example,

> the vowel /i:/ is spelt in 12 different ways: the most common spelling pattern (**EA**, as in **LEAF**) occurs in 39.5% of (English) words, the second most common (**EE**, as in **BEEF**) occurs in 38.6% of words, and the third most common (**IE**, as in **THIEF**) occurs in only 6.7% of words. (Barry & Seymour, 1988: 8)

The remaining ways (e.g. as in **ME**, **EKE**, **CLIQUE**, **KEY**, **SKI**, **KEITH**, **QUAY**, **PEOPLE**, **FOETAL**) occur very few times each. In sound–spelling contingencies, the clear distinction between regular and irregular is replaced by gradations based on frequency of occurrence. Notice, however, that the notion of regularity is not completely lost, for there is a very real sense in which **PEOPLE** and **SKI** are irregular while **LEAF** and **BEEF** are regular, though ambiguous.

Spelling Processes

Whatever its current status, the distinction between regular and irregular words has been theoretically valuable because it has helped provoke a distinction between two kinds of spelling process. Regular words should, in principle, be able to be spelt by a set of processes (*phonological processes*) that rely on only alphabetic knowledge and the rules and regularities of English spelling. In contrast, this same set of processes would not be able to spell irregular words because they violate these rules and regularities. Irregular words can be spelt only by a different set of processes (*lexical processes*) that use word-specific spelling knowledge (e.g. that *yacht* has a **CH** between the **A** and the **T** and that the vowel is spelt with an **A** rather than the more phonetically appropriate **O**). This postulation of two sets of separate, independent processes is the basis of the *dual process model* of spelling, to which we now turn.

According to the dual process model, the first of these routes or set of processes (the phonological route) which produces a spelling does so by breaking the word up into its component phonemes (e.g. **kuh–ah–tuh**) and then using knowledge of sound–spelling correspondences /k/ → **K**; /æ/ → **A**; /t/ → **T**) to assemble an appropriate spelling (**CAT**). This route or set of processes is variously referred to as: the phonological route, phonological spelling, assembled spelling, and phonetic spelling. Whatever one chooses to call it, its major feature is that it can produce correct spellings only for regular words. As we have said, irregular words will be incorrectly spelled because, by definition, they break the rules of English spelling. Should an irregular word be attempted, however, the spelling, though wrong, will reflect the sound structure of the target and will therefore be phonetically plausible (e.g. **SED** (*said*), **WUR** (*were*)). A second major feature of the phonological route is that it can produce a plausible, if not correct, spelling for non-words, where these are defined as being sounds which *could* be English words but happen not to be (e.g. *glub, pluft,* etc.). The spelling of any such non-word would be produced in the usual way, by breaking it down into its constituent phonemes and then applying knowledge of sound–spelling correspondences.

$$/g/ + /l/ + /\Lambda/ + /b/ \rightarrow G + L + U + B$$

Now, while there might be some variation in the way different people, especially children, spell the same non-word, the variations produced by the phonological route will all be plausible representations of the sound structure of the target.

The second route or set of processes (the lexical route) has been postulated to cope with the irregularities of English orthography. The critical feature of this route is that it uses word-specific knowledge stored in a word store or mental lexicon. Thus under *colonel* would be stored specific information about its idiosyncratic spelling (e.g. the speller might encode the spelling thus: that the vowel is represented by **O**, the final /l/ by **EL** (rather than, say, **LE**), and the **LO** as an idiosyncrasy). Similarly, under *mane* would be stored the information that the spelling is with an **A_E** rather than **AI**. This kind of information can be acquired only by acquaintance with the written form of the word (e.g. **COLONEL, MANE**) and would have to be consulted if the word was going to be correctly spelt. It is generally assumed that word-specific information about spelling is built up over the course of many exposures to the word in question. Thus, spellers will generally be more likely to know the spellings of frequently occurring irregular words (*high*) than of infrequently occurring irregular words (*sigh*). The fact that the lexical route produces spellings on the basis of knowledge specific to the word in question means that it is not capable of spelling non-words because these, by definition, have not been seen before.

A major source of evidence for dual process theory is cognitive neuropsychology. This is a branch of psychology which investigates brain damage (through surgery, disease, accidents, etc.) and its effects on a person's intellect. In this context, we are concerned with people who have suffered some kind of neurological damage which has affected their ability to spell. More specifically, we find that some patients perform in a way suggesting that the damage has affected only the phonological route (Shallice, 1981) while others perform in a way suggesting that the damage has affected only the lexical route (Beauvois & Dérouesné, 1981). The former are called *phonological dysgraphics*, the latter *lexical dysgraphics*. How does the existence of these two types of impairment support the dual process theory? The reason is simply the fact that, in each case, one of the routes has been knocked out while leaving the other (more or less) intact. This suggests very strongly that they are, as proposed, separate and independent.

We can see from this synopsis that dual process theory has the equipment to produce a spelling for any word or non-word, regular or irregular, homophonic or not. See Ellis (1984) for a carefully explained account of dual process theory (and dyslexia), and to the papers by Barry (Chapter 4) and Seymour (Chapter 3) in this volume for detailed but concise coverage of the model and relevant evidence.

A major problem for the dual process model is the evidence from spelling by analogy. This evidence casts doubt on the important assumption that the two routes are separate and independent. Spelling by analogy was first reported by Ruth Campbell (1983; 1985) who found that both adults' and children's spellings of non-words could be influenced by prior exposure to real words. Thus, for example, /preIn/ would tend to be spelt **PRAIN** if preceded by *brain*, but **PRANE** if preceded by *crane*. In each case the spelling is being produced *by analogy* with the real word and the real word is said to be acting as a *prime*. Perhaps the most intriguing example of the phenomenon of priming was obtained by Seymour & Dargie (1990) who found that the non-word /bəʊp/ would tend to be spelt **BOAP** if the prime had been *detergent* (presumably stimulating **SOAP**) and **BOPE** if it had been *vatican* (presumably stimulating **POPE**). Now, it is clear from such a phenomenon that *lexical* information is affecting the functioning of the *phonological* route. This should not happen given the assumption of dual process theory that the lexical route and the phonological route are separate and independent sets of processes. See the chapters by Barry and Seymour and the concluding chapter for further discussion.

Spelling Development

We suspect that the majority of readers of this book are most interested in the development of spelling. Accordingly, we turn first to a discussion of a particularly influential theory, followed by a brief discussion of other ideas.

What follows is only an outline of Frith's (1985) theory of reading and spelling development and the reader is urged to read the original paper. Two important aspects of the theory are firstly that the development of literacy can be divided into three main stages — the logographic, the alphabetic and the orthographic — and secondly that reading and spelling are closely related in a relationship that changes over the course of development.

In the *logographic stage* the child reads and spells on the basis of learned pairings between a visual representation of a word and its meaning, a notion which will be familiar to those acquainted with whole-word methods of reading. In this stage some features of the written form become stored in the child's mental lexicon as a *logograph* or pictorial representation. Now while in the very early phases of the logographic stage it seems likely that words like the distinctive *Harrods* or *MacDonalds* names are represented as pictures, letter identification develops rapidly. Thus for example, the child Alice (described in Harris and Coltheart, 1986) was able to read *Harrods* even when its distinctiveness was destroyed by alternating the case, i.e. HaRrOdS. Further evidence for the form a logographic representation

INTRODUCTION TO THE PSYCHOLOGY OF SPELLING

might take comes from the kinds of errors children make. Thus Seymour & Elder (1985) refer to one child who read *television* as *children* because *children* is a long word, and another who read *smaller* as *yellow* because *yellow* has two 'sticks' in it. According to Frith, spelling development in the logographic stage lags behind reading in the sense that logographic representations become available for spelling only some time after they have become available for reading.

It seems clear that using only logographic representations will result in an increasingly unmanageable memory load as vocabulary increases. Thus for example, adult Chinese people who don't read and write their logographic script on a regular basis complain that their expertise and their memory for the (logographic) symbols become eroded with time. This burdensome memory load, together with other factors, probably provides the impetus for movement to the next stage, the alphabetic stage.

The substantially alphabetic nature of English permits, in principle, any word or potential word to be spelt by learning the relationship between phonemes and graphemes. Frith claims that, in the *alphabetic stage* of development, the relationship between phonemes and graphemes is acquired first for spelling and then for reading. She argues that a desire to write, together with the fact that spelling is principally the writing of sounds, direct the child's attention to the phonemes of the language and to the relationship between these phonemes and the graphemes that spell them. Only when they have begun to master this alphabetic principle for spelling do they begin to acquire it for reading. This lag between spelling and reading suggests that there is a transitional phase when the child is reading by eye (logographically) but spelling by ear (alphabetically). Evidence for this comes from Bryant & Bradley (1980) who found that beginning readers/spellers could read but not spell irregular words like *light,* while being able to spell but not read regular words like *bun.* This was because they were reading using a logographic strategy but spelling using a phonological strategy.

The final phase of development according to Frith is the *orthographic stage* which is, once again, non-phonological. Increasing experience with the orthography permits the child to abstract out regularities or spelling patterns. Examples of such regularities are the morpheme spellings such as **PRE-**, **-ING**, and **-ED** and the spelling pattern **-IGHT**. The process becomes non-phonological again in that these clusters or spelling patterns become represented as independent orthographic units, free of the sounds they represent. Idiosyncratic spellings also become accurately represented. Thus the spellings of words such as *bough, cough, tough* and *laugh* are specific to them (they are not predictable from the sounds) and will have to be stored as such. In this final phase the relationship between spelling and reading is again reversed in that the child's orthographic skills are more advanced for reading than they are for spelling.

Another influential body of work comes from Bryant and his colleagues (e.g. Bryant & Bradley, 1985; Goswami & Bryant, 1990) although their work is not embodied in the form of a well-defined theory as is that of Frith. The substance of their work has to do with *phonological awareness* and its relationship to literacy and they argue that phonological awareness is a causal factor in the development of reading and spelling (see Goswami & Bryant (1990) for a comprehensive review). Generally speaking, their work suggests that the child's awareness of the sound structure of a language is the basis for their reading and spelling ability and that as this awareness becomes more defined and more sophisticated so does their skill in reading and spelling.

As one might expect this generalisation understates the complexity of the issue. One source of complication is the fact that phonological awareness is a complex ability. Being phonologically aware can mean anything from being able to judge whether or not words rhyme (*cat*, *bat* and *fat*, but not *pan*), through being able to break a word up in different ways (/bIt/ into /b/ + /It/ or into /bI/ + /t/), to being able to manipulate phonemes by adding, transposing or omitting them (e.g. /nIp/ → /pIn/ or /pIn/ → /In/). A helpful distinction, used to good effect by Ellis & Cataldo in this volume (Chapter 7), is that between *implicit awareness* (e.g. making judgements about sounds such as whether or not they rhyme) and *explicit awareness* (e.g. being able to inspect the sound structure by, for example, splitting the word up into its components), the intimation being that the latter reflects a more advanced stage of development than the former. Given this dimensional quality it is not surprising to find that a child's phonological awareness develops over time. Consider, for example, the subskill of segmentation. It seems that children can segment words into syllables before they can segment syllables into subsyllabic units called the *onset* and *rime*, and they can do this before they can finally segment these into phonemes (Trieman, 1985). This developmental sequence is pertinent to the development of literacy because of the hypothesis (put forward by Bryant and his colleagues, amongst others) that reading and spelling advance as a consequence of developing phonological awareness. The question is whether children read and spell on the basis of large phonological chunks such as onset and rime before they do so on the basis of phonemes. Reviewing the evidence is far beyond the scope of this volume. Suffice it to say that while no one would now dispute that phonological awareness is a causal factor in the development of reading and spelling, the evidence that children use phono–graphic (sound–spelling) *chunks* before they do phoneme–grapheme correspondences is more convincing for reading than it is for spelling. Currently, the evidence from spelling is more consistent with the idea that phonological spelling begins with a focus on phoneme–grapheme correspondences and only later makes use of larger chunks.

Another major aspect of Bryant *et al.*'s views is their conception of the relationship between reading and spelling. While they agree with Frith that reading and spelling are closely connected and mutually influential they don't subscribe to the notion that the direction of the causal relationship changes with each stage of development (in general they don't subscribe to the idea of stages of development). They argue (and admit that this is speculative) that reading and spelling begin on different paths (reading is 'visual' or 'global'; spelling phonological), and only after a time become connected in the child's mind, the result of which is that the child begins to apply 'global' strategies to spelling and phonological strategies to reading. Thus they do not accept Frith's contention that spelling is initially logographic but do agree that a phonological strategy is used for spelling before it is used for reading.

Individual Differences

Children differ in their spelling ability. There are good spellers and poor spellers. However, even though identifying poor spellers is no problem, identifying the reason for their problem is often less easy. As a preliminary classification we can distinguish three groups:

1. There are those whose spelling is poor because of some perceptual or motor disability such as deafness.
2. There are those whose performance in all spheres of educational activity, including spelling, is poor.
3. There are those whose problem is confined to literacy, and who are, in other respects, average or above average.

The first group consists of those with an identifiable physical disability likely to produce a spelling deficit. Given the phonological basis of spelling we might, for example, expect those with auditory perceptual disorders, such as the deaf, to be disadvantaged. The simplest reasoning would suggest that because the deaf have an impaired sound system they would rely entirely on visual memory when spelling and consequently be very poor spellers. Such simple reasoning, it turns out, is also naïve, as we shall see in the paper by Campbell, Burden & Wright (Chapter 11). We might also wonder if people with severe speech disorders are poor spellers. Bishop (1985) has looked at the spelling of dysarthrics. Dysarthrics are individuals with a motor speech impairment due to lesions in the central or peripheral nervous system. They are able to talk but the production of sounds is slow and distorted. They are often unintelligible and, in some cases, unable to speak at all. Could such a disability severely impair their spelling ability? The answer seems to be that it doesn't, for dysarthrics have no more problems with the spelling of either words or non-words than a matched group of physically disabled people. This indicates that the phonology used in spelling, and the processes of 'sounding out', are *not* at the level of the peripheral musculature responsible for speech but at the level of more abstract (phonemic) representations of the sound structure of the word.

The second group, those whose performance in school is generally poor have been called 'garden variety' (i.e. common) poor readers by Stanovich (Stanovich, Nathan & Zolman, 1988). Such evidence as there is for these children (and there are no studies that look at their spelling), suggests that they have no specific problem, phonological or otherwise. Thus, when compared to children of the same reading age (but who are chronologically younger) they showed no impairment in measures of vocabulary, phonological awareness, picture and word/non-word naming speed and use of context. It seems that they simply lag behind their peers.

The third group is the most intriguing. These consist of children, generally known as dyslexics, who, though comparable in all other ways, are significantly behind their peers in reading and spelling (by two years or more). Now dyslexia is a huge topic and the interested reader is referred to texts by Miles & Miles (1990), Snowling (1987), Bryant & Bradley (1985) and Ellis (1984). All we can do here is acquaint the reader with a few generalisations.

The problem in what is commonly called dyslexia (classic developmental, phonological, dysphonetic are but three other names) seems to be an enormous difficulty in converting sound to spelling and spelling to sound. According to Frith these people have failed to progress beyond the logographic stage of development because they cannot grasp the alphabetic principle. Given this, it is hardly surprising that one of their problems is the reading and spelling of non-words. Furthermore, if one assumes, after Frith, that they rely on their logographic knowledge, then the fact that they tend to treat regular and irregular words in the same way and to make 'visual' errors when reading and spelling comes as no surprise. Thus Temple (1986) reports a case of a boy of ten years with a spelling age of seven years whose spelling was non-phonological in that he made significantly fewer phonetically plausible errors (e.g. **WUR** for *were*) when spelling than children in a control group with the same spelling age (his reading was also significantly retarded). The root of the problem seems to be a poorly developed phonological awareness for, relative to children of the same spelling age with no problem (i.e. younger), they are poorer at tasks such as counting the number of phonemes in a word (Rohl & Tunmer, 1988), and deleting phonemes from words (e.g. /spIn/ → /pIn/) (Bruck & Trieman, 1989). In spite of their problems, however, it would be a mistake to assume dyslexics to be illiterate because some of them, for example the student R.E., develop highly efficient, non-phonological strategies (Campbell & Butterworth, 1985).

Implicit to Frith's theory, and to the criteria of dyslexia used by researchers, is the notion that dyslexia is a disorder which makes those who are dyslexic qualitatively different from all other readers and spellers, even from those who have substantial but lesser problems. Bryant & Bradley argued in 1985 that this had not been comprehensively demonstrated — that while investigators had compared various aspects of the performance of dyslexics to people of the same age (a chronological control group) and had shown them to *lag* behind, they had not always compared them with children of the same reading/spelling age (the reading/spelling age control group), a comparison which would have shown whether or not they were *deficient* in some respect. (Note that dyslexics could achieve the same reading/spelling age as a group of normal children by using completely different strategies.) Since this was pointed out, investigators (e.g. Temple, 1986) have been careful to use the appropriate comparison group, and as a consequence the evidence that dyslexics are qualitatively different from normal readers/spellers is stronger. Bryant *et al.*, however, still feel that there is some way yet to go before dyslexics can be regarded as a readily identifiable, qualitatively different subgroup, and hence tend to use the term 'backward reader' in preference to 'dyslexic' (see Goswami & Bryant (1990) for a recent exposition of their ideas).

Concluding Comments

There is much that has been omitted from this review. Most of the issues are more controversial and far more complex than has been suggested here. The last text to cover the whole area that was that of Frith (1980), but there is no more recent single text which can be recommended. Nevertheless, the reader should have been provided with enough information about the psychology of spelling to understand the papers to follow.

References

ALBROW, K. H. 1972, The English writing system: Notes towards a description. Schools Council Programme in Linguistics and English: Teaching Papers Series II. London: Longman.

BARRY, C. and SEYMOUR, P. H. K. 1988, Lexical priming and sound-to-spelling contingency effects in non-word spelling. *Quarterly Journal of Experimental Psychology* 40A, 5–40.

BEAUVOIS, M. F. and DÉROUESNÉ, J. 1981, Lexical or orthographic agraphia. *Brain* 104, 21–49.

BISHOP, D. V. M. 1985, Spelling ability in congenital dysarthria: Evidence against articulatory coding in translating between phonemes and graphemes. *Cognitive Neuropsychology* 2, 229–51.

BRUCK, M. and TRIEMAN, R. 1989, Phonological awareness and spelling in normal children and dyslexics: The case of initial consonant clusters. Unpublished manuscript cited in U. GOSWAMI and P. E. BRYANT (1990) *Phonological Skills and Learning to Read.* London: Lawrence Erlbaum.

BRYANT, P. E. and BRADLEY, L. 1980, Why children sometimes write words which they do not read. In U. FRITH (ed.) *Cognitive Processes in Spelling.* London: Academic Press.

—— 1985, *Children's Reading Problems.* Oxford: Basil Blackwell.

CAMPBELL, R. 1983, Writing nonwords to dictation. *Brain & Language* 19, 153–78.

—— 1985, When children write nonwords to dictation. *Journal of Experimental Child Psychology* 40, 133–51.

CAMPBELL, R. and BUTTERWORTH, B. 1985, Phonological dyslexia and dysgraphia in a highly literate subject: A developmental case with associated deficits of phonemic awareness and processing. *Quarterly Journal of Experimental Psychology* 37A, 425–75.

CHOMSKY, N. and HALLE, M. 1968, *The Sound Pattern of English.* New York: Harper & Row.

ELLIS, A. W. 1984, *Reading, Writing and Dyslexia: A Cognitive Analysis.* London: Lawrence Erlbaum.

FRITH, U. 1980, *Cognitive Processes in Spelling.* London: Academic Press.

—— 1985, Beneath the surface of developmental dyslexia. In K. PATTERSON, M. COLTHEART and J. MARSHALL (eds) *Surface Dyslexia.* London: Lawrence Erlbaum.

GOSWAMI, U. and BRYANT, P. E. 1990, *Phonological Skills and Learning to Read.* London: Lawrence Erlbaum.

HARRIS, M. and COLTHEART, M. 1986, *Language Processing in Children and Adults.* London: Routledge and Kegan Paul.

MILES, T. R. and MILES, E. 1990, *Dyslexia: A Hundred Years On.* Milton Keynes: Open University Press.

ROHL, M. and TUNMER, W. E. 1988, Phonemic segmentation and spelling acquisition. *Applied Psycholinguistics* 9, 335–50.

SCRAGG, D. E. 1974, *A History of English Spelling.* Manchester: Manchester University Press.

SEYMOUR, P. H. K. and DARGIE, A. 1990, Associative priming and orthographic choice in nonword spelling. *The European Journal of Cognitive Psychology* 2, 395–410.

SEYMOUR, P. K. and ELDER, L. 1985, Beginning reading without phonology. *Cognitive Neuropsychology* 3, 1–36.
SHALLICE, T. 1981, Phonological agraphia and the lexical route in writing. *Brain* 104, 413–29.
SNOWLING, M. 1987, *Dyslexia: A Cognitive Developmental Perspective*. Oxford: Basil Blackwell.
STANOVICH, K. E., NATHAN, R. G. and ZOLMAN, J. E. 1988, The developmental lag hypothesis in reading: Longitudinal and matched reading-level comparisons. *Child Development* 59, 71–86.
TEMPLE, C. 1986, Developmental dysgraphias. *Quarterly Journal of Developmental Psychology* 38A, 77–110.
TRIEMAN, R. 1985, Onsets and rimes as units of spoken syllables: Evidence from children. *Journal of Experimental Child Psychology* 39, 161–81.

Section One:
The English Spelling System

The two chapters in this section are concerned with the English spelling system. Upward argues that standard English orthography needs to be modernised, while Veltman argues that it is not as unmotivated as it seems.

Teaching Literacy First, Traditional English Orthography Second (Upward)

Upward's chapter is concerned with the modernisation of English spelling. He argues that, despite examples of patterning, standard English orthography is profoundly irregular, and that, far from expecting spellers to persevere until they master it, we should rectify its most troublesome irregularities.

In the second part of the paper he describes the success of early attempts to teach literacy skills in English by means of regularised spelling systems. One such system was Fonotypy, which was devised by Isaac Pitman in the mid-nineteenth century, but suffered from the fact that it used some novel symbols. Another, Nue Speling, was devised by the Simplified Spelling Society and used in a small number of schools during and after the First World War.

In the third part of the chapter Upward describes and reviews the success of the Initial Teaching Alphabet (i.t.a.) in the 1960s and 1970s. The evidence cited suggests that i.t.a. was effective, and he argues that it was abandoned for organisational rather than educational reasons.

He ends his chapter by arguing that initial teaching orthographies are only temporary palliatives for the problems caused by English orthography, and that a long-term solution requires it to be modernised, as other languages modernise their orthographies. He concludes with a discussion of some of the practical implications of reforming English spelling.

An Orthography as a Theory of a Language (Veltman)

Veltman's chapter has two purposes. The first is to argue that orthographies are essentially attempts at analysing the language they apply to. That is, by virtue of their having 'chosen' to represent particular units in the language and to make particular distinctions rather than others, they are theories of what is important in the language. The second purpose of Veltman's chapter is to show that Standard English Orthography, in addition to representing phonemes, morphemes and words, represents phonetic features. He seeks to conclude that graphotactical rules (rules that are 'in house' to the orthography, specifying which letter combinations are permitted, desirable, etc.) can be seen to be motivated if this notion of an orthography is applied.

Veltman argues that writing is not just a transcription system for sound but a functionally autonomous system for representing the language. Language, of course, has a number of components or levels (a *meaning* level, a *wording* level and a *sounding* level) and within each level there are units which the orthography may or may not represent, depending on the language in question. For example, there are words and morphemes at the wording level and phonemes, syllables and features at the sounding level.

Orthographies differ in their analytical focus (e.g. alphabet, syllabary, logography) and it is this focus which determines the principle on which a particular orthography is organised. English orthography has a multiple analytical focus in that, while it is principally alphabetic in nature, representing phonemes, it also represents morphemes and words from the wording level and, Veltman argues, distinctive features from the sounding level. Thus it spells morphemes such as -**ED** across variations in pronunciation, distinguishes between whole words such as *meet* and *meat,* and spells phonemes such as /**b**/ and /**p**/. It is this multiple focus which is the source of so many apparently unmotivated spellings. However, while multiple focus may make standard orthography difficult to learn it is, nevertheless, learnable. Multiple focus may even make it psychologically advantageous.

Phonetic features, Veltman continues, provide a basis for grouping phonemes. Phonetic features are aspects of sounds which, together, make up phonemes. Thus 'voicing' is a feature found in sounds such as /**b**/, /**d**/ and /**g**/, which distinguishes them from /**p**/, /**t**/ and /**k**/, respectively, by virtue of the fact that the vocal cords vibrate for the former but not for the latter. Another feature, applicable to vowel sounds, is laxness. Vowels such as /**I**/ (*bit*), and /**e**/ (*bet*) are lax vowels, and are distinguished from tense vowels such as /**i:**/ (*meat*) and /**eI**/ (*mate*) by characteristics such as their length (lax vowels are short, tense vowels long). Orthographically, we find that they are distinguished by the environments in which they can occur, e.g. lax, but not tense, vowels occur in the environment -/ŋ/ (*ring, bang, long*).

The major significance of phonetic features, Veltman argues, is that they permit classification of phonemes and that because of this a number of apparent inconsistencies can be explained. Veltman cites the occurrence of doubled consonants in certain words (*tapped, running, dinner*). Consonant doubling is usually learned as a complex graphotactical rule but a simpler explanation is that it protects the laxness of the preceding vowel, i.e. doubling occurs after lax vowels, signals this fact and hence can be considered to represent a phonetic feature. It can also, however, serve a lexical function in that it can signal the origin of a morphemically complex word (e.g. indicate that *tapping* is a derivative of *tap* and not *tape*) and distinguish between different words (*tapping* and *taping*).

Veltman's paper concludes with the comment that a number of spellings, apparently unmotivated if described in terms of graphotactical rules, make sense if we analyse them on the assumption that English orthography represents phonetic features as well as words, morphemes and phonemes.

1 Teaching Literacy First, Traditional English Orthography Second

CHRISTOPHER UPWARD

The Problem of English Spelling

It has never been easy to teach reading and writing in English. Ian Michael's history of English teaching (Michael, 1987) vividly describes the painful trying out of methods over some three centuries up to 1870, with shifting emphases on learning the ABC, reading through spelling, syllabic analysis, spelling lists, and dictations. He notes that there were 'complex difficulties with which teachers were struggling' as early as the sixteenth century.

Until the nineteenth century the writing system was fluid, with uncertainty even about the number of letters, their order, their names and when to use them. Today such questions are largely resolved, but there is still no agreement on the best method of teaching literacy skills. In recent decades controversy has raged over whether learners should begin with sound–symbol correspondences or with recognition of whole words in context. Both approaches are perceived to have drawbacks: a bottom-up, phonic approach stumbles over the mismatch between spelling and pronunciation, while a top-down, visual approach at worst results in inability to read or write unfamiliar words.

This methodological dilemma is inherent in the present condition of English spelling, which evolved without regard to learners' needs. Comparative literacy studies (Downing, 1973; 1988) show how serious the problem is. The author of this chapter recently found further confirmation that the root of the problem lies with English spelling rather than with the failings

TEACHING LITERACY FIRST, ORTHOGRAPHY SECOND

of pupils or teachers, when he studied the spelling of British language students writing in English and in German: far more misspellings were made in the students' mother tongue, English, than in German, which they were studying as a foreign language. But the ultimate proof will be described in later sections of this chapter: it has been repeatedly found that literacy skills are more easily acquired in English too, if the spelling is regular.

Despite present public concern about standards of literacy and especially spelling, there is widespread confusion on the subject. Even some eminent linguists fail to appreciate the nature of the problem. An often quoted remark by Chomsky & Halle (1968) states that English spelling is a 'near-optimal' system, because the spelling of related words like *courage/courageous* does not reflect their changed pronunciation. The Australian psychologist Valerie Yule (1978) effectively refuted this view, and indeed there are abundant counter-examples, both of word-pairs whose spelling does change with pronunciation, and of pairs whose spelling varies quite arbitrarily. The pair *explain/explanation* for instance changes ‹ai› to ‹a› as the pronunciation changes, while unmotivated variations occur between *comparison/comparative, enjoin/injunction, high/height, speak/speech*. No careful study of English spelling can avoid concluding that it is riddled with inconsistencies.

Confusion is similarly observed in official reports in the UK. The Kingman report (Department of Education & Science (DES) 1988), which set out basic principles for English in the National Curriculum, said that children should consider 'the regular patterning of word forms in English' (p. 20), and, as though this followed logically on, they should 'spell correctly' (p. 52); the difficulty with English spelling is, however, precisely that regular patterns offer little assistance with correct spelling.

The Kingman Committee (DES, 1988) was succeeded by the Cox Committee (DES, 1989), whose final report then passed to the National Curriculum Council. Unlike the Kingman Committee, the Cox Committee recognised that irregular spellings cause learners real difficulty; in §17.33 it said:

> . . . by the end of compulsory schooling pupils should be able to spell confidently most of the words they are likely to need to use frequently in their writing . . .; to make a sensible attempt to spell words they have not seen before . . . The aim cannot be the correct unaided spelling of any English word — there are too many words in English that can catch out even the best speller . . . specifying lists of increasingly irregular and unusual words . . . would be absurd. (DES, 1989)

These remarks, though more realistic than Kingman, beg some important questions. We note the repeated caveats in the first sentence — pupils are to spell 'confidently' rather than correctly, but their confidence is only expected to apply to 'most' of the words they are 'likely' to need to use 'frequently'; and if they wish to write words they have not seen before, then only a 'sensible attempt' can be expected (one wonders which incorrect spellings are 'sensible'). Finally, the 'correct unaided spelling of any English word . . . cannot be the aim'.

Though realistic, these recommendations are an admission of educational defeat: they are saying, children have to try and learn a system they cannot be expected to master. Yet in 1990–91 the call for 'correct spelling' was raised again by Kenneth Clarke, then Secretary of State for Education and Science, with examination candidates to be penalised in all subjects for poor spelling. In other words: we should penalise failure to achieve the impossible.

Not merely do Cox and Clarke implicitly contradict each other, but both raise some awkward questions. The Secretary of State was effectively asking for some examination candidates to be denied qualifications in, say, maths and physics, despite adequate subject knowledge; and he would take pupils and teachers away from their academic subjects to spend time learning irregular spellings instead. Is this what our society really needs? As for the Cox Report (DES, 1989), we must ask whether it is right that future generations should not be expected to use standard spellings for any but a core of common words. If most people no longer aim at standard spellings, won't the standard itself be undermined? If many people write *accomodate*, why should dictionaries only list *accommodate*? What spellings should foreigners be taught if native speakers constantly flout the taught conventions? Doesn't the world need standard spellings for its primary international language, which everyone can learn and use?

Confusion and contradiction persisted into 1990. In 1989 the National Curriculum Council's Consultation Report (NCC, 1989) moved towards specifying phonic training for beginners: the Level 1 Statement of Attainment in the Consultation Report said that 'Pupils should be able to: . . . write some letter shapes in response to speech sounds and letter names'. But in early 1990 the LINC (Language in the National Curriculum) programme was preparing material emphasising a visual approach and firmly stating that teachers should not 'sound out' spellings, or use spelling tests.

English spelling and public understanding of it thus both demonstrate serious confusion. This chapter will now describe an alternative approach to teaching literacy skills which has been used successfully in the past and attempts to avoid both kinds of confusion. Finally, the chapter will suggest a way of reducing the confusion of English spelling itself.

Teaching Literacy Skills via Regularised Spelling

An early, graphic statement of the psychological rationale of the 'literacy first, spelling second' approach was made by John Hart, one of the band of Elizabethans who in the sixteenth century took an active interest in the problems of written English. Sir James Pitman (Pitman & St John, 1969: 77) quotes Hart (1570) on teaching children their letters as follows:

> Vvich I finde as reasonable, as if a nurse should take in hand to teach a child, to go first upon high pattens or stiltes, or vpon a coarde, or on the hands, before he should be taughte as the naturall and reasonable order is . . . (Hart, 1570)

In other words, just as you would not teach a child tightrope walking or handstands before it can walk on its own two feet, so by analogy you should not teach the difficulties of written English before the child has mastered basic literacy skills. But how could you teach literacy skills other than by using the very spelling system which causes the difficulty? The answer was to devise a regularised spelling system for English, to be mastered by the beginner before attempting conventional spellings. From Hart's day to the present there has been a succession of orthographical innovators designing regularised systems, so all that was needed was for one of them actually to use such a system for teaching.

An early recorded example of this 'literacy first, spelling second' approach was the work of Isaac Pitman who had already devised a system of shorthand based on phonemic analysis of spoken English (its modern form is still associated with his name). He applied the same kind of analysis to creating a system of rationalised spelling, which he called Fonotypy. His shorthand abandoned the letters of the alphabet altogether, preferring simple strokes which could be written faster, but his Fonotypy was based on the Roman alphabet, augmented with a couple of dozen extra letters. Fonotypy was first used in the 1840s for teaching some 1,300 illiterate adults in Manchester.

The best documented instances of its use were, however, in the United States between 1852 and 1860. Perhaps at that time America was more open to such ideas because only some 25 years previously Noah Webster's first American dictionary had appeared with some simplifications of traditional British spelling. Sir James Pitman (Pitman & St John, 1969: 85) quotes from an 1852 report of the school committee of the town of Waltham, Massachusetts:

> We advocate Pitman's Phonetics simply as an aid in education, and as an introduction to ordinary orthography. It has been proved in repeated experiments that if a child, upon his first learning his letters, is taught the Phonetic Alphabet, and is confined to Phonetic books for the first six or eight months of schooling, he will at the end of his first year's schooling read common print, and *spell in common spelling* better than children ordinarily do at the end of four or five years' instruction. It has also been proved by repeated experiments, that if an adult of ordinary intelligence is ignorant of his letters, he may learn to read the Bible, or the newspaper in two months' time by giving his attention to Phonetics two hours a day for six weeks, and to common print for the remaining fortnight. (Pitman & St John, 1969: 85)

The biggest drawback to Fonotypy for teaching initial literacy skills was that it contained symbols that were not part of the conventional Roman alphabet. This factor complicated the provision of reading materials, required special training of teachers, and by its unfamiliar appearance could deter adults when they first saw the system. Most later generations of 'literacy first, spelling second' experimenters therefore preferred to develop a regularised writing system using only the conventional 26 letters of the alphabet. By World War I the Simplified Spelling Society (SSS) had produced a system called New Spelling (Nue Speling), of which a sample (in its revised, 1948 form) now follows:

> We rekwier dhe langgwej az an instrooment; we mae aulsoe study its history. Dhe prezens ov unpronounst leterz, three or for diferent waez ov reprezenting dhe saem sound, three or for uesez ov dhe saem leter: aul dhis detrakts from dhe value ov a langgwej az an instrooment. When we plaes dhis instrooment in dhe hand ov dhe chield, we duu not at dhe saem tiem teech it historrikal gramar. (Ripman & Archer, revised by Jones & Orton, 1948: 93)

In the years before and after 1920 the SSS was able to test this system in 16 schools in England and Scotland, and in 1924 it summarised its findings as follows:

> The reports . . . show . . . conclusively:
> (1) That children learn to read fluently matter in a simple phonetic spelling, and to write correctly according to the system, in the course of a few months;

(2) that, as a consistent spelling presents no bar to free expression, the original compositions of children who use a phonetic spelling are markedly superior in matter and manner to the compositions of children of the same age who use the traditional spelling;
(3) that, in reading aloud, the children who use a phonetic spelling acquire a clearer enunciation than children taught to read throughout in the current orthography;
(4) that, contrary to expectation the transition from the phonetic to the ordinary spelling is attended by no difficulty, and indeed, that children who pass from the former to the latter acquire something like proficiency in the ordinary spelling sooner than children do who are familiar with no other;
(5) that the better mental discipline introduced into the reading and writing lesson leads to improved work in other subjects of the School course.
(Simplified Spelling Society, 1924: 2)

The use of the SSS's New Spelling was resumed in some schools after World War II, but it was not until the 1960s that the 'literacy first, spelling second' approach was first implemented on a large scale.

The Initial Teaching Alphabet

As in the nineteenth century, it was a Pitman, this time Sir James, grandson of Isaac, who was the driving force behind the new wave of 'literacy first, spelling second' teaching. He believed that a rationalised English writing system for learners must replace all digraphs (pairs of letters representing single sounds, as ‹ch›, ‹sh›, ‹th›, ‹ng›, ‹ai›, ‹ee›, ‹oo›, ‹oi›, ‹ou› and above all the 'magic' ‹e› spellings as in *mate, mete, mite, mote, mute*) by single characters. Pitman therefore commissioned the design of an augmented alphabet, containing most of the conventional letters (some slightly adapted), but nearly 20 new ones as well, as shown in Table 1.1. It came to be known as the Initial Teaching Alphabet, or i.t.a. By this system, all native English words can be written directly from their pronunciation, and to read and write fluently children have to learn and practise little more than the letter shapes and sound–symbol correspondences.

During the 1960s i.t.a. was introduced to many hundreds of schools in the UK, and many more in the USA, Canada, Australia and Africa. Towards the end of the 1970s, however, it gradually began to drop out of use (for organisational rather than educational reasons), until by 1990 it had all

TABLE 1.1 *Initial Teaching Alphabet by rote*

No.	Character	Name	Example	No.	Character	Name	Example
1.	æ	ain	æbl	23.	y	yay	yellœ
2.	b	bee	but	24.	z	zed or	zω
3.	c	kee	cat			zee	
	d			25.	ʂ	zess	aʂ
4.	d	did	dog	26.	wh	whee	whie
5.	ee	een	eech	27.	ch	chay	church
6.	f	ef	fun	28.	th	ith	thin
7.	g	gay	gæt	29.	th	thee	then
8.	h	hay	hay	30.	ʃh	ish	ʃhip
9.	ie	ide	ies	31.	ʒ	zhee	meʒuer
10.	j	jay	jam	32.	ŋ	ing	siŋ
11.	k	kay	kiŋ	33.	ɼ	er	herɼ
12.	l	el	lip	34.	a	ahd	faɼher
13.	m	em	man		a	ask	
14.	n	en	not	35.	a	at	at
15.	œ	ode	œpen	36.	au	aud	autum
16.	p	pee	pæ	37.	e	et	egg
	q			38.	i	it	it
17.	r	ray	rat	39.	o	og	on
18.	s	ess	sit	40.	u	ug	up
19.	t	tee	top	41.	ω	oot	bωk
20.	ue	une	ueʂ	42.	ω	ood	mωn
21.	v	vee	vois	43.	ou	oun	out
22.	w	way	wet	44.	oi	oin	oil
	x						

Source: Pitman & St John (1969)

but vanished. Viewed from the 1990s, perhaps the most important thing about i.t.a. was that it was backed up by an extensive research programme (conducted by John Downing), whose findings were independently reviewed and confirmed by Warburton & Southgate (1969) on behalf of the Schools Council. Downing's (1967) own study, however, provides the key data on the standards achieved by pupils who learnt to read and write through i.t.a.

His statistical analysis of test results confirmed the central message of the relatively impressionistic conclusions from the earlier 'literacy first, spelling second' schemes: literacy skills are acquired faster, with better motivation and a sounder foundation, if the writing system uses regular sound–symbol correspondences. Downing (1967) found that the transfer to traditional orthography (t.o.) caused a setback, but pupils soon recovered, and years later their literacy skills were superior to those of pupils who have only ever learnt through t.o. There are, it must be acknowledged, anecdotal accounts of individuals who claim their long-term ability to spell was damaged by the i.t.a. medium, but these claims have not been substantiated by evidence that the problems are directly due to the 'literacy first, spelling second' approach.

Shortly before his death in 1987, Downing reflected (1987) on the psychology underlying the success of pupils who learnt through i.t.a. He explained it in terms of the transfer of skills: reading and writing are skills independent of any particular writing system, and once the learner has achieved fluency (automaticity) in them, they can be readily transferred to any writing system. I.t.a. enabled children to learn without being confused by spelling irregularities until they could transfer their skills to t.o. Downing (1987) also recalled an intriguing finding from his research 20 years earlier (1967: 233–4): a comparative study by one headmistress showed that pupils who learnt through i.t.a. performed other cognitive tasks better than those who learnt through t.o., which suggested that attempting to acquire basic literacy skills through a confusing medium such as t.o. may even damage a child's intellect more generally. The implications of this finding are serious and need further investigation.

Lessons for the Future

While acknowledging the achievements of i.t.a., Downing (1967: 235) also expressed an important reservation, saying that 'this definite conclusion that t.o. is a serious handicap does not mean that i.t.a. is the best means of overcoming the problem'. Bullock's (DES, 1975) view was similar:

> One obvious advantage of using a modified spelling system such as i.t.a. . . . is that it helps writing as well as reading. Children tend to learn quickly how to spell in i.t.a., and they then have ready access to almost every word in their spoken vocabulary . . . When groups of t.o. and i.t.a. children were matched in the main British experiments, the writing produced by the latter was of consistently higher quality. (Downing and Latham subsequently tested a sample of the children

originally involved in this experiment and found that the i.t.a. pupils remained superior in t.o. reading and spelling even after five years at school, i.e. well beyond the transition stage.) It is fair to add that many critics do not accept that such gains are attributable to the medium itself. (DES, 1975)

I.t.a. was always controversial, largely no doubt because it used unconventional symbols. On the other hand, now that concern with standards of literacy in the English-speaking world is perhaps greater than ever before, and confusion on the subject so widespread, the 'literacy first, spelling second' approach, which has repeatedly proved itself over more than a century, should be seriously considered. Could it be revived today?

Another initial teaching system could be designed that avoided the weaknesses of i.t.a. and exploited the latest insights into how writing systems work. By using only conventional letters, it would be an 'initial teaching orthography', like New Spelling. But even such an 'i.t.o.' would be only a makeshift solution, because like i.t.a. it would by definition be used only by beginners. Pupils would still face the disruption of transferring to t.o. and then all the difficulties of t.o. itself. Nevertheless, an i.t.o. could be useful; it would be also simple and flexible, as it could be implemented by individual teachers, or individual schools, or individual education authorities, or individual countries, without the need for worldwide co-ordination.

Despite its earlier sponsorship of New Spelling as an i.t.o., the SSS has always maintained that the writing system itself needs to be made easier for all users: readers and writers, young and old, beginners and professionals, native speakers and foreign learners. Unlike other languages, English has never attempted to control the evolution of its writing system, yet only such an approach goes to the root of the problems of literacy in English. Among the possible ways of tackling the issue is one currently under discussion in the SSS, known as Cut Spelling. Here is a sample, which also explains its rationale:

> Cut Spelng is a relativly new concept for modrnizing ritn english. It exploits th discovry that redundnt letrs cause lernrs th most trubl, and it therfor ataks that dificlty by removing those letrs. Typicl of th resultng spelngs ar: *det, iland, burglr, teachr, doctr, neibr, martr, acomodation, dautr, sycolojy*. Few letrs ar actuly substituted, wich means that th apearnce of text is chanjed far less than if evry sound wer respelt acordng to a fixd set of sound–symbl corespondnces. If u ar readng this, u wil hav been able to do so without much dificlty and without any practice or instruction at al. Cut Speling can save about 10% of letrs in ritn english, wich means that al riting is that much fastr

— a valubl saving of time for evry educationl establishmnt and evry producer of ritn text.

Using such a system for teaching literacy skills would not remove all the problems of learning English spelling, but it would help considerably. However, Cut Spelling is not intended as an i.t.o.: it is designed to be compatible with t.o., so that pupils can continue using it and benefiting from it throughout their lives. It is designed to go to the root of the problem, and modernise English spelling itself at last. That aim bears thinking about.

To conclude, a few observations about the implementation of spelling reform are called for, since the concept is generally unfamiliar in the English-speaking world. A natural and commonly expressed anxiety is that reform could involve such radical changes that adults would need to relearn their literacy skills and the whole structure of written English could be undermined. There have occasionally been such radical reform proposals (Bernard Shaw, for instance, advocated a completely new alphabet), but in literate societies spelling change has to be a gradual, continuous development towards the improved application of the alphabet to the language. A practical reform means that most adults go on writing largely as they were originally taught, while modernised spellings are increasingly introduced by the rising generation. People's spellings are then often a guide to their age. The new spellings have to be immediately recognisable to the older generation (e.g. as *acomodation* is for t.o. *accommodation*), and the old spellings likewise have to be immediately recognisable to young people. In this sense, the old and new spellings have to be compatible with each other, as both are encountered for many years. There can be no question of switching from *accommodation* to, say, *akomodaeshon* (the form used in Nue Speling).

A common misconception is that spelling reform means suddenly starting to spell words phonetically. While it is, in principle, true that the better a spelling represents the pronunciation, the easier it is to handle, and any reformed spellings would represent a step in that direction, as a global reform objective for English the concept of phonetic spelling is utopian. For a start, there would be the practical obstacle that the changes required would be so drastic that the old and new spellings would no longer have that essential quality of compatibility with each other. But more fundamentally, phonetic spelling presupposes an agreed standard pronunciation, which is something that the English language lacks — even in the UK, never mind as a world language.

In short, spelling reform should be seen in historical terms, as a normally unceasing but very slow process of evolution, without disruptive shocks. (The problem with traditional English orthography is that this natural process has been blocked for some 300 years, and the system has simply become out of date.) The Cut Spelling system illustrated above is designed to combine the maximum degree of regularisation with the minimum degree of disruption, but it may well be felt that even that proposal is too disruptive for instant introduction. As for possible mechanisms for introducing improved spellings into English, that is at present a wide field for speculation, and cannot be entered into here.

The one certainty at this stage is that the traditional orthography of English will not stay unchanged for ever, and that we would do ourselves and our descendants a great favour by grasping the nettle and seriously considering how it could best be updated for the twenty-first century.

Summary

Because English lacks a predictable correspondence between writing and pronunciation, learning to read and write it is uniquely difficult, though the implications have often not been recognised by educationists. Teachers mostly use the conventional irregular spellings to teach initial literacy skills, yet there is a long history to the alternative approach of teaching literacy skills first via a regular spelling system, and only teaching conventional spelling after fluency has been achieved. This chapter described the 'literacy first, spelling second' approach, its successes and its psychological rationale, and a plea was made for the English writing system to be modernised. The practical parameters of spelling reform were discussed in conclusion.

Note

This chapter derives from a paper originally entitled 'Positive Lessons from the Initial Teaching Alphabet'.

References

CHOMSKY, N. and HALLE, M. 1968, *The Sound Pattern of English*. New York: Harper and Row.
Department of Education and Science (DES) 1975, *A Language for Life* (The Bullock Report). London: HMSO.
—— 1988, *Report of the Committee of Inquiry into the Teaching of the English Language* (The Kingman Report). London: HMSO.

—— 1989, *English for Ages 5 to 16* (The Cox Report). London: Department of Education and Science and the Welsh Office.
DOWNING, J. 1967, *Evaluating the Initial Teaching Alphabet*. London: Cassell.
—— (ed.) 1973, *Comparative Reading (Cross-National Studies of Behavior and Processes in Reading and Writing)*. New York: The Macmillan Company.
—— 1987, Transfer of Skill in Language Functions. *Journal of the Simplified Spelling Society* Vol. 1, 2.
—— 1988, *Cognitive Psychology and Reading in the USSR*. Amsterdam: North-Holland.
HART, J. 1570, *A Methode or comfortable beginning for all unlearned, whereby they may bee taught to read English, in a very short time, vvith pleasure (The Epistle Dedicatorie, p. 2)*. London: Henrie Denham.
JONES, D. and ORTON, H. 1948, revision of W. RIPMAN and W. ARCHER *New Spelling*. London: Sir Isaac Pitman & Sons.
MICHAEL, I. 1987, *The Teaching of English from the Sixteenth Century to 1870*. Cambridge: Cambridge University Press.
NCC (National Curriculum Council) 1989, *English in the National Curriculum* (Consultation Report). York: NCC.
PITMAN, Sir J. and ST JOHN, J. 1969, *Alphabets and Reading*. London: Sir Isaac Pitman & Sons.
Simplified Spelling Society (SSS) 1924 (reprinted 1942), *The Best Method of Teaching Children to Read and Write (Reports of Experiments conducted in Sixteen Schools)*. London: Sir Isaac Pitman & Sons.
WARBURTON, F. W. and SOUTHGATE, V. 1969, *i.t.a.: An Independent Evaluation*. London: John Murray/W. & R. Chambers.
YULE, V. 1978, Is there evidence of Chomsky's interpretation of English spelling? *Spelling Progress Bulletin* Vol. XVIII, No. 4, Winter.

2 An Orthography as a Theory of a Language

ROBERT VELTMAN

Introduction

My aim is to reinterpret orthographies (roughly 'spelling systems') and the spellings that emerge from them, by showing that orthographies, in particular Standard English Orthography (SEO), are attempts at partially *analysing* the languages they respectively apply to, and are thus, in a weak sense, 'theories' of those languages. I will also show how phonetic features (as opposed to 'phonemes') constitute an area of linguistic structure which an orthography may exploit analytically and how SEO does this in a limited but striking way. I conclude that several apparently arbitrary graphotactic rules of English spelling, in particular the 'double consonant rule', which traditionally constitute the most difficult area for learners to cope with, can be motivated in a natural, non-arbitrary way, if the notion of 'an orthography as a theory of a language' is applied. Thus, it is hoped that this revised understanding of SEO will throw light on and perhaps contribute to a solution of some of the problems in the pedagogy of literacy.

I have tried to avoid the problem of 'spelling reform', but I found to my surprise, that my topic willy-nilly evokes it. However, whatever the pros and cons of that issue, this chapter is concerned with coming to terms with the present standard orthography.

Orthographical Principles

Orthographies are ways in which *scripts,* e.g. Roman, Arabic, Cyrillic, are organised to give rise to individual *spellings*. It is normally understood that only scripts which are organised according to *phonographic* principles, that is on the basis of sound–written symbol relationships, may have 'orthographies' and 'spellings'. Here letters or 'graphs' combine with each other linearly to represent a word in terms of the successive segments in which it is carefully pronounced; hence, **B-A-T-T-E-R-Y** gives us the word *battery*. Note that in the case of the double **T-T**, pronounced as a single sound or phoneme /t/, the presence of the second **T** has a radical effect on the representation of the pronunciation (*battery* versus *batery*); whereas in the word *matt* (as in 'matt emulsion paint'), the second **T** makes no difference to the pronunciation (**MATT** versus **MAT**) and has primarily a lexical function, that of distinguishing visually different words that have an identical pronunciation. It is this type of issue that I wish to address.

Chinese written symbols are known as 'characters'. They do not stand for meaningless sounds like /p/ or /æ/, but for whole words like k$\overline{ai}$, 开, meaning *open*. I would like to extend the concept of an 'orthography' to Chinese writing, because I wish to define an orthography as a way a script analyses a language, and analysing a language in terms of words is as legitimate and feasible as analysing it in terms of its sounds. It has been recognised for some time both among teachers and commentators that SEO analyses English lexically (i.e. in terms of word shapes) as well as phonologically (i.e. in terms of sounds). This tendency is apparent in related words whose stems do not alter 'shape', despite differences in pronunciation, such as *sign* and *signal,* in homonyms which SEO keeps apart orthographically, for example *meet* and *meat,* and in words whose spellings hardly reflect, for historical and etymological reasons, their pronunciation, such as *phlegm, deign* or *endeavour.*

Thus, orthographies have an essentially linguistic function and nature, in the sense that they represent one or, in the case of SEO in particular, more linguistic levels (see Table 2.1). SEO, like Spanish or Finnish orthographies, but unlike the Japanese syllabary and Chinese logography (i.e. character system), is assumed to comply largely with the alphabetic principle, a subprinciple of the phonographic orthographical principle, according to which each grapheme symbolises a different contrastive sound in the language, namely a phoneme, ideally on a one-to-one basis. Learners of the English spelling system are often led to a literal belief in this relationship and then are sometimes clumsily or abruptly disabused of it, with predictably sad results. My main point is that the word, the grammatical morpheme, and the phonetic feature, as well as the phoneme, figure also in the tie between grapheme and linguistic unit in SEO. The impression of 'inconsistency' in SEO can be traced to the association of SEO with more than one linguistic level and component, as Table 2.1 implies.

TABLE 2.1 *Language, its levels and organisational components and their relationship to orthography*

Linguistic level	Organisational component	Script example	
Sounding ('Expression')	*Phonology* feature phoneme syllable tone	SEO, Korean Han'gŭl SEO & all alphabets Japanese Kana Yoruba, Chinese Pinyin	→ O R T H → → →
Wording	lexicon grammar (incl. morphology)	SEO, Chinese charactery SEO	→ O G R A P H →
Meaning	semantics	Japanese Kanji	→ Y

In summary, then, scripts are organised in terms of orthographic principles, which relate graphemes (including devices of the apostrophe, punctuation and letter-case) or characters to one or more linguistic components.

One of the fundamental tenets of twentieth-century linguistic science is that linguists have a special responsibility towards the description of spoken language. Certain specific consequences have issued from this valid methodological demand. It has sometimes implied that the written language is derivatively related to the spoken language, and to the extent that the spoken language is conceived primarily as an inventory of phonemes, then speech is (a) equated with sounds, and (b) with a particular class of sounds — phonemes. But writing is rarely used, except in highly specialised circumstances for transcription, the inscribing of speech as it is uttered, a task to which phonology and phonemic analysis contribute. Therefore, writing is at least functionally autonomous of speech (Lyons, 1972: 62). Furthermore, if writing is at all derivative, it is derivative of language, of which phonology is but one element. Thus, a model of language as represented in Table 2.1 is more useful to the practitioner and ultimately the learner than a model where writing is one of the components of the level of expression, alongside speech and signing. Writing and orthography are much more than physical manifestations of language.

Linguistic Levels and Components

As Table 2.1 shows any human language has three main levels: meaning, wording and expression. Each contains, as indicated, one or more characteristic systems of organisation: meanings are derived via various semantic systems, some of which are more pragmatic, i.e. related to the real world and immediate situation, than others; wordings are generated by the interaction of the grammar and the lexicon ('vocabulary', 'word-store', 'dictionary'); and expression is realised by the systems underlying each of its sounded, written or signed manifestations, phonology, graphology and semology, respectively.

Phonology itself is a complex entity containing at least four organisational components: a featural one, a phonemic one, a syllabic one and a prosodic one. The first three are known to characterise the orthographical principles of different scripts (featural, alphabetic, syllabic), although prosodic features are marked in SEO by a number of graphetic and orthographic conventions, e.g. italics, high case lettering, punctuation (see

Vachek, 1989: 172). A number of alphabetic scripts devised for tone languages, such as Chinese Mandarin 'Pinyin', Yoruba, Vietnamese, mark lexemic tonal distinctions, e.g. Chinese Pinyin: *haŏ (good)*, *hào (number)*.

One of the reasons why it is so difficult to distinguish wording from expression is that you cannot talk about or cite a 'wording', e.g. a sentence, phrase or word, without giving it some form of expression! I am saying that a sentence, such as the one I am writing now, and the phrases and individual words it contains, actually exist *independently* of the form of expression, in this case the written form of expression, it takes. It exists, as it were, in an abstract, inaudible and invisible form, prior to its *realisation* in one of the three physical modes and channels described. In principle, the sentence mentioned could be spoken or written or signed. It just happens here to be written.

The point that grammar is separate from phonology is an important one, since it is commonly assumed that the orthographical representation of a language purely as sound correspondences suffices as a representation of that language, and that the alphabetic principle serves as a 'window', as it were, on the non-phonological compartments of a language. This is not so. Phonemics, embodied in the alphabetic principle of association between sounds of a language and alphabetic graphemes, may be more accurately thought of as a 'door' to language, facilitating in its own way the apprenticeship of literacy.

The view presented here of the relationship between an orthography and a language is one that does indeed accord priority to speech and phonology, but where orthography is not just an epiphenomenon at the end of a chain of command, but a set of systems that has the potential for characterising a language and *all* its levels and components. However, despite the claims of advocates of the 'reading for meaning' approach (e.g. Smith, 1978), orthographies do not as a rule (Japanese *kanji* characters being a well known exception) represent meanings. They represent aspects of pronunciation, grammatical morphology and vocabulary.

Analytical Focus

Orthographies are determined to some extent by the structure of languages they represent, thus you can speak only of 'an orthography as a theory of *a* language'. Orthography is not a 'linguistic theory' or 'theory of language'. Orthographies differ from each other, however, not only as function of differences between the represented languages (English, French,

AN ORTHOGRAPHY AS A THEORY OF LANGUAGE 35

etc.) but also in terms of their differing *analytical focus,* which if consistent enough can be adopted as an *orthographical principle,* e.g. featural script, alphabet, syllabary or logography. Examples of these are, respectively, Korean Han'gŭl, Castillian, Spanish, Japanese Kana and Chinese charactery. However, SEO is perhaps the prime example of *multiple analytical focus* — few orthographies are 'pure' — and sometimes this alternation of focus is prompted by competing needs (Sampson, 1985: 212–13): competent user versus learner, reader versus writer, native versus foreign learner/user, pre-printing versus post-printing literacy, older (not necessarily adult) versus younger learner, silent reading versus the practice of reading aloud (pre-printing, parents or teachers to children), and varying reading or spelling strategies.

It has been said of SEO that it is especially suitable for native, competent users, there being no need to indicate pronunciations (Chomsky, 1970). Users of SEO learn to tolerate a significant degree and quantity of lexical, sometimes arbitrary and etymologically-based spellings, e.g. **NIGHT, ENDEAVOUR, FOREIGN.** The SEO user world also tolerates a range of conventionalised variations in English spelling, notably US versus British. In 1755, Dr Johnson's dictionary appeared with the purpose of regulating hitherto inconsistent *private* English spellings. However, as any teacher knows, including teachers in tertiary education, there is repeated and predictable variation in spelling: homophones confused, e.g. *there/their* weak syllables spelled with **E** rather than **A**, e.g. **SEPERATE**.

There is, as Yule (1984: 22) suggests, a case for extending tolerance and even recognition to the commonest spelling 'mistakes'. Some mistakes are even historically justified: *scissors* spelled sometimes by learners as **SISSERS** or **SISSORS** corresponds more closely to an earlier spelling of **SISOURS**, before mistaken etymology was allowed to apply. Interestingly enough, in a few cases SEO incorporates some 'free' variation in spelling, e.g. **INQUIRY/ENQUIRY**, which does not entail variation in meaning as with **MEAT/MEET**, or reflect national differences, as does **LABOUR/LABOR** and other British–American divergences in spelling. At any given time a speller has a tacit but individualised knowledge of principles underlying spellings of his or her language, and thus can be said to be equipped with something like an *orthographical competence,* analogous with Chomsky's 'grammatical competence'. Despite the predictability of spelling mistakes revealing the existence of several 'private' SEO orthographies, the established system is learnable. Rules that in number and complexity go beyond mere letter–phoneme equivalence seem to be acquired not on exposure to formal instruction in spelling rules but through the act of reading, according to Krashen (1989). Moreover, as Sampson (1985) points out,

SEO has undergone very little change or 'reform' since the eighteenth century, while frequent reforms are characteristic of societies, where letter–phoneme consistency is deemed by authorities to be the hallmark of socially acceptable, perhaps non-elitist orthography (France and Spain both saw recent attempts at spelling reforms).

I would agree that SEO spelling is elitist in the sense that it poses problems that bring about marked differential individual success, socially stigmatising those who fall short of its norms in the public arena. But as Sampson (1985) points out, popular incentive for change may be largely absent, for reasons outlined above. One may also argue that there are equal risks of elitism, social stigma and failure, if the orthography were hitched to a particular regional or social accent and to a form of 'careful' pronunciation, where a spelling system would reflect the pronunciation of *February* as **/februːɛri/** (careful but unnatural) rather than **/febjuːɛri/** (common, natural pronunciation). SEO for all its half-hearted relationship with the phonemes of English has certain advantages in its very remoteness and compromise. What I am arguing for in promoting the investigation of the relationship between an orthography and the full range of linguistic levels and components is that these should be tapped so as to meet the resources of the learner, which include a significant linguistic element, transcending the set of phonemes of a language. Such resources are not necessarily concentrated at the non-phonological levels of language either. Other phonological areas need to be considered, such as the phonetic feature.

Provided the principle is accepted that a purpose of an orthography can be to represent a language with all its multi-level complexity, rather than simply the inventory of phonemes of a language (which in any case the 26-letter alphabet can hardly do with accuracy in the case of the 44 or 45 phoneme standard English received pronunciation), the teacher and learner may find the task less daunting. Moreover, the 'mould', to borrow a politically exploited metaphor, into which literacy teaching has over the years been poured, of phoneme- and word-based approaches, can be broken, if other linguistic components are explored and exploited in the teaching and learning processes, such as the syllable or — what I shall principally be concerned with now — the *phonetic feature.*

I want to explain how SEO spelling is learnable and how, paradoxically, some of the very features, such as double consonants (**NN** in *running*), digraphs (**TH, SH, PH, CH, WH**), the alternation of **C, K** and **CK** and 'silent' letters (**E** in *brave*), which are deemed 'graphotactic' and are commonly understood to offend logic and cause spelling failure, have a certain linguistic status and, possibly, 'psychological reality' enabling them with less difficulty than is often believed to become part of the individual speller's orthographical competence.

Phonetic Features in SEO

By now it should be understood that SEO is a 'theory' of the English language, in that it represents at least one linguistic level or level component of the language: expression (sounding — phonemes, phonetic features, prosodic elements); wording (lexicon and grammar); meaning (semantics) (see Halliday, 1989: 11). However, it was made clear that SEO analyses English in terms of four of these elements — phonemes, phonetic features, lexicon and grammar — SEO having a multiple analytical focus. The phonemic, lexical and grammatical functions of SEO have been well documented. What has tended to be overlooked in accounts, or at least interpreted differently from here, is the role of phonetic features in SEO. Accordingly, I shall omit further discussion of phonemic, lexical and grammatical focuses of SEO, and concentrate on phonetic features in SEO.

Perhaps the least documented aspect of SEO analytical focus is that concerned with phonetic features (as opposed to phonemes). A possible reason for this is the notion that phonetic features are sometimes predictable and thus would not, in principle, participate in distinguishing words or morphemes. Phonetic features are those articulatory positions or movements or acoustic qualities of oral sounds, which when combined are perceived as phonemes, the ultimately contrastive units of sound in language, which alphabetically based orthographies are purported to analyse the phonological component of language into. Thus the consonant phoneme /z/ is describable in terms of the following articulatory features (among others): voiced, alveolar, fricative. Teachers of spelling and reading have for centuries exploited a major distinction among phonetic features to classify sounds and letters of the alphabet, namely the consonant–vowel difference. Vowels may differ simultaneously in their 'height' and in the degree to which the front, centre or back of the tongue is raised in their articulation. Vowels may be 'tense' or 'lax': there are seven lax vowels in British English, five of them corresponding to the first set of sound values learners are taught to assign to the five vowel graphemes of SEO: /æ/ as in *bat*, etc. They, unlike the eleven or so tense vowels, may occur before the sound /ŋ/, as in *rang, length, ring, wrong, rung*. Tense vowels, on the other hand, often described as being 'long', may occur in open syllables, as in *may, my, toy, tea, tar*, etc. (Ladefoged, 1982: 207).

The major significance of phonetic features is that they permit the classification of phonemes: hence, a set of phonemes can be formed on the basis of, say, a common 'plosive' feature, or one can talk about 'nasal' consonants, or 'back' vowels. From the acoustic–auditory point of view, some sounds like /l/, /r/, /w/ and /j/ have vowel-like qualities and can thus be grouped together as approximants, as they are technically known.

Since alphabetic orthographical systems relate in principle to the inventory of the phonemes of their respective languages, it might easily be assumed that features, being only individual sound features that have to combine with other features to make phonemes, cannot be directly represented in such orthographies. However, Korean Han'gŭl, devised by King Sejong in 1444 for writing Korean (Chinese had hitherto been the language of literacy in Korea), is a featural script and orthography (Sampson, 1985: ch. 7), in which the forms of the letters and their rules of combination are determined explicitly by phonetic features. I am claiming here that SEO has a significant featural element and that a number of well-known features of SEO often dismissed as inconsistencies, or at least as resulting from quaint, graphotactic rules, can be explained if they are regarded as phonetic features rather than phonemes.

As suggested above, phonetic feature variation is suppressed in standard alphabetic orthographies especially those that are predictable. Several phonological processes in spoken English are largely ignored by the SEO spellings: for example 'weakening' of the vowel in unstressed vowels, is not recorded in the spelling, a cause of common spelling errors, such as **SEPERATE, DEPENDANCE, GRAMMER**; nor are 'co-articulations' orthographically signalled, where phonetic details are not indicated, such as the lip rounding of the /s/ in *soup* and lip-spreading of the /s/ in *seep*. Difference in voice is reflected, however, in the graphemic pairs **P–B, T–D, S–Z, CH–DG, SH–3** (in *leisure*), **K–G**; but **TH** spells both voiceless /θ/ and voiced /ð/ as in *thanks* and *that*. Some instructive facts emerge on close observation of palatalisation.

Several English words like *lewd, sue* and *pseudonym* are subject to alternative pronunciations, where the first vowel sound in these examples are variously pronounced as /u:/ or /ju:/. In other words, the vowel represented by **EW** in *lewd* may be 'palatalised' as /ju:/ to give /lju:d/ (lyood) as opposed to /lu:d/ (lood). Some English speakers, particularly North Americans and Norfolk country people, do not palatalise the /u:/ sound at all, they always say /lu:d/ for *lewd* and /nu:z/ for *news*. For the majority of British speakers words like *lewd* or *sue* are variably pronounced, though some words of this class like *suit* tend to be pronounced in one way rather

AN ORTHOGRAPHY AS A THEORY OF LANGUAGE

than the other (an older generation says /sju:t/). As we have just seen, this vowel appears to be spelled in a number of ways: **EW, UE, UI, EU** or just **U** as in *putrid*. The palatal element, phonetically /j/ is not directly, and certainly not consistently, represented. However, there are words, such as *goose, soup, through* or *tomb*, which have the /u:/ sound but are never pronounced as /gju:s/ (gyoose) etc. in any dialect. What one can say is that those /u:/ vowels in words like *knew*, whose /u:/ vowel can be palatalised, are normally spelled with an **E** or a **U** or both, but not an **O**. An analogy of a somewhat simpler nature is the use of **H** in digraphs, **SH, TH, PH, WH, CH** (and historically **GH**), where a fricative or 'hissing' quality is indirectly represented by **H**. 'It certainly is an art form' a colleague of mine recently said to me of SEO, a comment substantiated by the subtle way in which SEO marks such features of 'palatal' vowels and 'fricative' consonants.

The Double Consonant Rule

The double consonant rule in SEO illustrates how SEO exploits other phonetic distinctions in English, such as those between tense and lax vowels. The type of analysis proposed deconstructs graphotactic rules, like the double consonant rule. These have to be learned in an apparently arbitrary way in the apprenticeship of English spelling, since they are internal to the system and therefore are deemed not to reflect linguistic items. The evidence presented here suggests that at least some of these so-called graphotactic restrictions are linguistically motivated in respect of phonetic features.

Around 1200 AD an Augustinian cleric from the East Midlands, called Orm, produced a 10,000 line manuscript of a homily, which has become a landmark in the history of English spelling (Scragg, 1974: 29). The manuscript, since known as the *Ormulum,* contains a number of orthographical innovations, including one that distinguishes in modern SEO *taping* from *tapping,* and thus relates the former to the lexical item *tape* and the latter to *tap*. Scragg describes the purpose of the revised spelling as 'a desire to improve the delivery of the preachers who used the sermons by creating a phonemic spelling'. It is possible that the phonemes of the English of the time were represented by the revised spelling, but this is not to say that the spelling system Orm devised was organised through phonemes alone. The extra consonant has no phonemic value on its own. What it does, as in *tapping, running, dinner, blotted, penned,* is to 'protect' the fundamental lax ('short') value of the previous single vowel grapheme. This seemingly protective function of the doubled consonant, preventing it from tensing in the environment of **E** or **I** has an intriguing iconic, almost pictorial character.

English has double ('geminate') consonant sounds in words such as *unnecessary* or *tailless* (pronounced /ʌnnɛsəsɛri/, /teilləs/), but this 'doubling' of sound, although reflected in both pronunciation and spelling (**NN, LL**), occurs only across morpheme boundaries in English (unlike Italian or Russian), such as *un* and *necessary*. The double consonant grapheme rule of SEO, on the other hand, reflects a lot of linguistic information about English. It has a phonemic function, distinguishing between several pairs of vowel phonemes, e.g. /ei/ versus /æ/ in *taping* and *tapping*. The rule has a lexical function, as indicated above, in relating *taping* to the lexeme *tape* and *tapping* to the lexeme *tap*. It has a grammatical function, indicating the affixation of grammatical morphemes, such as *-ed* and *-ing* for verbs, *-er*, and *-est* for adjectives and adverbs and *-er* for 'agentive' nouns like *robber*. Lastly, it has the fundamental role of offering general information about the phonetic composition of the vowels concerned.

If what has just been said is correct, then why does the double consonant rule not apply in derived words with lax vowels like *sanity* and *agility*? After all, we ought to expect such words to be spelled **SANNITY** and **AGILLITY**, to ensure that the vowels are not tensed as in their related words *sane* and *agile*. The function of the rule is to differentiate words like *tap* and *tape* and *rob* and *robe,* and to bring together forms of the same word (or 'lexeme') like *tap* and *tapping* and *rob* and *robbing* in terms of their pronunciation. *Sane* and *sanity*, etc. are forms of the same lexeme but are pronounced differently, therefore there is no requirement that the vowel in question be 'protected'. Indeed, the rule applies quite obstinately to preserve the phonic relationship of related words even when basic graphotactic rules, such as the rule preventing the doubling of **V** are violated. After all, words like *quiver* and *revel,* given the laxness of their first vowel, should be spelled **QUIVVER** and **REVVEL**, to ensure they do not rhyme with *fiver* and *evil*, respectively. This rule is probably a response to the demands made on the orthography by typography to prevent confusion of **VV** with **W**. At least two words, according to various modern dictionaries, including a dictionary of spelling (Wileman & Wileman, 1990), are spelled with double **V**, *skivvy* and *navvy*. Could a minor graphotactic rule be operative in the case of words ending in **Y**? The word *bevy* according to the same sources shows only a single **V** in this environment. *The Guardian* newspaper of 26 January 1991 supports this textually with 'Nikki, one of the *bevy* of pin-ups that adorn jets in the Gulf' (but note how *Nikki* violates the double **K** graphotactic rule!). *Skivvy* has to contrast with *skive* (for skivvies hardly skive!) and *navvy* with *navy*. Therefore, it appears that **VV** is permitted before the **Y** suffix, *provided specific pairs of words need to be differentiated from each other*. The example of the restriction on double **VV** in SEO is interesting, because it shows what appears to be an essentially graphotactic rule, with no linguistic input whatever, ultimately shares considerable ground with morpho-lexical (see Stubbs (1986) for this useful term) and phonetic features.

Vallins (1954: 52) observes, as if it were an arbitrary fact, a certain 'regularity' associated with the rule: the final consonant doubles either in monosyllables (most of the examples given so far) or polysyllabic words with a stressed final syllable, e.g. *occur – occurred.* Thus in *happen, gallop, waver, focus, bias, clever,* the final consonant is not duplicated, when suffixing occurs, as in *happened, wavering, cleverest,* etc. This is entirely explicable in phonetic terms: unstressed syllables are weakened and pronounced as 'schwa' /ə/, which is a neutralisation of several different phonetic values. These unstressed syllables, therefore, as it were, have no phonetic 'value' worth protecting via duplication of the final consonant: hence, *pre'ferred* but *'proffered,* where the stress is on the first syllable.

The double consonant rule therefore reflects lexical, grammatical, phonemic and, indeed, phonetic knowledge of the English speller. It is thus an excellent example of the way an orthography acts as a 'theory' of a language.

Concluding Remarks

Most graphotactical rules of spelling are not taught. Spellers remember clearly only a handful of them: 'I before E except after C', 'final Y changes to I before affixes, unless Y is preceded by a vowel, as in *chimney*', and the 'double consonant rule'. But even the double consonant rule is taught usually with partial reference to grammar (adding of suffixes) and to phonetic features ('long' and 'short' vowels, syllable stress and quantity). However, subtleties like 'let double O in words like *book, cook,* etc., represent a long (tense) vowel' in order to account for the spelling of /k/ as K rather than CK, are rarely taught. (In most English accents, but not all, these words are pronounced with a lax (short) vowel /ω/ and not a tense (long) one /u:/.)

Graphotactical rules are a set of arbitrary restrictions that are internal to the orthographic system, most of which spellers actually know and use only unconsciously. These graphotactic rules, when grasped consciously, are treated for the most part prescriptively and are the particular targets of spelling reform. However, they include numbers of rules, such as the palatalisation rule or the double consonant rule or the /k/ realisation rules, which though defiant of explanation on the basis of a one-to-one grapheme–phoneme pairing, can be motivated particularly on the grounds of the assignment of general phonetic values rather than phonemic ones. The point about phonetic features is that they are general to sounds and in respect of an individual sound are not immediately accessible. They may not even have been consciously present in the minds of those who contributed to the development of SEO (although Orm probably realised the iconic significance of his double consonant rule). We know, however, that before the eighteenth century private spelling was highly idiosyncratic and that learners, 'poor' and even mature spellers do spell, idiosyncratically. This individual exploitation is explicable only through reference to the way spellers themselves analyse English words on the basis of a relative modicum of taught or assimilated sound–grapheme associations or word shapes acquired in reading (see Krashen, 1989), which provide clues to the way words are to be analysed. The rest of the analysis and synthesis depends on the way in which the speller relates his or her acquired knowledge of the orthography, a 'theory' of the English language, to the language itself as the speller re-creates it in writing.

References

CHOMSKY, C. 1970, Reading, writing and phonology. *Harvard Educational Review* 40, 2, 287–309.
HALLIDAY, M. A. K. 1989, *Spoken and Written Language* 2nd edn. Oxford: Oxford University Press.
KRASHEN, S. 1989, We acquire vocabulary and spelling by reading: Additional evidence for the input hypothesis. *The Modern Language Journal* 73, 4, 440–64.
LADEFOGED, P. 1982, *A Course in Phonetics* 2nd edn. New York: Harcourt, Brace, Jovanovich.
LYONS, J. 1972, Human language. In R. A. HINDE (ed.) *Non-Verbal Communication* (pp. 49–85). Cambridge: Cambridge University Press.
SAMPSON, G. 1985, *Writing Systems*. London: Hutchinson.
SCRAGG, D. G. 1974, *A History of English Spelling*. Manchester: Manchester University Press.
SMITH, F. 1978, *Reading*. Cambridge: Cambridge University Press.
STUBBS, M. 1986, The synchronic organization of English spelling. BAAL/LAGB Committee for Linguistics in Education Working Paper No. 10.
VACHEK, J. 1989, *Written Language Revisited,* Amsterdam: John Benjamins.
VALLINS, G. H. 1954, *Spelling*. London: André Deutsch.
WILEMAN, B. and WILEMAN, R. 1990, *Dictionary of English Spelling*. London: Harrap.
YULE, V. 1984, English, the international language handicapped by its spelling. *Language Monthly* 8, 22–3.

Section Two:
Spelling Processes

This section consists of four chapters: by Seymour, Barry, Funnell and Pattison & Collier. Seymour reviews the cognitive theories of spelling. Barry deals with spelling by analogy and the phenomenon of priming. Funnell focuses on proofreading and the differences between lexical information used for reading and spelling. Pattison & Collier argue that we shouldn't be surprised to find evidence of phonetic spelling because the way we test and measure spelling performance is weighted in its favour.

Cognitive Theories of Spelling and Implications for Education (Seymour)

Seymour's chapter begins by applying the notion of modularity to spelling: one module consisting of processes that produce spellings from sounds, the other consisting of processes that produce spellings from stored forms (the dual route model). The first source of evidence for this is disorders of spelling and, in particular, the phenomena of lexical and phonological dysgraphia in each of which one set of processes are largely preserved and the other largely destroyed. The second source of evidence is the English writing system which seems to need both a logographic and a phonological system.

Seymour then moves on to a discussion of theories of development. He points out that the sequential development of phonological awareness supports a stage theory of spelling development, a notable example of which is, of course, Frith (1985). He discusses two aspects of the logographic phase: whether or not it exists for spelling, and whether or not there are several stages of segmentation ability. He concludes that the evidence supports Frith but prefers his own model — that of a letter generator working out of a literagraphic lexicon. Similarly, in his discussion of the alphabetic stage, while the evidence is consistent with Frith's notion that spelling is phonological and precedes reading, he argues that his own model provides at least as good an account. Finally, the orthographic phase of Frith's theory is about skilled performance and Seymour moves on to a discussion of Morton's (1989) account of the relationship between Frith's model and the dual process model of skilled performance. Seymour examines the claims made, concluding that certain key aspects of the Frith–Morton model are questionable. The most important of these, damaging to the whole idea of two separate systems, is the fact that non-word spellings can be influenced by priming (i.e. prior exposure to real word spellings of the same sound).

Seymour goes on briefly to discuss a number of possible models and then specifies the criteria by which they should be evaluated, concluding that only a modified two-process model or a single-process literagraphic model can satisfy these criteria.

In the final major section Seymour moves on to the practical implications of his results. For assessment the purpose is to develop word and non-word lists which could then be used to identify a child's developmental level. He sketches out how these lists could be developed for spelling (he has already developed one for reading). Briefly, the words and non-words would be generated by combining building blocks consisting of initial consonant structures (**B- P- CL- PR-** etc.), vowels (**A E I O U**) and terminal consonant structures (**-B -P -ST -ND -FT** etc.). There would be at least two levels of difficulty (core words, expansions of the core) and the sample selected for testing would cover the range of spellings of each building block. There would also be homophone pairs and words and non-words composed of morphemic building blocks (e.g. **-ED -ING** etc.). For teaching he suggests using these lists in a programme which stresses the phonological basis of spelling and the integrity of the building blocks. The child would first learn the letter sounds; then how to spell words and non-words with simple high-contingency (frequent) correspondences; then be introduced to simple words with low-contingency correspondences to indicate the existence of 'exceptional' spellings; then to words and non-words with complex correspondences (with both high- and low-contingency spellings being introduced); and finally to words and non-words composed partly of morphemes.

Interactions Between Lexical and Assembled Spelling (in English, Italian and Welsh) (Barry)

Barry's chapter provides a detailed account of the priming phenomenon (alluded to in Seymour's paper) that gives the dual process model its problems. After briefly reviewing the model, Barry asks two questions of it.

First, are the two sets of processes completely independent of each other or do they interact? Second, given that dual route theory was devised partly to deal with the irregularities of English spelling, is there any evidence that two routes exist in languages with regular orthographies? Such languages shouldn't, in principle, need the lexical route as both reading and spelling could proceed using the assembled (phonological) route.

The answer to the first question has been reported in a previous paper (Barry & Seymour, 1988), which he here summarises. To understand the logic we need to note that many sounds in English can be spelled in many ways (henceforth 'multi-spelling sounds'), some being more common than others. In Barry & Seymour's terminology, a common spelling of a sound is a *high-contingency* spelling, while an uncommon spelling is a *low-contingency* spelling. Barry & Seymour required English speakers to spell non-words, a task in which spellers *have* to use the assembled spelling route. They were concerned specifically with how multi-spelling sounds would be spelled. They found two things. Firstly, that the spellings produced reflected the pattern of contingencies for each of the sounds in question. That is, high-contingency spellings were produced more frequently than low-contingency spellings. Secondly, that the speller could be influenced into producing a particular spelling by presenting (i.e. priming) them with a real word containing that spelling immediately before.

The modification to the dual route model Barry & Seymour propose is this; explained here for the spelling of a single, multi-spelling vowel. Through experience, a knowledge of the many spellings of this vowel will have been built up, with, for each spelling, some indicator of how common it is relative to the others. In other words a knowledge of the spelling contingencies of the sound. Their finding that the spelling of non-words reflects these spelling contingencies indicates that this knowledge is used by the processes of assembled spelling when spelling non-words. Furthermore, the fact that previous exposure to a particular spelling, embodied in the real word prime, influences the non-word spelling indicates that the choice of spelling by the assembling processes is affected by events that have taken place in the mental lexicon. In short, according to Barry & Seymour, there is an interaction between the assembled and lexical routes.

To answer the second question, Barry and various colleagues have also looked at Italian and Welsh. Although both these languages have overwhelmingly regular orthographies, in that most phonemes are spelled in only one way, they both also have one (Welsh) or two (Italian) vowels with two spellings. This permits us to test whether the dual route model (or rather Barry & Seymour's amended version) applies to these languages. Barry and his colleagues carried out the same type of experiment described above on native Italian and bilingual English/Welsh speakers using these ambiguities of Italian and Welsh orthography. They found the same effects for both of these as they did for English: firstly, that subjects' spelling of the multi-spelling vowel in the invented words reflected the spelling contingencies of the vowel, and secondly that the particular spelling produced was influenced (primed) by the real word spelling previously seen. Thus, as with English, Welsh and Italian literates (even though their orthographies are regular) have two routes for spelling, the assembled route and the lexical route, and the two interact in the way proposed by Barry & Seymour.

On Recognising Misspelled Words (Funnell)

Funnell's chapter is concerned with how we recognise correctly and incorrectly spelled words. She asks whether it is realistic to expect poor spellers to recognise their own misspellings. She cites evidence which suggests that a proofreading task permits correct-spelling identification but not misspelling detection. Indirect evidence from Type A (good readers/spellers) and Type B (good readers/poor spellers) subjects implies that misspelling detection is related to reading proficiency. Funnell argues, by contrast, that correct-spelling identification depends on the word being in the reading vocabulary while misspelling detection depends on the word being in the spelling vocabulary.

In the first study, Thomas, a ten-year-old good reader/good speller, was able, when presented with a mixture of correct and incorrect spellings, to identify all the correct spellings but only about half the misspellings. He was subsequently able to read all the words, suggesting that having the words in his reading vocabulary was not relevant to misspelling detection. However, when asked to spell them, he misspelled some, and a comparison revealed that he only detected a misspelling if he had been able to spell it. The suggestion that misspelling detection was dependent on having the word in his spelling vocabulary was confirmed in a second study.

Funnell goes on to argue that if spotting a misspelling requires knowing the spelling of a word, then words learned with the intention of only being able to read them should be missed in a detection task more often than words learned with the intention of only being able to spell them. In a second study she tested Helen, a poor reader/poor speller, who practised reading five words she initially couldn't read until she could (reading only group), and spelling five (different) words she initially couldn't spell until she could (spelling only group). In a subsequent detection task Helen correctly identi-

ical
INTRODUCTION: SPELLING PROCESSES

fied the *same* number (80%) of correct spellings from each group but while she detected all the misspellings in the spelling only group she only detected about 50% (guessing level) in the reading only group.

It seems then that misspelling detection is related to having the words in the spelling vocabulary while correct spelling identification isn't. What are the effects on detection, however, of having, or not having, a word in the reading vocabulary *which isn't in the spelling vocabulary*. Funnell argues that if detectability is based on the resemblance of the presented letter string to words in the reading vocabulary then correct spellings of known words should be more often judged as correct than correct spellings of unknown words. In contrast, and somewhat counter-intuitively, misspellings of known words should be detected *less* often (because of the misleading similarity to the mother word) than misspellings of unknown words (because these don't resemble particular mother words). This is what she found.

It seems, then, that correct-spelling identification is dependent on having the word in the reading vocabulary — being able to spell it as well makes no difference. In contrast, misspelling detection depends on whether or not it is in the spelling vocabulary. If the word is not in the spelling vocabulary then having the word in the reading vocabulary affects misspelling detection, but in a paradoxical way: the child is likely to make fewer detections when the word is known than when it is not known.

Funnell concludes her chapter with an explanation. Essentially, knowing a word well enough to read it doesn't require a precise specification of the spelling — letter identity information may be enough, with letter order information being more or less an irrelevance. In contrast, knowing a word well enough to spell it requires a complete specification of identity and order. In the detection task the incomplete specification of the 'reading representation' will be enough to identify correct spellings (there will be enough of a match between letter string and representation), and the additional information present if the word can also be spelled adds nothing. With misspellings, however, while the incomplete reading representation will be enough to detect a few errors, it will let substantial numbers through the net (again because there will be enough of a match between the misspelling and the representation). To pick up all the misspellings needs a full specification of the spelling and this comes only when the word can also be spelled.

The practical implication is clear: asking children to check for misspellings of words they can't spell is a futile exercise. A corollary is that good spelling is only really attained by learning how to spell — practising reading will not be sufficient.

Methodological Issues in the Investigation of Spelling and Spelling Development (Pattison & Collier)

Pattison & Collier begin by pointing out the importance that theories of spelling put on phonetic spelling. This approach seems justified, for even the deaf, who we do not usually associate with use of a sound system, show evidence of (pseudo)phonology in their spelling. However, they say, this theoretical emphasis may be misguided. Teaching, for example, emphasises other strategies, a fact which in itself should lead us to believe that phonetic spelling is not the only strategy available to children. They suggest that one reason why we find such pervasive evidence of phonetic spelling is because the tasks used to investigate spelling may actually promote its use to a greater than usual degree.

The authors' stated long-term purpose is to develop unbiased investigative instruments and, in particular, to develop more sophisticated spelling tests. They review the methods used to investigate spelling, pointing out the problems with each. Thus the most common, oral presentation (heard or lip read), may well bias the speller towards use of phonetic strategies and may also be inappropriate for some special needs groups such as the deaf.

They then go on to a critique of the ways in which spelling errors are classified, pointing out that mutually exclusive classification (an error is either phonetically plausible or not) takes no account of either the fact that multiple classifications may be justified (a phonetically plausible error (**BEAR** for *bare*) could equally be construed as visually plausible) or that errors vary in their magnitude.

They illustrate their position with a study in which the items to be spelled were presented either as pictures or orally and in which errors were multiply classified in the degree to which they were phonetic and visually plausible. They found that younger children (seven years) made more errors and more severe errors on both dimensions than did the group of older children (10 years). However, while in younger children there was a correlation between number and magnitude of error on both dimensions, for older children there was no such correlation for visual errors, suggesting that by this age they have either mastered the visual strategy or are not using it. Finally, they found that oral presentation led to greater phonetic accuracy than did pictorial presentation.

They conclude their chapter with a discussion of the practical implications of their work. They argue that the scope of tests of ability must be increased to take account of *how* spelling ability is tested (e.g. oral, picture presentation) and to classify errors in more than one way.

References

BARRY, C. and SEYMOUR, P. H. K. 1988, Lexical priming and sound-to-spelling contingency effects in non-word spelling. *Quarterly Journal of Experimental Psychology* 40A, 5–40.
FRITH, U. 1985, Beneath the surface of developmental dyslexia. In K. E. PATTERSON, J. C. MARSHALL and M. COLTHEART (eds) *Surface Dyslexia: Neuropsychological and Cognitive Analyses of Phonological Reading*. London: Lawrence Erlbaum.
MORTON, J. 1989, An information processing account of reading acquisition. In A. M. GALABURDA (ed.) *From Reading to Neurons*. Cambridge, Mass.: MIT Press.

3 Cognitive Theories of Spelling and Implications for Education

PHILIP H. K. SEYMOUR

Introduction

In asking me to contribute to this volume, the editors suggested that I might comment on current cognitive theories of spelling and their possible implications for educational practice. I see this as a task of discussing theories which purport to explain how knowledge of spelling might be represented in the brain, how this knowledge is built up during development, and what might be the conclusions from the theories, if true, regarding: (1) methods of investigation and research (diagnostic assessment of spelling), or (2) methods of instruction (the spelling curriculum).

Modular Framework

An assumption of the cognitive approach is that spelling competence is based on a number of internal processes (often termed 'modules'). These have a neural basis but are defined in terms of the functions they perform rather than their strict localisation in the brain. The modules and their interconnections constitute the cognitive architecture of the spelling system. Following Shallice (1988), Ellis & Young (1988), and others, we can distinguish between a peripheral process, concerned with the production of handwritten forms (writing), and central processes, which are involved in the storage and retrieval of spelling information. A widely held view is that there are two major central processes in spelling, one based on a lexicon of word forms and the other on a set of sound–letter (phoneme–grapheme) correspondences (see Morton, 1980; 1989; Seymour & Porpodas, 1980; Ellis, 1984; Patterson & Shewell, 1987; Ellis & Young, 1988). It is suggested that spelling output might be generated by a process of phoneme–grapheme conversion, by a direct connection between speech production and a store of orthographic word-forms, or through the mediation of meaning (semantics).

Evidence from Neuropsychology

The main empirical support for a dual system in spelling comes from case studies of acquired dysgraphia (loss of capacity due to brain damage in adulthood). The method has stressed the contrast between writing words, an index of the lexical process, and writing non-words, an index of the sublexical process.

Lexical dysgraphia. Beauvois & Dérouesné (1981) reported the case of R.G., who was able to write non-words to dictation while making numerous errors on words containing ambiguous segments. The difficulty was not due to a failure to comprehend the words and occurred in both written and oral spelling. Errors occurred on 'irregular' or ambiguous words and tended towards regularisation (production of phonetically plausible spellings). Performance on non-word lists was almost perfect.

Phonological dysgraphia. Shallice (1981) described the case of P.R. This patient was able to repeat a spoken non-word, immediately or after a delay, but made numerous errors (82%) when writing non-words to dictation. Word writing was largely preserved (6% errors) apart from occasional derivational substitutions (e.g. *ascend* → **ASCENT**). P.R. could not segment words into phonemes or write letters in response to their sounds.

This dissociation is so extreme as to be difficult to explain except by reference to an involvement of two functions which are separately realised neurologically and which are independently vulnerable to damage (Shallice, 1988; Ellis & Young, 1988).

There is some evidence for the same kind of dissociation in childhood disorders of spelling (developmental dysgraphias). Boder (1973) described two patterns of dyslexic disorder:

1. in *dysphonetic dyslexia* there is an inadequate grasp of sound–symbol relationships, resulting in reliance on visual memory and production of deviant spelling errors;
2. *dyseidetic dyslexia,* by constrast, is marked by a poor memory for word-specific details and a reliance on sound–letter associations.

Additional case descriptions have been published by Campbell & Butterworth (1985), Coltheart, Masterson, Byng, Prior & Riddoch (1983) and others. Two further examples are presented by Seymour (1990) and by Seymour & Bunce (in press). One case, D.K., showed a 'phonological dysgraphia' (non-word spelling markedly more impaired than word spelling), while the other, R.C., showed the opposite pattern (word spelling more impaired than non-word spelling), i.e. a lexical dysgraphia.

Writing Systems

More abstract arguments for the modular scheme are provided by linguistic analyses of English orthography (see Kavanagh & Mattingly, 1972; Reber & Scarborough, 1977; Frith, 1980; Henderson, 1982; Coltheart, 1984). The major distinction here is between *logographic* systems, in which signs are used to represent whole words or meanings, and *phonographic* systems, in which signs represent component sounds. Figure 3.1 sets out a classification scheme (see Coltheart, 1984) which shows an evolution from the representation of meanings or words by pictographs or logographs towards the representation of component sounds at the level of whole syllables or phonemes (cf. Gleitman & Rozin, 1977). The scheme can be used to describe the historical development of writing systems or to classify the systems which are currently in use.

Examples of modern logographic scripts are provided by Chinese and by the Kanji symbols used by the Japanese. Although these systems have a complex internal structure (Martin, 1972; Morton & Sasanuma, 1984), they do not encode a relationship between the elements of visual form and the elements of pronunciation in a systematic way (cf. discussion by Harris & Coltheart, 1986).

In English, the arabic numerals form a set of logographs. A child who has learned that the symbols **1**, **2** and **3** correspond to the names *one*, *two* and *three* and their associated concepts has no basis for predicting what shapes might be used for *four*, *five* and *six* until someone who knows tells and shows him or her. Thus, learning to write a logographic script appears to be a matter of establishing a large store of correspondences between the words used in the spoken language and their conventional graphic representations.

In a phonographic system symbols are used to represent component sounds of words, either syllables, as in the Japanese Kana syllabaries, or vowel and consonant phonemes, as in the Greek and Roman alphabets. The symbols constitute sets of logographs which must be paired with arbitrarily

COGNITIVE THEORIES OF SPELLING

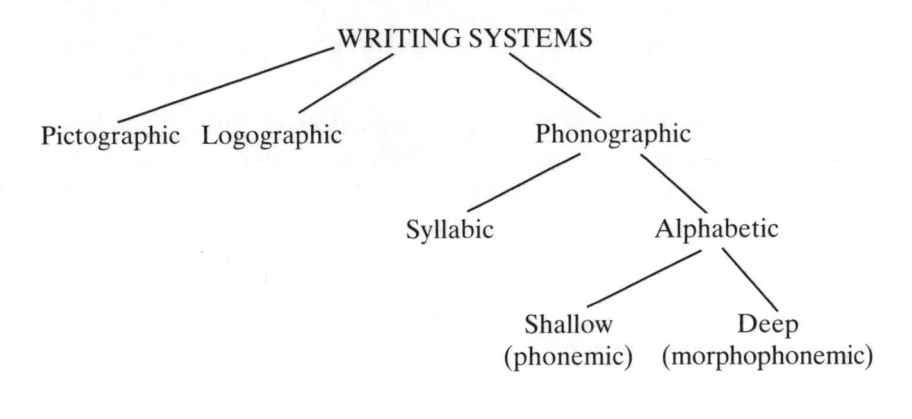

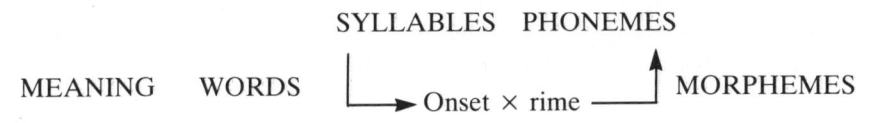

```
                    WRITING SYSTEMS
                   /      |       \
Pictographic  Logographic         Phonographic
                                  /          \
                             Syllabic      Alphabetic
                                           /        \
                                        Shallow    Deep
                                       (phonemic) (morphophonemic)
```

```
                           SYLLABLES   PHONEMES
MEANING    WORDS          └─► Onset × rime ─┘   MORPHEMES
```

FIGURE 3.1 *Classification scheme for different types of writing system, with an indication of the level of 'phonological awareness' required for mastery of each script*

assigned sounds and names. If the size of the set of sounds is relatively small a massive reduction in the number of sound–symbol pairings which must be learned becomes possible. To exploit such a system the learner must be able to segment speech into units of the appropriate size (syllables or phonemes). If the relation between the speech elements and the written symbols is reliable and consistent, knowledge of the sound–symbol pairings plus the necessary segmentation ability should be sufficient for the correct spelling of any word in the language.

So-called 'shallow' alphabets, such as Serbo-Croat, Italian and Finnish, approximate this condition which is often the aspiration of spelling reform movements, including the Initial Teaching Alphabet (i.t.a.). However, the conditions are not met by complex ('deep') alphabetic systems such as English or French where the relation between sound and symbol is a diverse (one-to-many) mapping and the spelling encodes higher order features such as lexical identities, distinctions between homophones, and morphological structure (Henderson, 1982; Coltheart, 1984; Ellis, 1984). In these 'morphophonemic' scripts, a knowledge of sound–symbol pairings plus segmentation ability is not sufficient for mastery of spelling. Additional knowledge of specific lexical items is required plus some understanding of morphemic structure and the conventions governing its representation of the orthography.

As an illustration of the first requirement, Table 3.1 lists a number of words which all contain an /əʊ/ vowel. The capacity to choose among the arbitrarily varying spellings, including the distinctions among homophones, implies the availability of a store in which the conventionally correct letter sequence for each word is represented. It is arguable that *all* words must be contained in this store, since even the most regular forms could be written in a less obvious way and must therefore have the fact of their regularity stored as a lexically specific feature.

TABLE 3.1 *Examples of different spellings of the vowel /əʊ/ in words, including contrasting spellings of homophones, with frequencies (per cent) of items exemplifying each spelling in the lexicon*

Words					
DOPE	BOAT	MOST	BOW	THOUGH	MAUVE
NOTE	ROAST	GHOST	OWN	MOULT	
DOSED	SOAP	ROLL			
WROTE					

Homophones					
NO	TOW	SO	DOE	SOLE	GROAN
KNOW	TOE	SOW	DOUGH	SOUL	GROWN
		SEW			

Frequencies in the lexicon (per cent words)

O-E	31.0	OU	1.0
O	26.0	EW	0.8
OW	16.0	OWE	0.8
OA	15.0	OUGH	0.5
OE	4.0	AU	0.2

These comments suggest that the spelling of English might be based on a logographic store in which each word is independently defined as a sequence of letter identities. An alternative possibility is that the store defines morphemes (word stems, prefixes, suffixes) together with some principles of combination. A complex form, such as **UNAPPRECIATIVELY** might be stored as a sequence of 16 letter identities or might be constructed from the component morphemes:

Prefix	Stem	Suffix
un	preci	ate
ad		ive
		ly

with the help of some rules of orthographic morphology, e.g. the copying of the initial **P** of the stem onto the prefix in place of the **D**, and the suppression of the **E** of **ATE** before **IVE**.

Developmental Implications

Rozin & Gleitman (1977) argued that the evolution of writing systems might be echoed in the phonological development of children (a progression from larger to smaller elements). This idea is incorporated into Figure 3.1 as a suggestion that the level of phonological awareness which has been achieved constrains the type of script which can be mastered. The progression has been complicated by:

1. insertion of a division into onset units (initial consonant structures) and *rime* units (vowel + terminal consonant structures) between syllables and phonemes (Treiman, 1983; 1987; Goswami & Bryant, 1990); and
2. the indication that a grasp of morphological structure may be necessary for mastery of a morphophonemic script.

The hypothesis provides a justification for theories of spelling development which envisage a progression through a sequence of stages. For example, Frith (1985) proposed that literacy development might involve the establishment of three distinctive *strategies* for dealing with written language, which she labelled as 'logographic', 'alphabetic' and 'orthographic'. The logographic strategy entails recognition of whole words in reading (see Seymour & Elder, 1986) and the establishment of a capacity for written production of isolated words, generally including the child's own name. The alphabetic strategy is a non-lexical procedure, involving the use of discrete sound–letter and letter–sound associations. An orthographic strategy reflects a mature understanding of the spelling system and involves the recognition or production of abstract letter arrays which correspond to morphemes.

Frith suggests that the ordering of the strategies is the same for reading and spelling although the phasing may be asynchronous. In particular, it is argued that the alphabetic strategy may be adopted for spelling before it appears in reading. (The opposite relation is proposed for the orthographic strategy.) Goswami & Bryant (1990) have commented that the scheme ignores the stages of development which may intervene between whole words and phonemes, notably subsyllabic units such as onset and rime. They also question whether spelling passes through a logographic phase at all (i.e. the alphabetic approach may be present from the start). On this view, the bearing of the writing system × phonological awareness theory on literacy development might be somewhat different for reading and spelling. For reading, the relevant progression might be from whole words through syllables and subsyllabic structures, whereas, for spelling, phonemic segmentation might be a start point for progression towards awareness of larger, morphologically defined structures.

To answer the question about a logographic phase in spelling we need an operational definition. We might infer the presence of 'logographic spelling' if complete or partial word knowledge was demonstrated in the absence of an alphabetic capability. For example, in a recent study of children at the start of their first school year, I verified that all members of the class could write their own names *before* they were able to write the letters in response to dictated sounds. Seymour & Evans (1988) reported the case of a ten-year-old child, A.T. with a genetic anomaly (Klinefelter's syndrome), who possessed no effective alphabetic abilities in either reading or spelling. Non-words could not be read (visual or semantic word substitutions predominated) and could not be written to dictation. A.T. typically responded by fluent production of a sequence of letters which often contained orthographic illegalities. Some of these matched the target on the initial letter (e.g. *dar* was written as **DEEY** and **FDEEDE**), or, very occasionally, on an internal sound (e.g. /ku:nd/ → **NOONRS** and **RAROOE**). Similar responses occurred in attempts at writing dictated words. However, a few words were correctly written (e.g. *milk, jam, zoo*), and others were correct on one occasion but not on the other, sometimes suggesting partial retrieval of the correct form (e.g. *blue* → **BLUE** and **BULE**; *eight* → **CHER** and **EIGTH**).

In interpreting the results, Seymour & Evans suggested that A.T. had developed a *literagraphic lexicon,* a store of letter forms which generated a sequential output when an instruction to write to dictation was detected. Under normal circumstances, the effect of learning to spell will be to place constraints on the output of the letter generator. These could take account of lexical identities for known words or of sounds contained in the target. In addition, the generator might internalise permissible letter sequences (graphotactics). In A.T.'s case, these constraints operated in only the most minimal form. None the less, the data may illustrate the arrest of development at an early (pre-alphabetic) point and thus provide information about the beginnings of the spelling system.

COGNITIVE THEORIES OF SPELLING

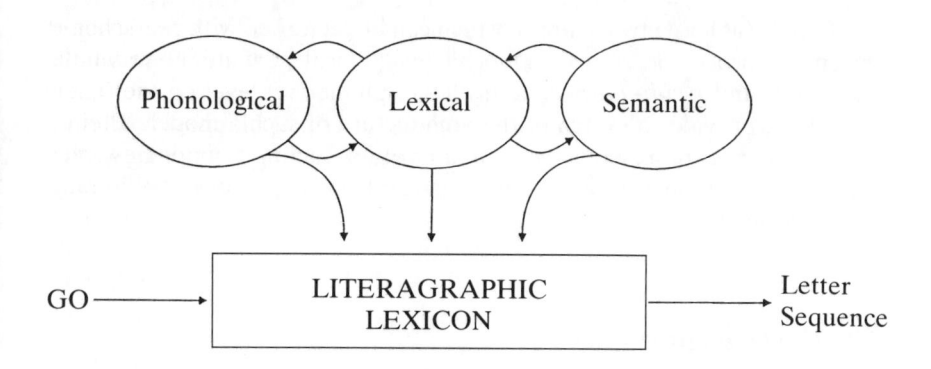

FIGURE 3.2 *Diagrammatic representation of literagraphic lexicon model of spelling in which letter sequence output is dominated by semantic, lexical and phonological constraints*

For the alphabetic phase, there is substantial evidence from the work of Read (1986) and others that early spelling is typically phonologically motivated, often via a primitive model of the orthography (e.g. use of letter names for vowel lengthening). Frith's contention that the alphabetic strategy may appear earlier in spelling than in reading leads to the prediction that children should find it easier to write non-words than to read them. In a recent study (see Seymour, 1990), S. Kinnison taught pre-schoolers, aged about four years, simple sound–letter associations. The children made plausible attempts at writing dictated C–V–C non-words but were consistently less successful when given the same items to read. Bryant & Bradley (1980) used a similar argument to explain why children sometimes succeeded in writing words they could not read. This phenomenon was also observed in the nursery school study and in the investigation by Seymour & Elder (1986). It could arise if an alphabetic (sound–letter) strategy was applied in spelling while a logographic (whole word recognition) strategy was applied in reading.

The evidence considered so far suggests that distinct logographic and alphabetic functions may be identifiable in early spelling. This could be taken as an indication of the earliest stages in the emergence of a two-process (lexical and sub-lexical) modular system of the kind described by Ellis & Young (1988). However, the literagraphic lexicon model of Seymour & Evans (1988) suggests a slightly different interpretation. In this account, there is a single system which generates orthographic output, even though the constraints imposed on the output (i.e. the sequence of letter identities) come from (at least) two sources, which can be identified with two levels of the speech processor, roughly a *morphemic* (lexical, semantic) level on the one hand, and a *sub-morphemic* (syllabic, phonemic) level on the other. Figure 3.2 provides a sketch of the architecture of such a model. The linguistic system is represented as a number of interacting components, each capable of imposing a distinctive constraint on the output of the letter sequence generator.

The Orthographic Phase

The contrast between these positions has an important bearing on the discussion of the advanced orthographic system which underlies fully competent spelling. It is a requirement of the developmental models that they should define a trajectory which ends by putting in place the 'cognitive architecture' of the mature (adult) system. The dual and single process models of the orthographic system imply different developmental trajectories.

A trajectory leading to the dual process model is set out by Morton (1989). It consists of a series of diagrams, each representing the 'cognitive architecture' established at a given point in Frith's (1985) six-step sequence. Two points of importance are: (1) the alphabetic process is shown as surviving into maturity as the non-lexical phoneme–grapheme translator; (2) the early logographic system is discarded during the alphabetic stage and is subsequently replaced by an entirely new, morphologically organised word store (the graphemic output logogen). The final diagram in the sequence is formally similar to the two-process model adopted by Ellis & Young (1988).

A virtue of Morton's account is that it makes question-provoking proposals about the histories of the different processing modules. Is it true that the early and later word stores are functionally unrelated to one another? If so, early word learning might be thought to be unimportant. To support such a conclusion we would need: (1) operational definitions of logographic and orthographic spelling; and (2) a demonstration of the discontinuity of the two systems. According to Frith and Morton, the distinction lies in the incorporation of morphology. One proposal, therefore, might be that morphologically complex words can be spelled only via an orthographic system. However, as has already been noted, logographic storage of complex words is perfectly possible. It therefore seems unlikely that a simple contrast between mono- and polymorphemic word sets could establish whether a competent speller was relying on a logographic or on an orthographic store.

COGNITIVE THEORIES OF SPELLING

It might be argued that an orthographic system would generalise its knowledge to the writing of complex forms which had not previously been seen or written. This could include the writing of complex non-words. However, if we found that polymorphemic non-words were written 'orthographically' (i.e. with observation of principles of orthographic morphology), this would suggest that non-words were processed via the lexical system and would undermine the assumptions of the modular dual process view.

This brings us to a second question. Is it true that the lexical and sub-lexical aspects of spelling are handled by functionally distinct systems? If so, we might conclude that there are two tasks in the teaching of spelling, one being the establishment of a set of phoneme–grapheme associations, and the other the building up of a store of word-forms. However, there are reasons to doubt the functional separation of the lexical and sub-lexical processes:

- Word and non-word spelling may be correlated
  1. In a study of word and non-word spelling by Primary 7 children (aged about 11 years) in Dundee, accuracy scores on words and non-words were significantly correlated. There were no instances of a major dissociation of the kind reported for the neurological cases of acquired dysgraphia.
  2. The spellings of the phonological dysgraphic subject, D.K., described by Seymour & Bunce (in press) were analysed in terms of accuracy levels on individual initial and terminal consonant structures which occurred in the items used for word and non-word spelling. The error hierarchies for words and non-words were significantly correlated.

- Non-word spelling is affected by lexical priming
  1. Campbell (1983) has shown that hearing a word containing an ambiguous segment influences the immediately following spelling of a non-word (thus, /preIn/ is likely to be written **PRANE** after hearing *crane*, and **PRAIN** after hearing *brain*). This 'priming effect' indicates that a word, which is presumed to be processed by the lexical systems, can influence the spelling of a non-word, thought to be dealt with by the sub-lexical process.
  2. Seymour & Dargie (1990) have shown that the priming effect can be mediated associatively. Adult subjects listened to a mixed list of words and non-words in a writing to dictation task. On some occasions the word was associatively related to another word which shared a vowel–consonant rhyme with the immediately following non-word. The associate influenced non-word spelling (e.g. /bəʊp/ was likely to be written as **BOAP** following *detergent* but as **BOPE** following *vatican*). This reinforces the conclusion that non-word spelling is achieved via a system which is not isolated from lexical–semantic processes.

These comments place question marks over the key assumptions of the Frith–Morton model: (1) it is not certain that the logographic–orthographic distinction can be upheld; (2) we can no longer feel sure that non-words are written via an independent sub-lexical channel.

Sound–Spelling Contingency

Barry & Seymour (1988) attempted to look further at these issues by examining the relation between lexical priming and the frequencies with which particular grapheme clusters occurred as orthographic realisations for phonemes or phoneme clusters. For this purpose, the orthographic lexicon was treated as a three-dimensional framework within which monosyllables (and disyllables with an unstressed second component) could be represented. The frame was defined by initial consonants (IC), vowels (V), and terminal consonants (TC), somewhat along the lines of the *Phonetic Lexicon* published by Rockey (1973). We examined all combinations of sets of initial and terminal consonant structures with each of about 20 vowels and entered the words (homophones included) in a segmented format. This yielded a three-dimensional (3D) lexicon of syllables (i.e. an IC × V × TC combination) together with tabulations of the frequencies of vowel spellings and consonant spellings summed across the rows and columns of each matrix.

One outcome of this exercise was the notion of 'sound–spelling contingency' — essentially the pre-eminence of the association between a sound (consonant or vowel structure) and its most popular orthographic form. To illustrate, most short vowels have a single dominant form (e.g. /o/ → **O**, but occasionally **A**, **OU**), whereas many of the long vowels map onto a wide diversity. Table 3.1 includes a summary for the vowel /əʊ/, showing that even the popular forms **O-E**, **OA**, have relatively low frequencies, and that there are numerous minor correspondences, some very infrequent, e.g. **EW**, **AU**. A low frequency of the dominant form was said to involve a low contingency.

Barry & Seymour (1988) reported an analysis of the relationship between lexical priming and sound–spelling contingency. The main question was whether a prime containing a low contingency form would influence the spelling of a non-word. The result was that both priming and contingency affected the probability of choice of letters in non-word spelling and that the effects were additive, i.e. low contingency forms were used infrequently but priming exerted a constant increment. Seymour & Dargie (1990) obtained essentially the same outcome with associative priming. The increment in usage due to priming seemed to be a constant addition to an underlying variation which was related to contingency.

It seems, therefore, that the choice of letters in non-word spelling is influenced by at least two factors: (1) the presence of lexically derived priming; and (2) the frequency of occurrence of sound–letter correspondences in the language. It is perhaps worth noting that this latter relation may not be an exact one. Seymour & Dargie found that the distribution of choices in non-word spelling was not identical to the distribution in the lexicon for most of the vowels they considered.

Theoretical Implications

One possibility is that the standard model runs into difficulties because it over-emphasises the functional *modularity* of processing systems and underplays developmental influences. The apparent incompatibilities might be reconciled if we could assume:

1. The later (orthographic) word store is built onto a phonologically structured organisation, deriving from the early stages of alphabetic (phoneme–grapheme) writing.
2. Both words and non-words are written via a single system of correspondences which has the features of (i) reflecting the hierarchy of sound–letter choices in written English, and (ii) being open to modification by lexical influences.

There are various ways in which these changes might be implemented. One implication is that the lexical/non-lexical distinction should be abandoned altogether and that we should consider a single channel or network which encodes information about words and more general correspondences. This might be approached by adapting models which have been developed to describe print–sound associations in reading, e.g.

1. *Connectionist model.* Seidenberg & McClelland (1989) have described a computer simulation of the learning of print–sound associations which is based on a network of connections between orthographic units, hidden units, and phonetic units. The network was trained on a vocabulary of 2,000 or so monosyllables using a back propogation algorithm which minimised the error between the target and the generated response. A version of this model which operated in reverse, i.e. was trained to substitute orthographic forms for phonetic forms, might learn to spell English words and might show some generalisation to non-words. It is also possible that the model would reproduce the contingency and priming effects.

2. *Multi-level process.* Shallice (1988) has described a two-channel model of reading, which envisages a semantic process and a phonological process which carries information about print–sound correspondences at various levels, including morphemes and syllabic and subsyllabic structures (consonant clusters, rimes, etc.). He suggests that an analogous arrangement might exist for spelling, i.e. a semantic route combined with a single, multi-level orthographic channel.
3. *Orthographic framework.* Seymour (1987) proposed that the orthographic lexicon is built on a 3D model of the syllable, involving IC, V and TC dimensions (a phonologically based organisation). The incorporation of specific words (lexicalisation) and orthographic conventions was represented as the copying of data from the dimensions of the orthographic input lexicon required for reading.
4. *Literagraphic lexicon.* An alternative proposal can be derived from Seymour & Evans' (1988) account of the primitive spelling system displayed by the Klinefelter case, A.T. In this view, the essential basis of the spelling process is a letter sequence generator which operates under constraints of various kinds, the most important being phonological and lexical. Under phonological constraint, certain letters have raised probabilities of production when a particular element (perhaps syllabic) is active in the phonological system. A lexical constraint raises the probabilities for the letters contained in an active word or morpheme.

Criteria for Evaluation of Models

These models — or indeed any other relevant accounts of the spelling process — can be evaluated by considering how well they explain:

1. the dissociation of word and non-word spelling found in 'acquired dysgraphia', including the selective loss of non-word writing in phonological dysgraphia, and
2. the facts of non-word spelling, especially: (i) the ability of competent spellers to produce plausible forms for dictated non-words; and (ii) the evidence that letter choice in non-word spelling is subject to lexical influences (contingency and priming effects).

The connectionist model can be 'lesioned' by removal of hidden units. This produces a simulated 'surface dyslexia', i.e. a loss of low frequency irregular forms and preservation of the more basic correspondences. 'Phonological dyslexia', involving the preservation of words and loss of ability to

COGNITIVE THEORIES OF SPELLING

assemble pronunciations for non-words, does not occur. It is likely that the same considerations would apply to a connectionist model of spelling, i.e. it would have difficulty in accommodating phonological dysgraphia unless another pathway (e.g. via the semantic level) was implemented.

Work on a connectionist spelling model by Gordon Brown and colleagues at the University of Wales, Bangor, supports this conclusion (Brown & Watson, 1991). The model (a single channel network analogous to Seidenberg & McClelland's (1989) reading model) learned 'regular' words (which shared spellings with other words) more quickly than 'irregular' words (containing infrequent, low contingency spellings). It was the irregular forms which were lost when the model was lesioned. We might note that regularity was defined in terms of rimes (V + TC segments) and involved the identification of lexical 'friends' (rhyming words having the same spelling) and lexical 'enemies' (rhyming words having different spellings).

Besner (1990) has shown that the Seidenberg & McClelland model is much worse at non-word reading than human subjects. If this is true of the spelling model, the central proposal that a lexically trained network will generalise its peformance to unfamiliar non-words will be questioned. Gordon Brown's simulation is not, as yet, helpful on this point, since he focused on the spelling of words of varying regularity and did not test non-words.

Shallice's multi-level process would be expected to succeed with non-words because it contains distinct sub-morphemic correspondences. However, damage would affect the vulnerable morphemic levels, producing a 'lexical dysgraphia'. 'Phonological dysgraphia' occurs when all levels of the orthographic route have been damaged and surviving spelling proceeds via a semantic route.

Similar comments apply to the 'orthographic framework' model. The framework encodes both lexical specifics and general correspondences (though in a different format from Shallice's multi-level system) and so might be expected to perform successfully on words and non-words. Damage could affect the lexical specifications while leaving the outer dimensions intact, producing a 'lexical dysgraphia'. The reverse pattern (damage to the margins with preservation of the 'lexical' centre) would not be possible without disabling the system entirely. Hence, the model could not accommodate 'phonological dysgraphia' without the addition of a semantic (or logographic) route which could take over if the framework was destroyed.

The 'literagraphic lexicon' model would also predict the abolition of all spelling if the letter generator was damaged. However, the model allows that the alternative sources of constraint (or their outputs) could be selectively impaired. This would make possible both 'lexical' and (non-semantic) 'phonological dysgraphia'. The system would be capable of spelling words and non-words and would be expected to show lexical and associative priming effects.

It is apparent from these arguments that it is too early to make a confident choice among the possible cognitive models of spelling. However, it seems that the standard dual process model (Ellis & Young, 1988; Morton, 1989) has difficulty with the priming and contingency data and that the single process connectionist account runs into problems with non-word spelling and the preservation of word knowledge in phonological dysgraphia. On these grounds, I would be inclined towards a cautious bet on either:

1. a two-channel process, including a semantic level and an orthographic level structured according to the connectionist scheme or Shallice's multi-levels or my own orthographic framework, or
2. a 'literagraphic lexicon' which operates under the influence of two (or more) independent sources of constraint.

We now need to turn to the possible implications of these models for education, i.e. for the assessing and teaching of spelling.

Implications for Testing

A recurrent theme has been the contrast between a generalised knowledge of sound–letter correspondences and a knowledge of specific lexical items or morphemes. For diagnostic purposes the distinction is captured by the use of structurally comparable word and non-word lists as materials to be routinely used in testing. It seems desirable that the lists should reflect the content of the orthographic framework, including the structures (sounds and spelling patterns) by which it is defined as well as the lexical entries.

Two approaches to the identification of orthographic content have been mentioned. One is based on the onset/rime distinction of Treiman (1987) and presents the framework as a *two-dimensional* (2D) structure described by the combination of a set of initial consonants with a set of rimes (vowels + terminal consonants). The other possibility is a *three-dimensional* (3D) structure, defined by the combination of sets of initial consonants, vowels and terminal consonants. In what follows I will use the 3D (IC × V × TC)

COGNITIVE THEORIES OF SPELLING

framework which I have employed in my own research, though it would clearly be possible to make out the case for an analogous approach based on the 2D framework.

Seymour (1990) and Seymour & Bunce (in press) have set out a possible content for a 3D orthographic input lexicon, using a four-level developmental progression. An analogous proposal for spelling might distinguish two main levels, namely:

1. *Core.* An IC × V × TC structure consisting of simple (single phoneme) initial consonants, short (checked) vowels, and simple terminal consonants.
2. *Expansion.* The same structure with the addition of initial consonant clusters, terminal consonant clusters, and lengthened vowels, perhaps divided into three or more sub-levels.

In order to take account of 'contingency' (Barry & Seymour, 1988) lexical items might be selected from each structure so as to reflect the frequency of the orthographic realisation of the IC, V and TC components, say at three levels (high, medium, low). The non-word set would, of course, be based on alternative combinations of the IC, V and TC phonological structures occurring in the words.

In addition to these 'orthographic' lists, I would include a set of homophone pairs, stratified according to frequency of occurrence and regularity.

Using this procedure, the availability of an 'orthographic framework' could be determined from the accuracy levels for non-words or for high contingency words on lists representing the 'core' or the 'expansions'. Note that accuracy could be expressed simply in terms of the number of items correct or by reference to the component IC, V and TC structures. An index of 'lexicalisation' (the incorporation of word-specific information) is provided by: (1) any advantage for high contingency words over comparable non-words; (2) success on words containing medium or low contingency correspondences; and (3) the proportion of homophone pairs correctly discriminated when writing to dictation with the support of a disambiguating context.

This assessment deals only with the heart of the orthographic system (spelling of monosyllables and disyllables). In order to deal with a morphemically structured store of the kind described by Morton (1989) lists of affixed items are required. These would contain complex words, stratified by frequency, with inclusion of the major prefixes and suffixes, together with a non-word list formed by recombination of the stem and affix components.

A procedure of this kind might be used to measure the degree of orthographic development achieved by an individual and also to pinpoint areas of weakness. The occurrence of major discrepancies between word and non-word spelling (as shown by cases D.K. and R.C. described by Seymour & Bunce, in press) would support the diagnosis of developmental forms of phonological and lexical dysgraphia, i.e. dysphonetic versus dyseidetic categories of Boder (1973).

Implications for Teaching

Previous approaches to the teaching of spelling have emphasised the building up of a store of word-forms using study procedures such as the look–cover–write–check technique of Peters (1967) or the method of simultaneous letter naming and cursive writing used by Lynette Bradley (see Bryant & Bradley, 1985). Both methods apear to be based on a 'logographic' model of the store in which words are represented as lists of letter identities. In Peters' account the representational code is considered to be visual and practices designed to encourage cross-referencing between words containing common letter sequences are recommended. The approach is in conflict with the theories discussed here in so far as it plays down the importance of phonology, orthographic structure, and morphology. From the examples given, it is clear that words are not thought to be grouped by sound and that the letter groups used in cross-referencing often cut across orthographic or morphemic boundaries (Peters, 1967).

The connectionist model (Seidenberg & McClelland, 1989; Brown & Watson, 1991) is based on a training procedure of the form: hear–write–look–compare. The learner writes individual spoken words, sampled according to frequency from a large representative corpus and compares feedback of the correct form with each attempt. No explicit mention of orthographic or morphemic structures is necessary since these aspects will emerge as the statistical properties of the input are internalised. Whether this is also true of Shallice's (1988) multi-level model is unclear, though comments on the early acquisition of the basic correspondences suggest that initial 'phonic' instruction may be envisaged.

My own preference for the orthographic framework and literagraphic lexicon models leads to a curriculum in which there is a strong emphasis on the phonological basis of spelling together with a stress on the integrity of orthographic and morphemic structures. A curriculum designed to promote the formation of such a system might include the following steps:

COGNITIVE THEORIES OF SPELLING 67

1. *The letter generator.* The foundation consists of procedures for forming letters and producing sequential written output. It is probably preferable if the letters are labelled by their 'sounds' rather than their conventional names.
2. *The alphabetic core.* The aim here is to establish a 'phonological constraint' on the output from the letter generator. This might initially apply only to the first sound but needs to extend across the three positions of C–V–C syllables containing simple elements. It presupposes segmentation of the syllable into phonemes. Control of output may be supported by sounding of letters. Establishment of this basic structure is indicated by correct writing of non-words or high contingency words sampled from the core IC × V × TC structure.
3. *Lexicalisation of the core.* This requires exposure to words which fall within the IC × V × TC structure but which have a discrepant (low contingency) spelling. Although these words might be learned as isolated 'exceptions', it would be preferable to make the contrast between the word and its more obvious (high contingency) form explicit, so that each word is assigned a place within the framework.
4. *Expansion of the core.* The presumption is that the core elements can be elaborated to accommodate consonant clusters and also ambiguities and positional constraints. Thus, /dz/ may be **J** or **G** in the IC position but **DGE** or **GE** in the TC position. The expansion is viewed as an elaboration of the original core structure, with complex consonants built on to simple ones (e.g. the expansions **PR** and **PL** are located with **P**). Lexicalisation, resulting from encounters with written words, will produce hierarchies of sound–spelling 'contingencies' (cf. the distribution of /əʊ/ spellings in Table 3.1).
5. *Morphological structure.* The aim at this level is to make it apparent that seemingly complex words are built up by the recombination of syllabic elements, including prefix and suffix structures and word stems. Some directive emphasis on the analysis of words into stem and affix morphemes seems desirable.

Conclusion

Although there is as yet no generally acknowledged cognitive theory of spelling and spelling development, this review has revealed a common preoccupation with the contrast between the lexical (word) knowledge which is essential for a 'deep' alphabetic script such as English and the rules or regularities by which sounds are related to letters. The attempt to draw implications from some of the current theories has led to proposals for a graded, orthographically based assessment procedure and curriculum which might be evaluated in future research.

Summary

Cognitive theories aim to describe the psychological processes which support spelling competence. A standard view has been that two processes are involved, one concerned with translation from sounds (phonemes) to letters (graphemes), and the other with the storage of word-specific (lexical) information. Support has been provided by cases of 'acquired dysgraphia' and by linguistic considerations. A discussion of spelling development and of lexical effects in non-word writing suggested some modification of this view, particularly the idea that spelling may be achieved by a single orthographic framework which operates under different kinds of constraint. Implications for assessment and teaching were considered.

References

BARRY, C. and SEYMOUR, P. H. K. 1988, Lexical priming and sound-to-spelling contingency effects in non-word spelling. *Quarterly Journal of Experimental Psychology* 40A, 5–40.

BEAUVOIS, M.-F. and DÉROUESNÉ, J. 1981, Lexical or orthographic agraphia. *Brain* 104, 21–49.

BESNER, D. 1990, Does the reading system need a lexicon? In D. A. BALOTA, G. B. FLORES D'ARCAIS and K. RAYNER (eds) *Comprehension Processes in Reading*. Hillsdale, NJ: Lawrence Erlbaum.

BODER, E. 1973, Developmental dyslexia: A diagnostic system based on three atypical reading–spelling patterns. *Developmental Medicine and Child Neurology* 21, 504–14.

BROWN, G. D. A. and WATSON, F. L. 1991, Spelling-to-sound and sound-to-spelling translation in developmental dyslexia. Paper presented to meeting of the British Dyslexia Association, Oxford.

BRYANT, P. E. and BRADLEY, L. 1980, Why children sometimes write words which they do not read. In U. FRITH (ed.) *Cognitive Processes in Spelling*. London: Academic Press.

—— 1985, *Children's Reading Problems*. Oxford: Blackwell.

CAMPBELL, R. 1983, Writing non-words to dictation. *Brain and Language* 19, 153–78.

CAMPBELL, R. and BUTTERWORTH, B. 1985, Phonological dyslexia and dysgraphia in a highly literate subject: A developmental case with associated deficits in phonemic processing and awareness. *Quarterly Journal of Experimental Psychology* 37A, 435–75.

COLTHEART, M. 1984, Writing systems and reading disorders. In L. HENDERSON (ed.) *Orthographies and Reading*. London: Lawrence Erlbaum.

COLTHEART, M., MASTERSON, J., BYNG, S., PRIOR, M. and RIDDOCH, J. 1983, Surface dyslexia. *Quarterly Journal of Experimental Psychology* 35A, 469–95.
ELLIS, A. W. 1984, *Reading, Writing and Dyslexia*. London: Lawrence Erlbaum.
ELLIS, A. W. and YOUNG, A. W. 1988, *Human Cognitive Neuropsychology*. London: Lawrence Erlbaum.
FRITH, U. (ed.) 1980, *Cognitive Processes in Spelling*. London: Academic Press.
—— 1985, Beneath the surface of developmental dyslexia. In K. E. PATTERSON, J. C. MARSHALL and M. COLTHEART (eds) *Surface Dyslexia: Neuropsychological and Cognitive Analyses of Phonological Reading*. London: Lawrence Erlbaum.
GLEITMAN, L. R. and ROZIN, P. 1977, The structure and acquisition of reading, I: Relations between orthographies and the structure of language. In A. S. REBER, and D. SCARBOROUGH (eds) *Toward a Psychology of Reading*. Hillsdale, NJ: Erlbaum.
GOSWAMI, U. and BRYANT, P. 1990, *Phonological Skills and Learning to Read*. London: Lawrence Erlbaum.
HARRIS, M. and COLTHEART, M. 1986, *Language Processing in Children and Adults*. London: Routledge and Kegan Paul.
HENDERSON, L. 1982, *Orthography and Word Recognition in Reading*. London: Academic Press.
KAVANAGH, J. F. and MATTINGLY, I. G. (eds) 1972, *Language by Ear and by Eye: The Relationship Between Speech and Reading*. Cambridge, Mass.: MIT Press.
MARTIN, S. E. 1972, Non-alphabetic writing systems: Some observations. In J. F. KAVANAGH and I. G. MATTINGLY (eds) *Language by Ear and by Eye: The Relationships Between Speech and Reading*. Cambridge, Mass.: MIT Press.
MORTON, J. 1980, The logogen model and orthographic structure. In U. FRITH (ed.) *Cognitive Processess in Spelling*. London: Academic Press.
—— 1989, An information processing account of reading acquisition. In A. M. GALABURDA (ed.) *From Reading to Neurons*. Cambridge, Mass.: MIT Press.
MORTON, J. and SASANUMA. S. 1984, Lexical access in Japanese. In L. HENDERSON (ed.) *Orthographies and Reading*. London: Lawrence Erlbaum.
PATTERSON, K. and SHEWELL, C. 1987, Speak and spell: Dissociations and word-class effects. In M. COLTHEART, G. SARTORI and R. JOB (eds) *The Cognitive Neuropsychology of Language*. London: Lawrence Erlbaum.
PETERS, M. 1967, *Spelling: Caught or Taught?* London: Routledge and Kegan Paul.
READ, C. 1986, *Children's Creative Spelling*. London: Routledge and Kegan Paul.
REBER, A. S. and SCARBOROUGH, D. (eds) 1977, *Toward a Psychology of Reading*. Hillsdale, NJ: Erlbaum.
ROCKEY, D. 1973, *Phonetic Lexicon: Of Monosyllabic and some Disyllabic Words with Homophones, arranged according to their Phonetic Structures*. London: Heyden.
ROZIN, P. and GLEITMAN, L. R. 1977, The structure and acquisition of reading, II: The reading process and the acquisition of the alphabetic principle of reading. In A. S. REBER and D. L. SCARBOROUGH (eds) *Toward a Psychology of Reading*. Hillsdale, NJ: Erlbaum.
SEIDENBERG, M. and MCCLELLAND, J. L. 1989, A distributed developmental model of word recognition and naming. *Psychological Review* 96, 523–68.
SEYMOUR, P. H. K. 1987, Developmental dyslexia: A cognitive experimental analysis. In M. COLTHEART, G. SARTORI and R. JOB (eds) *The Cognitive Neuropsychology of Language*. London: Lawrence Erlbaum.

—— 1990, Developmental dyslexia. In M. W. EYSENCK (ed.) *Cognitive Psychology: An International Review*. Chichester: Wiley.

SEYMOUR, P. H. K. and BUNCE, F. (in press) Application of cognitive models to remediation in cases of developmental dyslexia. In G. HUMPHREYS and J. RIDDOCH (eds) *Cognitive Neuropsychology and Cognitive Rehabilitation*. London: Lawrence Erlbaum.

SEYMOUR, P. H. K. and DARGIE, A. 1990, Associative priming and orthographic choice in nonword spelling. *The European Journal of Cognitive Psychology* 2, 395–410.

SEYMOUR, P. H. K. and ELDER, L. 1986, Beginning reading without phonology. *Cognitive Neuropsychology* 3, 1–36.

SEYMOUR, P. H. K. and EVANS, H. M. 1988, Developmental arrest at the logographic stage: Impaired literacy functions in Klinefelter's XXXY syndrome. *Journal of Research in Reading* 11, 133–51.

SEYMOUR, P. H. K. and PORPODAS, C. D. 1980, Lexical and non-lexical processing of spelling in dyslexia. In U. FRITH (ed.) Cognitive *Processes in Spelling*. London: Academic Press.

SHALLICE, T. 1981, Phonological agraphia and the lexical route in writing. *Brain* 104, 413–29.

—— 1988, *From Neuropsychology to Mental Structure*. Cambridge: Cambridge University Press.

TREIMAN, R. 1983, The structure of spoken syllables: Evidence from novel word games. *Cognition* 15, 49–74.

—— 1987, On the relationship between phonological awareness and literacy. *European Bulletin of Cognitive Psychology* 7, 524–9.

4 Interactions Between Lexical and Assembled Spelling (In English, Italian and Welsh)[1]

CHRISTOPHER BARRY

Introduction

The dual-route model of spelling production proposes separable lexical and assembled (or 'phonic') spelling systems. This chapter considers the functional independence of, and interactions between, these two routes and concentrates upon the experimental demonstrations of lexical influence on assembled spelling in adults. As well as evidence from the notoriously (but wonderfully) deep orthography of English, the chapter also considers evidence from spellers of the shallow (or regular) orthographies of Italian and Welsh.

The Dual Route Model of Spelling

The dual route model of spelling production is widely accepted as a theoretical framework for understanding how English readers spell both familiar and new words. The model proposes that there exist two separable processing systems or 'routes' (i.e. functional sequences of processes), which are assumed to operate in parallel:

1. The *lexical* (or word-specific) route retrieves the spellings of known words from an orthographic (or graphemic) output lexicon.
2. The *assembled* route (which is sometimes called the 'non-lexical' route) constructs spellings using some form of sound-to-spelling conversion process. This is frequently referred to as the 'phoneme-to-grapheme correspondence' system, although it is logically possible for the units of conversion to be either phonemes or combinations of sounds (e.g. /**ng**/ → **ING**).

All known words can be spelled by the lexical route because all words are assumed to have representations in the output lexicon. However, it is entirely possible that only the spellings of very familiar words are stored and that low-frequency words may need to be spelled using the assembled system. Alternatively, it is possible that only certain components of any particular word's spelling are stored (such as irregular spelling of vowels, e.g. that *yacht* contains **ACH**) and the remainder, perhaps the consonants for instance, are spelled by the assembled process.

Words with regular (or predictable) sound-to-spelling correspondences could be, and all new words (and non-words) must be, spelled by the assembled system. (Note that a non-word such as *mant* is simply a potential new word.)

The dual route model has received support from a number of sources. Its a priori plausibility derives from the facts that normal spellers of English can produce both correct spellings of the many frankly irregular words (such as *colonel*) and phonologically plausible spellings of non-words. Irregular words could not be spelled correctly by any purely non-lexical sound-to-spelling conversion and so some lexical knowledge must be functional. Non-words require some process of non- or at least *sub*-lexical sound-to-spelling conversion process because, by definition, they have no full representation in the lexicon. Support for the model has also accrued from the success of the similarly structured dual route model of reading. Indeed, the basic framework for understanding spelling production has been adapted, *mutatis mutandis*, from models of word recognition in reading.

However, the most persuasive empirical support for the dual route model of spelling production for adults has come from cognitive neuropsychological investigations of patients with acquired disorders of spelling competence following neurological damage, the *central dysgraphias*. (Given the paucity of research into normal, correct spelling production of words by adults, neuropsychological evidence has figured really quite strongly.) In particular, the notion that the two routes are *separable* has been supported by the dissociations observed within, and the double dissociation between, patients with phonological and surface dysgraphia.

There exist patients with *phonological dysgraphia* (see, for example, Shallice, 1981; Roeltgen, Sevush & Heilman, 1983) who are selectively impaired at spelling non-words (such as *pog*) — a task which, by definition, requires the operation of the assembled spelling system — but can spell most words accurately. For example, Shallice's patient, P.R., could correctly spell 94% of words, but only 18% of non-words. Phonological dysgraphics are interpreted as having an intact lexical spelling system and an impaired assembled system.

There also exist patients with *surface dysgraphia* (sometimes called lexical agraphia) who may spell non-words correctly (i.e. in a phonologically plausible fashion) but produce many errors spelling words with ambiguous or irregular sound-to-spelling correspondences. Surface dysgraphics misspell words in a phonologically plausible fashion, as if they were non-words, e.g. *monsieur* spelt as **MESSIEU** (Beauvois & Dérouesné, 1981), *flood* spelt as **FLUD** (Hatfield & Patterson, 1983), *phase* spelt as **FAZE** (Goodman & Caramazza, 1986) and *clay* spelt as **CLAI** (Baxter & Warrington, 1987). These patients may be interpreted as having an impairment in retrieving lexical (i.e. word-specific) orthographic representations and so rely upon the operation of their preserved assembled spelling route. For orthographies with inconsistent sound-to-spelling relationships (such as English and French) such reliance would produce incorrect, but typically phonologically plausible, spellings for irregular words.

Are the two routes independent and are both needed in other languages?

There are two questions arising from the dual route model which will form the basis for the remainder of this chapter. The first concerns the issue of the functional independence of the two routes. The neuropsychological dissociations found in surface and phonological dysgraphia show reasonably clearly that the lexical and assembled routes are *separable:* neurological damage can selectively impair one functional spelling system and leave the other relatively intact. However, whether the two routes are *functionally independent* in normal spellers — who, of course, are assumed to possess both — is a separate question. One way this question has been addressed is by considering whether there are effects of lexical knowledge upon the assembled spelling system — and specifically by studies of the lexical priming of non-word spelling. However, the question may also be addressed by considering the effects of the assembled system on the spelling of words. It is possible that, for skilled adult spellers, assembled spelling is used only as a 'back-up' system, when spellers either do not know a word or are uncertain of its correct spelling. The contribution of assembled spelling for the efficient spelling of words is limited by orthographic regularity, which brings us to the second issue to be considered by this chapter, namely whether the dual route model is applicable to other languages.

Perhaps the strongest claim concerning the role of assembled spelling is that a lexical system need not exist and that all words are spelled by phonological segmentation, followed by the application of an assembled, phoneme-to-letter conversion process. Although implausible for the irregular orthography of English, this would be quite possible for languages with consistent (or 'shallow') orthgraphies. Most of the neuropsychological evidence for the dual route model has come from the erroneous spelling performance of writers of languages with inconsistent orthographies (most notably English and French). The question therefore arises whether separate lexical and assembled spelling systems are necessary for languages with shallow orthographies (such as Italian, Finnish, Serbo-Croatian and, closer to home, Welsh). English orthography is highly inconsistent — and may be argued to 'need' a dual route model — but Italian and Welsh are highly regular and so a more parsimonious account would be that *only* an assembled spelling system is necessary.

Lexical influences upon assembled spelling in English

The phonological dysgraphic patient, P.R., studied by Shallice (1981), commented that when he attempted to spell non-words, he often used a word as a mediator. For example, he spelled /sim/ as **SYM** and reported that he had thought of, and used as an analogy, the word *symbol* (which is an irregular word as /i/ is only very rarely spelled **Y** in English words). This analogy strategy often led P.R. to produce errors, however, as in *na* spelt as **GN** (via *gnat*). It is, of course, quite possible that P.R. was using a lexical analogy strategy in order to compensate for his primary deficit of (normal) assembled spelling. However, P.R. may have been using his (impaired) assembled spelling system in which lexical knowledge is *normally* consulted within some form of analogy process. This view suggests that the assembled spelling route does not operate independently as a set of non-lexical abstract sound-to-spelling conversion rules.

The idea that assembled spelling in normals is a function or property of the lexical spelling system was explored in an important paper by Ruth Campbell (1983). She presented people with lists of spoken words and non-words and they were instructed to write down only the non-words. (This may be seen as a 'lecture' task, in which subjects write down only the nonsense they don't already understand!) She found that the spelling of a previously heard word biased normal subjects' spelling productions for rhyming non-words. For example, subjects who heard *sweet* and then /priːt/, tended to spell the non-word as **PREET**, whereas subjects who heard *treat* followed by /priːt/, tended to spell it as **PREAT**. Campbell (1983: 153) concluded from these lexical priming effects that 'skill at assigning letters to sounds *never* becomes independent of lexical skill in adult readers' and so supported a lexical analogy model of assembled spelling.

Barry & Seymour (1988) extended Campbell's (1983) study by manipulating, within the prime words used in the experiment, what they called 'sound-to-spelling *contingency*', i.e. the frequency with which spelling patterns represented vowel sounds in words. Consider the vowel **ee**: this is actually spelled in 12 different ways, as in **LEAF, BEEF, THIEF, ME, THEME, CLIQUE, KEY, SKI, KEITH, QUAY, PEOPLE** and **FOETAL**. The most common spelling, **EA**, occurred in 40% in the corpus of monosyllabic words Barry & Seymour analysed and the second most common, **EE**, occurred in 39% of words. They called **EA** and **EE** *high-contingency* spellings of the vowel and the others (like **IE**, which occurred in only 7% of words) *low-contingency* spellings. Clearly, the term 'contingency', more so than 'regularity', better captures the widely distributed nature of English sound-to-spelling correspondences.

Barry & Seymour compared normal subjects' spellings of non-words in both a priming task (like that used by Campbell) and a free-spelling task in which only non-words were presented. They compared four priming conditions (see Table 4.1):

1. The prime word contained the most commonly occurring spelling pattern for its vowel. For instance, the vowel *ah* is spelled as in **LANE** in 43% of words.
2. The prime word contained the second most commonly occurring (but still high-contingency) spelling pattern for its vowel. For instance, the vowel *ah* is spelled as in **BRAIN** in 20% of words.
3. The prime word contained a rarely occurring (i.e. low-contingency) but phonologically plausible spelling of its vowel. For instance, the vowel *ee* is spelled as in **THEME** in only 4% of words but the major phonological correspondence of **E-E** is *ee*.
4. The prime word contained a low-contingency and phonologically irregular spelling of its vowel (i.e. the spelling is not one which, if produced, would be pronounced regularly as the target sound). For instance, the vowel *ee* is spelled as in the word **KEY** in less than 1% of words but the major phonological correspondence of **EY** is not *ee*. (If /**di:**/ were to be spelled as **DEY**, it should not be pronounced as *dee*.)

As can be seen in Table 4.1, two clear effects were found. First, non-word spelling was indeed lexically primed; the frequency of production of the critical spelling patterns was significantly higher in the priming than in the control conditions. For example, /**toup**/ was spelled as **TOAP** more often following the presentation of the priming word *soap* than when the non-

TABLE 4.1 *Design and results of Barry & Seymour (1988)*

	% production of critical spellings	
	Priming	Control
High-contingency and most common *lane*→ /**tein**/ = **TANE**	70	49
High-contingency and second most common *brain*→ /**tein**/ = **TAIN**	52	33
Low-contingency but phonologically plausible *theme*→ /**pi:m**/ = **PEME**	36	14
Low-contingency and phonologically 'irregular' *key*→ /**di:**/ = **DEY** (or **DUAY**)	18	1

word was presented alone. Second, non-word spellings were strongly determined by sound-to-spelling contingency: people were more likely to produce more high-contingency (i.e. common) than low-contingency (i.e. rare or 'irregular') spelling patterns, and this was equally true for both the priming and the control conditions. For example, the non-word /**pi:m**/ was spelled as **PEAM** or **PEEM** (with the two most common spelling patterns for the vowel) more often than as **PEME** or **PIEM** (which contain phonologically plausible but very rarely occurring spelling patterns for the vowel).

Barry & Seymour's model of assembled spelling

In order to account for their data, Barry & Seymour proposed a model of normal assembled spelling in which a set of probabilistic sound-to-spelling correspondences relate vowel phonemes to weighted lists of alternative spelling patterns, which are ordered by sound-to-spelling contingency. For example, /**ei**/ → **A-E** (0.43), **AI** (0.20), **AY** (0.13), **A** (0.13), **EY** (0.03), **EI** (0.02), others (0.06), where the figures in brackets represent the 'weights' or probability of that pattern being produced. They proposed that these correspondences are abstracted from lexical knowledge but are represented (and may be implemented) separately of it (i.e. as a non-lexical assembled spelling route). They claimed that the selection of a spelling pattern from such lists is *normally* open to lexical influence, as demonstrated by the lexical priming effects. Finally, they suggested that once a spelling pattern has been selected, there is a tendency to repeat it. This model suggests that lexical priming effects upon non-word spelling can be interpreted within a dual-route model of spelling production, in which the two routes operate in functional interaction, rather than within a single 'lexical analogy' model.

This model has found support in a number of subsequent studies. Baxter & Warrington (1987) report the case of a pure surface dysgraphic patient who appears to spell words in a very similar fashion to how normal subjects spell non-words and so shows a clear effect of sound-to-spelling contingency (see Barry, 1988). Burden (1989) found that both good and poor adult spellers showed both lexical priming and contingency effects. Seymour & Dargie (1990) extended the effect to also show semantically mediated priming: subjects who heard the word *coffee* tended to spell the non-word /sti:/ as **STEA** (via *tea*) whereas those who heard *forest* tended to spell it as **STEE** (via *tree*).

The Barry & Seymour model was presented in terms of *phoneme*-to-spelling associations but their data (and those of Campbell and Burden also) came from effects of priming of non-words by *rhyming* words. It might be argued that in these experiments subjects implemented a task-specific strategy of explicitly biasing spelling on the basis of detected rhymes. However, the model should also predict that lexical priming effects would also occur from non-rhyming words that share the same vowel (as in *hole* → /**voup**/, and not only *hope* → /**voup**/). This expectation was tested and confirmed by a recent experiment (Barry, in preparation), in which non-words in the lecture task were preceded by prime words which either rhymed with or only shared the same vowel as the following non-word. With both rhyme and same vowel primes, there were prime words which contained: (1) the most commonly occurring spelling of its vowel (e.g. *boot/mood* → /**vu:t**/); (2) the second most commonly ocurring spelling of its vowel (e.g. *gain/rail* → /**tein**/) or (3) a low-contingency but phonologically plausible spelling of its vowel (e.g. *theme/these* → /**zi:m**/). There were also control conditions in which non-words were preceded by unrelated words. As can be seen from the results presented in Table 4.2, two effects were found. First, there was a clear effect of sound-to-spelling contingency. Second, there was a priming effect which was large for rhyming words and, although smaller, was also present for non-rhyming words sharing only the same vowel. Priming can occur from the spellings of vowel phonemes and not only from rhymes, which supports Barry & Seymour's model of *vowel*-to-weighted lists of spelling patterns.

TABLE 4.2 *Priming non-word spelling by rhyming words versus words with only the same vowel*

	% production of critical spellings with		
	Most common	2nd most common	Low contingency
Control: preceded by unrelated word *lamp* → /**vuːt**/	51	40	3
Primed by rhyming word *boot* → /**vuːt**/	65	64	23
Primed by word with same vowel *mood* → /**vuːt**/	58	48	9

Necessity of a Separate Lexical System in Regular Orthographies?

The lexical priming effects show that the assembled spelling system does not necessarily operate independently of lexical spelling knowledge in normal, adult English spellers. It may be argued that, for languages with regular orthographies, all words are spelled by a non-lexical, assembled spelling process and so a lexically specific spelling process need not actually exist. Indeed, it might be argued that the notorious inconsistency of English forces at least some interaction between lexically derived knowledge and the assembled spelling system. It is quite possible that such interaction is entirely unnecessary for spelling languages with regular orthographies, such as Italian, where a more parsimonious account of spelling production would require only the existence of a non-lexical sound-to-spelling conversion process.

English orthography is 'deep'. English sound-to-spelling correspondences are extremely inconsistent: whole words are spelled inconsistently (as there are many homophones, e.g. **SAIL-SALE**), rhyming segments are spelled inconsistently (e.g. /ein/ as in **SANE, TRAIN, REIGN, REIN**), and virtually all phonemes — and particularly vowels — are spelled inconsistently (e.g. /ei/ is spelled as in **LATE, WAIT, DAY, BASS, THEY, EIGHT, FEINT, GREAT, REIGN, FETE, STRAIGHT** and **GAUGE**). Furthermore, because there are more spelling patterns than there are phonemes and as most spelling patterns have more than one pronunciation, spelling English non-lexically is even more inconsistent than reading it. In stark contrast, Italian orthography is 'shallow': words are generally spelled as they are pronounced, using highly predictable correspondences. Further, and again in clear contrast to English, spelling Italian non-lexically is even more consistent than reading it, due to the presence of *sdrucciole* words in Italian with irregular syllabic stress assignments which complicate non-lexical reading but have no effect on spelling consistency.

There are only two cases of inconsistently spelled phonological segments in Italian words. First, in only a few words, the letter **I** is phonologically redundant when it occurs between the letters **C** and **E** (as in **CIELO** and **SUPERFICIE**). As a consequence of this, the phonological segment *chey* is spelled inconsistently in the words **SPECIE** and **PECE**, although **CE** is (by a considerable extent) the most common spelling correspondence of this segment. Second, the phonological segment *koo* is spelled inconsistently in Italian, as in the words **CUORE** and **QUANDO**, with **CU** being (by a small majority) the most common spelling.

These two instances of spelling inconsistency compromise the accuracy of any non-lexical spelling system only for an extremely small minority of words — perhaps no more than 20 or so — but they do permit experimental investigation of lexical priming of non-word spelling in Italian. If words are spelled using only an assembled spelling process (as is logically possible for the vast majority of Italian words), there should be *no* effects whatsoever of any lexical influence upon spelling Italian non-words. This expectation is explored in an experiment conducted on over 100 native Italian undergraduates of the University of Ferrara (full details in Barry & De Bastiani, submitted for publication a). Non-words containing the inconsistently spelled segments *chey* and *koo* were constructed and were presented preceded by a prime word which: (i) contained that segment spelled with the most commonly occurring pattern (e.g. *pece → te-chey,* and *cuoco → koo-odo*); (ii) contained the less commonly occurring spelling (e.g. *specie → te-chey,* and *quota → koo-odo*); or (iii) did not contain the segment at all, to provide a control, baseline condition (e.g. *colore → te-chey,* and *gioco → koo-odo*). (The experimental pairs were embedded in a long list of words and non-word fillers, all spoken at a rate of one item every four seconds and the subjects were instructed only to write down the non-words.)

Two predictions could be made if the model advanced by Barry & Seymour to account for assembled spelling in English were also applicable to the regular orthography of Italian. First, there should be a contingency

TABLE 4.3 *Priming non-word spelling in Italian*

	% production of critical spellings with	
	Most common spelling	*Alternative spelling*
-/*chey*/	**-CE**	**-CIE**
Control: preceded by unrelated word *collegio → besicé*	97	3
Primed by word with **-CE** spelling *radice → besicé*	95	5
Primed by word with **-CIE** spelling *superficie → besicé*	81	19
/*koo*/-	**CU-**	**QU-**
Control: preceded by unrelated word *trota → kwona*	74	26
Primed by word with **CU-** spelling *cuoco → kwona*	73	27
Primed by word with **QU-** spelling *quota → kwona*	37	63

effect, in that people would be more inclined to produce the lexically most frequent spelling. Second, there should be a priming effect, in that the prime word should bias the production of the critical spelling pattern. Both predictions were supported by the experiment, the results of which are shown in Table 4.3 (which sums over the non-words with each critical segment). For the segment *chey* almost all spellings were with the **CE** pattern in the control condition. When primed by a word with a **-CE** pattern, there was no change in the distribution of the spellings produced (but there was a ceiling effect). When primed by a word with a **-CIE** pattern, there was a clear (and significant) priming effect (from 3% to 19%). For the segment *koo,* about three-quarters of the spellings were with the **CU** pattern in the control condition (and this mirrors, to a first approximation, the fact that there are more words in Italian with this spelling). When primed by a word with the **CU**- pattern (i.e. the most commonly produced in the control condition), there was *no* priming effect (74% versus 73%). When primed by a word with the **QU**-pattern, there was a substantial priming effect (from 26% to 63%).

This experiment shows quite clearly that there can be lexical priming of non-word spelling in the shallow orthography of Italian, at least for the less common spelling patterns. Barry & De Bastiani (submitted for publication b) have studied three cases of phonological dysgraphia in Italian patients: the fact that there exist patients who can spell words but not non-words suggests that there must be a separate lexical system for spelling Italian. The data from the lexical priming experiment suggest further that the lexical and assembled spelling systems interact functionally. In order to see whether this result extends to other shallow orthographies, a similar experiment was conducted in Welsh.

Welsh orthography, like Italian, is also extremely regular phonologically. Welsh spelling-to-sound conversion rules are simple and direct, although there exist some context sensitive rules (e.g. the letter **Y**, which can also exist as a word, is pronounced differently depending upon its position within a word). Welsh sound-to-spelling correspondences are also regular, but there is one inconsistently spelled phoneme in Welsh words: when in the final syllable of a word, the letters **I**, **U**, and **Y** are pronounced by South Walians in the same way. Therefore, /i/ may be spelled as in *ticedi, teledu* and *tararndy* (and in *morfil, helbul* and *ceffyl*). These words rhyme in Welsh (and are, indeed, perfectly regular for reading). (For North Walians, U and Y — but not I — are pronounced identically, and therefore *teledu* and *tararndy* rhyme but *ticedi* does not.) The fact that /i/ can be spelled in one of three different ways means that spelling Welsh non-lexically is actually harder than reading it. This (unique) instance of spelling inconsistency in Welsh was utilised in an experiment run by Aled Davies at UWCC (full details in Barry & Davies, in preparation). Non-words were constructed with the vowel /i/ (as pronounced by South Walians) and were presented (again embedded in a longer list of filler words and non-words) in the 'lecture' task. The non-words were preceded by one of four conditions:

1. a rhyming word with a **I**-spelling (e.g. *morfil* → *derfil*; *ennill* → *ffalill*);
2. a rhyming word with a **U**-spelling (e.g. *helbul* → *derfil*; *cynnull* → *ffalill*);
3. a rhyming word with a **Y**-spelling (e.g. *ceffyl* → *derfil*; *sefyll* → *ffalill*); and
4. a control (unrelated) word which did not contain the vowel /i/ (e.g. *coleg* → *derfil*; *myned* → *ffalill*).

Twenty-four native (i.e. first language) Welsh speakers were tested and the stimuli were presented (at a rate of about one item per four seconds) by

TABLE 4.4 *Priming non-word spelling in Welsh*

	% production of critical spellings with		
	I-spelling	**U**-spelling	**Y**-spelling
Control: preceded by unrelated word *coleg → derfil*	56	14	30
Primed by word with **I**-spelling *morfil → derfil*	55	10	35
Primed by word with **U**-spelling *helbul → derfil*	29	36	35
Primed by word with **Y**-spelling *ceffyl → derfil*	33	14	53

a native South Walian speaker. Immediately after the Welsh experiment, the subjects (all of whom were fluent bilinguals) were also presented with a similar experiment in English, in which non-words containing inconsistently spelled vowels were preceded by:

1. a rhyming word containing the most commonly occurring spelling of the vowel (e.g. *cheat* → /**di:t**/; *boot* → /**pu:t**/);
2. a rhyming word containing the second most commonly occurring spelling of the vowel (e.g. *fleet* → /**di:t**/; *flute* → /**pu:t**/);
3. a rhyming word containing a low-contingency but phonologically plausible spelling of the vowel (e.g. *Crete* → /**di:t**/; *fruit* → /**pu:t**/); and
4. a control (unrelated) word which did not contain the vowel /i/ (e.g. *nurse* → /**di:t**/; *cloud* → /**pu:t**/).

The results from the Welsh experiment are shown in Table 4.4. In the control condition, the most commonly produced spelling pattern was **I**. When primed by a word with the **I**-pattern, there was *no* change in the pattern of the spellings produced (56% versus 55%), an absence of priming which is clearly not due to any ceiling effect. When primed by a word with a U-pattern, there was a clear (and significant) priming effect, from 14% to 36% (at the expense of **I**-spellings). When primed by a word with a

LEXICAL INFLUENCIES UPON ASSEMBLED SPELLING 83

TABLE 4.5 *Priming non-word spelling in English in Welsh/English bilinguals*

	% production of critical spellings with		
	Most common	2nd most common	Low contingency
Control: preceded by unrelated word *nurse*→ /**di:t**/	56	41	3
Primed by word with most common spelling *cheat*→ /**di:t**/	73	17	9
Primed by word with second most common spelling *fleet*→ /**di:t**/	51	49	0
Primed by word with low-contingency spelling *Crete*→ /**di:t**/	38	25	38

Y-pattern, there was also a significant priming effect, from 30% to 53% (also at 'the expense of' **I**-spellings). As in the results from Italian, there is no priming effect for the spelling pattern which was the most commonly produced in the control (unprimed) condition (which also tends to be the most commonly occurring spelling of the inconsistent phoneme in Welsh words). There are — and again just like Italian — clear priming effects from words with lower-contingency spellings.

The results from the English experiment are shown in Table 4.5. For English, there were clear priming effects for *all* spellings. When primed by a word with the most commonly occurring spelling pattern of its vowel, there was a significant priming effect (from 56% to 73%). When primed by a word with the second most common spelling pattern, there was a priming effect (from 41% to 49%), but, unfortunately, this failed to reach significance. When primed by a word with a low-contingency but phonologically plausible spelling, there was a significant priming effect (from 3% to 38%).

Conclusions

The shallow orthographies of Italian and Welsh, like the deep orthography English, show lexical priming of non-word spelling. Italian and Welsh, desite their orthographic regularity, are not spelled purely non-lexically. These results suggest that just because an orthography *allows* reasonably efficient assembled spelling does not mean that it *requires* that process. There is no support for the general notion, advanced by Turvey, Feldman & Lukatela (1984) from their work on the reading of Serbo-Croatian, that a shallow orthography constrains spellers to a 'phonologically analytic strategy'. The model of assembled spelling proposed by Barry & Seymour (1988) to account for performance in English also appears to be applicable to 'shallow' orthographies. The dual routes of spelling production interact in both deep and shallow orthographies.

The close similarities between the priming effects found in Italian and Welsh are quite striking: there was priming only for those spelling patterns which were *not* the most commonly produced in the control, free-spelling conditions. The 'most preferred' spellings of these sounds — which are the higher-contingency spellings in words — showed no lexical priming. For English, however, as Barry & Seymour have found, *all* spellings showed priming, even the most commonly produced. Furthermore, when tested in English, the Welsh speaking bilingual subjects showed the same results as monolingual English speakers. The explanation of this difference in results must therefore reflect orthographic-specific processes and not simply between-group differences. For Italian, there are only two inconsistently spelled phonological segments and each has only two possible spellings. For Welsh, there is only one inconsistently spelled phoneme, which has (for South Walians) only three possible spellings. It is quite likely that spellers of these languages have somehow 'flagged' these instances (as they have probably experienced difficulty with them) and know explicitly how they can be spelled. In contrast, for English, virtually all sounds are spelled inconsistently, often with a large range of spelling alternatives. It is unlikely that most spellers of English will be aware of all the possible spelling alternatives for each sound. It is therefore plausible that their assembled spelling systems represent *all* spellings, but without any particular ones coming to attain any special, 'highlighted' preference (other than that determined by the constant fluctuations of lexical exposure, i.e. contingency effects). For Italian and Welsh, however, it is likely that the most common spelling comes to attain a more fixed value, resulting from the speller's experience of the particular difficulty it represents (because these are the almost unique 'exceptions that prove the rule').

It is not clear what practical implications can be derived directly from these results, except to alert people to the inherent dangers of teaching sound-to-*single* spelling rules for the vowel phonemes of English. One-to-one correspondences are generally regular for many consonants and for the five so-called 'short' vowels in English (as in **PAP, PEP, PIP, POP, PUP**) — which Barry & Seymour refer to as 'consistent' vowels, in that their most common spelling occurs in over 90% of words in their corpus. However, it is a very easy matter to muster many blatant exceptions to virtually all correspondences. Spellers of English will, unfortunately, always need to know how to spell individual words rather than only sounds.

Given the close similarities between the results for Italian and Welsh, and the differences in patterns of lexical priming effects between these two shallow orthographies and those in English, it appears that a language's orthography does indeed affect spelling performance: the detailed means whereby lexical knowledge influences assembled spelling are somewhat different in shallow and deep orthographies. However, there is functional interaction in both and the data discussed in this chapter provide no support for the notion that orthographic regularity 'demands' non-lexical spelling.

Note

1. This chapter attempts to offer a more general overview of the functional interaction between the lexical and assembled spelling systems within the dual route model than the paper presented at the Newcastle Conference (by Barry, De Bastiani & Davis) which reported detailed experimental results (entitled 'Lexical priming of nonword spelling in English, Italian and Welsh').

    The experimental work in Italian was conducted in collaboration with Pierluigi De Bastiani (Clinica Neurologica, University of Ferrara, Italy) and the Welsh subjects were tested by Aled M. Davies (a graduate of the School of Psychology, UWCC).

References

BARRY, C. 1988, Modelling assembled spelling: Convergence of data from normal subjects and 'surface' dysgraphia. *Cortex* 24, 339–46.
—— in preparation, Lexical priming of nonword spelling: the effects of rhyme.
BARRY, C. and DE BASTIANI, P. submitted for publication a, Lexical priming of nonword spelling in Italian.
—— submitted for publication b, Phonological dysgraphia in Italian.
BARRY, C. and DAVIES, A. M. in preparation, Lexical priming of nonword spelling in Welsh.

BARRY, C. and SEYMOUR, P. H. K. 1988, Lexical priming and sound-to-spelling contingency effects in nonword spelling. *Quarterly Journal of Experimental Psychology* 40A, 5–40.

BAXTER, D. M. and WARRINGTON, E. K. 1987, Transcoding sound to spelling: Single or multiple sound unit correspondence? *Cortex* 23, 11–28.

BEAUVOIS, M. F. and DÉROUESNÉ, J. 1981, Lexical or orthographic agraphia. *Brain* 104, 21–49.

BURDEN, V. 1989, A comparison of priming effects on the nonword spelling performance of good and poor spellers. *Cognitive Neuropsychology* 6, 43–65.

CAMPBELL, R. 1983, Writing nonwords to dictation. *Brain and Language* 19, 153–78.

GOODMAN, R. A. and CARAMAZZA, A. 1986, Dissociation of spelling errors in written and oral spelling: The role of allographic conversion in writing. *Cognitive Neuropsychology* 3, 179–206.

HATFIELD, F. M. and PATTERSON, K. E. 1983, Phonological spelling. *Quarterly Journal of Experimental Psychology* 35A, 451–68.

ROELTGEN, D. P., SEVUSH, S. and HEILMAN, K. M. 1983, Phonological agraphia: Writing by the lexical-semantic route. *Neurology* 33, 755–65.

SEYMOUR, P. H. K. and DARGIE, A. 1990, Associative priming and orthographic choice in nonword spelling. *European Journal of Cognitive Psychology* 2, 395–410.

SHALLICE, T. 1981, Phonological agraphia and the lexical route in writing. *Brain* 104, 413–29.

TURVEY, M. T., FELDMAN, L. B. and LUKATELA, G. 1984, The Serbo-Croatian orthography constrains the reader to a phonologically analytic strategy. In L. HENDERSON (ed.) *Orthographies and Reading: Perspectives from Cognitive Psychology, Neuropsychology, and Linguistics*. London: Lawrence Erlbaum.

5 On Recognising Misspelled Words

ELAINE FUNNELL

Introduction

Poor spellers often complain that however carefully they read over their work, some spelling mistakes always slip through. This chapter investigates this phenomenon, and asks how we recognise correctly spelled and misspelled words, and whether it is realistic to expect poor spellers to be able to recognise their own misspellings.

How do we know when a word is *correctly* spelled? A common strategy, when unsure of a spelling, is to write down several alternative spellings of the word and to select the one that 'looks' right (Morton, 1980). Experiments have shown that in multiple-choice tasks, people can usually select the correct spellings, even of words they themselves are unable to spell (Tenney, 1980). So, the evidence suggests that we know when a word is correctly spelled because we recognise it when we read it.

How then do we know when a word is *misspelled?* Is a reading test sufficient for this task too? The available evidence suggests that it is not.

Frith (1980) found that a group of children who were poor spellers, but good readers, failed to spot some misspellings, particularly those that changed both the sound and letter pattern of the word (e.g. **DEVOLEPING**). In a further study of a 15-year-old boy, who was a good reader but poor speller, Frith (1984) found that in a proofreading task, he missed 50% of the misspellings of quite common words (e.g. **SPLEDID**; **QUICKLEY**; **WSA**). Children who were good readers and spellers were reported by Frith (1980) to make fewer mistakes in these tasks.

In a rather different study conducted by Campbell (1987), two university students, who always misspelled particular words in the same way, were asked to distinguish between the correct spelling and their own misspelling of each of these words. Campbell found that although the students were able to recognise the correct spellings of the words (which they could not themselves spell), they failed to spot about 50% of their own consistent misspellings, identifying them instead as correctly spelled words.

There are various attempts to explain why apparently good readers fail to spot misspellings. Campbell argued that consistently made misspellings were represented in the subject's reading lexicon and so had the status of words. Thus any reading check would accept the misspelling as correct.

Frith (1980) suggested that good spellers and poor spellers differed in the way they read. Reading, she argued, can proceed by 'partial cues' (such as knowledge of some salient features of a word), or by 'full cues' (in which identity and position of all the letters in the word is known). Frith proposed that while reading by partial cues would lead to fast, efficient processing, the dearth of detailed information about letter identities and letter position would inevitably result in poor spelling. Furthermore, written misspellings would be missed more often by partial cue readers than by full cue readers.

Later, Frith (1985) used a three-stage model of reading and spelling acquisition to explain the difference between the two spelling groups. She suggested that good readers who were good spellers processed words at the most advanced, *orthographic* stage of processing, in which morphemes are represented as 'abstract letter-by-letter strings'. Good readers who were poor spellers read at the orthographic stage too, but spelled at the preceding *alphabetic* stage, in which sounds are decoded sequentially into letters.

Frith divided the orthographic stage of reading into two sub-stages: (1) a strong stage, sufficiently detailed to allow written words to be recognised and misspellings to be detected, and (2) a preceding, weak stage, sufficient for recognising written words, but insufficient for detecting misspellings. Frith suggested that good readers who were good spellers read at the strong stage, and so detected misspellings, while good readers who were poor spellers read at the weak stage, and so overlooked misspellings. Clearly, Frith views the ability to detect misspellings as a consequence of *reading* proficiency.

The Study: The Ability to Distinguish Correctly Spelled Words and Misspelled Words

The ability to distinguish correctly spelled words and misspelled words was investigated further, and the results are given in this chapter. Two young subjects were studied: Thomas, a good reader and speller for his age; and Helen, a poor reader and speller. Through a variety of tasks, it was shown that the ability to spot a *misspelling* depended upon whether or not the subject could spell the word correctly. In addition, being able to recognise a *correct spelling* depended upon whether or not the word was within the subject's reading vocabulary. It is argued that correct and misspelled words call upon different processes for their recognition, and that an explanation based upon reading alone is insufficient to explain the findings.

Experimental investigation

Thomas: a good reader and speller

Thomas was 10:4 years old at the time of this study. He had been treated earlier for lack of eye dominance which had been corrected. An assessment of his strengths and weaknesses showed that he had an average IQ (WISC-R full scale 97: verbal 98; performance 96); that his oral reading was advanced for his age at 11:9 years (Schonell Word Reading Test (Schonell & Goodacre, 1974)); and that single word spelling was level with his age at 10:5 years (Schonell Word Spelling Test (Schonell & Goodacre, 1974)). He read and spelled 82% and 75% of nonsense words respectively (e.g. *flom, crogamp*), demonstrating good phonic skills. Visual memory was very poor: he scored at the thirteenth percentile on the Delayed Visual Recall Test (Elliott, Murray & Pearson, 1983), but verbal memory was average at 6 digits (Dempster, 1981).

The standard of Thomas' written work was of concern, so he was asked to write two to three lines about anything at all. The sample he produced contained two spelling errors (**FREIND, SWIMING**), two incomplete words, and a number of other errors. A week later, he was given his text typed out for him to correct. He failed to correct his spelling errors, but spotted the incomplete words and corrected missing capital letters and an uncrossed **T**. Since his spelling was at the level expected for his age, his failure to spot his own spelling mistakes was a surprise and considered to be worth investigating.

Mark the Spelling Test 1   In this test, correctly spelled and misspelled words were presented in written lists for Thomas to mark as correct or incorrect. The 39 words selected for this test were drawn from the reading test of the British Ability Scales (Elliott *et al.,* 1983) and were well within the *reading* vocabulary of a typical ten-year-old. The spellings of 19 words were changed so that nine looked wrong but sounded right (e.g. **SPAWT, CARF**)

TABLE 5.1 *Mark the Spelling Test 1 — Percentage of correctly marked correct and incorrect spellings made by Thomas and Helen*

	Correct spellings ($n = 20$)	Incorrect spellings	
		Look wrong Sound right (e.g. **SPAWT**) ($n = 9$)	Look right Sound wrong (e.g. **EMENY**) ($n = 10$)
Thomas			
Session 1	100	78	50
Session 2	100	67	40
Helen	95	78	40

and ten looked right but sounded wrong (e.g. **CAPRET, CHIAN**). Correct and incorrect spellings were mixed together and typed as a list in two columns on a plain sheet of paper. The test was given twice at an interval of three weeks.

Table 5.1 shows that Thomas spotted all the correct spellings but detected only 58% of the *total set* of misspellings, marking the remainder erroneously as correct (a difference that was significantly greater than chance: $z = 4.29$, $p < .001$). The results confirmed that Thomas was poor at detecting misspellings of words.

Since the misspellings in this test were not Thomas's own, it was of interest to know how many of the misspelled words he himself could spell. He was twice given all the words to spell to dictation, in tests spaced two weeks apart. He was also asked to read aloud the correct and incorrect spellings given in the test 'as if they were all words'.

Thomas read all the items correctly, including reinstating the misspellings to the original words (e.g. he read **CAPRET** as *carpet*, and **SPAWT** as *sport*). However, he misspelled ten words at least once. When his ability to spell the words was compared to his ability to mark the correct and incorrect spellings, it was found that correct spellings were recognised whether or not he himself could spell them. In contrast, misspellings were detected only if he could spell the word reliably himself (see Table 5.2).

The results of this test supported the initial observation that Thomas failed to spot spelling mistakes. However, the number of words he mis-

TABLE 5.2 *Mark the Spelling Test 1 — Proportion (and percentage) of correct judgements of correct spellings and misspellings according to Thomas's ability to spell the word*

	Words	
	Can spell	Cannot spell
Correct judgements:		
Correct spellings	15/15 (100)	5/5 (100)
Incorrect spellings	9/14 (64)	0/5 (0)

TABLE 5.3 *Mark the Spelling Test 2 — Number (and percentage) of misspellings correctly detected according to whether Thomas could correctly spell the word on two occasions, one occasion, or no occasions*

	Can spell twice (n = 8)	Can spell once (n = 8)	Cannot spell (n = 8)
Misspellings detected:			
Session 1	6 (75)	4 (50)	2 (25)
Session 2	6 (75)	2 (25)	3 (37)

spelled in this test was small and, for this reason, a second test was carried out.

Mark the Spelling Test 2 Forty-eight words were selected from the Schonell reading and spelling tests, half of which were presented misspelled. Of these 24 misspelled words, Thomas had previously spelled eight correct on 2/2 occasions; eight correct on 1/2 occasions; and eight correct on 0/2 occasions. Thomas' ability to spell the remaining 24 correctly spelled words was not investigated. Correct and misspelled words were presented mixed together in a typed list for Thomas to mark as correct or misspelled. The test was presented twice in sessions ten days apart.

The results presented in Table 5.3 confirmed earlier findings. If Thomas could spell the words 2/2 times, he spotted 75% misspellings, whereas, if he misspelled the word at least once, only 34% misspellings were spotted in total (a difference significantly greater than chance: $z = 2.32$, $p < .05$). He judged correctly 81% of the correctly spelled words.

In the next part of the study, predictions based on the findings reported above were tested. It was argued that if it is necessary to know the spelling of a word in order to spot a misspelling, then experimental words taught in either a reading or spelling task, should vary in how well their misspellings are detected. Misspellings of words taught only in reading should be overlooked more often than misspellings of words taught for spelling. The second young subject took part in this section of the study.

Helen: a poor reader and poor speller

Helen was 12:6 years at the time of testing. Oral reading age (tested by the Schonell Graded Reading Test) was more than two years below chronological age, at 10:1 years. Reading of text was poor also: on the Neale Reading Test (Neale, 1966) her age levels were 9:4 for accuracy; 9:5 for comprehension; and 8:7 for speed. Her spelling age was also depressed at 9:3 years (Schonell Graded Spelling Test). Phonic decoding skills were better developed for spelling than reading: she could spell to dictation 80% of nonsense words, but could orally read only 48%. Real word spelling mistakes showed some use of phonics (e.g. *type* → **TIPE**; *welfare* → **WELLFAIR**), but reading errors were rarely phonetically correct, most being visually similar words (e.g. *pint* → *print*; *borough* → *bought*). Visual memory, tested by the Delayed Recall of Designs (Elliott *et al.*, 1983), was above average at the 67th percentile, and verbal memory was average at six digits. IQ was not tested.

Helen scored at a similar level to Thomas on the Mark the Spelling Test 1 (see Table 5.1). She recognised 95% of correct spellings, but only 58% of the full set of incorrect spellings. She was able to read all the words in the test correctly (re-instating the misspellings to the correct word). Her ability to spell the words in this test was not investigated. Instead, Helen was taught to read or to spell a selection of novel words, and subsequently tested on her ability to detect correct and incorrect spellings of these words.

Learning tests: reading and spelling Five words that Helen had failed to read (or to spell) correctly were selected from the Schonell Reading Test, and five words that she had failed to spell correctly (but may have been able to read) were selected from the Schonell Spelling Test. The aim was to teach her to read the words she had previously failed to read, and to spell the words she had previously failed to spell. The words varied in length from six

TABLE 5.4 *Proportion of correctly sorted spellings made by Helen according to the mode of learning (reading or spelling)*

	Learned to read	Learned to spell
Correct spellings	8/10	8/10
Misspellings: Total types	7/15	14/15
Omitted letters	4/5	5/5
Added letters	3/5	5/5
Misordered letters	0/5	4/5

to nine letters. Words in the *read* condition were slightly longer than those in the *spell* condition (at an average of 8.8 and 7.7 letters respectively).

The words were printed on individual cards and arranged into sets for reading or spelling. She was given the words to take home to learn. She was asked to read through the word set every day and to spell the spelling set every day, using methods of her own choice.

On retesting, a week later, she read the five *read* words correctly and spelled the five *spell* words correctly. She estimated that it had taken about three trials to learn to spell the words, which she had accomplished by looking at each word, writing it down from memory and then checking back to see if her spelling was correct.

Helen was then given a sorting test of correct spellings and misspellings of the ten words. For each word there were two instances of the correct spelling and three instances of a misspelling (totalling 50 spellings in all). Misspellings either omitted a letter (**ANTQUE**), misordered letters (**ANTQUIE**) or added/substituted letters (**ANTICQUE**). Spellings were printed on individual cards and mixed together, making sure that different spellings of the same word were distributed throughout the set.

As Table 5.4 shows, correct spellings were recognised on 80% of occasions and performance was unrelated to mode of learning (i.e. reading or spelling). In contrast, mode of learning had a marked effect on her ability to detect misspellings: almost perfect scores in the *spell* condition contrasted with chance performance in the *read* condition (a difference which was significantly greater than chance: $z = 2.35, p < .01$).

Letter length did not appear to affect the results in the reading condition. Equal numbers of errors were made to the two shortest words of seven and eight leters and the two longest words of ten letters (three errors in each case).

The results suggest that the ability to detect *misspelled* words depends upon knowing how to spell the word. Knowledge of spelling therefore appears to be an essential requirement for spotting misspellings. In contrast, and somewhat paradoxically, recognising the *correct* spelling appears to be unrelated to spelling ability; both children were able to judge the majority of correct spellings to be correct, quite independently of their ability to spell the words (see Tables 5.2 and 5.4). In order to explain this finding, it is suggested that judgements about correctly spelled words were based upon *reading* knowledge.

It seems likely that when Thomas and Helen were unsure of how to spell a word, their judgements about spellings were based upon the visual similarity of the letter string to their memory of the word-form experienced through reading (and stored in a mental dictionary, or lexicon). Thus, if a letter string resembles a familiar written word-form in the mental lexicon, that may be enough for it to be judged to be a correctly spelled word. If true, then correct spellings of *familiar* words (that the subject cannot spell), are likely to be accepted as correctly spelled words more often than correct spellings of *unfamiliar* words, which have not previously been read, and for which there will be no record in the mental lexicon. Misspellings may also resemble word-forms in the lexicon, in which case, misspellings that resemble *familiar* words may be misjudged to be correctly spelled words, while misspellings that resemble *unfamiliar* words may be less likely to be misjudged as correctly spelled words.

In order to test this theory, Thomas was asked to judge the spelling of correct and incorrectly spelled familiar and unfamiliar written words. It was predicted that if the judgement of correct/incorrect spelling depends upon the similarity of the letter string to a word-form stored in the mental lexicon, then correct spellings of familiar words would be more likely to be judged to be correct than would the correct spellings of unfamiliar words. Similarly, Thomas should be more likely to misjudge the incorrect spellings of familiar words to be correctly spelled than to misjudge the incorrect spellings of unfamiliar words.

Sorting spellings of familiar and unfamiliar written words   Twenty words were selected from the Schonell Word Reading Test: ten familiar written words which Thomas had read successfully in a previous reading test, but had been unable to spell, and ten unfamiliar written words which he had failed to read and to spell. For each word, three misspellings were constructed (an omitted letter, misordered letters and added or substituted letters), together with two instances of the correct spelling.

When Thomas was asked to sort correct and incorrect spellings into two sets, the predictions made above were confirmed. He judged as correct 18/20 correctly spelled familiar words compared with only 8/20 correctly spelled unfamiliar words, a difference which was significant ($z = 2.94$, $p < 0.01$). Furthermore, he misjudged 16/30 misspelled familiar words to be correctly spelled, compared with 7/30 misspelled unfamiliar words; again, the difference was significant: $z = 2.11$, $p < .05$. The results suggest that judgements about correct *and* incorrect spellings of words *that the subject cannot spell* are influenced by previous experience with reading the words.

Discussion

The results of the investigations reported in this chapter have revealed different processing requirements for recognising correctly spelled words and detecting misspellings. First, in order to recognise a *correct* spelling, the word must be within the subject's reading vocabulary. This appears to be a sufficient condition for recognising the correct spelling, since both subjects detected the great majority of correct spellings, quite independently of knowing how to spell the word. Second, in order to detect a *misspelling,* the subject needs to know how to spell the word. Knowing the spelling appears to be an essential requirement for detecting misspelled words, for when the subjects in this study did not know the spelling of the word, misspellings of familiar written words were likely to be accepted as correct. It should be emphasised here that 'knowing the spelling' refers to the *lexical* spelling, rather than to a correct spelling assembled on the basis of sound-to-letter correspondences.

A significant consequence of the activity of these two processes is that misspellings that resemble words that the subject can read, but cannot spell, are likely to be accepted as correctly spelled words.

Theories put forward so far to account for difficulties in detecting misspelled words appear unable to account for the data. Campbell (1987) has suggested that the consistent misspellings made by her subjects, and subsequently judged by them to be correct, were represented in the lexicon and so masqueraded as correctly spelled words. In this study, misspellings were presented that were not the subjects' own, and so had no status in the lexicon. Campbell's theory is therefore not directly relevant to this study.

Frith (1980; 1984; 1985) emphasised differences in reading strategies as an explanation for why some good readers spotted misspellings while other good readers did not. Good readers who detected most misspellings were argued to be reading by full cues, or at a strong orthographic level, while those that overlooked many misspellings read by partial cues, or at a weak orthographic level. However, in this study, Thomas was a good reader and speller, yet he still had difficulty in detecting some misspelled words. Moreover, the ability to detect a misspelled word was tied very closely to the ability to spell the particular word in question; a pattern that emerged in both subjects, despite the fact that one subject was a good reader and speller, while the other was poor at both tasks.

In a modification of Frith's theory, it might be argued that those words that the subjects could spell had been read by full cues (or at the orthographic stage), while those that the subjects could not spell had been read by partial cues (or at a sub-orthographic stage). However, this would change the developmental theory from one of different reading levels across *subjects* to different reading levels across *words,* and would no longer provide a straightforward account for the difference between those good readers who are good spellers and those who are not.

Instead, it is suggested that in a reading task, words are identified on the basis of their distinguishing properties: that is, those properties required to distinguish a particular written word from all others in the subject's reading vocabulary. For beginner readers, with very small written word vocabularies, words may be identified simply on the basis of an unusual feature, such as a hyphen (Seymour & Elder, 1986). As the reading vocabulary increases, more features will be required to distinguish any particular word, and in some instances where a set of words (e.g. *tea, eat, ate*) share the same letters but in varying order, the relative position of each letter in the word may need to be marked. It is suggested therefore that in reading, the distinguishing features are marked in the lexicon and that, in many cases, this will result in an incomplete orthographic description of the word. As a consequence, a misspelling that preserves the salient features is likely to be positively identified as a word, since it will match the orthographic description established through reading.

It would be unwise at this stage to speculate about what the distinguishing features for reading any particular word are likely to be, but preliminary evidence suggests that the linear ordering of letters is a less salient feature for reading (at least initially) than letter identities. Thomas and Helen made consistently more errors in detecting misspellings when these contained misordered rather than substituted letters (see Tables 5.1 and 5.4). Beginner readers largely ignore letter order (Frith, 1985) and are not apparently disconcerted when letters belonging to words within their reading vocabulary are re-ordered (Stuart, 1986). In a study in which university students, who may be presumed to be advanced readers, were asked to spell the name *Gandhi,* it was found that they tended to re-position the letter **H** next to the **G** (Campbell & Coltheart, 1984), suggesting that the letter identities had been coded through reading the word, but without a complete description of their relative positions.

In contrast to reading, spelling entails learning about the letter identities and the exact linear position of the letters in the word. Assuming that reading and spelling access a single orthographic lexicon (Allport & Funnell, 1981), it is suggested that learning to spell a word fills out the limited orthographic description established through reading into a complete linear description. Once the spelling of a word has been learned, misspellings will be detected since they will fail to match the completely specified orthographic description in the lexicon.

This theory has obvious similarities to that of Frith (1980; 1984), but the difference in the ability to detect misspellings found for good and poor spellers, that is accounted for by Frith in terms of *reading* by partial or full cues, is explained here as differences in *reading* by partial cues and *spelling* by full cues. In this theory the puzzle of children who read well but fail to detect misspellings is explained in terms of the different orthographic descriptions established in tasks of reading and spelling, rather than in terms of different ways of reading. This theory has the advantage that both poor spelling and the failure to detect misspellings can be accounted for by a single factor: that is, poor spelling.

No account will be given here as to why some children are good spellers and others are not, nor why most children know the spellings of some words and not other words. While there is evidence to suggest that some spelling knowledge can be acquired as a by-product of reading (Tenney, 1980), educational practice suggests that good spelling is acquired through spelling activities, and can be a prolonged procedure. Certainly the results of this study suggest that it is learning to spell (rather than learning to read), that is important for becoming a good speller.

The most immediate lesson from this study, which will be of concern to teachers, is that children who are poor at spelling will fail to detect many misspelled words however carefully they check their work by reading it through. It appears therefore that the traditional practice of asking children to check their work for misspellings is unlikely to be helpful. The conclusion seems clear: reading and spelling establish different types of orthographic description in the lexicon, with the result that good reading does not necessarily inform spelling. Good spellers are good because, somehow, they have learned how to spell.

Summary

This chapter is about how correct spellings and misspellings are recognised. Two young subjects had difficulty detecting the misspellings of words they themselves could not spell. However, they had no difficulty with recognising the correct spellings of these words, so long as the words were familiar. It is argued that being able to read a word is insufficient to enable misspellings to be detected reliably, because reading does not establish a full orthographic description of the word in the lexicon. Only when a word can be spelled will the orthographic description in the lexicon be sufficiently complete to detect misspellings. As a consequence, when checking their written work, good readers who are poor spellers will tend to overlook the misspellings of words they cannot spell.

References

ALLPORT, D. A. and FUNNELL, E. 1981, Components of the mental lexicon. *Philosophical Transactions of the Royal Society of London* B295, 397–410.
CAMPBELL, R. 1987, One or two lexicons for reading and writing words: Can misspellings shed any light? *Cognitive Neuropsychology* 4, 487–99.
CAMPBELL, R. and COLTHEART, M. 1984, Gandhi: The nonviolent road to spelling reform? *Cognition* 17, 185–92.
DEMPSTER, F. N. 1981, Memory span: Sources of individual and developmental differences. *Psychological Bulletin* 89, 63–100.
ELLIOTT, C. D., MURRAY, D. J. and PEARSON, L. S. 1983, *British Ability Scale.* Windsor: NFER-Nelson.
FRITH, U. 1980, Unexpected spelling problems. In U. FRITH (ed.) *Cognitive Processes in Spelling.* London: Academic Press.
—— 1984, Specific spelling problems. In R. N. MALATESHA and H. A. WHITAKER (eds) *Dyslexia: A Global Issue.* The Hague: Martinus Nijhoff.
—— 1985, Beneath the surface of developmental dyslexia. In K. E. PATTERSON, J. C. MARSHALL and M. COLTHEART (eds) *Surface Dyslexia.* London: Lawrence Erlbaum.
MORTON, J. 1980, The logogen model and orthographic structure. In U. FRITH (ed.) *Cognitive Processes in Spelling.* London: Academic Press.
NEALE, M. D. 1966, *Neale Analysis of Reading Ability.* London and Basingstoke: Macmillan Education Ltd.
SCHONELL, F. J. and GOODACRE, E. 1974, *The Psychology and Teaching of Reading* 5th edn. London: Oliver & Boyd.

SEYMOUR, P. K. E. and ELDER, L. 1986, Beginning reading without phonology. *Cognitive Neuropsychology* 3, 1–36.
STUART, K. M. 1986, *Phonological Awareness, Letter–Sound Knowledge and Learning to Read*. Doctoral thesis: Birkbeck College, University of London.
TENNEY, Y. T. 1980, Visual factors in spelling. In U. FRITH (ed.) *Cognitive Processes in Spelling*. London: Academic Press.

6 Methodological Issues in the Investigation of Spelling and Spelling Development

H. M. PATTISON and J. COLLIER

Introduction

Research on spelling and spelling development is of theoretical and practical importance. Many children never attain good spelling skills and the reasons for this are still unclear. Up until the 1980s spelling was a neglected area of research. The modelling of cognitive processes underlying spelling is still largely parasitic on reading research, particularly on research on reading single words aloud.

In common with theories of reading and reading development, theories of spelling and spelling development stress the importance of phonological skills. Frith's influential model of spelling and reading development (1980; 1985), based on analyses of the performance of children at different stages of development and of children with reading and/or spelling problems, suggests that phonological skills are necessary for progression from the logographic stage to the alphabetic stage. However, in the logographic stage the child relies on a visual representation, and at the orthographic stage, visual, semantic and syntactic representations would be important in addition to phonology.

Theories of the processes involved in spelling words also emphasise the importance of phonology. It is hypothesised that words are broken down into component sounds which may then be converted to orthographic form (e.g. Frith, 1980). Dual route models of spelling (e.g. Ellis, 1982) postulate one route for spelling in which an analysis into sounds takes place. Such a route, it is suggested, could be used to spell unfamiliar words. There is controversy over the nature of this phonetic analysis; whilst some would suggest it uses sound-to-spelling rules others, notably Goswami (1988), provide evidence that spelling involves the use of analogies to familiar words. The second route postulated in dual route models is a 'lexical' route to spelling whereby the output orthography of familiar words is derived directly, without recourse to an analysis of their component sounds.

The emphasis on phonology in spelling research has stimulated an interest in the performance of the hearing-impaired, particularly the congenitally deaf, because they would be expected to have an impaired phonology. If phonology is essential for the development of spelling, and also for the spelling of new words, one would expect the hearing-impaired to perform poorly on spelling tasks. However, researchers have found that deaf subjects tend to be better spellers than their reading levels would predict (Hoemann *et al.*, 1976; Markides, 1976). There are several ways of interpreting this finding and it should be interpreted with caution. It is very difficult to measure the spelling levels of the hearing-impaired on standardised tests in a way that is comparable to the measurement of those of the hearing, as most standardised tests use oral presentation of words. However, there is evidence (Pattison, 1986) that hearing-impaired children who are better spellers (and better readers) tend to use knowledge that looks like phonology in their spelling. This pseudo-phonology could be derived from lip-reading or from articulatory feedback. On the other hand, poorer hearing-impaired spellers do not seem to use such knowledge. They display different patterns of error than those shown by reading-age matched hearing children. Notably, they produce far more real word substitutions than hearing children, and these tend to be visually similar to the target word (Pattison, 1983). Dodd (1980) also concluded that the hearing-impaired children she tested did not normally use phonology in spelling. So other spelling strategies may be available to children who have poor phonology, though it remains to be demonstrated that such strategies could lead to normal levels of spelling performance.

In spelling research then, great emphasis is placed on the importance of phonology. However, less emphasis seems to be placed on phonology in the teaching of spelling. Here a variety of ways of looking at spelling may encourage the development of spelling skills relying on different aspects of word structure. Below, for example, are some of the techniques suggested by the National Curriculum Council (NCC) to help children master spelling conventions:

- encouraging the development of visual memory;
- encouraging children to identify a word by its initial letter and look for it in an alphabetical word bank or dictionary;

- using 'spell checker' computer programs;
- teaching the children to 'look, cover, remember, write, check' in memorising new words. (DES, 1990)

These techniques encourage a visual analysis of words to be spelled rather than a phonetic analysis. Most of the techniques suggested by the NCC are not new, and some, e.g. look, cover, remember, write, check, are very commonly found in classrooms. It is not surprising that spelling teaching emphasises visual and other information in spelling since the correspondences between sound and spelling are much less consistent than those in reading (Hatfield & Patterson, 1983), and, particularly at the early stages of learning, an emphasis on sound-to-spelling correspondences could be confusing.

It is noteworthy that the spelling tasks that children are given in research projects and as tests of their spelling progress may not fit well with the way they have been taught spelling and, as we shall argue below, may actually encourage strategies for spelling that would not always be used by the child.

The Importance of Measuring Spelling

The measurement of spelling performance and development is important for theoretical and educational reasons. Theories of spelling make predictions about how spelling should develop and what errors children should make. Clearly then, to test theories, spelling data must be collected and compared with the theoretical predictions. This may involve collecting data from a wide age range of children, and also from particular groups such as the hearing-impaired or backward spellers. The type of children to be tested must be considered when deciding what is the most appropriate and valid form of measurement in any particular case.

From an educational point of view, when monitoring the development of spelling and the efficacy of teaching methods it is necessary to assess when, and in what ways, failure occurs. Of great importance, is the availability of reliable and valid measuring instruments. The few standardised tests of spelling that are available tend to be fairly unsophisticated and dated. One does not find in spelling testing the sophisticated approach that characterises much of the measurement of reading and speech.

Our current work on the measurement of spelling and analysis of spelling errors has two motivations: (1) we wish to test theories of spelling and using measuring procedures and analyses of errors that will not bias our findings, and (2) we feel there is a need for a new standardised test of spelling.

Ways in which spelling is measured

The measurement of performance on some spelling tasks could introduce confounding variables into spelling research. Also, some spelling tasks may be more appropriate than others in monitoring the progress of spelling development. Below are the main ways in which spelling has been measured in research projects, together with criticisms of these measuring procedures.

Dictation

1. Written spelling to dictation of lists of real words (Barron, 1980; Temple, 1986; Bruck & Waters, 1988).
2. Written spelling to dictation, or from lip-reading, of lists of real words plus short sentences for context (Baron *et al.*, 1980; Dodd, 1980).
3. Written spelling to dictation of real word and non-word lists (Temple, 1986).
4. Written spelling to dictation or from lip-reading of non-word lists (Dodd, 1980; Marsh *et al.*, 1980; Campbell, 1985).
5. Oral spelling to dictation of lists of real words (Temple, 1986).

Oral presentation of words to be spelled is also commonly used to assess the progress of a child's spelling, e.g. using the Schonell test (Schonell & Goodacre, 1974).

The auditory reception of words to be spelled may affect the strategy used by children in spelling. It is possible that many children would normally use a stored representation of the visual pattern of the word rather than relying solely on a representation of the sound-to-spelling correspondence of the word, particularly at early and late stages of their spelling development. Note that this is not to say that children who use such a strategy are relying on reading to check spelling, but rather that the nature of the representation they are using is not phonetic. Dictation obviously emphasises the sound of words which may encourage phonetic strategies. This is an argument also made by Cromer (1980) with respect to language-disordered children's normal spelling strategies.

Such testing may not fit in with the way the child has been taught to spell if that teaching has particularly emphasised the visual aspects of words (see the extracts from NCC guidance for teachers, above).

A final criticism of such testing is that it is inappropriate for some special needs groups, notably the hearing-impaired, and some physically disabled children for whom difficulties in using a pen may lead to an unfair strain on auditory memory. Since the performance of the hearing-impaired is important for evaluating theories of spelling, some method of measurement which equates the spelling task for the hearing and hearing-impaired would be preferable. Dodd (1980) did use oral dictation to hearing-impaired subjects, but they were reliant on lip-reading; it is difficult to judge how similar this would be to hearing the words.

Reading text and searching for spelling errors (Everhart & Marschank, 1988)

Spelling error detection tests obviously rely on reading performance so reading and spelling cannot be evaluated as separate skills. Since it is generally thought that reading and spelling develop to some extent separately initially (Frith, 1980), this seems an inappropriate way of testing spelling performance. In addition, it is of dubious educational merit to expose children to incorrectly spelt words.

Spontaneous spelling

1. Spontaneous spelling in natural script (Wing & Baddeley, 1980).
2. Spontaneous spelling in stories with vocabulary restricted by a title or event to be described (Cromer, 1980; Pattison, 1986; Everhart & Marschank, 1988).

Children's writing is also, of course, routinely used by teachers to monitor spelling progress.

The measurement of spelling performance in natural script tends to be imprecise. First, even when the subject matter of a story is restricted, there may be ambiguity in the identification of target words, particularly in the worst spellings. Secondly, it is difficult to compare the performance of different children when they may have been attempting words of different complexity and difficulty. Thirdly, poor spellers may recognise their deficit and 'play safe' by using words they are more certain about, giving an unrealistic picture of their spelling competence.

Analysis of Errors

Of equal importance to the spelling task which a child is asked to perform is the way in which errors are analysed. The two most common forms of analysis are: (1) right or wrong classification 'target words pre-coded, usually as irregular and regular in spelling to sound correspondence' (Dodd, 1980); and (2) mutually exclusive classification in a more or less sophisticated fashion (Cromer, 1980; Dodd, 1980; Temple, 1986). These two forms of analysis are essentially the same, and open to the same criticisms: an inability to spell irregular words is usually interpreted as a reliance on phonology, thus errors are pre-classified into mutually exclusive classes according to the type of words in which they occur. Analyses which involve the classification of spelling errors in an all or none fashion as an error on one characteristic of written language, may be oversimplified, lose information and beg the theoretical questions they are supposed to address.

Even in the most sophisticated error classification, errors are classified as a failure of a particular hypothesised component of the process. This form of classification obviously assumes a particular model of spelling made up of several components. Errors are seen as a failure of one of these components. In the simplest classification an error may be classified as a phonetic error or a visual error (Bruck & Waters, 1988). So the spelling of *bear* as **BARE** would be classed as a correct sound analysis but a failure in visual analysis or memory, i.e. a phonetically plausible error. However, one could equally well argue that this is a visual error, since it has the correct word shape and the correct letters. Unsurprisingly, such classification often leads to a large number of errors defined as 'unclassifiable' (e.g. Temple, 1986).

Hierarchical classification (e.g. Cromer, 1980) is classification where errors are first considered on their proximity to one aspect of the target word, e.g. sound, then another, e.g. visual appearance, then another, e.g. morphology, and so on. Hierarchies tend to assume a model of spelling which places primary importance on phonology, it is only if the error cannot be categorised as a phonetically plausible error that other classifications are considered.

In addition mutually exclusive error categories do not yield information on the extent of the error. For example an error may be classed as phonetically plausible or not, but if it is not, to what extent is it not? For example, whilst one would consider **BARE** to be a phonetically plausible rendering of *bear*, one would also consider **BRAE** to be a more phonetically plausible spelling than **RABER**.

Suggestions for Different Ways of Measuring and Analysing Spelling

We have attempted to overcome the problems inherent in the methods of measurement described above, which either use linguistic stimuli which may bias strategies, or which produce errors which are not restricted enough to carry out an analysis of individual differences or produce a test that is repeatable. The spelling task we decided on was to use pictorial word lists, where children have to write the names of the pictures. Pictures are often used in tests of speech production and of reading and it is surprising that they are not used more often as stimuli for spelling. We recognise that pictures may be ambiguous, but we have found that by careful selection of the words used and of the pictures chosen to represent those words, ambiguity is reduced to a negligible level.

We have also attempted to overcome the problems inherent in classifying errors. No matter how sophisticated the classification system is, information is lost by deciding an error belongs to one and only one category. One loses information about the extent of error within its class, and the extent to which it could also be seen as belonging to a different class.

We believe that there is no need to categorise errors, and rather we have adopted and extended a method of analysis used by Pattison (1983; 1986). This involves the multi-dimensional scaling of errors. In the study reported below we used a three dimensional analysis whereby *every* error was measured on its phonetic and visual accuracy, and also on its orthographic legality. This method of analysis could be used to analyse errors from a range of spelling tasks, not only the picture naming task, but also writing words to dictation or spontaneous writing. So it could be used to look for different strategies in different spelling tasks.

A Preliminary Study

We carried out a study in which we investigated the written spelling of normal seven- and ten-year-old children. We used both oral and pictorial presentation of words to be spelled. A set of words was selected from vocabulary norms for six- to ten-year-old children. The word list contains a wide variety of spelling patterns. The variety comes not only from the number of sounds and letters represented, but also from the inclusion in the list of:

- words containing consonant clusters, e.g. *castle, apple*;
- words with silent letters, e.g. *comb, sword*;
- the same sound represented by different letters, e.g. /k/ in *candle, kangaroo, bucket* and *anchor*, /əʊ/ in *boat, comb* and *bow*;
- the same letter(s) representing different sounds, e.g. **OW** in *owl* and *bow*, **CH** in *chair, anchor* and *parachute*.

INVESTIGATING SPELLING AND SPELLING DEVELOPMENT

Pictures representing each word were reproduced in booklets for individual presentation to the children. The pictures were simple black-and-white line drawings, though these did vary in style as they were drawn from several sources. A pilot study confirmed that the pictures finally used in the test elicited the correct spoken names from children in the age groups we tested. The same words were presented orally for spelling to the same children on a later occasion.

All errors were analysed using three metrics:

The phonological error score. The phonological target score was obtained by counting the number of phonemes in the target word and adding this to the number of syllables. The error score was then obtained by counting the number of incorrect graphemic representations of the phonemes in the word and adding to this the number of syllables above or below the number in the word, this total was then divided by the target score.

For example, **CLOW** for *clown*.

Clown has a target score of 5 (four phonemes, one syllable), **CLOW** has one phoneme omitted and the correct number of syllables. The phonological score is thus 1 divided by 5 giving 0.2. Note that a graphemic representation of a phoneme was counted as correct if a word using those letters to represent that sound (regardless of the position of sound in the word) would be likely to be within the vocabulary of a child of 12 or less.

The visual error score. The visual target score was obtained by counting the number of letters in the target word and adding this to the number of up-strokes (as in the lower-case letters **b** and **l**) and down-strokes (as in the lower-case letters **p** and **y**). The error score was then obtained by counting the number of incorrect letters and adding to this the number of up-strokes and down-strokes above or below the number in the word, this total was then divided by the target score. Each word was divided into beginning, middle and end sections, and a letter would be counted as correct only if it occurred in approximately the correct place.

For example, **CLOW** for *clown*.

Clown has a target score of 6 (five letters, one up-stroke), **CLOW** has one letter omitted and one up-stroke in the right place. The visual score is thus 1 divided by 6 giving 0.17.

The orthographic score. The orthographic score was obtained by simply counting the number of letter combinations, or letter positionings that broke the rules of English orthography, with reference to Wijk (1966) and Venezky (1970), e.g. starting a word with the letters **CK**. This metric proved to be problematical and the results of this analysis will not be described in great detail. The metric has been replaced in current work with a 'phonographic' metric which is described in the final section.

It was perfectly possible for an error to score 0 on a metric, e.g. spelling *swan* as **SWON** would score 0 on the phonological metric, but 0.25 on the visual metric; similarly, spelling *boat* as **BAOT** would score 0 on the visual metric, but 0.5 on the phonological metric.

Results

The seven-year-old children produced not only significantly more spelling errors than the ten-year-olds, but also errors which were significantly further from the target word, both phonetically and visually, and more highly illegal according to the rules of English orthography. Qualitative analysis of errors revealed a significantly different relationship between patterns of spelling errors and the overall spelling proficiency between the seven-year-old children and the ten-year-old children (see Table 6.1). The seven-year-old children who were poor spellers, as demonstrated by the total number of errors they made, consistently produced errors that scored high error value scores on all three dimensions. The ten-year-olds showed a different pattern whereby the number of errors a subject made was not significantly correlated to their mean visual error value, but was correlated to their mean phonological score suggesting that phonological aspects of spelling were more important in determining success in spelling for the ten-year-olds.

TABLE 6.1 *The relationship between error scores and overall spelling performance (picture presentation)*

		7 year olds	10 year olds
(a)	Mean number of errors	25.5	7.7
(b)	Mean phonological score	0.276	0.149
	correlation between (a) and (b)	0.651**	0.570*
(c)	Mean visual score	0.314	0.190
	correlation between (a) and (c)	0.717**	0.238^{NS}

** = ($p < 0.005$)   * = ($p < 0.01$) ^{NS} = not significant

When we examined the effect of the mode of presentation, we found that the ten-year-olds consistently produced less errors with the oral presentation, but the mean difference was very small (0.78 errors). There was no significant difference in the number of errors produced by the seven-year-olds in the two conditions (see Figure 6.1). However, for both age groups, oral presentation of stimuli led to the production of errors which were significantly more phonologically accurate than pictorial presentation of stimuli (see Figure 6.2).

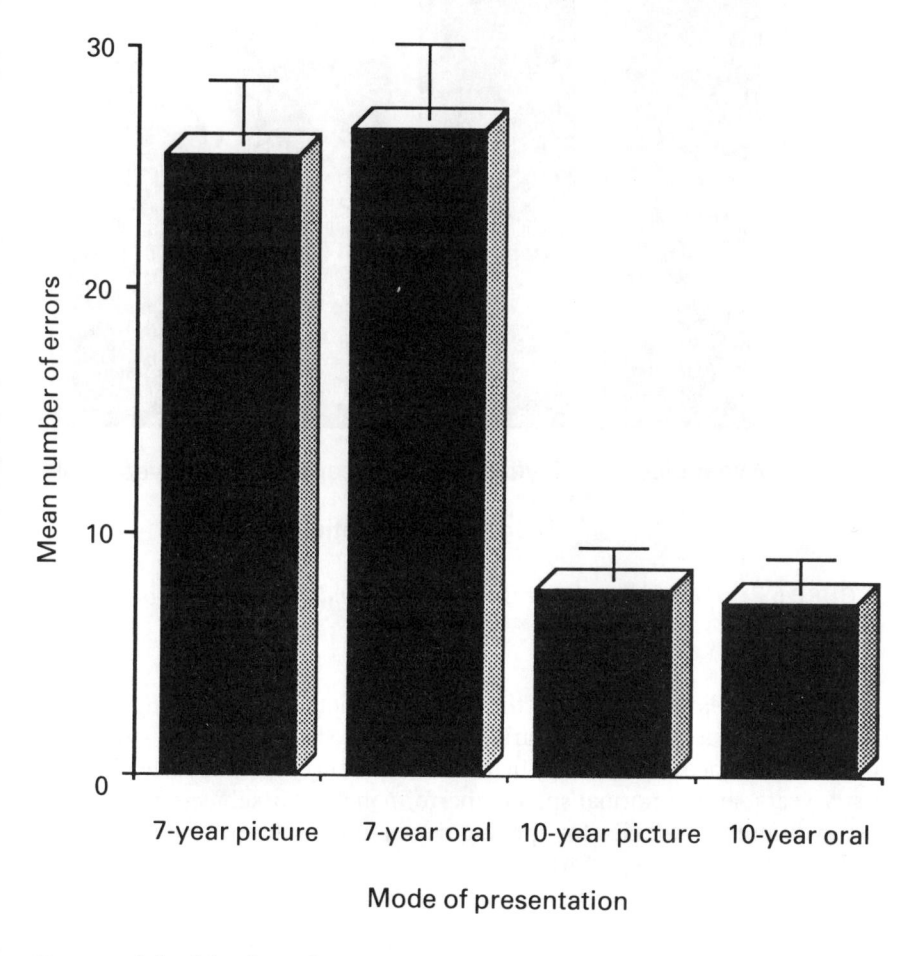

FIGURE 6.1 *Number of errors with picture and oral presentation*

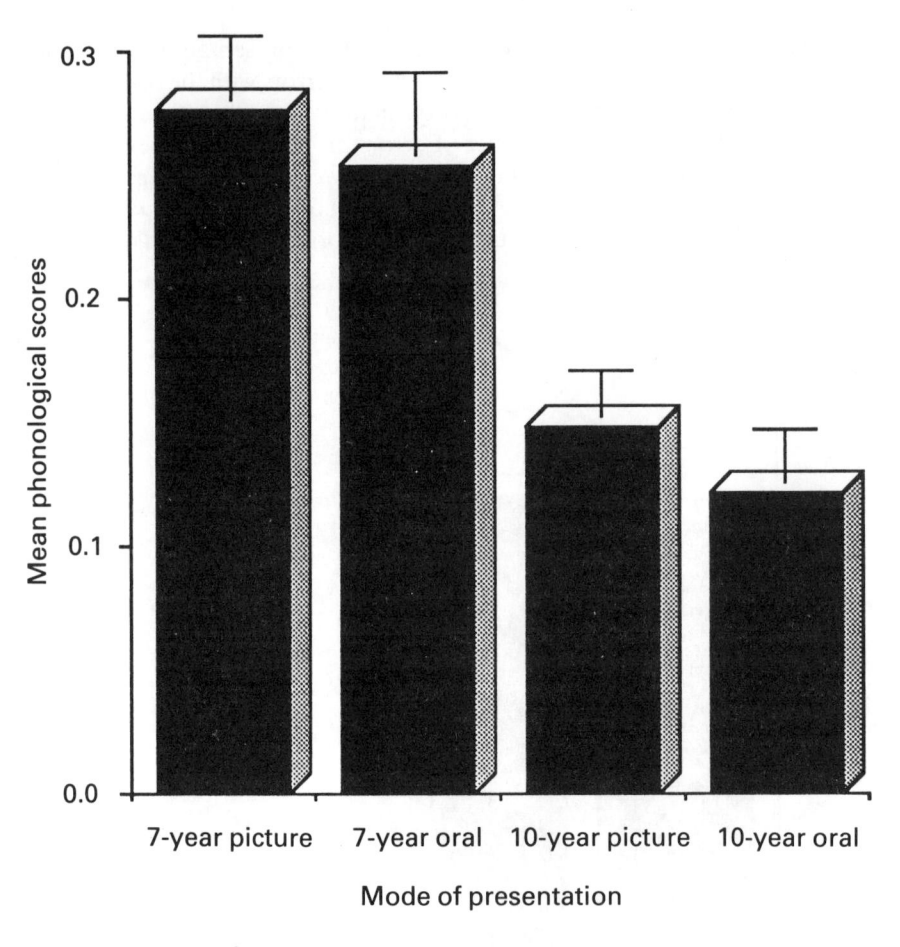

FIGURE 6.2 *Phonological scores with picture and oral presentation*

These findings suggest that the traditional methods of assessing spelling may introduce a confounding variable, and hence lead to the over-emphasis of the importance of phonology in the development of spelling, at least in the early years, and in normal spelling performance. Our subjects seem to be using different strategies for spelling depending on the particular spelling task they are asked to perform.

Practical Implications

The results of our research to date have obvious practical implications for the testing of spelling in educational assessment and research. Firstly, we have shown that the way spelling is tested affects spelling performance. Thus children may be able to make use of the sound of words when spelling to dictation to make their spellings more phonologically accurate, giving an inflated impression of their phonological skills. Secondly, we have argued that categorising errors loses information and may be misleading, but the multi-dimensional system of analysis that we have developed is time-consuming and requires a degree of linguisitic knowledge. Any standardised assessment based on this system would have to be supported by extensive databases of pre-analysed errors. Finally, we have argued that if the spelling development and performance of various special needs groups are to be assessed accurately, it is important that they should be tested under the same conditions as other children. We have demonstrated that it is possible to test spelling by using picture presentation of words to be spelled and this overcomes communication problems associated with spelling to dictation and allows children to work at their own pace.

Current Research

We are using the test developed in the work described above to measure the spelling of a sample of 700 children aged between six and eleven years. We want to build up a database of the levels of spelling performance and the types of error made by this age group. The test has been improved by adding a few more words to extend the range of words to be spelled and new pictures have been drawn specifically for the test by one artist. We are also replacing the orthographic metric. The new 'phonographic' metric is a context-sensitive phonological measure, where the position of a spelling pattern within the word is taken into account. In future we also hope to be able to use the test and analyses to look at spelling development longitudinally, and in special groups, particularly the hearing-impaired.

Summary

Theories of spelling and spelling development place great emphasis on phonology, and research tends to use methods of measurement and analysis which reflect this. However, such methodology could encourage the use of particular, not necessarily preferred, strategies in spelling and lead to analyses of errors which fail to answer the theoretical questions they purport to address. The way in which errors are typically analysed tends to overemphasise the importance of particular types of information for spelling. We have used pictorial and oral presentation of words to be spelled and have found that these two methods of presentation lead to differences in error rate and types of error produced. These methodological issues obviously have implications for theories of spelling and spelling development. A multidimensional scoring system for spelling errors has allowed us to analyse errors without having to classify them a priori as a failure of a particular part of an hypothesised spelling system.

References

BARON, J., TREIMAN, R., WILF, J. F. and KELLMAN, P. 1980, Spelling and reading by rules. In U. FRITH (ed.) *Cognitive Processes in Spelling*. London: Academic Press.
BARRON, R. W. 1980, Visual and phonological strategies in reading and spelling. In U. FRITH (ed.) *Cognitive Processes in Spelling*. London: Academic Press.
BRUCK, M. and WATERS, G. 1988, An analysis of the spelling errors of children who differ in their reading and spelling skills. *Applied Psycholinguistics* 9, 77–92.
CAMPBELL, R. 1985, When children write nonwords to dictation. *Journal of Experimental Child Psychology* 40, 133–51.
CROMER, R. F. 1980, Spontaneous spelling by language-disordered children. In U. FRITH (ed.) *Cognitive Processes in Spelling*. London: Academic Press.
DES (Department of Education and Science) 1990, *English in the National Curriculum*. London: HMSO.
DODD, B. 1980, The spelling abilities of profoundly pre-lingually deaf children. In U. FRITH (ed.) *Cognitive Processes in Spelling*. London: Academic Press.
ELLIS, A. 1982, Spelling and writing (and reading and speaking). In A. ELLIS (ed.) *Normality and Pathology in Cognitive Functions*. London: Academic Press.
EVERHART, V. S. and MARSHCHANK, M. 1988, Linguistic flexibility in signed and written language productions of deaf children. *Journal of Experimental Child Psychology* 46, 174–93.
FRITH, U. 1980, Unexpected spelling problems. In U. FRITH (ed.) *Cognitive Processes in Spelling*, London: Academic Press.
—— 1985, Beneath the surface of developmental dyslexia. In K. PATTERSON, J. MARSHALL and M. COLTHEART (eds) *Surface Dyslexia*. London: Lawrence Erlbaum.
GOSWAMI, U. 1988, Children's use of analogy in learning to spell. *British Journal of Developmental Psychology* 6, 21–33.
HATFIELD, F. M. and PATTERSON, K. E. 1983, Phonological spelling. *Quarterly Journal of Experimental Psychology* 35A, 451–68.
HOEMANN, H. W., ANDREWS, C. E., FLORIAN, V. A., HOEMANN, S. A. and JENSEMA, C. A. 1976, The spelling proficiency of deaf children. *American Annals of the Deaf* 121, 489–93.

MARKIDES, A. 1976, Comparative linguistic proficiencies of deaf children taught by two different methods of instruction. *Teacher of the Deaf* 74, 307–47.
MARSH, G., FRIEDMAN, M., WELCH, V. and DESBERG, P. 1980, The development of strategies in spelling. In U. FRITH (ed.) *Cognitive Processes in Spelling*. London: Academic Press.
PATTISON, H. M. 1983, Reading and writing in hearing-impaired children. Ph.D. thesis, University of Reading.
—— 1986, Orthographic skills in the hearing-impaired. In G. AUGST (ed.) *New Trends in Graphemics and Orthography*. Berlin: Walter de Gruyter.
SCHONELL, F. J. and GOODACRE, E. 1974, *The Psychology and Teaching of Reading* (5th edn). London: Oliver & Boyd.
TEMPLE, C. 1986, Developmental Dysgraphias. *The Quarterly Journal of Experimental Psychology* 38A, 77–110.
VENEZKY, R. L. 1970, *The Structure of English Orthography*. The Hague: Mouton.
WIJK, A. 1966, *The Rules of Pronunciation for the English Language*. London: Oxford University Press.
WING, A. M. and BADDELEY, A. D. 1980, Spelling errors in handwriting: A corpus and distributional analysis. In U. FRITH (ed.) *Cognitive Processes in Spelling*. London: Academic Press.

Section Three: The Development of Spelling Ability

The papers in this section are concerned with several aspects of the development of spelling. Ellis & Cataldo deal with the relationship between phonological awareness, reading and spelling. Goulandris is concerned with the relationship between early spelling ability and later literacy. Huxford, Terrell & Bradley focus on the relationship between phonological reading and phonological spelling. Taylor & Martlew compare children and adults in their spelling of vowel sounds.

Spelling is Integral to Learning to Read (Ellis & Cataldo)

Ellis & Cataldo are concerned with the relationship between reading, spelling and phonological awareness. They point out that while there are correlational studies, these, by their nature, don't show the direction of causality, e.g. they don't indicate whether the ability to read leads to the ability to spell or vice versa. The purpose of the research they report is to identify the direction of the causal relationships between this trio.

A significant feature of the study is the distinction between implicit and explicit phonological awareness. Implicit awareness seems to require only the ability to recognise relationships between sounds, e.g. the identification of rhyme or alliteration. It does not require the ability to examine and manipulate the phonemic structure of a word. This comes with explicit awareness, which enables the child, for example, to segment the word in a number of ways, e.g. *c-at, ca-t,* or *c-a-t.* Given that the alphabetic principle requires phoneme–grapheme correspondence knowledge, a child showing explicit awareness is more likely.to have a grasp of it than a child with only implicit awareness.

Ellis & Cataldo followed a group of children over two years. They were tested at the beginning of the first year of school (four to five years old), again towards the end of the first year, at the beginning of the second year, and finally at the beginning of the third year. On each occasion they were given tests of implicit awareness, explicit awareness, reading, spelling, letter–sound associations and various tests of intelligence.

Using a sophisticated statistical methodology called LISREL, Ellis & Cataldo have been able to determine the direction of causal relationships. Whether, over a given time period, *Ability A is the basis for the development of Ability B* or whether *Ability B is the basis for the development of Ability A*. What they found was this:

1. In the *early* phase of the children's development both reading and spelling ability developed on the basis of their implicit awareness. While this suggests that both are dependent on a knowledge of phonological relationships it does not mean that they have grasped the alphabetic principle, which specifically requires phoneme–grapheme knowledge.
2. In the *early and intermediate* phases, spelling (but not reading) ability developed on the basis of explicit awareness. This, together with the first result, suggests that while reading in these first two phases was pre-alphabetic, spelling was partly dependent on the acquisition of the alphabetic principle (which requires the awareness of phonemes found in explicit awareness). Furthermore, reading ability developed on the basis of spelling ability, which suggests that spelling is the mediator by which reading becomes alphabetic.
3. In the *last* phase, spelling continued to develop on the basis of explicit awareness. Reading and spelling ability ceased to develop on the basis of implicit awareness and reading became, for the first time, dependent on explicit awareness. This suggests that knowledge of the alphabetic principle had now become pivotal to reading.

Having dealt with the main body of data, Ellis & Cataldo go on to look at how the children's spelling errors changed. They selected those who had made more than five errors and looked at the nature of these. They use a classification system which indicates the degree to which a spelling is phonetic, and found that, over time, even though the total number of errors the children made decreased, the proportion of phonetic errors increased. Thus they began by producing only the first letter consistently and then over time produced larger and larger chunks of phonetically appropriate spellings with fewer and fewer random letters. The final piece of evidence for the relationship between awareness and spelling is that while this spelling change is taking place, explicit, but not implicit awareness, is also improving.

INTRODUCTION: DEVELOPMENT OF SPELLING ABILITY 117

Finally Ellis & Cataldo consider the implications of their work. They argue for reading programmes whch deal with a range of tasks involving phonics, spelling, comprehension and interpretation and suggest that those with reading problems, particularly, be given awareness training.

Alphabetic Spelling: Predicting Eventual Literacy Attainment (Goulandris)

The issue addressed by Goulandris is whether spelling ability, especially the ability to recall the precise spellings of words, is based on underlying competence in alphabetic skills. She suggests that visual memory alone does not explain children's ability to recall word spellings. She proposes that new words are learned by referring to orthographic memory, a memory system in which recurrent spelling patterns are gradually abstracted by using basic sound–spelling mappings as a framework. For this framework to be available the child must have acquired at least rudimentary alphabetic skills. She cites evidence from invented spellings and stage-based error analyses.

Goulandris then turns to the relationship between reading and spelling during early development, citing evidence which indicates them to be based on different strategies and which suggests that spelling ability promotes reading ability. The purpose of the experiments she reports is to determine whether alphabetic skills are evident from the beginnings of spelling and whether skill in non-word spelling will predict subsequent general reading and spelling ability.

The use of a phonetic strategy can be deduced from the spelling of high-frequency regular and irregular words. If the child's early attempts are phonetic then regular words should be largely correct, irregular words largely wrong and misspellings of the latter regularisations. Conversely, there should be no difference between the two types of words if the child is either an advanced speller (good alphabetic skills and good word specific knowledge) or just beginning (poor alphabetic skills and primitive logographic representations). In the first case the overall number of errors would be small, in the latter the number would be large.

In the first experiment she tested children with reading ages of 5.5 and 8 years on high-frequency regular and irregular words. While both groups made more errors on irregular words, the older group got more regular words right and made more regularisation errors. This indicates that the older group were more advanced in the acquisition of alphabetic skills than the younger.

In the second study she investigated the possibility that the ability to use phonic rules for spelling predicts eventual reading and spelling ability. Two months after experiment one she gave the same children a non-word spelling test. The children's spelling attempts were classified as phonetic, semi-phonetic or non-phonetic. At the end of the summer term of the following academic year she gave the children standardised reading and spelling tests.

Verbal intelligence, non-word spelling, and reading and spelling ability in the first year are all potential predictors of reading and spelling ability in the second year. What she found was that non-word spelling ability was a powerful predictor even after the effects of these other predictors had been allowed for.

Goulandris concludes by drawing our attention to the importance of alphabetic expertise in the development of literacy and particularly to its importance in the acquisition of the rules, regularities and word specific knowledge which comprise spelling knowledge. The practical implications of her work, she concludes, lie in the active promotion of phonological awareness and in the teaching of sound–spelling correspondences. She warns, however, against the over promotion of alphabetic expertise, because there is a point at which the child must move on and develop an orthographic expertise if he or she is to become an accomplished speller.

'Invented' Spelling and Learning to Read (Huxford, Terrell & Bradley)

Huxford, Terrell & Bradley begin by drawing our attention to the opposition between the compositional and secretarial aspects of writing. On the one hand it is clearly desirable that children be encouraged to develop writing as a medium of expression. On the other hand, having to spell correctly is a demand which might hamper fluency and stifle the desire to write. A solution to the problem is to let children invent their own spellings initially, and only gradually increase the demand for correct spelling.

Can invented spellings be justified on other grounds? Citing previous evidence as well as a case study, Huxford *et al.* point out that early in development children can spell some words which they can't read and that these words are spelt phonologically. This, together with other evidence, suggests that children can spell phonologically before they can read phonologically. The first implication of this is that teachers shouldn't expect children who seem advanced in writing to be able to use all reading strategies. Secondly,

INTRODUCTION: DEVELOPMENT OF SPELLING ABILITY

children should be encouraged to spell earlier than they currently are. That is, they should be encouraged to invent spellings, which being phonological in character, will promote development of (phonological) reading.

Before such an approach can be advocated we need to be sure that children can spell phonologically before they can read phonologically. The purpose of the study was to collect *longitudinal* evidence for this.

The research tested young children's ability to read and spell nonwords, which can only be spelt using a phonological strategy. They were all single syllables, with two or three phonemes and simple phoneme–grapheme correspondences (e.g. *pez, ak*). Children were all in the age group 3:6 to 5:6 years when they began the study and were selected on their ability to identify the *first,* and only the first, sound of a word. They were tested on their ability to read and spell these non-words at eight-week intervals until they reached the same criteria of achievement. These were: (a) their ability to hear *all* the sounds in the words for spelling purposes, and (b) their ability to use a decoding strategy to read.

Children varied in the time they took to reach these criteria. To look at the relative development of their reading and spelling ability at various times, their performance at the beginning, the end and three intermediate points were calculated. The results were that at each of these times the children could spell significantly more words correctly than they could read. For example, when they were spelling three-letter non-words they were only just beginning to read two-letter non-words.

Huxford *et al.* conclude with a discussion of the practical implications. Inventing spellings uses a phonological strategy in which sounds are first isolated and then represented using letters, a skill that is clearly related to reading. Furthermore, as spelling is the pacemaker for reading, encouraging children to invent spellings may not only permit fluency in their writing but also may be useful in reading. Finally, the level of expertise reached in spelling (e.g. three-letter words) may be used as an indicator of the *maximum* level of reading the child has achieved.

Developmental Differences in Phonological Spelling Strategies (Taylor & Martlew)

Taylor & Martlew are concerned with the development of phonetic (phonological) spelling strategies. They argue that there are two aspects to development. First, children have to learn that phonetic spelling is a necessary but not sufficient strategy to cope with English spelling and therefore have to develop other strategies. Second, they have to acquire a phonetic strategy. The evidence (Read, 1986) suggests that children initially make judgements about sounds that adults don't seem to make (e.g. regarding the (**tr**) and /tʃ/ sounds as equivalent). These judgements are crucial if children are to avoid, for example, spelling different sounds in the same way. Taylor & Martlew point out the possibility that children and adults use similar phonetic strategies which may seem to differ not because of phonetic judgement differences but because adults' judgements are overridden by their knowledge of English orthography. Taylor & Martlew's experiment seeks to investigate putative differences of phonological awareness by comparing the vowel spellings of adults and children.

In their experiment they tested 32 adults and 46 children (between the ages of eight and nine years) in a dictation task using real words. The participants were asked to *spell the words as they sounded,* not as they were actually spelt. They used words in which there were five different spellings of the /iː/ phoneme and two spellings of the /ɒ/ phoneme. For each of these phoneme spellings there was one high-frequency word and one low-frequency word.

The results indicated that both groups broke words up into phoneme-sized units (rather than larger groupings). Secondly, there was no effect of word frequency indicating that strategy being used was phonetic and that there was no interference from the child's knowledge of the spellings. Thirdly, they found that for adults the dominant spelling of /iː/ was **EE** and that of /ɒ/ was **OR**. For the children, in contrast, **EE**, **EA**, and **I** were dominant spellings of /iː/ (depending on the word) while **OR**, **AW** and **O** were dominant spellings of /ɒ/ (again depending on the word). Fourthly, they found that while the range of spellings used for /i/ was the same, children used a greater range of spellings for /ɒ/. Finally, adults preferred the **EE** spelling of /iː/ to either the **E** or **I** spellings, a preference that was significantly less marked for the children. Similarly, adults preferred the **OR** spelling of /ɒ/ to the **O** spelling to a greater degree than did the children.

Taylor & Martlew interpret the variability in children's spelling as indicating a search for invariant correspondences. Adults have learned the dominant correspondences for a given sound and tend to use them rather than other less frequent possibilities. They go on to argue that children's use of **E** and **I** to spell /iː/ and of **O** to spell /ɒ/ could be due to two sources. First, to their educational experiences, which Taylor & Martlew reject. Second, to a failure to distinguish between /iː/ and /I/ and between /ɒ/ and /ɔː/. Consider /iː/ and /I/: they are similar in that they are both produced at the front of the mouth but are different in that the first is long and tense while the second is short and lax. What is probably happening, they argue, is that the child is focusing on the former feature (the place of articulation) but ignoring the latter features (the length and laxness) and, as a result, is treating them as equivalent sounds. As a consequence the child spells /iː/ with spellings normally used for /I/ (i.e. **E** and **I**). The same argument applies to /ɒ/ and /ɔː/. One of the consequences of development, of course, will be the ability to distinguish between the members of each pair by attending to the length and laxness of the sounds as well as to their place of articulation.

In their final section Taylor & Martlew discuss the implications of their work. First, that differences as well as similarities between vowel sounds should be pointed out. Secondly, that children should be taught about phoneme–grapheme correspondences, focusing on the most dominant. Thirdly, they recommend some teaching of the history of English orthography.

Reference

READ, C. 1986, *Children's Creative Spelling*. London: Routledge and Kegan Paul.

7 Spelling is Integral to Learning to Read

NICK ELLIS and SUZANNE CATALDO

Introduction

Although the importance of phonological awareness (PA) in the acquisition of reading has been established (Bradley & Bryant, 1983; Ellis & Large, 1987; 1988; Frith, 1985) the causal pathways between the two abilities have eluded clear determination (Bryant & Goswami, 1987; Shanahan & Lomax, 1986). Furthermore, research that examines the relationship of phonological awareness to the emergence of literacy has often neglected spelling as an important agent that independently influences and is influenced by phonological awareness and reading. Whilst it has been acknowledged that use of a phonological strategy plays a fundamental role in spelling before it becomes important in reading (Smith, 1978; Bryant & Bradley, 1980; Frith, 1980; Snowling & Perin, 1983; Juel, Griffith & Gough, 1986), comparatively little attention has been focused on the possible interactions among reading, spelling and phonological skills. There are some recent correlational and longitudinal studies which now identify spelling as an independent contributor to the emergence of reading (Morris & Perney, 1984; Tornéus, 1984; Mommers, 1987; Cataldo & Ellis, 1988), and these support theoretical analyses that assign spelling the major role in promoting insight into the alphabetic nature of the written language (Bryant and Bradley, 1980; Frith, 1985; Juel, Griffith & Gough, 1986). Such correlational studies provide evidence of a strong relationship between early reading and spelling and between spelling and phoneme awareness (Snowling & Perin, 1983; Juel, Griffith & Gough, 1986; Ellis & Large, 1987); however, the form of causal connections cannot be determined from correlations alone.

The use of phonological awareness in children's early efforts in spelling encourages them to approach the printed word as a sequence of phonetic cues to pronunciation (Liberman & Shankweiler, 1979; Frith, 1985). As children refine their ability to detect and isolate the sound content of spoken words through repeated practice in spelling, so they build a store of knowledge about the relationships among sounds, letters and pronunciations that can be applied to the task of reading (Chomsky, 1977; Ehri & Wilce, 1987; Juel, Griffith & Gough, 1986). Thus, practice in spelling enhances the knowledge-base from which novice readers draw information in their attempts at phonetic-cue reading.

Frith (1985) provides a theoretical framework within which spelling and reading interact to advance the learner towards increased proficiency in each ability. In her model, spelling plays a fundamental role in the movement from a visual, or logographic reading strategy to an alphabetic approach: alphabetic spelling is the pacemaker for the use of an alphabetic strategy in reading. Early spelling practice involves dividing spoken words into phonemes and representing these phonemes with letters. In this way experience in spelling words affords the opportunity for making comparisons between the phonetic information in individual letters and sounds as they are embedded in the spoken word. Through repeated practice in spelling, the child may come to appreciate the subtle relationship between a symbol in the written word and its corresponding sound in the context of the spoken word. The discovery of this relationship is the key to alphabetic insight. The crux of the problem is 'knowing how to combine the letters into units appropriate for speech' (Liberman & Schankweiler, 1979: 141). Early efforts in spelling may provide the opportunity to experiment in a very concrete way with the properties of this abstract concept. As children struggle to decompose words into individual phonemic units, they commonly experiment with various articulatory rehearsals of word parts and they search for distinguishable articulatory units that correspond to letter-sound units. This process of their separating sounds in a word through consciously monitoring their own articulations may serve a dual purpose: it may both help the development of phonological awareness and enhance knowledge of the alphabetic principle.

The idea that explicit and productive knowledge of the sound content of words comes to reading via spelling may account for the power of spelling to predict reading in some studies (Shanahan & Lomax, 1986; Mommers, 1987; Ellis & Large, 1987; 1988). But now we need a broader and more detailed description of the interactive development of all three components, reading, spelling, and phonological awareness, in order to clarify the details of precisely how spelling mediates the influence of phonological awareness on reading. In terms of educational practice, it is vital to explore how the early development of spelling and phonological awareness help children across the threshold to literacy.

A Longitudinal Study of the Development of Spelling, Reading and Phonological Awareness

In our longitudinal study (Cataldo & Ellis, 1988; 1990; Ellis & Cataldo, 1990) we examined the growth of reading, spelling, and phonological awareness, from the formulative stage of each skill through the early stages of its development. We followed a group of children as they progressed through the earliest stages of literacy acquisition. By charting their development in spelling, reading and phonological awareness, we were able to analyse the factors which contribute to the early formation of these skills as well as the sequences of interaction which facilitate later strategy shifts in each ability.

Method

Subjects

Forty children were selected from reception or infant classes of three schools in North Wales. They were English speaking and were taught reading and spelling in English. Initial testing commenced when the children were between four and five years old and most of them failed to demonstrate even rudimentary skill in reading or spelling. The children were assessed on three subsequent occasions; once when most were at the end of their first year in school, again in the autumn of their second year and finally at the beginning of their third school year.

Procedure

The children were tested individually in reading, spelling, phoneme segmentation, auditory categorisation, letter-sound knowledge, STM and full Wechsler Pre-school and Primary Scale of Intelligence (WPPSI) (Wechsler, 1967). Tests of reading, spelling and phonological awareness were repeated when most of the children were finishing their first year at school. The full set of tests (excluding the WPPSI) was readministered the following autumn. One year later, when the majority of the children were beginning their third school year, a final administration of the reading and spelling tests was given. Each of the tests, testing procedures and scoring methods is described briefly below. For a more detailed description of procedures see Cataldo & Ellis (1988).

Tests of reading and spelling The reading and spelling tests consisted of phonemically regular, consonant–vowel–consonant (C–V–C) words. All words contained short vowels.

(C–V–C) Reading test: This consisted of 96 C–V–Cs; half of these were real words and half were nonsense words. Two scores were taken for each subject; number of words read correctly and number of phonemes correct in each 'word' response. The second scoring method was used to measure reading at the first testing time, when the majority of the children were performing at floor level with the first measure.

(C–V–C) Spelling test: Each child was asked to spell 32 of the words in the reading test. This subset consisted of 16 real words and 16 nonsense words. As in the reading test, two scores were taken for spelling: at the initial testing we used number of letters spelled correctly, thereafter, the measure was the number of words spelled correctly.

Tests of phonological awareness Two different types of phonological tasks were chosen, a rhyme detection task and a phoneme segmentation task. Recent work suggests that the level of phonemic awareness demanded by the phonological tasks influences the strength of the relationship between reading and phoneme awareness (Backman, 1983; Goswami & Bryant, 1990). Stanovich, Cunningham & Cramer (1984) asked children to perform tasks involving the analysis of words for explicit sound content (non-rhyming tasks) and for the perception of overall similarity of sound content (rhyming tasks). They found that the non-rhyming, or analytic and productive phonological tasks formed a cluster of related skills that did not correlate with the rhyming tasks. Snowling & Perin (1983) found that children's ability to perform a segmentation task was not significantly different from their ability in spelling, the close connection between these skills indicating the necessity of explicit PA in spelling. Thus there seem to be two, developmentally different, measurable levels of PA. Children's first awareness of the sound properties of speech is implicit and perceptual. Spontaneous play with rhyming and nonsense words is thought to reflect an overall sensitivity to the sound content of words (Chukovsky, 1968; Slobin, 1978; Clark, 1977). At this point they are not yet able to consciously reflect on language (Shankweiler, Liberman & Savin, 1972). Valtin (1984) describes a three-stage model for the development of phonological awareness. Initially the child is not aware of the sound value of speech. During the next stage, 'children become increasingly able to abstract the language from the action and the meaning context and to think about some of the properties of the form of language. Their knowledge of language units is still implicit, however, and related to psycholinguistic units of speech' (Valtin, 1984: 214). Once the child achieves conscious awareness, he or she demonstrates explicit phonological awareness and can reflect upon, produce and manipulate phonemic units within spoken words.

That growth in phonological awareness follows a developmental continuum from implicit to explicit levels raises the question of how children utilise these different types of phonological awareness in their reading and spelling strategies. We used two different phonological tasks in order to examine this question. The minimal requirement for success in rhyme detection is a global awareness of the sound property in words, while successful performance of phoneme segmentation tasks requires an explicit awareness of individual sounds within words.

Implicit Phonological Awareness: Test of auditory organisation (Bradley, 1980). This has three conditions: (1) initial (comprised of words that begin with the same sound), (2) final (with words that end with the same sound), and (3) medial (containing words that share the same vowel sound). The child listens to a series of four words and is asked to identify the 'odd one out' (the word that does not share a common sound component with the other three words).

Explicit Phonological Awareness: Phoneme segmentation test (Elkonin, 1973; Helfgott, 1976). Each child was asked to perform three types of segmentation on eight real and eight nonsense C–V–C words given in spoken form. In the intial segmentation task subjects were asked to segment words into two parts; the initial consonant and the remaining vowel–consonant portion (C–VC). For the final segmentation task, the children were asked to segment the final sound from each word by producing the initial CV component followed by the final phoneme (CV–C). The complete segmentation task required each child to segment words into three distinct sound components (C–V–C).

Letter–sound associations Knowledge of isolated letter–sound associations alone does not account for success in learning to read and spell. However, it does contribute to the development of reading (Ellis & Large, 1988) and use of letters helps children learn to segment words into constituent phonemes (Hohn & Ehri, 1983).

Test of letter–sound knowledge. The child was asked, 'What sound does this letter make?' for each of the 26 lower-case letters.

Wechsler Pre-School and Primary Scale of Intelligence (WPPSI) Five verbal and five performance tests were given to each child. Full scale scores on this test were used in the initial matching of groups for training and for purposes of partialling out the effect of IQ in the LISREL analyses.

LISREL analysis methodology In this study, LISREL (Jöreskog & Sörbom, 1984) was used to formulate a descriptive model that identifies significant contributors to the early growth of literacy. We fitted exploratory low constraint time-interval type models (Cataldo & Ellis, 1988; Ellis, 1990) where each ability could result from an effect of *any* ability measured at the previous time. With standardised data, pathweights represent the amount of change in a variable (in standard deviation (sd) units) caused by one sd of change in another variable. For a complete description of the data see Ellis & Cataldo (1990) and Cataldo & Ellis (1988).

Results and discussion

By broadening the phonological awareness–reading paradigm to include spelling, we are able to see a clearer picture of the early interaction among these abilities. Our model of reading and spelling development describes three measured phases of development. Phase One spans the children's first year in school. Phase Two charts the development from spring of the first school year to autumn of the second year. Phase Three looks at development from the beginning of the second year in school to the beginning of the third year. The Phase One pathweights from spelling to reading real words (0.31) and nonsense words (0.23) identify spelling as an important contributor to the early formation of reading. This pattern of influence is repeated in the second phase (spelling to reading real words 0.64 and nonsense words 0.60). The pronounced influence of spelling on reading contrasts with the contribution of reading to spelling (Phase 1: 0.10 real words, 0.06 nonsense; Phase 2: 0.14 real, 0.00 nonsense). Implicit PA initially predicts early attempts to read (0.36, 0.41) as well as to spell (0.38, 0.31) but loses its influence on both reading and spelling in the following two phases. In contrast to the diminishing predictive power of implicit PA, explicit PA consistently predicts spelling in all three phases, this influence increasing with phase. Explicit PA emerges as a strong predictor of reading only in Phase Three.

To summarise, the early flow of information between reading and spelling appears to be unidirectional: knowledge gleaned from spelling is contributing to reading. Similarly, both implicit and explicit PA affect spelling development with explicit PA increasing its influence as the contribution of implicit PA diminishes. Later in the developmental sequence, explicit PA begins to contribute directly to reading. The pattern of interactions among abilities in Phase One clarifies the different roles of implicit and explicit PA in the early formation of reading skill. Implicit information about the sound properties of words directly affects early reading attempts: explicit knowledge of phonemic content influences reading via spelling experience. Beginners may be using implicit PA both to help them detect acoustic properties that define a word by its sound boundaries and to detect sounds with salient qualities, and their use of these rudimentary sound strategies allows them to form associations between sounds in spoken words and pronunciations and to call upon these associations to perform phonetic-cue reading (Ehri & Wilce, 1985). The first evidence of the direct influence of explicit PA on reading occurs in Phase Three, when explicit PA predicts ability to read non-words. In earlier phases explicit PA does not influence reading directly but acts as the strongest predictor of spelling both real and nonsense words. In turn, spelling is the most consistent predictor of reading.

This early interactive sequence describes the pattern of growth from pre-alphabetic to alphabetic stage reading. While implicit knowledge of the sound properties of words helps children forge initial connections between the printed word and the perception of its pronunciation, spelling acts as a mediator for the use of explicit PA until the child begins alphabetic stage reading by directly applying explicit PA to reading. Our data suggests that as children practise spelling they develop proficiency in the use of the alphabetic principle and apply this knowledge to the task of reading. The emergence of explicit and productive PA as a significant predictor of reading marks the entry into the alphabetic stage of reading.

Examination of the Phase Three pathweights suggests that children apply a strategy reliant on letter-sound knowledge and, to a lesser degree, explicit PA to read real words, but letter-sound knowledge and explicit PA jointly predict nonsense word reading. While learners appear to use a pre-alphabetic strategy with real words, they utilise a true alphabetic approach to nonsense words. Here we see evidence of the selective use of strategies for different purposes. Children are able to shift from one level of reading strategy to another, depending on the demands of the task. Beginners attempt to read unknown words via a strategy of combining context, visual and phonetic cues, and only when this fails, switch to deciphering. Initially, deciphering is used exclusively for reading unknown words when other strategies fail, but with practice children integrate this alphabetic approach into their repertoire set of strategies and eventually the beginner comes to appreciate the general usefulness of this deciphering strategy.

A Longitudinal Study of Pattern and Prediction of Spelling Errors

The idea that children's misspellings reflect a developing sense of phonetic properties in words was pioneered by Read (1971: 1975; 1986) who found evidence that young inventive spellers used a system of grouping sounds together according to shared phonetic features. Thus they might represent a particular vowel sound in their spelling by subsituting a letter whose *name* shared a salient phonetic feature with the sound. His exhaustive studies of invented spellings attuned further research to the analysis of misspellings in an attempt to uncover a developmental sequence for spelling that reflects a heightening awareness of the internal sound structure of words, and this has led subsequent researchers to categorise developmental strategies in spelling. Henderson & Beers (1980) analysed samples of children's creative writing and assigned each error to a category according to the completeness of phonetic information mapped by the misspelling. They charted movement from pre-phonetic to phonetic stages of spelling. As a result of their work and that of Gentry (1982), it is now generally agreed that children move through distinct stages of spelling, namely: pre-communicative, semi-phonetic, phonetic, transitional and correct spelling. It is the first three of these developmental stages that are relevant to the question of how phonological awareness plays a role in children's early spelling. Pre-communicative spellings are characterised by the strategy of randomly selecting letter strings to represent words. Although at this stage children can produce letters in writing, their spellings reflect a complete lack of letter-sound or letter-name knowledge. Semi-phonetic spellings contain a partial mapping of phonetic content. Phonetic spellings contain a complete description of the sequence of sounds in pronunciations.

Our results indicate that as spelling begins to take form, the beginner relies on a phonological strategy based on a perception of the overall sound content of words. In turn, these early endeavours in spelling contribute to an awareness of the general sound properties of words. In the next stage, as children begin to demonstrate proficiency in spelling with increasingly complete phonemic descriptions, the novice is more analytic in his or her approach to pronunciations. This progression from holistic to analytic phonological strategy is analogous to the movement from semi-phonetic spelling proposed by Gentry (1982). In the above study we measured first-stage spelling by the number of phonemes correctly represented and second- and third-stage spelling by number of words correctly spelled. Recognising that children's misspellings provide valuable insight into the formation of spelling ability, we next explored the relationships among different groupings of misspellings and different levels of PA.

Method

Subjects

Only those subjects who produced at least five spelling errors were included in this analysis.

TABLE 7.1 *Categories of spelling error*

Description of each error type with examples from data.
(Example spellings followed by pronunciation of target word in / /.)

First letter strategy	Boundary sounds strategy	Partial sequential strategy	Sequential strategy	Correct mapping
Initial consonants	Initial–final consonants	C–V segment	C–V–C unit incorrect V	C–V–C unit + extra
C /kɒd/	CD /kɒd/	CO /kɒd/	REF /rif/	NOLME /nɒl/ FISS /fis/
Initial consonant plus incorrect letter(s)	Initial–final consonants + extra letters	C–V segment + incorrect final consonants	C–V–V–C unit one or two incorrect V	Correct spelling
CGTZNY /kɒd/ CAN /kɒd/	GBC /gʌb/ WDNGIST /wid/ BSI /bis/	COT /kɒd/	HIED /hid/	COD /kɒd/
	Initial–final consonant embedded in string	C–V segment extra letter	C–V–C+ extra letter (V incorrect)	
	MWDS /wid/ BERBO /rʌb/	COWZO /kɒd/	DELL /dæl/ BASUS /bis/	
	Initial + final consonant at bounds of string	C–V segment embedded in letter string		
	FOATL /fʊl/ SRRN /sæn/ WAESD /wid/	MNOP /nɒl/		

Notes on scoring: When scoring children's early attempts to spell it was necessary to evaluate letter-forms that were either crudely formed or printed in the opposite direction. In the former case, we relied on notes taken for each child during testing. Letters printed in the reverse direction were scored correctly. Children frequently printed the letters **S, H, R, A, C** and **P** in the opposite direction. In the case of the letters **B** and **D**, it was decided to score 'reversals' as correct responses due to the frequency with which children verbally segmented the proper sound (/b/ or /d/), pointed to the correct letter (**B** or **D**), and proceeded to produce the letter in the opposite direction.

Procedure

We classified misspellings in five categories that reflect increasing insight into the phonetic structure of the word. Our hierarchical classification of spelling errors (Table 7.1) is based on work by Henderson (1980), Morris (1983) and Gentry (1982). The most rudimentary spelling skill, first letter strategy, preserves only the information for the initial letter. Closer approximations have both boundary sounds intact. The highest level of informed error are partial-sequential and sequential errors where only the middle phoneme is in doubt: the representation of consonant sounds is 'safer' than vowel sounds in that consonant sounds are more reliably 'matched' to letters on a one-to-one basis than are vowel sounds. In Table 7.2 we show the mean number of such errors made at each testing time and the mean percentage of the child's total errors which this category of errors comprised. Table 7.3 shows the mean performance on the explicit and implicit phonological awareness tests for each sound position.

TABLE 7.2 *Mean raw scores for each category of spelling errors at the four testing times*[a]

	* *Categories of error*[b]				
	1st letter intact /cat/ = C	*Boundary intact* /cat/ = CT	*Partial sequential* /cat/ = CA	*Sequential (C–V–C intact)* /cat/ = CET	
Beginning year one $n = 38$	5.7 18%[c]	0.39 1%	0.55 2%	0.31 2%	(Total 23%)
End year one $n = 35$	7.4 23%	1.2 5%	1.3 5%	0.71 4%	(Total 37%)
Beginning year two $n = 30$	9.4 31%	1.3 7%	2.4 10%	1.3 6%	(Total 54%)
Beginning year three $n = 17$	4.0 15%	1.9 8%	1.8 12%	2.3 19%	(Total 54%)

[a] This sample includes only those children with five or more spelling errors.
[b] For a complete description of each error category in terms of the early development of spelling see text.
[c] The percentage figures reflects the mean per cent of the child's total errors that were made in this category.

TABLE 7.3 *Phonological awareness as a function of time and position*

	Initial /k–æt/	Final /kæ–t/	Complete /k–æ–t/	Total
Mean number of items correct on *explicit segmentation* at each testing time				
Beginning year one	2.6 sd 4.6	0.78 sd 2.8	1.8 sd 4.2	5.3 sd 8.9
End year one	7.0 sd 6.7	1.4 sd 3.0	5.0 sd 6.1	13.6 sd 13.8
Beginning year two	11.3 sd 5.7	3.3 sd 5.6	9.0 sd 5.5	23.7 sd 14.0
Mean number of items correct on *implicit segmentation* at each testing time				
Beginning year one	3.0 sd 1.6	3.8 sd 2.0	4.4 sd 2.0	11.10 sd 4.2
End year one	3.6 sd 1.8	4.11 sd 1.5	4.0 sd 2.2	12.0 sd 4.0
Beginning year two	4.6 sd 2.2	4.3 sd 2.1	5.1 sd 2.4	14.14 sd 5.6

Results and discussion

The following general patterns emerged:

- When children in this age band make a spelling error which bears any phonetic resemblance to the target, it is more often the case that only information for the initial consonant is preserved. Responses which are not totally correct, yet which approximate more than this to the correct phonetic analysis are more rare. The next most typical responses are those where both boundary sounds are correct (either with or without an incorrect intervening vowel).
- Table 7.2 refers only to phonetic-based categories of spelling errors (not all error types). By the time the children are at the beginning of year three the total numbers of errors has declined. Errors which fall into this hierarchical classification system become predominant (54% at the beginning of years two and three versus 23% at the beginning of year one) — the children are indeed moving from being pre-communicative to semi-phonetic spellers. And this progression is also found within the semi-phonetic

stage: the lowest phonemic content errors (first letter intact) decline with age, and, in percentage terms at least, higher order errors (sequential and partial sequential) which preserve more of the phonetic content come to the fore.

Thus the proportion of phonetic-based spelling errors increases with age, as the proportion of other error types concomitantly declines. Furthermore there is development within phonetic-based errors from 'first letter intact' errors to sequential and partial sequential errors where more of the phonetic representation is preserved.

- The patterns of ability on explicit segmentation are highly positionally determined: children are most accurate at segmenting the initial sound from the rest. This contrasts dramatically with performance on the implicit task where children seem to be roughly as accurate at identifying the 'odd one out' whatever the position, initial, medial or final, of its errant sound, but with a slight tendency for them to have most difficulty with the alliterative task of the implicit initial condition.
- There is little measurable developmental improvement on the implicit segmentation task. In contrast there are large improvements in explicit segmentation skill during year one and the transition to year two.

In contrast to the pattern for implicit segmentation, that of explicit phoneme segmentation doubly mirrors that of spelling: it follows both its developmental surges and its positional sensitivity. Thus, although implicit phonological awareness is the precursor of early developments in spelling, reading and explicit phonological awareness, it is the growth of *explicit* phonological awareness that allows the acquisition of alphabetic spelling. Awareness of rhyme and alliteration is not sufficient for accurate spelling, rather the child has to be able to explicitly segment the sounds of a spoken word, to strip it apart sound by sound, and then look for the graphemes that represent these sounds. In turn, spelling makes this ability relevant to the child for the first time, both grow through practice, and the alphabetic insight is gained. This insight is then available to allow its application in reading and the child shifts from a logographic to an alphabetic strategy of reading (see also Frith, 1985; Ehri & Wilce, 1987).

Conclusions

Our results describe the ways in which spelling acts as a mediator for the influence of explicit phonological awareness on reading. Children's very first efforts at reading are characterised by a visual or logographic strategy where letters are analysed for salient graphic cues to rapid word recognition;

this is the pre-alphabetic stage. When a small number of pronunciations can be accessed in this manner, the child may embark upon a more advanced strategy of using associations between partial phonetic cues in the spoken word with letters in the printed version and subsequently utilise these associations to recognise the words. Children appear to use implicit and perceptual PA to help them make these rudimentary sound analyses of pronunciation. In addition, spelling practice may contribute to the store of associations between the spoken words and letter-sound constituents in printed words. At first, spelling may encourage children to focus on the first letter of printed words and to begin to analyse this first letter, in the reading task, for phonetic cues to pronunciations. Thus, the practice of turning attention to the first letter-sound unit in spelling may influence children to discriminate between stored pronunciations on the basis of the first letter of the printed word. This method of early word recognition is described by Marsh *et al.* (1981) as 'discrimination net substitution'. As visual and phonetic cue strategies make increasing demands on the child's memory, the efficiency of this strategy decreases. Conversely, as the source of knowledge about letter–sound associations, and the relationships between letters in printed words and sounds in spoken words swells, the child is discovering that he or she can rely on the use of this knowledge for successful word recognition. Our studies support the idea that the transition from pre-alphabetic stage reading to alphabetic stage reading is facilitated by spelling. By employing explicit and productive PA in spelling practice, the child gains familiarity with the alphabetic nature of writing and builds a reliable fund of information about letter–sound correspondences and explicit phonemic content in words. Spelling affords the opportunity to forge a meaningful link between phonological awareness and letter-sound knowledge. This connection is a prerequisite to the development of phonological strategies in reading. Furthermore, the data suggest that progress from the pre-alphabetic stage of literacy to the alphabetic stage involves an overlapping of strategies and in this sense there is no one 'reading' but rather a cascade of very different strategic blends of information processing skills being used at different points in a fast-changing stream of the development of reading (Ellis & Large, 1988; Ellis, 1989).

Implications for Teaching

These are but a few more words contributing to 'The Great Debate' (Chall, 1967) concerning the 'best' ways of teaching reading, at the core of which vie methods based on look-and-say phonics, spelling and meaning. Over the decades each has ascended and waned in almost predictably recurrent cycles.

The alphabet method, in spite of occasional protest, was almost universally used from the Greek and Roman times until some thirty years ago, and of course has not been discarded even yet. In this method the child learned first the names of the large and small letters and their order in the alphabet. This was task enough, uninteresting as it was to many, to keep them employed for some months, or even in some cases for a year or more. Then the combinations like *ab, eb, ib* were spelled out and pronounced, and then three-letter combinations like *glo, flo, pag,* etc., in all of which the early pages of the old spellers abounded . . . Spelling the word preceded its pronunciation, until it was well known. It was assumed that there was a necessary connection between naming the letters of a word and pronouncing that word. (Huey, 1908: 254–5)

Just how naming the letters was supposed to assist in pronouncing the word it is difficult to see. The value of practice in learning to spell doubtless had much to do with blinding centuries of teachers to its uselessness for the reading of words and sentences. However, in dealing thus constantly with the letters and their combinations, the pupil necessarily acquiried a familiarity with *the sounds represented by each letter,* whether purposely these taught or not. And thus this method always combines something of phonics as well . . . The phonic method, used by the Jansenists in the Port Royal Schools, long neglected but advocated again by Thornton in 1790 . . . *It is a spelling method, but the word is spelled by its elementary sounds and not by the letter-names. The word is slowly pronounced until its constituent sounds come into consciousness, and these sounds are associated with the letters representing them. Drill in this sound analysis trains the articulation, trains the ear and the ability to sound the letters of any new word, and gives the power to pronounce it by blending the sounds suggested.* (Huey, 1908: 266, our emphasis)

In 1908 Huey decries the spelling methods which involve the names of letters but he does acknowledge the advantages of training in phonics. Yet at the same time he equivocates and is concerned about teaching which concentrates on the 'mechanics' of reading:

It seems a great waste to devote, as at present, the main part of a number of school years to the mere mechanics of reading and spelling. The unreasoned and unreasonable devotion to our irrational English spelling in itself robs the child of probably two whole years of school life . . . the results too often show only mechanical, stumbling, expressionless readers, and poor thought-getters from what is read. The mechanical reading is thought to come from learning reading as mere word-pronouncing; the stumbling and hesitation, from the over-attention to form as against content, especially from the early and too constant analysis of the reading process in phonics. (Huey, 1908: 301–2)

In response to such criticisms, from the 1930s on, modal reading tuition was based on principles which

> include as major goals, *right from the start,* not only word recognition, but also comprehension and interpretation, appreciation, and application of what is read to the study of personal and social problems . . . Drill or practice 'in isolation' (i.e. apart from the reading of sentences or stories) should be avoided; instead, phonics should be 'integrated' with the 'meaningful' connected reading. In addition, the child should not isolate sounds and blend them to form words. Instead, he should identify unknown words through a process of visual analysis and substitution. (Chall, 1967: 13–15)

The pendulum followed its natural return in America in the mid-1950s with Flesch's (1955) popular *Why Johnny Can't Read* — which challenged the then prevailing emphasis on sight-method teaching and which advocated a return to a phonic approach as the best, nay only, method to use in beginning instruction — and in Britain with the evaluation studies of Daniels — Diack (1956) — which demonstrated a superiority of their 'phonic-word method' over the current mixed methods.

And again, two decades later, the position swings back away from phonics and spelling to Smith's (1978) 'psycholinguistics guessing game':

> Reading is not 'decoding to sound'. (Smith, 1978: 83)

> Mediated word identification . . . strategies . . . include the use of phonics (spelling–sound correspondences). Attempting to decode isolated words to sound is unlikely to succeed because of the number, complexity, and unreliability of phonic generalisations. Phonic rules will help to eliminate alternative possibilities only if uncertainty can be reduced by other means, for example, if the unfamiliar words occur in meaningful contexts. Spelling–sound correspondences are not easily or usefully learned before children acquire some familiarity with reading. (Smith, 1978: 150)

> Of course, spelling is a problem, both in school and out, but it is a problem of writing, not of reading . . . Knowing how to spell does not make a good reader because reading is not accomplished by the decoding of spelling . . . I am not saying that knowledge of spelling is not important, only that it does not have a role in reading, and that undue con-

cern with the way in which words are spelled can only interfere with a child's learning to read. (Smith, 1978: 143)

Our present results lead us firmly to believe that Smith is wrong in these claims, and, taken with the work of Bradley & Bryant (1983; 1985), Downing (1973), Ehri (1979), Elkonin (1973), Frith (1980; 1985) and Miles & Miles (1975), they constitute an impetus back to methods of reading teaching which involve spelling and phonics. This direction is furthermore reaffirmed by the accumulation of evidence from evaluative studies of differing teaching methods that phonic and spelling-pattern training is particularly effective. Thus Chall's (1967) exhaustive meta-analysis of the studies performed between 1910 and 1965 concludes:

(1) a code (phonics) emphasis tends to produce better overall reading achievement by the beginning of the fourth grade than a meaning emphasis, with greater accuracy in word recognition and oral reading from the very beginning, and better vocabulary and comprehension scores by mid-second grade. With a code emphasis the child seems to initially read more slowly because of the greater emphasis on accuracy; however, by the third or fourth grade when he is more fluent his rate is equal to, or may ultimately exceed, that produced by a meaning emphasis.

(2) Systematic-phonics programmes that rely on direct teaching of letter–sound relationships are as successful as, or perhaps more successful than, programmes that rely on 'discovery' — the so-called linguistic approaches that do not teach letter–sound correspondences directly. (Chall, 1967)

We find, similarly, in Bradley & Bryant's (1983) training study that when children who were backwards in reading at four and five years old were trained on sound categorisation they showed markedly greater improvements in reading over the next two years than those who were given semantic categorisation training. However, those children who were given sound categorisation and, with the help of plastic letters, were additionally taught how each common sound was represented by a letter of the alphabet, showed even greater improvement. Furthermore, less than ten hours of such training spaced over two years led to these superiorities in reading being sustained through until the children were 13 years old (Bradley, 1989). We can conclude from these results that phonic training is particularly effective for individuals who are retarded in reading, and, furthermore, training in sound categorisation is even more effective when it is linked to spelling and involves an explicit connection with the alphabet.

Our results demonstrate the growth of cognitive skills which explain these findings. Explicit phonemic awareness is an important factor in the first stages of spelling development, emerging only later as a significant contributor to reading. The early influence of explicit phoneme awareness on spelling, in conjunction with the major contribution of spelling to beginning reading, indicates that experience in spelling promotes the use of a phonological strategy in reading. Thus training phonics and spelling to individuals who have not yet acquired these particular phonological skills nor related them to spelling patterns will eventually help them to become proficient readers. In saying this we are not advocating a return to Huey's (1908) 'mere mechanics of reading and spelling. The unreasoned and unreasonable devotion to our irrational English spelling', we are certainly not suggesting spelling by letter names, rather we promote the notion of reading programmes which include the wide range of goals from word attack skills, through comprehension to interpretation and which are tailored to the needs of the particular child and particular stage (Ellis & Large, 1988; Frith, 1985) of reading development. However, we do believe that it is advisable for beginning readers and those who are backward or specifically retarded to be assisted in developing facility in dissecting a word's sound structure so as to foster symbol–sound and sound–symbol association. At times this must involve the direct teaching of these associations.

The other conclusion concerns the early identification of children at risk. The work of Bradley (1989) demonstrates that the younger the child the more effective is remedial intervention. We do not need to wait until children are seven or eight years of age or older to identify that they are falling substantially behind in their reading development. Our present description of the growth of reading skill identifies its precursors as phonological skills and early spelling. We can therefore use young children's problems in these areas as indices predictive of risk of later reading delay.

Summary

Early interactive processes of development in reading, spelling and implicit and explicit phonological awareness were assessed in a group of children at four time-points as they progressed through their first three years in school. Causal path analyses demonstrate a role of spelling in the early stages of reading acquisition, as well as differential contributions of implicit and explicit phonological awareness to both reading and spelling. They also suggest a developmental cascade from implicit to explicit phonemic awareness in the normal acquisition of phonological knowledge and associated skills. An analysis of the children's spelling errors at these stages demonstrates that spelling changes in nature from being pre-communicative, through semi-phonetic in nature, and these changes are associated with the children's increasing phonological awareness.

The implications of these findings for teaching are clear: the teaching of spelling and phonological awareness is an integral and important part of early reading instruction.

Acknowledgements

We thank the headteachers, teachers and pupils of St Gerards Convent School, Bangor, Our Ladies Roman Catholic School, Bangor, and Llandegfan Primary School, Anglesey for their constant help, encouragement and patience throughout the three years of this project. Parts of this work are also reported in our chapter in P. D. PUMPHREY and C. D. ELLIOTT (eds) *Primary School Pupils' Reading and Spelling Difficulties: Current Research and Practice*, Basingstoke: Falmer Press, 1990, and in our article in *Language and Education*, 1991.

References

BACKMAN, J. 1983, The role of psycholinguistic skills in reading acquisition: A look at early readers. *Reading Research Quarterly* 18, 466–79.
BRADLEY, L. 1980, *Assessing Reading Difficulties: A Diagnostic and Remedial Approach*. London: Macmillan Education.
—— 1989, Specific learning disability: Prediction — intervention — progress. Paper presented to the Rodin Remediation Academy International Conference on Dyslexia, University College of North Wales, September, 1989.
BRADLEY, L. and BRYANT, P. E. 1983, Categorizing sounds and learning to read — a causal connection. *Nature* 301, 419–21.
—— 1985, *Rhyme and Reason in Reading and Spelling* International Academy for Research in Learning Disabilities, No. 1. Ann Arbor: The University of Michigan Press.
BRYANT, P. E. and BRADLEY, L. 1980, Why children sometimes write words which they do not read. In U. FRITH (ed.) *Cognitive Processes in Spelling*. London: Academic Press.
BRYANT, P. E. and GOSWAMI, U. 1987, Phonological awareness and learning to read. In J. R. BEECH and A. M. COLLEY (eds) *Cognitive Approaches to Reading*. Chichester: Wiley.
CATALDO, S. and ELLIS, N. 1988, Interactions in the development of spelling, reading and phonological skills. *Journal of Research in Reading* 11, 2, 86–109.
—— 1990, Learning to spell, learning to read. In P. D. PUMPHREY and C. D. ELLIOTT (eds) *Children's Difficulties in Reading, Writing and Spelling: Challenges and Responses*. Basingstoke: Falmer Press.

CHALL, J. (1967) *Learning to Read: The Great Debate*. New York: McGraw-Hill.
CHOMSKY, C. 1977, Approaching reading through invented spelling. In L. B. RESNICK and P. A. WEAVER (eds) *The Theory and Practice of Early Reading* Vol. 2. Hillsdale, NJ: Erlbaum.
CHUKOVSKY, K. 1968, *From Two to Five*. Berkeley: University of California Press.
CLARK, E. V. 1978 Awareness of language: Some evidence from what children say and do. In A. SINCLAIR, R. J. JARVELLA and W. J. M. LEVELT (eds) *The Child's Conception of Language*. New York: Springer-Verlag.
DANIELS, J. C. and DYACK, H. 1956, *Progress in Reading*. University of Nottingham: Institute of Education.
DOWNING, J. 1973, *Comparative Reading: Cross National Studies of Behaviour and Processes in Reading and Writing*. New York: Macmillan.
EHRI, L. C. 1979, Linguistic insight: threshold of reading acquisition. In T. G. WALLER and G. E. MACKINNON (eds) *Reading Research: Advances in Theory and Practice* Vol. 1. New York: Academic Press.
EHRI, L. C. and WILCE, L. C. 1985, Movement into reading: Is the first stage of printed word learning visual or phonetic? *Reading Research Quarterly* 20, 163–79.
—— 1987, Does learning to spell help beginners learn to read words? *Reading Research Quarterly* 22, 47–65.
ELKONIN, D. B. 1973, USSR. In J. DOWNING (ed.) *Comparative Reading*. New York: Macmillan.
ELLIS, N. C. 1989, Reading development, dyslexia and phonological skills. *The Irish Journal of Psychology* 10, 4, 551–67.
—— 1990, Reading, phonological processing and STM: Interactive tributaries of development. *Journal of Research in Reading* 13, 2, 107–22.
ELLIS, N. and CATALDO, S. 1990, The role of spelling in learning to read. *Language and Education* 4, 1–28.
ELLIS, N. and LARGE, B. 1987, The development of reading: As you seek so shall you find. *British Journal of Psychology* 78, 1–28.
—— 1988, The early stages of reading: A longitudinal study. *Applied Cognitive Psychology* 2, 47–76.
FLESCH, R. 1955, *Why Johnny Can't Read and What You Can Do About It*. New York: Harper and Brothers.
FRITH, U. 1980, Experimental approaches to developmental dyslexia: An introduction. *Psychological Research* 43, 97–110.
—— 1985, Beneath the surface of developmental dyslexia. In K. PATTERSON, J. MARSHALL and M. COLTHEART (eds) *Surface Dyslexia*. London: Lawrence Erlbaum.
GENTRY, J. R. 1982, Analysis of developmental spelling in GNYS AT WORK. *The Reading Teacher* 36, 192–200.
GOSWAMI, U. and BRYANT, P. 1990, *Phonological Skills and Learning to Read*. Hove, Sussex: Lawrence Erlbaum.
HELFGOTT, J. A. 1976, Phonemic segmentation and blending skills of kindergarten children: Implications for beginning reading acquisition. *Contemporary Educational Psychology* 1, 157–69.
HENDERSON, E. H. 1980, Developmental concepts of words. In E. H. HENDERSON and J. W. BEERS (eds) *Developmental and Cognitive Aspects of Learning to Spell: A Reflection of Word Knowledge*. Newark, Del.: International Reading Association.

HENDERSON, E. H. and BEERS, J. W. (eds) 1980, *Developmental and Cognitive Aspects of Learning to Spell: A Reflection of Word Knowledge*. Newark, Del.: International Reading Association.
HOHN, W. E. and EHRI, L. C. 1983, Do alphabet letters help pre-readers acquire phonemic segmentation skill? *Journal of Educational Psychology* 75, 752–62.
HUEY, E. B. 1908, *The Psychology and Pedagogy of Reading*. Cambridge, Mass.: MIT Press.
JÖRESKOG, K. G. and SÖRBOM, D. 1984, *LISREL VI User's Guide*. Uppsala: Department of Statistics.
JUEL, C., GRIFFITH, P. L. and GOUGH, P. B. 1986, The acquisition of literacy: A longitudinal study of children in first and second grade. *Journal of Educational Psychology* 78, 243–55.
LIBERMAN, I. Y. and SHANKWEILER, D. 1979, Speech, the alphabet, and teaching to read. In L. B. RESNICK and P. A. WEAVER (eds) *Theory and Practice of Early Reading*. Hillsdale, NJ: Erlbaum.
MARSH, G., FRIEDMAN, M. P., WELCH, V. and DESBERG, P. 1981, A cognitive-developmental theory of reading acquisition. In T. G. WALLER and G. E. MACKINNON (eds) *Reading Research: Advances in Theory and Practice* Vol. 3. New York: Academic Press.
MILES, T. R. and MILES, E. 1975, *More Help for Dyslexic Children*. London: Methuen Educational.
MOMMERS, M. J. C. 1987, An investigation into the relationship between word recognition, reading comprehension and spelling skills in the first two years of primary school. *Journal of Reading Research* 10, 122–43.
MORRIS, D. 1983, Concept of word and phoneme awareness in the beginning reader. *Research in the Teaching of English* 17, 4, 359–73.
MORRIS, D. and PERNEY, J. 1984, Developmental spelling as a predictor of first-grade reading achievement. *The Elementary School Journal* 84, 4, 441–57.
READ, C. 1971, Preschool children's knowledge of English phonology. *Harvard Educational Review* 41, 1–34.
—— 1975, *Children's Categorizations of Speech Sounds in English*. Urbana, Ill.: National Council of Teachers of English.
—— 1986, *Children's Creative Spelling*. London: Routledge and Kegan Paul.
SHANAHAN, T. and LOMAX, R. G. 1986, An analysis and comparison of theoretical models of the reading–writing relationship. *Journal of Educational Psychology* 78, 116–23.
SHANKWEILER, D., LIBERMAN, I. Y. and SAVIN, 1972, General discussion of papers. In J. F. KAVANAGH and I. MATTINGLY (eds) *Language by Ear and by Eye*. Cambridge, Mass.: MIT Press.
SLOBIN, D. J. 1978, A case study of early language awareness. In A. SINCLAIR, J. JARVELLA and W. J. M. LEVELT (eds) *The Child's Conception of Language*. New York: Springer-Verlag.
SMITH, F. 1978, *Understanding Reading: A Psycholinguistic Analysis of Reading and Learning to Read* 2nd edn. New York: Holt, Rinehart and Winston.
SNOWLING, M. and PERIN, D. 1983, The development of phoneme segmentation skills in young children. In J. SLOBODA (ed.) *The Acquisition of Symbolic Skills*. London: Plenum Press.
STANOVICH, K. E., CUNNINGHAM, A. E. and CRAMER, B. B. 1984, Assessing phonological awareness in kindergarten children: Issues of task comparability. *Journal of Experimental Child Psychology* 38, 175–90.

TORNÉUS, M. 1984, Phonological awareness and reading: A chicken and egg problem? *Journal of Educational Psychology* 76, 6, 1,346–58.

VALTIN, R. 1984, The development of metalinguistic abilities in children learning to read and write. In J. DOWNING and R. VALTIN (eds) *Language Awareness and Learning to Read*. New York: Springer-Verlag.

WECHSLER, D. 1967, *Manual for the Wechsler Preschool and Primary Scale of Intelligence*. New York: The Psychological Corporation New York.

8 Alphabetic Spelling: Predicting Eventual Literacy Attainment

NATA KYRTSIS GOULANDRIS

Introductory Review

Competent spellers are able to spell a large number of words automatically and effortlessly. The accumulation of this lexical store, often referred to as word-specific knowledge, is widely recognised but the mechanisms involved when word spellings are learned, recalled and retrieved have so far eluded explanation. It is evident that the processing requirements for beginners and skilled spellers must differ substantially. Young children who have no knowledge of orthography will need to rely initially on non-orthographic memory mechanisms for recalling word spellings (Morton, 1987) while skilled adults can learn new words by referring to a variety of orthographic regularities.

Establishing how beginners learn to spell new words is crucial for understanding spelling acquisition and for planning effective spelling instruction. Therefore, this chapter explores the relationship between young children's mastery of phonic spelling strategies as exemplified in their attempts to spell nonsense words and their subsequent overall levels of attainment in reading and spelling. The hypothesis of interest is whether spellng competence, in particular the ability to recall word specific spelling information, requires underlying phonic skills or whether adequate spelling knowledge can be accumulated without a basic grasp of sound–letter relationships.

Learning sound–spelling associations may play a vital role in the acquisition of both reading and spelling skills. Frith (1985), for example, proposes that spelling is a 'pacemaker' in the acquisition of literacy, providing the initial impetus in the child's acquisition of sound–letter associations or 'alphabetic skills'. Children's first attempts to use phonics are instigated by their desire to spell words. Once they have acquired some proficiency in alphabetic spelling they are able to transfer their knowledge of correspondence rules to reading.

It is generally accepted that skilled spellers can spell in one of two distinct ways (Ellis, 1984). The first is the lexical, or whole word, strategy, in which the precise spelling of a word is retrieved from the lexicon, or word memory store. This 'direct' route is used when the word is familiar and has been learned. The second, often referred to as the sub-lexical or phonological route, is used primarily for assembling unfamiliar word spellings. The required word is broken down into its component speech sounds (phoneme segmentation) and phoneme–grapheme rules are used to generate a plausible spelling. The two processes have their limitations. A speller who uses the sub-lexical route can generate spellings which sound like the required word but which often differ markedly from the conventional spelling. A speller can use the lexical route to access correct spellings of highly irregular words such as 'yacht' and 'colonel' but would not be able to find an entry for an unfamiliar word.

This dual-route model of spelling, does not specify how a new word is learned and placed in the lexicon. Word specific spelling information could conceivably be recalled using visual memory. There is, however, insufficient empirical evidence to support the view that visual memory plays more than a peripheral role in the early acquisition of whole word spellings although the possibility, particularly in the earliest stages of spelling learning, cannot be dismissed. It has also been suggested that visual imagery may be an important factor in the learning and recall of word spellings (Radakar, 1963; Peters, 1985). Research demonstrating that adults who are good visualisers are not necessarily good spellers has, however, provided contradictory evidence (Sloboda, 1980). In fact, Tenney (1980) reported that spellers are more likely to select the correct phonologically plausible spelling, e.g. **CONSENSUS/CONCENSUS; FROLICKING/FROLICING**, when they can look at the alternatives than when they imagine them, apparently employing phonological and morphological information to help them select the correct option.

A more convincing explanation of whole word learning is that spellers retrieve information from 'orthographic memory' (Barron, 1980) and that this spelling information is coded using precise 'letter by letter' data (Frith, 1980). Visual memory for everyday objects and shapes can then be contrasted

ALPHABETIC SPELLING

to orthographic memory, a specialised memory system which facilitates the learning of written language. Frith (1985) proposes that orthographic representations depend on the child's understanding of basic sound–letter rules. Once young spellers are able to use sound–letter rules competently they can begin to code and recall words in orthographic units, chunking words into common letter sequences such as **ING, TURE, TION** or as morphemes, e.g. **ANTI, TRACT**.

A similar view is advocated by Ehri (1985) who considers that correct spellings are mastered when the learner is able to fuse the visual and phonological representations of the word. The sounds in the word's pronunciation must be linked to its spelling by mapping at least a proportion of the letters to the speech sounds in the word's pronunciation.

/m/	/æ/	/p/		/k/	/a:/	/p/	/e/	/t/
|	|	|		|	|	|	|	|
M	A	P		C	AR	P	E	T

Even irregular words can be recalled more efficiently when the predictable letters are noted and the unexpected letters singled out and learned.

/y/	/ɒ/	/t/		/s/	/e/	/d/
|	|	|		|	|	|
Y	A	CHT		S	AI	D

According to both of these theories, initial learning of words would require at least moderately proficient phonic skills for this mapping procedure to take place.

There is considerable research supporting the view that children rely on their knowledge of words' pronunciations in their initial spelling attempts (Read, 1986). Error analyses demonstrate that spelling attempts gradually evolve from non-phonetic renderings in which few of the target word's speech sounds are represented, to partially phonetic in which most of the consonants are retained, to phonetic but unconventional spellings. These are, in turn, gradually superseded by the correct orthography (Snowling, 1987).

Some pre-school spellers are able to use their awareness of speech sounds and their partial knowledge of letter names to construct a surprisingly successful albeit unconventional spelling system, e.g. **ADE LEFWTS KRAMD NTU A LEVATR** for *eighty elephants crammed into an elevator*

(Gentry, 1981) or **R U DF** (*are you deaf?*) written to a mother who was otherwise preoccupied (Bissex, 1980).

Bryant & Bradley's (1980) striking finding that six- to seven-year-old children could read some words they could not spell and spell other words which they could not read demonstrated forcefully that beginners approach reading and spelling in different ways. Whereas these as yet unskilled readers recognised words visually, they spelled words by sound, applying elementary sound–letter rules. What is more, they seemed unable to decode words, although they could sound out and read some nonsense words like **WEF** and **BIF** quite proficiently. Indeed, when the researchers tricked the children by embedding the regular words which the children had previously been unable to read amongst a list of nonsense words, the children decoded the unfamiliar words with little difficulty, demonstrating latent ability to use alphabetic skills for reading.

The role of spelling in the promotion and extension of reading skills has also been studied by Cataldo & Ellis (1990) and Ellis & Cataldo (Chapter 7 this volume) who examined the relationship between children's unconscious awareness of speech sounds (implicit phonology), their ability to make use of this knowledge (explicit phonology) and the development of reading and spelling ability during their first three years at school. They reported that spelling plays an important function in the advancement of early reading ability as well as promoting both types of phonological awareness.

The use of early invented spellings in kindergarten to predict reading ability in first grade has been reported by Mann, Tobin & Wilson (1987) who consider invented spellings to be a measure of children's phonological awareness. Novices who have no experience of written language are obliged to abstract fundamental sound–letter associations basing their analyses on their perception of the phonetic and articulatory properties of spoken words. Thus the ability to construct a rudimentary spelling system requires an extremely high level of phonological competence and is a most exacting test of a child's ability to use phonological information.

The experiments reported here examined the role of early alphabetic spelling. The first experiment sought to determine whether alphabetic knowledge is evident from the commencement of spelling acquisition. The second experiment considered whether proficient generation of phonetic spellings will predict children's spelling and reading competence in the following year. If orthographic memory relies initially on existing alphabetic skills, evidence of early phonetic spelling should be associated with later *general* spelling competence. If, in turn, inventing phonetic spellings precipitates the realisation that correspondence rules can be used to decode new words when reading, early alphabetic spelling ability should also presage word recognition skills in the early years.

Experimental Studies

Forty children were selected from an inner city infants and primary school. The youngest group was approximately six years old, had an average reading age of 6:9 and a mean spelling age of 5:6. The older group was approximately 7:6, had a reading age of 8:6 and a spelling age of 8:1.

The children were grouped by spelling age, with 20 in each spelling age group. A battery of standardised tests was administered consisting of the Schonell single word reading and spelling tests, and the British Picture Vocabulary Scale (Dunn, Dunn, Whetton & Pintillie, 1982), a test of receptive vocabulary which was used as an approximate measure of verbal intelligence. The children were subsequently asked to read and spell high-frequency regular and irregular words. A non-word reading and spelling test based on the regular words was administered two months later. The Schonell single word reading and spelling tests were administered again at the end of the following academic year.

Orthographic Regularity

It is possible to classify words according to their degree of orthographic regularity, the extent to which they can be spelled accurately using sound–letter rules. Regular words (e.g. *net, pin, carpet,* and *zigzag*) can be spelled easily if the speller is familiar with basic sound–spelling associations, while irregular words, e.g. *who, island, yacht* will invariably be spelled incorrectly if the speller has not learned their unique spellings or if sound–letter rules are applied. By comparing children's ability to spell regular and irregular words it is possible to discern whether children are using phonological or whole word strategies. It is, for example, possible to detect if children are relying on phonics, first by looking for a regularity effect in which regular words are spelled more accurately than irregular words and secondly by regularisation errors which occur when a speller tries to use sound–letter rules to spell irregular words, spelling *what* as **WOT**, *you* as **U**, or *school* as **SKOOL**. If children are not using correspondence rules for spelling, they will be equally successful at spelling both regular and irregular words.

In this first experiment two alternative hypotheses are examined.

1. If children learn spellings by relying primarily on visual skills, then young spellers will find irregular words which cannot be spelled using correspondence rules just as easy to spell as regular words, providing that the words are equally familiar to the children and contain the same number of letters.
2. If, on the other hand, children rely predominantly on letter–sound associations when they are first learning to spell, they will spell regular words more proficiently than irregular words.

The children were asked to spell 24 high-frequency words of which 12 were regular, e.g. *run, like, still, little* and 12 irregular, e.g. *you, said, write, pretty*. These were words which they had seen often in their reading and were likely to have tried to spell. The words were presented in random order along with a further ten words used in another experiment not reported here.

The beginners spelled an average of 4.1 (34%) of the regular words but only 1.85 (15%) of the irregular words correctly. The children who had attained a spelling age of 8, spelled 10.6 (88%) of the regular words and 7.25 (60%) of the irregular words correctly. Statistical analysis using a 2-way ANOVA indicated that there was a significant difference between the groups ($F(1,38) = 153.97, p < .001$). Furthermore, there was a significant effect of regularity ($F(1,38) = 102.47, p < .001$), demonstrating that both groups found the regular words easier to spell than the irregular words (see Figures 8.1 and 8.2). However, although both groups found regular

TABLE 8.1 *Mean number of correct spellings on high-frequency regular and irregular words for spelling age 5:6 and spelling age 8 (SpA = 8–9 years), maximum = 12*

	Regular	Irregular
SpA 5:6		
Mean	4.10	1.85
sd	(2.19)	(0.88)
SpA 8:0		
Mean	10.60	7.25
sd	(1.31)	(2.22)

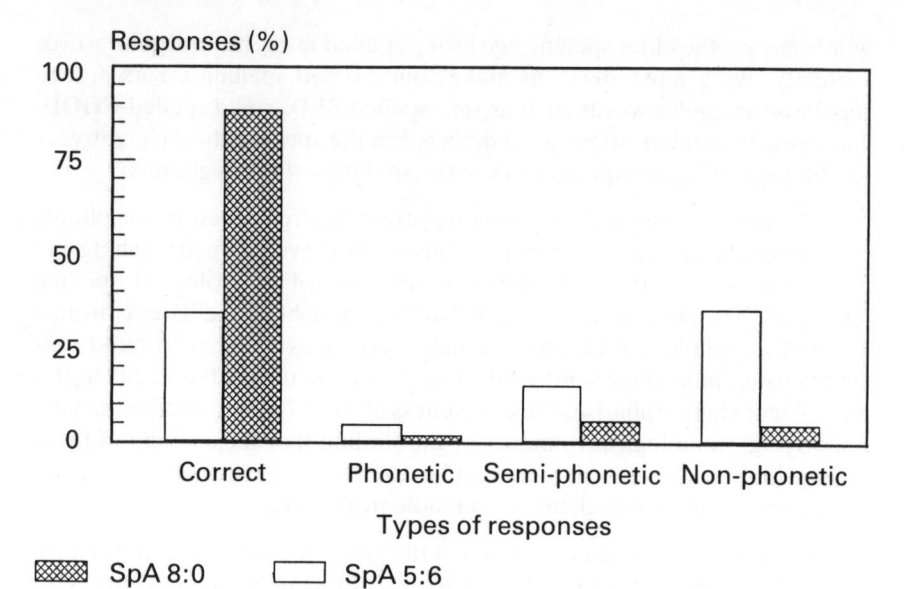

FIGURE 8.1 *Spelling of regular words*

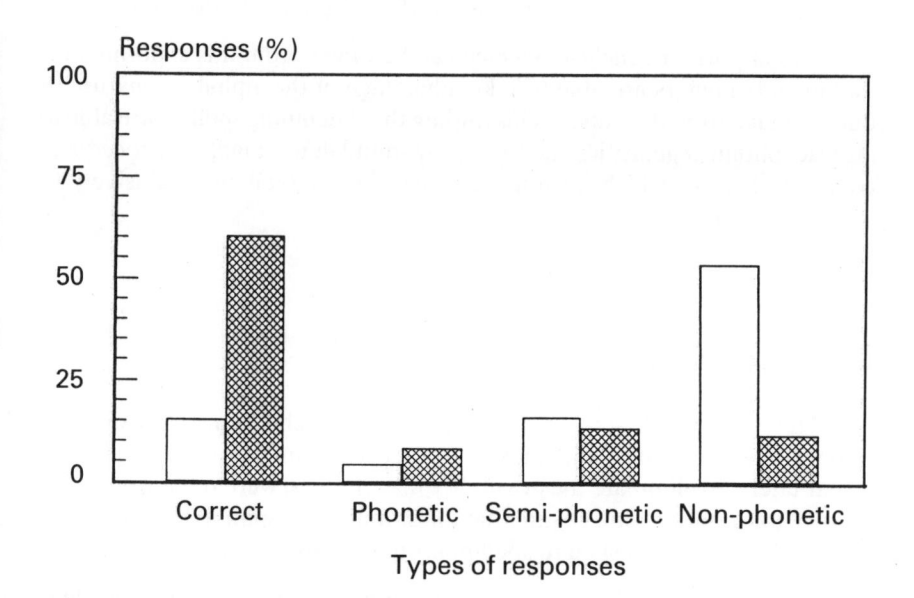

FIGURE 8.2 *Spelling of irregular words*

words easier, the older spelling age group spelled many more regular words correctly, were more likely to make sound-based spelling errors and to regularise irregular words such as *said* spelled **SED**, *could* spelled **COOD**. Twenty-one regularisations were detected in the spellings of the eight-year spelling age group compared to 11 in the spellings of the beginners.

These results support the view that young children depend upon phonic mediation in early spelling attempts. This was true even though teaching had been eclectic and did not emphasise the use of phonological spelling strategies. The children in this study had been taught by the 'Breakthrough Method', a whole-word method which encourages learners to build sentences using individual word cards and then copy the sentence. Since this type of teaching emphasises the uniqueness of word spellings rather than the underlying phonological framework, the finding that the spelling of these young children showed a definite regularity effect suggests that it is the spelling process itself which elicits the phonological strategy.

The error data revealed a trend in the types of errors the children produced. The eight-year-old spellers made predominantly phonetic errors for both types of words. In contrast, younger spellers were more likely to produce non-phonetic spellings although their errors became increasingly phonetic as their spelling skill increased. (See Figures 8.1 and 8.2.)

The important conclusion which can be drawn from this experiment is that even beginners are able to take advantage of the alphabetic nature of our language from the outset. This finding that beginning spellers are able to abstract phonic regularities and to employ sound–letter mapping procedures counters theories which attribute the learning of spellings exclusively to visual processing.

Non-word Spelling

This experiment set out to explore whether children's ability to use phonic strategies can predict their overall spelling and reading competence a year later. To eliminate the possibility that children were relying on word-specific information, and ensure that the stimuli corresponded to unfamiliar words, children were asked to spell nonsense words.

If early spelling ability requires a phonological foundation on which to base recall of orthographic structure, non-word spelling should be significantly associated with later spelling ability. If the acquisition of alphabetic skills for spelling initiates the use of phonics for reading, non-word spelling should also predict eventual reading ability. This hypothesis was tested using the children's spelling scores a year after the administration of the regularity spelling tests. Moreover, if initial spelling learning is based on the child's ability to map the phonological representation of a word to its orthographic representation, then children who are particularly poor at spelling non-words may fail to develop normal spelling skills even if reading is within the normal range.

Two months later, the children who had participated in the first experiment were asked to spell 12 non-words derived from the regular words described above. As several children had either left the school or were not available when the standardised tests were administered in the following year, follow up data only for 27 children in the original sample is reported here.

The nonsense stimuli were formed by altering one letter in the original word, so that for every set of three words one word was changed at the beginning, one in the middle and one at the end, e.g. *and* was altered to *ind*, *run* to *rin*, *bed* to *bep*, *like* to *sike*, *make* to *mafe* and *good* to *goot*. Only the first letter was altered in the words containing more than one syllable, e.g. *little* became *gittle*, *family* became *hamily*.

Non-word spelling was introduced by discussing the concept of nonsense words and encouraging the child to make up examples. The child, tested individually, was instructed to spell the nonsense words so that anyone who read them would pronounce them correctly. The child was asked to repeat each nonsense word before attempting to spell it, to ensure that the target was heard accurately and that the spelling errors were not attributable to inattentiveness or incorrect hearing.

Spelling responses were classified as phonetic, semi-phonetic and non-phonetic. Any spellings which could conceivably be sounded out as the target were considered *phonetic* spellings, e.g. **COF**, **COFF**, **COPH**, **COGH**, **KOPH**, **KOGH** etc. *Semi-phonetic* spellings represented the consonant structure of the target but were incomplete phonetic representations frequently containing deletions of consonants in clusters, e.g. *stiss* → **SIS**, omissions of nasals, e.g. *thenk* → **THEK**, omission or incorrect use of vowels, e.g. *sike* → **SIK**; *mafe* → **MAF**, or voicing errors (Snowling, Stackhouse & Rack, 1986). *Non-phonetic* spellings were impossible to recognise unless one knew the target, e.g. *stiss* → **MNNTY**; *gittle* → **TENEY**; *mafe* → **LIKEF**. Non-word spelling proficiency was calculated by adding the number of phonetic and semi-phonetic spellings produced by each child.

Results of non-word spelling

Although the Schonell Graded Word Spelling Test does not contain many irregular words, it includes numerous ambiguous words such as *week, pie, boat, year, dream, sight, mouth, brought*, which require word-specific knowledge for spelling accuracy. The children's scores on this test have, therefore, been taken to indicate their overall spelling ability reflecting both their encoding skill and their word-specific knowledge.

A series of partial correlations (a type of multiple regression) was computed to see if there was a relationship between children's ability to spell non-words in the first year and their subsequent reading and spelling ability. The predictor variables were always placed in the same fixed order with the British Picture Vocabulary Scale (BPVS) score partialled out first to eliminate statistically the difference in the children's levels of verbal intelligence. For those who are not interested in the details of statistical analyses, a summary of the results can be found at the end of this section.

The first analysis was a simple correlation between the test scores. This examined the relationship between verbal intelligence as measured by the BPVS, reading age, spelling age, non-word spelling in the first year, and reading and spelling ages a year later. The results indicated that the best predictor of reading age in the second year was reading age in the first year — a result which is not likely to astonish most reading teachers! Spelling age in the first year also predicted the children's reading ability in the subsequent year. However, non-word spelling also proved to be an important predictor of both eventual reading and spelling achievement.

A partial correlation was then computed in which the differences between the children's scores on the BPVS were statistically eliminated to control for differences in the children's verbal IQ. Controlling for verbal intelligence did not greatly alter the relationships between the variables seen in the previous analysis. Reading age in the second year was highly correlated to reading age, spelling age and phonetic non-word spelling in the previous year ($p < 0.001$). Although reading and spelling age in the first year predicted spelling performance in the second year ($p < 0.05$), non-word spelling competence proved to be a significantly better predictor of spelling age in the second year than the previous year's reading and spelling age scores ($p < 0.001$).

Reading facility is likely to contribute substantially to the learning of spelling. In order to evaluate the effect of non-word spelling competence as a predictor, it was decided to eliminate the influence of the children's initial reading ability in the first year as well as controlling for differences in verbal intelligence. Consequently, BPVS and reading age in the first year were partialled out. The effect of this statistical manipulation is impressive. Spelling age in the first year no longer correlates with later literacy attainment whereas non-word spelling is a significant predictor of future reading and spelling ability. Finally, if we then eliminate statistically all the differences between the children in the initial year of testing except for their ability to spell non-words phonetically (namely their verbal intelligence and their initial reading and spelling ability), non-word spelling remains a significant predictor of success for both reading and spelling in the second year.

If, on the other hand, we eliminate all the individual differences attributable to the children's proficiency with non-word spelling a very different picture emerges. Whereas both reading age and spelling age in the first year are significant predictors of reading age in the following year, there are no significant predictors of spelling age in the second year.

Summary of Results

Statistical tests were used to identify the best predictors of reading and spelling in the following year. When all the other influential variables had been eliminated, the children's early level of proficiency in non-word spelling proved to be the best predictor of their reading and spelling performance in the second year. To summarise the steps:

1. *When no variables were partialled out.* Reading age (RA), spelling age (SpA) and non-word spelling predicted reading ability the following year. Only non-word spelling predicted spelling ability in the following year.
2. *When verbal intelligence was partialled out.* RA, SpA and Non-word spelling predicted reading. RA, SpA and Non-word spelling predicted spelling, with non-word spelling proving marginally superior.
3. *When verbal intelligence and reading age were partialled out.* Non-word spelling predicted reading and spelling better than spelling age.
4. *When verbal intelligence, reading age and spelling age were partialled out.* Non-word spelling still predicted reading and spelling in the second year.

In conclusion, although non-word spelling is a reasonably good predictor of eventual reading ability when we have taken account of variations in verbal intelligence reading age in the previous year is a better predictor. However, non-word spelling ability is certainly the most sensitive predictor of spelling ability in the subsequent year.

Discussion

These experiments sought to evaluate the importance of alphabetic spelling competence and its influence on the overall development of reading and spelling in the early years. The results indicate clearly that a child's ability to generate phonetic spellings is closely associated and predicts eventual acquisition of reading and spelling skills. The ability to produce phonetic or semi-phonetic non-word spellings was shown to predict overall spelling ability a year later, even on ambiguous words which required precise word specific information. Indeed, phonetic non-word spellings predicted future ability more reliably than overall spelling ability in the previous year. This finding endorses theories of literacy development which propose that orthographic knowledge is dependent on a framework of alphabetic expertise, and that the learning of word specific knowledge is facilitated by competent use of sound–letter rules.

The predictive role of non-phonetic spelling in the development of reading was less striking but is nevertheless important. Since readers are more likely to use a visual lexical route, children's earlier reading attainment and ability to recognise a corpus of words is clearly an important predictive variable. However, non-word spelling is also a significant predictor, reflecting the child's ability to decode novel words.

Why is the ability to use alphabetic knowledge such an important predictor of later spelling proficiency? A child who can perceive the link between speech sounds and letters can gain information about spellings by referring to his or her spoken language system. As alphabetic knowledge is gradually acquired, it can become a framework upon which orthographic spelling conventions can be overlaid, reducing the memory requirements of the learning process. A child with even a modicum of alphabetic skills has the potential to set up expectations of a word's likely spelling. The discrepancy between expectations and the correct spelling may enable the child to learn new spellings more effectively. The gradual accumulation of lexical knowledge will in turn provide the learner with data permitting the coding of words according to non-phonemic regularities, such as lexical or morphemic regularities.

It seems unlikely that the predictive role of invented spellings will persist for more than a few years in children whose literacy skills is progressing normally. A child who has acquired substantial word-specific information will no longer rely on simplistic sequential correspondence rules. Overall spelling competence will consequently depend on alternative mechanisms for encoding orthographic information.

Research evidence demonstrates a strong link between poor phonological processing and the most serious type of spelling disorder (Snowling, Stackhouse & Rack, 1986; Snowling & Hulme, 1989). Some individuals with severe phonological deficits can learn to spell adequately despite a seriously impaired phonological system (Campbell & Butterworth, 1985) by relying on visual memory, kinaesthetic memory or by rote learning. However, it remains unlikely that severe phonological processing deficits can coexist with proficient spelling.

Whereas these studies indicate that alphabetic competence provides the beginning speller with vital clues about word spellings, and may form the foundations upon which orthographic memory is constructed, such spelling knowledge is rudimentary and incomplete. The complexity of English orthography precludes spelling accuracy if the speller relies exclusively on alphabetic spelling. Indeed excessive dependence on sound–letter rules in an older child is a diagnostic sign of a different type of spelling deficit (Goulandris & Snowling, 1991). However, initial spelling competence proceeds more smoothly and productively once alphabetic skills have been acquired.

Practical Implications for Classroom Practice

Children who are unable to apply alphabetic skills or are virtually incapable of producing some phonetic invented spellings by the second year of schooling, may be seriously at risk even if their reading appears 'normal'. Reading is a more flexible skill than spelling because a written word can be recognised using several alternative strategies. Some children excel at predicting words through context and picture cues but are often unable to identify whole words out of context or to sound out unfamiliar words. These individuals usually have poor phonological skills and are consequently unable to invent plausible spellings using sound–letter rules.

Children may find it difficult to grasp the fundamental principles of initial spelling for a number of different reasons and careful assessment is essential for effective remediation. One frequent cause of spelling difficulties is poor phonological processing, the inability to recognise and be able to manipulate speech sounds in words. Children with deficient phonological processing need to be helped to listen to words and identify rhymes and later to make up rhymes. They need practice in dividing words into smaller units such as syllables (*rab/bit; ba/na/na*); onset and rime units (*c/ap; tr/ap; str/ap*); and phonemes (/k/ /æ/ /p/; /k/ /ei/ /k/). Games requiring the recognition or identification of common speech sounds in initial, final or medial positions of words such as 'I spy', picture matching, picture sorting, dominoes, lotto or snap can be used to develop phonological awareness in an entertaining way.

Secondly, children may not realise that there is a relationship between speech sounds and the letters used to represent words in written language. More explicit teaching or sound–letter rules can help children understand the underlying alphabetic link between spoken and written words and give children viable strategies for inventing spellings. There are also children who have learned correspondence rules but cannot understand how this knowledge can be applied to spelling. They will need explicit instruction to help them realise that word spellings are not arbitrary but are governed by orthographic conventions.

It must be stressed that using phonics to produce invented spellings is only a first step in the complicated process of learning about English spelling. Alphabetic spelling skills can initially assist children to select the appropriate letters. At a more advanced level, they enable a speller to sequence sounds and syllables correctly. However, once basic acquisition of alphabetic skills is completed, spelling instruction must steer the child away from over-reliance on sound strategies to learning words in terms of larger orthographic units using spelling patterns (**ING, TURE, TION**), morphemic units (**ED, GRAPH, AUTO**), and lexical families (**SIGN, SIGNAL, SIGNATURE, SIGNIFY**).

It is inevitable that psychologists and educators should ask if nonword spelling practice should be included in the spelling curriculum. I do not believe it is necessary to do so. Spelling nonsense words provides a pure measure of a child's ability to segment phonemes, and apply sound-spelling rules. It can, therefore, be used as a quick measure of those skills. However, on a day to day basis, it is equally easy and, I would argue more productive, to teach beginners spellings grouped according to rhyming word families (e.g. b*oat*, c*oat*, g*oat*, fl*oat*) than to teach meaningless nonwords. Children want to write real words and can see no point in writing nonsense.

At the outset, teachers may wish to introduce three-letter words grouping them in word families to stress the fact that rhyming words often have similar spellings (e.g. h*en*, p*en*, m*en*, t*en*, or b*ut*, c*ut*, h*ut*, n*ut*). In this way children can be given instruction in listening to the sounds of words, identifying the dissimilar phonemes and in applying sound–letter rules. Children should also be helped to understand that it is possible to construct spellings of unfamiliar words by referring to the sounds in the words and encouraged to invent their own spellings. As skill develops the child should be encouraged to recall *orthographic patterns* and not to rely exclusively on transcribing sounds. If the teacher introduces spellings in groups of visually, and phonologically similar words (e.g. *ought*, b*ought*, f*ought*, b*rought*, th*ought*) children will be encouraged to identify similar orthographic patterns.

Summary

This chapter considers the hypothesis that there is a fundamental relationship between children's ability to construct phonetic invented spellings and their overall spelling and reading ability in the following year. Forty children with a spelling age of 5.5 years and 8 years were administered a spelling test comprising regular and irregular words. The regular words proved easier for both groups. Error analysis showed that spelling attempts became progressively more phonetic as spelling competence increased.

A test of non-word spelling was administered two months later. At the end of the following academic year standardised reading and spelling tests were repeated with 27 of the original sample. Partial correlations demonstrated that when verbal ability was partialled out, the ability to produce phonetic or semi-phonetic non-word spellings predicted overall spelling ability a year later on the Schonell Spelling Test. This test includes numerous words with ambiguous spellings which require precise orthographic information and cannot be accurately spelled using sound–letter rules alone. Non-word spelling also predicted reading ability in the second year.

These findings support theories which propose that the ability to use phonic skills for spelling facilitates the construction of a normally functioning orthographic system, by providing a framework of regularity against which the inconsistencies of English spelling can be recalled and coded (Ehri, 1985).

References

BARRON, R. W. 1980, Visual and phonological strategies in reading and spelling. In U. FRITH (ed.) *Cognitive Processes in Spelling.* London: Academic Press.

BISSEX, G. L. 1980, *GNYS at Work: A Child Learns to Write and Read.* Cambridge MA: Harvard University Press.

BRYANT, P. E. and BRADLEY, L. 1980, Why children sometimes write words which they do not read. In U. FRITH (ed.) *Cognitive Processes in Spelling.* London: Academic Press.

CAMPBELL, R. and BUTTERWORTH, B. 1985, Phonological dyslexia and dysgraphia in a highly literate subject: A developmental case with associated deficits of phonemic awareness and processing. *Quarterly Journal of Experimental Psychology* 37A, 435–75.

CATALDO, S. and ELLIS, N. 1990, Learning to spell, learning to read. In P. D. PUMPHREY and C. D. ELLIOTT (eds) *Children's Difficulties in Reading, Writing and Spelling: Challenges and Responses*. Basingstoke: Falmer Press.

DUNN, L. M., DUNN, L. M., WHETTON, C. and PINTILLIE, D. 1982, *British Picture Vocabulary Scale* (BPVS). Windsor: NFER-Nelson.

EHRI, L. 1985, Sources of difficulty in learning to read and spell. In M. L. WOLRAICH and D. ROUTH (eds) *Advances in Developmental and Behavioural Paediatrics* Vol. 7 (pp. 121–95). Greenwich, Conn.: JAI Press Inc.

ELLIS, A. W. 1984, *Reading, Writing and Dyslexia*. London: Lawrence Erlbaum.

FRITH, U. 1980, Unexpected spelling problems. In U. FRITH (ed.) *Cognitive Processes in Spelling*. London: Academic Press.

—— 1985, Beneath the surface of developmental dyslexia. In K. E. PATTERSON, J. C. MARSHALL and M. COLTHEART (eds) *Surface Dyslexia*. London: Routledge and Kegan Paul.

GENTRY, J. R. 1981, Learning to spell developmentally. *The Reading Teacher* 34, 378–81

GOULANDRIS, N. K. and SNOWLING, M. J. 1991, Visual memory deficits. A plausible cause of developmental dyslexia? *Cognitive Neuropsychology* 8, 2, 127–54.

MANN, V. A., TOBIN, P. and WILSON, R. 1987, Measuring phonological awareness through the invented spellings of kindergarten children. *Merrill-Palmer Quarterly* 33, 365–91.

MORTON, J. 1987, An information processing account of reading acquisition. Paper delivered to the From Neurons to Reading Symposium, Florence, June.

PETERS, M. L. 1985, *Spelling: Caught or Taught. A New Look*. London: Routledge and Kegan Paul.

RADAKAR, L. D. 1963, The effect of visual imagery upon spelling performance. *Journal of Education Research* 56, 370–2.

READ, C. 1986, *Children's Creative Spelling*. London: Routledge and Kegan Paul.

SLOBADA, J. A. 1980, Visual imagery and individual differences in spelling. In U. FRITH, (ed.) *Cognitive Processes in Spelling*. London: Academic Press.

SNOWLING, M. J. 1987, *Dyslexia. A Cognitive Developmental Perspective*. Oxford: Basil Blackwell.

SNOWLING, M. J. and HULME, C. 1989, A longitudinal case study of developmental phonological dyslexia. *Cognitive Neuropsychology* 6, 379–401.

SNOWLING, M. J., STACKHOUSE, J. and RACK, J. P. 1986, Phonological dyslexia and dysgraphia: A developmental analysis. *Cognitive Neuropsychology* 6, 309–39.

TENNEY, Y. J. 1980, Visual factors in spelling. In U. FRITH (ed.) *Cognitive Processes in Spelling*. London: Academic Press.

9 'Invented' Spelling and Learning to Read

LAURA HUXFORD, COLIN TERRELL and LYNETTE BRADLEY

Introduction

'. . . and then he must've eaten his way round to the back . . .' Tom aged three, is reading about how his hamster had made a nest inside his father's favourite chair. The page is filled with wavy lines — his own writing. Although Tom's written thoughts are unrecognisable, he can think in sentences; an ability required in writing but rarely in talking. Tom knows that people make wavy lines on paper when they want to remember what to buy from the supermarket or in order to leave a message. Young children know they can also write, and they do.

One of the issues addressed by those who took part in the Writing Projects in the United States and Britain was how we can prevent the complexities of our writing system from stifling children's natural urge to get meaning down on paper (Graves, 1983; Dyson, 1985; 1988; Sulzby, Barnhart & Hieshima, 1989; D'Arcy, 1989). Research into young children's understanding of the writing/reading process (Clay, 1975; Ferreiro, 1986; Ferreiro and Teberosky, 1982) and the continuing research into the 'process' of writing at various centres (Freedman et al., 1987) have provided a basis for 'English in the National Curriculum' (DES, 1989). While acknowledging the interrelatedness of the four language modes — talking, listening, reading and writing — a distinction is recognised between writing, as composing, and the secretarial skills (Smith, 1982). 'The main principle is that the secretarial aspect should not be allowed to predominate in the assessment while the more complex aspects of composition are ignored' (DES, 1988: 46). The practice of encouraging children to develop their compositional skills at an early age by allowing them to evolve or 'invent' their own spellings for words has been endorsed by the National Curriculum, Non-

Statutory Guidance. 'Teachers will need to be aware of the steps which can be identified in learning to spell correctly, and which can be used to support a child to develop from invented spelling, towards conventional accuracy' (DES, 1989: C17).

Tom's elder sister, Rachel, had used a mixture of the letters from her own and Tom's names, and sometimes numbers, to write messages until she grasped that letters represent sounds. At this stage, in common with many children who have been encouraged to write freely, she would use the correct initial letter of a word, e.g. **F** for *friend*, followed again by a selection of letters which she considered appropriate (Gentry, 1981). As her ability to hear sounds in other positions in a word improved and her knowledge of letters increased, she was able to include more correct letters. She progressed, over a period of time, from **FCHD**, through **FRD** and **FRED** to **FREND**. At this point it seemed appropriate to draw her attention to the additional **I**. It has been shown that children are able to hear sounds within words at an early age and that they are resourceful in their choice of letters with which to represent those sounds (Read, 1971; Chomsky, 1970). In Figure 9.1 the child has used the letter **O** as the nearest equivalent to the vowel sound in *corn* and *called* and **S** to represent the final consonant in *which*. He has also, in exaggerating the articulation in the word *we*, included a **Y**.

Frith (1985) suggests that the ability to 'invent' spellings appears at an earlier stage in children's development than the ability to combine sounds in order to read words. (She maintains that in the first instance young children use a visual strategy to read.) Bryant & Bradley (1980) found a category of

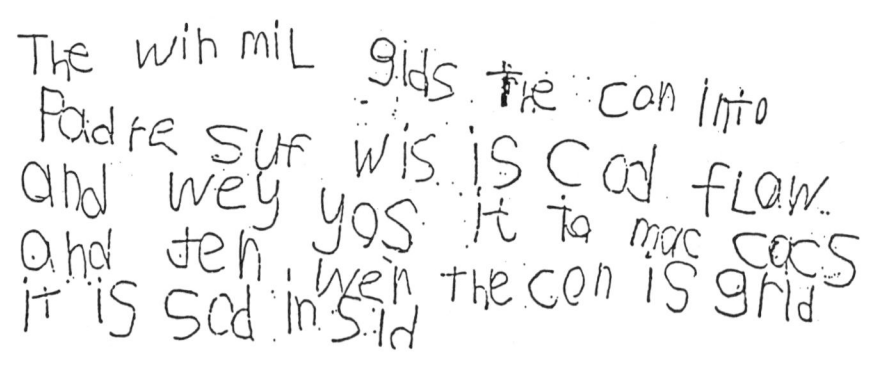

The windmill grinds the corn into powder stuff which is called flour, and we use it to make cakes and then when the corn is ground it is stored inside.

FIGURE 9.1   *Example of a child's invented spelling (age five years)*

'INVENTED' SPELLING AND LEARNING TO READ 161

words (e.g. *bun, mat, leg, pat*) which children were able to spell better than they could read. More recently, Cataldo & Ellis (1988) ran a longitudinal study in which children showed an ability to spell certain words earlier than they could read them.

At the age of four, Rachel could write her own name and a limited number of words from memory. Her written vocabulary was greatly increased, however, by her attempts to write words as they sound. She was aware of the most common sounds which each letter represents. She knew the short sounds of vowels as well as their names, so words like *man, tip, we, on, picnic,* and later, *kind, print, cold, must* and *drag* were, by coincidence, correct. She would also write **DA** (*day*), **SUM** (*some*), **SED** (*said*), **MARID** (*married*). Rachel could generally read what she had written. Certainly, when she was able to hear, and therefore write, all three sounds in a word such as *dig*, her messages could also be interpreted by other people. It was assumed that she could read all the words she was capable of writing. However, when she received messages which included words which she had written correctly herself a few days before, she was not always able to read them. It transpired that the words which she had spelled according to their sounds were those which she subsequently found difficult to read. She would, therefore, guess these words on the basis of the context of the message. When presented with the same words in isolation, her attempts at assimilating the individual sounds in order to read a word were often unsuccessful.

The possibility that children can write some words which they cannot read has certain implications. In the first place parents and teachers would be aware that although children may appear to be advanced in writing, they should not necessarily expect them to be able to use the full range of possible strategies for reading. Secondly, if it were established that children were able to 'spell using sounds' (i.e. use a phonological strategy) before using a corresponding strategy for reading, perhaps children should be encouraged to write at an earlier age than is at present considered appropriate. Before initiating a change in approach, further research of a longitudinal nature was required.

The Study

In order to investigate the relationship between reading and spelling strategies, a longitudinal study was established to examine children's abilities to read and spell two- and three-letter short-vowelled words. It was necessary to isolate the phonological strategies for both spelling and reading — strategies where sounds, rather than the visual properties of words are manipulated. The spelling strategy was that of using letters which correspond to the sounds children can hear in words in order to write, i.e. 'invented spelling'. (On being asked to write *hip*, child says and writes **H, I, P**.) The reading strategy was that of 'decoding', where children blend or merge letters in order to identify a word. (Child reads the word *hip* presented on a card.) It was not anticipated that children would necessarily need to 'sound' each letter before merging them together into a word. It has been shown that young children can decode words by analogy to known words, for example, knowledge of the words <u>can</u> and <u>cat</u> can enable <u>cap</u> to be read (Goswami, 1986).

The words used in the tests were limited to those in which there was direct, one sound to each letter (and one letter to each sound) correspondence. If, therefore, children knew the basic sounds represented by consonants and the short form of the vowels, their efforts at spelling and reading would be expected to result in a conventional response. The same words were used in both spelling and reading tests, and therefore administered on different days, so that a direct comparison could be made between the two abilities. To ensure that the children would not be able to employ a visual strategy and read or spell the words as 'sight' words, non-words such as *pez* and *ak* were devised. These 'words' were presented to the children as objects on a fictitious planet so that a meaningful reading and writing experience was maintained. As the children were only four or five years old at the beginning of the study they were asked to make the words using lower-case plastic letters instead of writing them. Children's phonological ability, independently of letters, was also measured. In order to assess children's phonological development against other factors of experience and ability measures of age, reading, spelling, alphabetical knowledge, verbal ability, memory and hearing were taken.

The criterion for entry into the study was an ability to hear the initial sound in a word. Some children could identify more than just the initial sound in some words, and three children were able to combine sounds in order to read a two-letter (vowel–consonant) word. Knowledge of letters was not a condition of entry to the study. A few children met the entry criterion at 3:6 years of age, most at 4, but some were 5:6 before being included. Forty-three children from two primary schools took part. Their mean score on British Picture Vocabulary Scales (BPVS) (Dunn *et al.*, 1982) was 99 (sd 14.9). Each child was tested at approximately eight-week intervals. Three parallel lists were constructed to reduce practice effects. In order to minimise test-order effects half the children were presented with the reading

TABLE 9.1 *Mean scores in phonological spelling and reading, at initial test, three intermediate points (a, b and c) and final test*

Developmental stage	Spelling	Reading
Initial test	2.18	0.18
a	4.11	1.31
b	6.21	2.66
c	8.15	4.66
Final test	11.50	8.58

test followed by the spelling test, and the other half, vice versa. The children were tested individually within a game-like format. There were three practice items. Encouragement but no feedback was given during testing.

Testing was discontinued when the children demonstrated that they could both hear sounds in words for spelling purposes and use a decoding strategy to read. Inadequate letter knowledge prevented some children from achieving maximum scores. The length of time between initial and final testing varied considerably. Seven children were tested only once more after entering the study whereas others required over a year to progress to an equivalent level. The average length of time taken was 28 weeks. Whilst for seven children there are only two sets of scores available for analysis, for the remainder there are between three and eight sets at intervals throughout their development. This discrepancy in time was of less interest than the relative development of the phonological strategies used in reading and spelling. Each child's scores for reading and spelling were, therefore, plotted individually and readings taken at three equivalent developmental points. The mean scores for the whole group at initial and final testing and at each of the three intermediate levels are shown in Table 9.1.

Mean spelling scores were consistently and significantly higher than reading scores ($p < 0.001$). At the point at which there was the greatest discrepancy between phonological spelling and reading ability, children could spell, on average, 3.5 more words (out of a total of 12) than they could read. Inevitably, as children remained in the study until they could read and spell most of the words, the discrepancy between the two scores was reduced in the final test.

Results suggest that throughout early development, children use a phonological strategy more effectively for spelling than for reading and confirm similar conclusions of Bryant & Bradley (1980) and Cataldo & Ellis (1988). The phonological spelling process requires identification of the sounds in a word followed by correct matching of the corresponding letters. The inverse of this process is required for decoding. Blending of the appropriate sounds takes place after recognition of the letters or letter-string has occurred. Both phonological ability and letter knowledge are therefore prerequisites for using a phonological strategy for spelling or reading. Although certain children made steady progress in phonological ability, their lack of knowledge of letters impeded their spelling and reading. Conversely, some children had sufficient letter knowledge but could hardly use it as they were unable to hear more than the initial sound in the word. The combination of letter knowledge and phonological ability proved to be important in children's progress in these particular tests of reading and spelling but it does not account for the disparity between the two different skills.

As letter knowledge is common to both reading and spelling, and spelling appears to be the more easily achieved skill, it suggests that the phonological ability of hearing individual sounds in words required for spelling is also a prerequisite for reading. However, the length of time from the point at which children could spell two-letter non-words until they were able to read three-letter non-words ranged from 8 to 51 weeks — an average of 21 weeks; 65% of the children achieved it in under five months while three children required over nine months. At the point at which children were spelling three-letter non-words, they were beginning to link short vowels and consonants to read two-letter non-words such as *ap* and *ez*. Reading three-letter (consonant–vowel–consonant) non-words was the final skill to be mastered within this battery of tests. Even though children could identify correctly the three letters in a word, e.g. **P–E–Z**, they could not necessarily combine them in the correct order to produce the word. A test using real words produced a similar response.

Practical Implications

Children use a variety of strategies for reading, including visual recognition of words and semantic and syntactic cues in addition to a phonological strategy. Spelling can be achieved through both visual and phonological means. When children 'invent' spellings they are using a phonological strategy — isolating sounds and representing them with letters. As it appears that these skills are also used in reading, it follows that encouraging children to 'invent' spellings may not only aid fluency in their writing but may also be useful in reading. Furthermore, activities which enhance children's knowledge of letters and improve their phonological ability will benefit both spelling and reading.

If, as has been shown, the ability to use a phonological strategy for spelling precedes that for reading, it would seem unreasonable to expect children to 'sound out' and blend those sounds to produce words until they have a degree of phonological spelling ability. In fact, children's spelling ability could be used as an indicator of potential to use a decoding strategy for reading. However, the study indicated a delay between the onset of an ability to 'invent' spellings and the ability to decode, sometimes of many months. It can be concluded from the growing body of research that a child who can spell phonologically may be able to decode, but that one who cannot spell will be unable to decode.

These data indicate, but cannot confirm, a causal connection between the ability to use a phonological strategy for spelling and an equivalent strategy for reading. Further research is required in which groups of children are encouraged to employ different strategies for spelling, and are then assessed for an ability to use a phonological strategy for reading. Other studies, however, show an influence of spelling on reading (e.g. Cataldo & Ellis, 1988; Ehri & Wilce, 1987). Mann, Tobin & Wilson (1987) found that 'invented spelling', as a measure of phonological awareness, was a good predictor of early reading ability. There are also a number of studies (e.g. Lundberg, Frost & Peterson, 1988; Bradley, 1988) which show that increasing children's phonological skills can improve their reading ability. When children invent their own spellings they are, in effect, exercising their ability to analyse words phonologically at the same time as developing their letter knowledge. As there is a body of research to show that this sort of practice helps reading, it is a logical supposition that inventing spellings may also contribute to children's reading.

By creating her own form of words rather than asking for words to be spelled for her, Rachel was able to get her ideas down on paper fairly quickly and coherently. She enjoyed writing. Gradually she assimilated the correct forms of words. Her teachers drew her attention to irregularities in words and also common letter combinations. She was encouraged to look for letter patterns within words and developed an interest in word forms. In order to recall the spellings of certain difficult words she relied on mnemonics. Now eight years old, she continues to concoct her own spellings for words she has not learned, but now it is with an extended knowledge of the orthography rather than merely conversion from sound to letter. If, after looking at the word she is still unsure, she checks with the dictionary. On the whole, her ability to compose does not seem to have been hampered by mastering the 'writing code'.

Summary

The National Curriculum Non-Statutory Guidance implies that young children should be encouraged to write, in the first instance, using their own invented spelling. Proponents of this method recognise that this includes a phonological element. A longitudinal study was undertaken to examine the relationship between the phonological strategies used in reading and invented spelling. Forty-three children, entering a sample at ages ranging from 3:6 to 5:6, were tested and retested at approximately eight-week intervals on a series of measures of phonological ability. Results indicate that a phonological strategy for spelling is acquired prior to an equivalent strategy for reading. Teaching implications were discussed.

References

BRADLEY, L. 1988, Making connections in learning to read and to spell. *Applied Cognitive Psychology* 2, 3–18.

BRYANT, P. E. and BRADLEY, 1980, Why children sometimes write words which they do not read. In U. FRITH (ed.) *Cognitive Processes in Spelling* (pp. 355–72). London: Academic Press.

CATALDO, S. and ELLIS, N. 1988, Interaction in the development of spelling, reading and phonological skills. *Journal of Research in Reading* 11, 86–109.

CHOMSKY, C, 1970, Reading, writing and phonology. *Harvard Educational Review* 40, 2, 287–311.

CLAY, M. 1975, *What Did I Write?* Auckland: Heinemann.

D'ARCY, P. 1989, *Making Sense, Shaping Meaning*. London: Heinemann Educational.

DES (Department of Education and Science) 1988, *English 5–11* (The Cox Report). London: HMSO.

—— 1989, *English in the National Curriculum*. London: HMSO.

DYSON, A. H. 1985, Individual differences in emergent writing. In M. FARR (ed.) *Children's Early Writing Development* (pp. 59–125). Norwood, NJ: Ablex Publishing Company.

—— 1988, Negotiating among multiple words. *Technical Report No. 15*. Center for the Study of Writing, University of California, Berkeley and Carnegie Melon University.

DUNN, L. M., DUNN, L. M., WHETTON, C. and PINTILLIE, D. 1982, *British Picture Vocabulary Scale* (BPVS). Windsor: The NFER – Nelson.

EHRI, L. C. and WILCE, L. S. 1987, Does learning to spell help beginners learn to read words? *Reading Research Quarterly* 22, 47–65.

FERREIRO, E. 1986, The interplay between information and assimilation in beginning literacy. In W. TEALE and E. SULZBY (eds) *Emergent Literacy* (pp. 15–49). Norwood, NJ: Ablex Publishing Company.
FERREIRO, E. and TEBEROSKY, A. 1982, *Literacy before Schooling*. Exeter, NH: Heinemann.
FREEDMAN, S. W., DYSON, A. H., FLOWER, L. and CHAFE, W. 1987, Research in writing: Past, present and future. *Technical Report No. 1*. Center for the Study of Writing, University of California, Berkeley and Carnegie Melon University.
FRITH, U. 1985, Beneath the surface of developmental dyslexia. In K. E. PATTERSON, J. C. MARSHALL and M. COLTHEART (eds) *Surface Dyslexia* (pp. 301–30). London: Lawrence Erlbaum.
GENTRY, R. 1981, Learning to spell developmentally, *The Reading Teacher* 34, 4, 378–81.
GOSWAMI, U. 1986, Children's use of analogy in learning to read: A developmental study. *Journal of Experimental Child Psychology* 42, 73–83.
GRAVES, D. 1983, *Writing: Teachers and Children at Work*. London: Heinemann Educational.
LUNDBERG, I., FROST, J. and PETERSON, O-P. 1988, Effects of an extensive program for stimulating phonological awareness in pre-school children. *Reading Research Quarterly* 23, 3, 263–84.
MANN, V. A., TOBIN, P. and WILSON, R. 1987, Measuring phonological awareness through the invented spellings of kindergarten children. *Merrill-Palmer Quarterly* 33, 3, 365–91.
READ, C. 1971, Preschool children's knowledge of English phonology. *Harvard Educational Review* 41, 1–34.
SMITH, F. 1982, *Writing and the Writer*. London: Heinemann Educational.
SULZBY, E., BARNHART, J. and HIESHIMA, J. 1989, Forms of writing and rereading from writing: A preliminary report. Technical Report No. 20. Center for the Study of Writing, University of California, Berkeley and Carnegie Melon University.

10 Developmental Differences in Phonological Spelling Strategies

EMMA TAYLOR and MARGARET MARTLEW

Introduction

Literacy research has tended to focus largely on reading. However, the advent of major changes to the UK's educational system and the criticism of current literacy skills signals a need for thorough investigation of spelling strategies. In particular, more research on the development of spelling strategies is required. If children differ from the adults who teach them in the spelling strategies they employ, this would have important implications for teaching practice. An explicit identification of children's spelling strategies, and an understanding of how and why these differ from those used by adults, would enable teachers to modify or develop their pupils' inappropriate strategies. For example, an understanding of children's spelling may help to identify the causes behind common spelling errors and subsequently appropriate methods for their correction. Since much of spelling instruction relies on emphasising the relationship between sound and spelling, we feel that the development of phonetic spelling strategies is a particularly important research area.

The spelling task

Phonetic, visual and lexical strategies are used in spelling but there is some debate as to the relative importance of each to good spelling. Whether strategies prove appropriate or inappropriate will depend upon how well adapted they are to the task they attempt to tackle. Since spelling involves an accurate representation of the English orthography, an examination of this orthography may shed some light on potentially helpful spelling strategies. The English orthography has been described as consisting of two major systems (Pyles & Algeo, 1982). One system is comprised of words and morphemes, whilst the other contains phonemes. However, theorists disagree as to which system is fundamental to contemporary spelling structure. Read (1986) argued that spelling represents phonemes rather than morphemes. However, Chomsky (1970) stated that spelling embodies abstract lexical meanings. Venezky's (1970) conclusion, that phonological, morphological and syntactical patterns all coexist and interact within the orthography, offers a compromise between the former opposing views.

Another means of making sense of the complex structure of the orthography is to look at its historical origins and development. Our present orthography developed from Old English (eighth century to twelfth century). Old English was based upon an Irish modification of the Roman alphabet and, like both Latin and Greek, was a phonetic system in that spellings had a one to one relationship with sounds (Scragg, 1974). Over the following centuries foreign influences, including loan words, the use of French after the Norman conquest and the great vowel shift in the fifteenth century changed the pronunciation and grammar and thus destroyed the phonetic nature of Old English.

There is a phonetic component to the English orthography rendering phonetic strategies as potentially useful to the spelling task. The use of such strategies can circumvent learning each word's graphemic pattern and help in the spelling of unfamiliar words (Mann, Tobin & Wilson, 1987). However, our current orthography is not a purely phonetic system and therefore the use of phonetic strategies alone would not be enough to guarantee good spelling.

Spelling strategies

Given that phonetic patterns do exist within our orthography, it is not surprising that both adults and children use phonetic spelling strategies (e.g. Liberman *et al.*, 1974; Frith & Frith, 1980). Although research in this area is scarce and often contradictory, a review indicates that phonetic spelling may develop in two ways. Firstly, unlike children, adults appear to have learnt that phonetic strategies are not adequate to cope with the irregular nature of our orthography. Whilst most children rely solely on phonetic strategies (Marsh *et al.*, 1980), adults have access to other strategies, e.g. rote learning, should a phonetic approach fail in spelling (Marsh *et al.*, 1980; Sloboda, 1980).

Secondly, whilst both adults and children do adopt a phonetic approach to spelling, there is evidence that this differs between the groups. Read (1986) examined a sample of creative spellings by pre-school children and found that even at this early age children were segmenting words into spelling–sound correspondences. For example, children used alphabetic letters to represent sounds, e.g. **LADE** for *lady* and **FAS** for *face*. In addition, the children were making consistent judgements about the relatedness and relative salience of phonetic properties. For example, children recognised the similarity in the sounds of /t/ in *trip* and the /tʃ/ in *chip* (both are affricated sounds), e.g. **CHRAC** for *truck*.

Read also found that children tended to use spellings of short vowels for their long counterparts. Read concluded that children perceive and use phonological properties that adults no longer distinguish. However, Read provides no indication as to whether such phonetic judgements are made by older subjects or whether they are unique to pre-school creative spellers. Treiman (1985) provided evidence that older children do still make such judgements. She administered spelling, phoneme recognition and phoneme deletion tasks to kindergarten, first and second grade children. In all age groups, some children recognised the similarity between affricated sounds and again tended to prefer the spelling /tʃ/ for /tr/ in words such as *truck*. This tendency was strongest amongst children who knew little about standard spelling. She concluded that children are aware of phonetic details which are inaccessible to adults and that the phonetic judgements they make could interfere with their learning of spelling–sound relationships.

Whilst both Read and Treiman have demonstrated that children's spellings do reflect classification of speech sounds, without drawing a direct comparison between child and adult samples they cannot safely conclude that adults do not make similar phonetic judgements but, for example, override these with visual strategies. The current experiment sought to investigate such differences by directly comparing adults' and children's phonetic judgements or strategies.

The Experiment

Hypotheses

Using a phonetic dictation task, the current experiment was designed to investigate the development of phonetic spelling strategies. In particular, we expected to find that spelling involves a basic strategy of dividing words into constituent phonemes and a subsequent search for their invariant spelling correspondences. However, we predicted that this strategy develops with age in that it becomes more finely tuned to the demands and rules of our spelling system.

Procedure

Thirty-two adults and 46 children were given a dictation task. The adults were all literate, aged 20–70 years and came from a variety of geographical localities, educational backgrounds and socioeconomic statuses. The children were taken from two Sheffield schools and were aged eight to nine years.

Subjects were asked to spell a list of 14 words as they sounded, i.e. as the presenter pronounced them. It was emphasised that this was not a test and that any answer, including correct spellings, would be acceptable. Only one experimenter read the test words to the subjects; a female with a standard English accent.

In our orthography, grapheme–phoneme correspondences alternate according to the graphemic environment (Venezky, 1970). In the current experiment, the 14 test words consisted of seven pairs (one high frequency and one low-frequency word for each pair — see Table 10.1) containing seven such grapheme–phoneme correspondences. Two pairs spelt the phoneme /ɔ:/, one with the **AU** spelling the other with the **AW** spelling. These two spellings of /ɔ:/ have equal distributions in the orthography. Five pairs spelt the phoneme /i:/ with **EA**, **EE**, **IE** (frequent spellings in the orthography) and **EI** and **I** (infrequent spellings in the orthography). See Table 10.1.

TABLE 10.1   *Test words*

	Frequency	
Phoneme	*High*	*Low*
	belief	niece
	agree	canteen
/i/	clean	conceal
	police	sardine
	receive	conceit
/o/	awful	dawn
	audience	trauma

To establish whether familiarity with a word influenced phonetic spelling, one word of high and another of low frequency was chosen for each alternation (Francis, Kucera & Mackie, 1982).

To prevent interference with phonological spelling, no homophones or morphemes were included. The words were taken from Venezky (1970) and Craigie (1928).

Results

In the analysis only the spellings used to represent the phonemes /iː/ and /ɔː/ were extracted from each word. Means of the numbers of participants using each grapheme–phoneme correspondence are given in Table 10.2.

Chi goodness of fit tests were used to establish whether certain grapheme–phoneme correspondences were more prevalent than others in each word. See Table 10.3.

Word frequency had little effect upon the choice of grapheme–phoneme correspondences. This indicates that familiarity with the lexical representations of the words did not interfere with the phonetic spellings subjects were trying to produce. The only influence of frequency detected in either subject group was children's maintenance of **I** as the dominant correspondence for /iː/ in the high frequency *police* but not in low frequency *sardine*.

A number of differences in the spellings of children and adults were apparent. Although all subjects segmented words into phonemes and tended to prefer the use of one graphemic unit for each phoneme, this tendency was stronger for adults. Whilst the prevalent correspondence in children's spelling varied from word to word, adults consistently used the same correspondence regardless of the surrounding graphemic environment. See Table 10.3. Thus **EE** was the dominant graphemic unit used by adults for the phoneme /iː/ whilst children used **EE, I** and **EA**. Similarly, **OR** was the single main spelling used by adults to represent /ɔː/ whilst children used **O, OR** and **AW** depending on the individual word.

In addition, children tended to use a larger range of graphemic unit for each phoneme than adults. See Table 10.2. Although both groups used the same range of spellings for /iː/, unlike adults who only used **AU, AW** and **OR** to represent the phoneme /ɔː/, children used seven spellings; **AU, AW, OR, O, U, OO** and **AL**.

TABLE 10.2 *Means and percentages for grapheme–phoneme correspondences used to represent /iː/ and /ɔː/*

	Adults	Children
Grapheme correspondence for /iː/		
EE	25.3 80.3%	19.1 42.5%
EA	2.1 6.5%	7.7 17.1%
EI	0.7 1.5%	0.9 2.0%
IE	0.2 0.6%	1.5 3.0%
I	1.4 4.4%	8.3 18.4%
E	1.8 5.6%	7.2 16.0%
Grapheme correspondence for /ɔː/		
AU	2.7 8.4%	3.2 7.2%
AW	8.5 18.8%	8.5 19.3%
OR	20.5 64.1%	16.7 37.9%
O	—	10.7 24.3%
OO	—	2.0 4.5%
AL	—	1.0 2.3%
U	—	2.0 4.5%

TABLE 10.3 *Results from Chi goodness of fit tests with major spellings*

Word	Adults df	x		Children df	x	
belief	4	51.7 **	EE	4	7.3	
niece	3	66.7 **	EE	4	17.7 *	EE
clean	2	28.9 **	EE	4	49.2 **	EE
conceal	2	25.8 **	EE	3	13.3 *	EE & EA
police	3	44.7 **	EE	3	39.9 **	I
sardine	3	43.2 **	EE	3	16.9 **	EE & I
agree	1	24.5 **	EE	2	46.2 **	EE
canteen	3	73.5 **	EE	2	43.2 **	EE
receive	2	33.2 **	EE	3	12.8 *	EE
conceit	2	15.4 **	EE	4	20.9 **	EE & EA
awful	2	18.8 **	OR	3	14.5 *	OR
dawn	2	16.9 **	OR	2	6.53 0.05	AW
trauma	2	4.8		3	11.9 *	O
audience	1	10.1 *	OR	2	14.1 **	OR

* = $p < 0.01$, ** = $p < 0.001$

Finally, children preferred different grapheme–phoneme correspondences from adults, namely **E** and **I** for /i:/ and **O** for /ɔ:/. Chi square tests of association and one tailed fisher exact probability tests were performed on each word. Two by two contingency tables contained row categories of adults and children and column categories of **E** combined with **I** and **EE**, and **OR** and **O**.

EE was significantly associated with adults and **E** and **I** with children in *belief* ($x = 19.9$, df $= 1, p < 0.001$); *niece* ($x = 10.7$, df $= 1, p < 0.001$); *police* ($x = 29.4$, df $= 1, p < 0.001$); *sardine* ($x = 6.6$, df $= 1, p < 0.01$) and *receive* ($x = 19.5$, df $= 1, p < 0.001$).

OR was significantly associated with adults and **O** with children in *trauma* ($x = 19.6$, df $= 1, p < 0.001$); *awful* ($p < 0.001$) and *audience* ($p < 0.01$).

Discussion

Both adults and children are able to employ phonetic strategies in spelling. Subjects treated the phonemes /i:/ and /ɔ:/ as separate entities in each word illustrating that subjects divided words into their constituent phonemes. In addition, subjects tended to use legitimate and usually major graphemic correspondences to represent phonemes regardless of their correct spellings and the word frequency. Thus a phonetic strategy may involve splitting words into constituent phonemes and subsequently searching for and committing to memory consistent grapheme correspondences for each phoneme, i.e. grapheme–phoneme correspondences.

However, the findings indicate that this search appears to develop in two ways. Firstly, children have not yet learnt to associate one major graphemic unit with each phoneme but instead represent phonemes using a large range of often legitimate grapheme–phoneme correspondences. Children were less consistent than adults in their use of grapheme–phoneme correspondences. Whilst adults use major grapheme–phoneme correspondences, i.e. **EE** for /i:/ and **OR** for /ɔ:/, children's preferred correspondences varied according to the word being spelt. In addition, children used a greater range of spellings for the phoneme /ɔ:/. We propose that this inconsistency may be caused by an unskilled search for invariant grapheme–phoneme correspondences in the orthography. Children appear to know that /i:/ and /ɔ:/ are represented by a number of spellings and use these randomly.

Secondly, whilst both adults and children split words into constituent phonemes, the findings indicate that adults use different phonological judgements from children when presented with the same task. This is illustrated in the difference in grapheme–phoneme correspondences employed by the two groups. Unlike children, adults consistently use **EE** and **OR** to represent /iː/ and /ɔː/. Both are major correspondences to these phonemes (Christopherson, 1956; Venezky, 1970) and, out of all the possible alternatives, have the fewest legal pronunciations in English spelling (Schonell, 1951), i.e. **EE** and **OR** are nearly always pronounced /iː/ and /ɔː/ respectively and are rarely used to spell other phonemes. Adults appear to have represented the most frequent and consistent grapheme–phoneme correspondences within the English orthography.

Unlike adults, children also used **E** and **I** to spell /iː/ and **O** to spell /ɔː/. There are two possible explanations for this finding: (1) the children's spelling education influences their use of spelling–sound correspondences; (2) children represent different invariant features of our orthography than adults in their spellings.

All children were taught using the Schonell's (1951) spelling method. Reference to the spelling lists used by Schonell showed that the phoneme /iː/ is infrequently spelt by **I** or **E** and that, up to the age of ten, no cases of /ɔː/ are represented by **O**. We therefore conclude that education does not provide an adequate explanation for the use of these spellings.

The second explanation is that children make different phonetic judgements from adults and these affect their choice of grapheme correspondences for individual phonemes. The phonemes /i/ and /ɔː/ are both vowel sounds. Vowels are classified according to where in the mouth they are formed, i.e. front or back: to the shape of the lips which forms the vowel sound, i.e. open or closed: to the muscle tension in the tongue and to the length of the sound, i.e. long or short. The phonemes /I/ and /iː/ are both front vowels and the phonemes /ɒ/ and /ɔː/ are back vowels but both pairs differ in length and tension as well as spellings (see Table 10.4).

Children appear to be recognising the similarity between long and short vowels and generalising the spellings of short vowels to their long counterparts. Whilst adults realise that vowel sounds which differ in length and tension are spelt differently from each other, children have not grasped this rule. In addition, children used the letter name **E** to represent /iː/. This indicates that children have learnt to associate individual phonemes with graphemes, in this case the alphabetic letter **E**, but have not yet learnt major legitimate correspondences for this sound in our spelling system. These results are consistent with the developmental stages in vowel spelling outlined by Bees & Gentry, 1974, cited in Read, 1986); the omission of the vowel; use of the letter name or lax/tense pairing of correspondences; an

TABLE 10.4 *Differences between vowel pairs*

	/iː/	/ɪ/	/ɔː/	/ɒ/
Pronunciation	*deep*	*dip*	*poured*	*pod*
Position	front	front	back	back
Length	long	short	long	short
Tension	tense	lax	tense	lax
Major spellings	**EE** *feet* **EA** *feast*	**I** *fit*	**OR** *gored* **AW** *law* **AU** *haul*	**O** *god* **A** *wander*
Alternative spellings	**E** *eve* **IE** *field* **EI** *deceit* **I** *machine*	**E** *pretty* **IE** *sieve* **EI** *foreign*	**OUGH** *fought* **AR** *warm* **A** *all*	**OU** *cough* **AU** *because*

incorrect standard correspondence and finally the standard spelling. The present results also replicate Read's findings (Read, 1986) that children spell long vowels like their short vowels and spell long vowels with their letter name, e.g. the use of **E** to represent /iː/. The current experiment indicates that these tendencies noted in a sample of pre-school creative spellers continue up to school age.

The use of the same spelling for long/short vowel sounds occurred in Old English and has been demonstrated in previous studies. The apparent strength of this tendency suggests that phonetic judgements about vowels may be made according to the motor movements used in producing the sounds themselves, i.e. according to whereabouts in the mouth phonemes are formed.

To summarise, a phonetic strategy may involve splitting words into constituent phonemes and subsequently searching for and committing to memory consistent grapheme correspondences for individual phonemes. However, this basic strategy differs with the age of the speller in two ways. First, children, unlike adults, have not learnt to associate one major graphemic unit with each phoneme. Secondly, children make different judgements from adults about which properties of phonemes should be represented in spelling. These interfere with their choice of grapheme–phoneme correspondences. Finally, we suggest that such phonetic judgements may be made on the basis of where a vowel sound is formed in the mouth, i.e. of motor co-ordination.

Implications for Future Research and Teaching Practice

The current experiment asked subjects to perform an unnatural task; ignored the role of pronunciation differences between subjects and simplified analysis by focusing only on the spelling of certain phonemes in each word. However, the fact that these findings replicate others and indicate differences between adults and children point to the area of developmental differences in phonetic spelling strategies as an important one for future research. In particular, this experiment indicates that the judgements children make about the relations between different phonemes and how these judgements interfere with the spelling task need to be investigated.

The findings also have important implications for teaching practice. Phonetic strategies may be useful to the early speller and the evidence suggests that these are indeed employed. Children bring their own phonetic judgements to spelling linking phonemes to specific spellings. Therefore, whilst teaching spelling–sound correspondences may be a useful approach, care should be taken to emphasise the *differences* as well as the similarities between sounds in words. For example, teachers might consider focusing on the differences in sound and in spelling between vowel pairs such as /iː/ and /I/ and affricated consonants such as /t/ in *truck* and /tʃ/ in *church*.

Unlike adults, children may be confused by the many spelling alternatives to different vowels. Teachers could help children by emphasising the most common grapheme–phoneme correspondences complementing this by emphasising the importance of the visual pattern of irregular spellings. As we have argued, phonetic strategies are not enough to guarantee good spelling and children should be encouraged to develop a visual awareness of words.

Above all, since spelling strategies are dictated by the nature of the English orthography itself, teachers may like to consider the importance of teaching children a little about the history of our orthography. This could include, for example, giving simple descriptions of the origin of irregular words or grouping words according to similarities in origins, sound and spelling. This may help children to understand, and even enjoy, the sometimes illogical nature of our spelling system.

Summary

An examination of the structure and history of the English orthography indicates that phonetic strategies are vital to the spelling task. Psychological literature concerning changes in phonetic strategies in spelling is scarce and findings are contradictory. This experiment was designed to establish the role of phonetic strategies in spelling in children and adults.

Twenty-eight adults and 46 children were asked to spell 14 test words correctly and as they sounded. Results indicate that spelling involves a search for invariant phonetic features but that the representation of these features varies with spelling age.

References

CHOMSKY, C. 1970, Reading, writing and phonology. *Harvard Educational Review* 40, 287–309.
CHRISTOPHERSON, P. 1956, *An English Phonetic Course*. London: Longman.
CRAIGIE, W. A. 1928, *English Spelling — its Rules and Reasons*. London: George Harrap.
FRANCIS, W. N., KUCERA, H. and MACKIE, A. W. 1982, *Frequency Analysis of English Usage and Lexicon and Grammar*. Boston: Houghton Mifflin.
FRITH, U. and FRITH, C. 1980, Relationship between reading and spelling. In J. F. KAVANAGH and R. L. VENEZKY (eds) *Orthography, Reading and Dyslexia*. Baltimore: University Press.
LIBERMAN, I. Y., SCHANKWEILER, D., FISCHER, F. W. and CARTER, B. 1974, Explicit syllable and phoneme segmentation in the young child. *Journal of Experimental Child Psychology* 18, 201–12.
MANN, V. A. TOBIN, P. and WILSON, R. 1987, Measuring phonological awareness through the invented spellings of kindergarten children. *Merill Palmer Quarterly* 33, 365–75.

MARSH, G., FRIEDMAN, M., WELCH, V. and DESBERG, P. 1980, The development of strategies in spelling. In U. FRITH (ed.) *Cognitive Processes in Spelling*. London: Academic Press.

PYLES, J. and ALGEO, J. 1982, *The Origin and Development of the English Language*. New York: Jovanovich.

READ, C. 1986, *Children's Creative Spelling*. London: Routledge and Kegan Paul.

SCHONELL, F. J. 1951, *Essentials in Teaching and Testing Spelling*. London: Macmillan.

SCRAGG, D. G. 1974, *A History of English Spelling*. Manchester: Manchester University Press.

SLOBODA, J. A. 1980, Visual imagery and individual differences. In U. FRITH (ed.) *Cognitive Processes in Spelling*. London: Academic Press.

TREIMAN, R. 1985, Phonemic awareness and spelling: Children's judgements do not always agree with adults'. *Journal of Experimental Child Psychology* 39, 182–201.

VENEZKY, R. L. 1970, *The Structure of English Orthography*. The Hague: Mouton.

Section Four: Spelling Problems

Introduction

There are two papers in this section. Campbell, Burden & Wright look at the spelling of the born-deaf while Burden examines the reading and spelling ability of Type B spellers, people who are poor spellers but allegedly good readers.

Spelling and Speaking in Pre-lingual Deafness: Unexpected Evidence for Isolated 'Alphabetic' Spelling Skills (Campbell, Burden & Wright)

Intuitively, we would not expect the born-deaf to have developed a notion of the sound system of the language. For example, we would not expect them to have much conception of phonemes, syllables or words; or of concepts such as rhyme, alliteration and spoonerism; or to be able to play word games based on the sounds of words; or to have a grasp of the alphabetic principle. We would expect their literacy to be based on their visual rather than their alphabetic skills. This paper suggests that such intuitions would be wrong.

They begin by reviewing the deaf's performance on tasks where some knowledge of the sound system and/or the alphabetic principle seems to be required. The picture is less than clear. On the one hand the evidence suggests that deaf children can behave like hearing children. For example, they can make rhyming judgements and are confused by homophones. On the other hand we know from studies of developmental (phonological) dyslexia that people can become remarkably proficient readers and spellers without phonological awareness or alphabetic skills. The question is whether the deaf's apparent knowledge of a sound system and alphabetic principle is genuine or an artefact of compensatory strategies like those shown by some dyslexics.

To answer the question Campbell, Burden & Wright look at the effect of (a) word frequency, and (b) spelling regularity on deaf children's spelling. The logic of their experiment is this: the less well known a word the less the speller can rely on visual memory (the lexical route) and the more he or she has to rely on generating the spelling using phonology and sound–spelling correspondences (the phonological route). Similarly, the more irregular a word the more the speller has to rely on visual memory because generating the spelling will produce misspellings, albeit phonetically plausible ones. These manipulations are therefore a source of information about how children are spelling, but to find out what the deaf are doing we need to compare their performance with the hearing. Should we, however, be looking at children of the same chronological age or the same reading age?

Children of the same chronological age should have advanced well into the orthographic stage of Frith's model and so be unaffected by irregularity when the word is familiar, and to some unknown degree when the word is unfamiliar, producing plausible but incorrect spellings in the latter case. Children of the same reading age (though chronologically younger), should still be in the alphabetic stage of spelling and so be substantially affected by irregularity, certainly for the unfamiliar words but also for the familiar words.

Overall, the deaf performed at a level between the two hearing groups. They were poorer at spelling than their chronological age controls (confirming the problem their disability causes) but better than their reading age controls (suggesting that their spelling is more advanced than their reading). They were clearly affected by irregularity, and produced plausible spellings, suggesting the use of phonology and the alphabetic principle rather than a visual strategy.

Campebll, Burden & Wright interpret the deaf's advanced (relative to reading) phonological spelling to mean that the Frith/Seymour model, with its linkage between reading the spelling, doesn't hold, and that spelling and reading in the deaf develop along separate and normal (though delayed) paths. They speculate that the deaf might not use phonology automatically when reading, as they do in spelling, but uncouple the two to pursue a visual reading strategy. They conclude we should not assume that the deaf cannot acquire the alphabetic principle but should encourage them to do so.

Why Are Some 'Normal' Readers Such Poor Spellers? (Burden)

Burden's paper is concerned with people who seem to be good readers but poor spellers (Type B spellers). Their spelling tends to be phonetic, with

INTRODUCTION: SPELLING PROBLEMS

a disregard for spelling rules and the finer points of English spelling. They are poor at identifying spelling errors, even their own, and find it difficult to select the correct spelling from a number of possibilities. The question is whether these people have only a spelling deficit, or whether they also have a (hidden) reading problem. Burden seeks to distinguish between two explanations of Type B spellers.

The first, that of Frith, argues that their problem is with spelling; that even though they do have a slightly different reading strategy which relies on partial cues to word identity they are perfectly competent readers, functionally indistinguishable from normal and even good readers. Their neglect of the detailed structure of words only becomes evident in their spelling, which generally fails to take account of the many rules and idiosyncrasies of English spelling.

The second explanation is that of Bruck & Waters, who argue that Type B spellers have a pervasive problem which affects both their spelling *and their reading*. They have difficulty in converting spelling to sound (reading) and sound to spelling (spelling). However, the problem is not at the phoneme–grapheme level but with larger chunks, where the relationship is a more sophisticated one, e.g. silent E spellings of long vowels, e.g. *make, tone, like*. Bruck & Waters argue that Type Bs tend to be slower and more reliant on context *when reading* than other good readers. They are, in effect, mildly dyslexic.

As Burden points out, Frith's theory predicts that Type B spellers should not differ from good readers/spellers (Type As) on reading tasks, including those where non-words are used, but will differ on spelling tasks, especially when the words are irregular. In contrast, according to Bruck & Waters, Type Bs should be slower and less fluent than type As on reading tasks, including non-words, and spell more poorly, particularly when higher level correspondences are involved.

Burden's experiment supports the view of Bruck & Waters. She found Type As to be both speedy and accurate when reading real words, being only slightly affected by low frequency or irregularity. In contrast, Type Bs were significantly affected (both speed and accuracy) by regularity of spelling when the words are low frequency. When reading non-words, Type Bs were slower, less accurate, less consistent and more affected by word length and word structure. In spelling they again differed. While type As were slightly affected by low frequency irregular words, Type Bs were significantly affected by word frequency, irregularity and these two factors acting interactively. They also differed in the kinds of errors they make in both reading and spelling. She also found that Type Bs had more problems with a phonological awareness task (a powerful predictor of reading and spelling skill) and were worse on a test of text reading speed and comprehension. She concludes that Type B spellers are indeed mildly dyslexic and that their *reading* problem is concealed by the development of compensatory strategies.

Burden concludes with the implications of her research. She suggests how Type B children can be identified on the basis of a growing discrepancy between spelling and other language abilities; poor phonological awareness; poor non-word spelling and reading; poor proofreading; and their often inaccurate and slow oral reading. With respect to remediation, she suggests structured phonics training and the teaching of literacy using word families, morphemic structure and a greater reliance on visual strategies.

11 Spelling and Speaking in Pre-lingual Deafness: Unexpected Evidence for Isolated 'Alphabetic' Spelling Skills

RUTH CAMPBELL, VIVIAN BURDEN and HELEN WRIGHT

Introduction

People born deaf are generally very poor readers and writers. One contributory reason (though believed by some to be a minor one) could be that they are unable to use the sound-to-letter mappings of English script (the alphabetic principle) to help guide their reading and, particularly, spelling. A number of people have been reported who cannot use the alphabetic principle in reading and writing, despite good hearing and normal speech development. They are phonologically dyslexic. Such people can reach high levels of literacy, but with a qualitative pattern to their reading and spelling that differs from most people. It is feasible that the deaf tend to use such non-alphabetic methods — that they resemble phonological dyslexics.

We have been examining born-deaf school leavers to see to what extent they show the signature of such non-alphabetic processing in their spelling (and in other tasks). Far from behaving like phonological dyslexics these deaf students relied on the aphabetic principle to a marked extent. This has been demonstrated for *some* deaf people. But this general finding gives rise to two questions:

(1) is the alphabetic principle really dependent on hearing speech — or is it more abstract: an ability to extract regularities from the flow of written letter-based texts?

(2) how do we use this knowledge that such detailed *internal* structures are available to teenage deaf people to improve their language skills?

In most literate readers and writers of English, whether children or adults, there is quite a close link between three particular cognitive skills. These are:

- phonological skills, such as spoonerising (*Phil Collins* becomes *Kill Follins*), 'sound-stripping' games (*pie* becomes *eye*, *store* becomes *tore*, *spare* becomes *pair*, etc.), or finding the odd-man-out in three words such as *pool*, *stool* and *poor*;
- immediate verbal memory — tasks like remembering lists of spoken or written numbers or letters in sequence; and
- reading and spelling — here, reading and spelling has a circumscribed meaning: just the decoding operations of matching the written letters to the intended words are what is being considered.

When we find someone who is poor at one of these tasks, we often (but not invariably) find that ability to do the other tasks is compromised too. In this chapter we consider what the implications of this triad of skills are in considering how reading and writing might be acquired in people who are born deaf, and how this relates to skilled spelling and reading in people who are not deaf.

People deprived of aural language from birth are typically in the same range of tested non-verbal intelligence as hearing people (Furth, 1966), but their language capacities may be much reduced. In particular, reading and writing in the 'typical' deaf child will seem to be several years behind that of comparably aged hearing children, so that the deaf 16-year-old very often leaves school with a reading age of around eight to ten years. One aspect of their poor reading might be related to the triad of skills outlined above. Perhaps in the absence of hearing one cannot develop phonological skills sufficient to support reading, writing and short-term memory. Certainly a number of studies with the deaf suggest they can be poor at the tasks related to reading and writing ability. But on the whole the work we have been engaged in suggests a very different pattern.

It would be wrong to claim that people born deaf necessarily fail to acquire phonological structures that can support and interact with reading and writing. A number of lines of evidence converge in indicating that the born-deaf might be slow at developing phonological competence, but that the basic cognitive structures to support it need not wither because of lack of auditory nourishment. However, this evidence is partial and selective: deaf people, as a group, do not perform like hearing people on tasks that tap phonological segmentation and awareness; their abilities are circumscribed and partial, and it is in trying to explain this partiality that problems arise.

However, among the 'suggestive facts' are these: the phonological development of the deaf child need not be particularly aberrant, although it is often very badly delayed (see Dodd (1987) for case histories). Thus, deaf children often make the same sorts of mistake in their first utterances as do hearing children; simplifying and deleting 'difficult' consonants in clusters, for instance. These studies have been performed on orally raised children exposed solely or primarily to the seen speech of the language community into which the child is born; where sign is the first language of the child, the phonological status of speech becomes less important in communication and systematic studies are lacking. In adults and in school children, Conrad (1964; 1972) noted that some deaf people made phonological confusions in recalling lists, just like hearing people (for instance **C-V-D-T** would be harder to recall than **P-L-B-J**). We (Campbell & Wright, 1988) following several others (Hanson & Fowler, 1987; Waters & Doehring, 1989; Dodd, 1987) have found that the deaf can make rhyme judgements on words and pictures. They can also use homophony (*rain* and *reign* sound alike, though they are written differently) in a number of tasks (Waters & Doehring, 1989; Dodd, 1987; Dodd & Hermelin, 1977).

Some of the most impressive evidence for the phonological skills of the deaf comes from studies in Belgium performed by Jacqueline Leybaert and her colleagues (Leybaert, Alegria & Morais, 1982; Leybaert, Alegria & Fonck, 1983; Leybaert, 1987). These concern the Stroop Colour Word phenomenon. If one is asked to name the colour in which a word is written (or printed) the name of the word can interfere with naming the colour. This is most pronounced when the word is itself a colour word other than the colour carrier. So seeing the word *blue* which is printed in red requires the response 'red' . . . but this seems to be blocked by the word *blue* which slows the response down. The deaf show just such effects in their colour naming of written words. But even more suggestive of phonological work is the effect of seeing the letter string **BLOO**. This isn't a real word, though it sounds like the colour word. This, too, blocks naming the colour — and to a similar extent in the deaf as in hearing subjects.

These elegant studies tell us that in looking at words both deaf and hearing people cannot inhibit the 'wrong' word-related sounds from starting to be produced. Furthermore, when the letter string is pronounced like the interfering word that too cannot be suppressed. The activation of speech sounds associated with letters seem, in these conditions, to be as automatic in deaf as in hearing people. Similarly, Dodd (1987) reports that when asked to check a piece of written text and to cancel every occurrence of the letter G some deaf subjects, like the hearing subjects in the same study, systematically 'missed' silent-Gs (NI̲GHT, REI̲GN) suggesting automatic phonological recoding of written text in this subgroup of deaf students, at least.

In a study we have shown (Campbell & Wright, 1990) that deaf teenagers are just like children of similar reading age in the way that they remember lists of pictured items like *caterpillar, umbrella, bat, bee*. Baddeley, Thomson & Buchanan (1975) first showed that in adult hearing people the number of words one could recall in order was determined by the spoken length of the word — even when the word was written (or seen in picture form — Schiano & Watkins, 1981). That is, that the spoken length of the item can affect span. One remembers longer lists of shorter words. In children, this sensitivity to word length develops during the early (primary) school years, suggesting that young children do not necessarily remember lists by saying them to themselves (Hitch, 1990). So in the (hearing) eight to nine-year-olds we looked at we found somewhat ambivalent evidence for word-length effects: when they recalled the items they had seen by pointing to the pictures in sequence or by sorting picture cards in order, there was no word length effect, but when they named the items at recall there was a word-length effect, with more short-name items recalled. Deaf teenagers (16–17 years) behaved *exactly* like these much younger, reading-age matched children on this task.

In one place where we had expected to find effects of phonological structure, we found none (Campbell & Wright, 1990). This was a task that had been reported to be sensitive to sound structure in some deaf children (Dodd & Hermelin, 1977). They are presented with pairs of pictured items to remember and later, one of each pair is shown and the child has to find the one that matched it (paired associate memory). When the pictures rhyme (i.e. pictured *fly* and *eye*) are children better than when they don't (e.g. *eye* and *bat*)? Hearing children certainly are, but we found no deaf child or teenager who *spontaneously* used the *implicit* rhyme clue in this task.

So the general picture presented by deaf teenagers is a rather confused one when it comes to assessing the depth and range of their phonological skills in reading, remembering and playing language games. On the whole, using pictured stimuli, we found that we could guide deaf subjects into using speech-based structures, but that they did not necessarily use them spontaneously. Also, their phonological skills seemed to resemble those of reading-age, not real-age hearing controls. This suggested to us that *experience with reading and writing* has generated the phonological skills that the deaf child shows. Very often one assumes that the link must be the other **way round**,

SPELLING AND SPEAKING IN PRE-LINGUAL DEAFNESS 189

with awareness of phonological structures needed to support the early stages of reading and writing (e.g. Liberman, 1973). Like several other investigators, we found quite marked individual differences in our deaf subjects: good speakers and good lip-readers were usually also good at the tasks outlined here (see Dodd (1987) for more on this link).

Short — Or Other — Cuts to Reading and Writing

These studies did not look directly at reading and writing. But some work with Brian Butterworth made us wonder whether, in fact, it was necessary for reading and writing in the deaf to be related in any way to their phonological and short-term memory skills. That work concerned a single university student, R.E. (Campbell & Butterworth, 1985; Butterworth, Campbell & Howard, 1986). She had excellent hearing and normal speech acquisition but extremely idiosyncratic reading and writing. She was completely unable to read or write new or nonsense words: even simple ones like *sast* or *bilk*. We found that she had no useful notion of the mapping of sounds to letters: for example, she thought there were four sounds in the spoken word *ache,* and she was unable to spoonerise sounds, though she could move *letters* around (i.e. she could turn *pool* into *loop,* but *Phil Collins* spoonerised to *Chill, something*). She was poor at immediate recall of heard letters and numbers, but improved with written material and also when she closed her eyes and visualised the spoken numbers or letters. It seemed to us that this young woman had no access to phonological structures in her own speech and hearing — despite perfect speech perception and production. This was a really 'central' problem of phonological awareness. But she did have good visual memory for letters and their positions in words and this meant that she was able to use 'look and say' methods in learning to read and spell — and to do so very successfully. Her spelling was as good as that of other undergraduates; she spelled words like *phlegm* and *accident* correctly. But her errors did not look like 'normal' spelling errors. She did not make errors that sounded like the target word but, rather, respected most of the visual written aspects of the word — an example could be **RTHYTM** for **RHYTHM**. R.E.'s extreme 'un-phonological' reading and writing *style,* rather than any quantitative measures of reading and writing skill, indicate a label of dyslexia. Moreover, just this pattern of abilities and debilities, with preserved word reading and spelling but no sensitivity whatever to letter–sound mappings, has been described in cases of acquired dyslexia following brain injury in a previously fully literate person, where it is labelled 'phonological dyslexia'. Characteristic of phonological dyslexia (and the corresponding writing style of phonological dysgraphia) are (1) failure to read and write new or non-words; and (2) no sensitivity in reading or spelling to the regularities of English spelling. Irregular words such as *sponge, crypt, rough,* are as well managed as regular ones like *like, freeze, spring.*

Now, it has sometimes been reported that this is the sort of pattern observed in deaf reading and writing. For example, it is widely thought that the deaf are less likely than hearing people to be misled by irregular mappings of sounds to letters. Consequently, in spelling English, they may be less impaired in spelling words where the sound-to-letter correspondence is not predictable (irregularly spelled words). In one of the first reported experimental studies of reading and writing in the deaf, Gates & Chase (1927) reported that the deaf could often spell better than might be predicted from their reading level — and the reason was just this 'failure to be misled by sound in spelling'. More directly, Waters & Doehring (1990) in a careful study of word reading in deaf youngsters find that this group, unlike their hearing controls, were no faster at recognising regularly spelled than irregular words and showed no sensitivity to rhyme when pairs of words were presented. The task, in each case was lexical decision; the subject sees a word or non-word on a screen and responds by pressing a button 'yes' for a word, 'no' for a non-word. Thus this task is a task of speed of processing at the level of word recognition. Similar findings — of a failure in sensitivity to the letter–sound regularities of English — have been reported in a number of other studies with deaf people and have led to such conclusions as the following:

> That profoundly deaf people can read at all is sometimes taken as evidence that speech recoding in normal readers is optional. (Conrad, 1972)

> However . . . they do not read very well . . . Since they have not experienced speech sounds, recoding into a phonological code is precluded from deaf readers . . . (Rayner & Pollatsek, 1979: 211)

The studies described so far lead us in two quite different directions: on the one hand there is some evidence that the deaf *can* use phonological knowledge in memory and reading tasks, and we make the suggestion that lip-reading, speaking and exposure to print have encouraged this — for some deaf people at least. On the other hand we have evidence that in English it is possible to reach a high level of literacy without obvious reliance on letter–sound mappings and with no apparent phonological skills at all (R.E.) so that we should not be surprised if the deaf take this 'Chinese', somewhat idiographic, route to literacy, although they may not have R.E.'s compensating excellent visual memory to support all tasks. There is some evidence for this, too. There is little sign of sensitivity to letter–sound regularity in deaf subjects when they perform written word recognition tasks, and their spelling (and possibly reading) are often considered to be less vulnerable than that of their hearing peers to letter–sound mappings that mislead.

We needed to do some direct studies ourselves to establish how normal, severely deaf, orally-trained British teenagers might use phonology in one aspect of literacy: spelling.

Spelling in Deaf Teenagers: A Systematic Study

We had several reasons for looking in detail at word spelling skill in the deaf: firstly, we knew we could construct stimuli (pictures) that corresponded to words that we could match carefully for degree of regularity in English as well as frequency. Word frequency is a powerful predictor of reading speed and can sometimes interact with word regularity in word recognition tasks (Waters, Seidenberg & Bruck, 1984). As far as we could tell, this had not been attempted in tasks of spelling in children at different levels of reading skill, let alone in deaf readers. So our first priority was to present stimuli which we knew would tell us something clear about the role of spelling–sound regularity, and its relationship with frequency of exposure to the word, in hearing and reading-age-matched deaf students.

Secondly, we had some insights into spelling in the deaf from previously published work. Dodd (1980) reports that, although the bulk of the literature on spelling and deafness tended to favour the phonological-dysgraphic or 'Chinese' type of story — with an emphasis on deaf childrens' failure to be swayed by regular sound–spelling patterns — she herself found plenty of evidence that many deaf children were quite 'phonological' and not at all 'Chinese' in their spellings. For example, deaf subjects were quite competent at spelling lip-read nonsense words to dictation: they knew quite well which letters stood for particular phonemes or seen syllables (R.E., by contrast, could not do any spelling of nonsense words). So we knew that, at the very least, the picture we would find could be mixed, and that it was possible that the deaf (or some of them) *might* show regularity effects in spelling pictured words.

Thirdly, we were interested in the developmental contingencies is between word-reading and word-writing. Frith (1985) and Seymour (Chapter 3, this volume) have developed a model of the possible stages of reading and spelling mastery. In their models, learning to read and to spell involve similar processes in aligned but not completely congruent stages (also see

Burden, Chapter 12, this volume). In the very first, *logographic* stage (following Frith's terminology) reading proceeds in a partial and idiosyncratic way; the child uses knowledge of some letters, such as the ones she knows in her own name, but also other knowledge, as in Seymour & Elder's (1986) example of the rising-six-year-old who 'knew' the word *yellow* 'because it's the only word with two sticks in the middle'. Such knowledge can support *some* word recognition, but may be insufficient to spell a word that one can 'read'. But at this stage it is possible for children sometimes to spell words that they cannot read, since they may have knowledge of at least some letter–sound correspondences sufficient to produce words they have not seen before (see Bryant & Bradley, 1980; Pring, 1992). Thus there can be a stage in the early years of reading and writing when reading may proceed rather 'visually' (logographically) while, concomitantly, the child's knowledge of letters and sounds (and how to blend and separate them) could support some spelling. This spelling must, however, be *alphabetic* in nature, that is, only the simplest mappings between sounds and letters occur (i.e. 'buh, ah, duh spells *bad*'). This, then, is the first non-correspondence between spelling and reading styles and can be observed in some if not all children learning to read and write in English. Following this early logographic stage in reading, which can be accompanied by some alphabetic spelling, most[1] children spend a year or two reading and writing in a very alphabetic fashion; at this stage they are usually better at reading regular words like *rave* than irregular ones like *have,* and their spelling shows a similar, very regular, quality, with homophone confusions and 'regularisations' (e.g. **SHOOE** for **SHOE**). But during this period (typically taking the child to about the age of ten years), the child will be reading correctly a good number of irregular words that require fuller knowledge of English orthography. Now a second 'slip' between reading and writing stages can sometimes occur, so that a child might read *rough* correctly, but still spell it **RUFF** when writing it. The child's *reading* is becoming richer in its ability to handle the peculiarities and higher-order rules of English (*orthographic* is the label Frith gives to this, final stage in word-decoding), while spelling appears to still be more simply *alphabetic* in nature.

So we can see that in these descriptions of literacy acquisition there is a strong hint that the *alphabetic* stage, where simple letter to sound mappings are adhered to, starts earlier and persists longer in spelling than in reading. It is as if spelling could be considered to be intrinsically 'more alphabetic' a task than reading.

Now let us think again about reading, writing, phonological segmentation and deafness. If spelling 'stays alphabetic' while reading tends to move through a more restricted alphabetic phase (see Seymour, Chapter 3 this volume; Burden, Chapter 12 this volume) and if the deaf can handle the phonological letter–sound principles on which the alphabetic stage must rest, we can start to investigate how children aged between 7 and 11, as well as the deaf, spell words that vary systematically in their degree of regularity, when everything else (such as frequency) is held constant. How, exactly, does the student manage words with different degrees of regularity at different levels of reading skill and does the deaf student, of matched *reading age* to the hearing children, show similar or different patterns of sensitivity?

One aspect of this investigation was prompted by Burden's findings (Chapter 12 this volume) with adult good readers who are poor spellers. Surprisingly perhaps, these people do not, when viewed in a developmental light, show a particularly deviant pattern of reading and spelling. When tested on naming speed for written words as a function of the regularity and frequency of the words' spelling, such readers showed regularity effects across different word frequency categories to a greater extent than good reader-spellers and they were *more,* not less, likely to generate regularised responses in reading irregular words aloud (i.e. pronouncing *have* to rhyme with *save*). It could be that they are 'stuck' at a reading and writing level that shows evidence of alphabetic rather than orthographic structure. But that study lacked evidence from normal children at this hypothesised stage; in particular a clear, detailed picture of the ability of the seven to ten-year-old to spell words as a function of their regularity was missing.

These then are the grounds we had for testing carefully the extent to which deaf students used alphabetic principles in spelling known words. If regularity effects were absent, in line with Waters & Doehring's (1990) findings in word recognition, then we would suspect that an important stage in early literacy acquisition was not generally available to the deaf. This could either derail or slow down the acquisition of literacy, and examining the errors produced in spelling would suggest which was more likely. The deaf might produce spelling errors like those of R.E. — that is, errors that respected the look, but not the sound of the target word, suggesting a derailment. Or they might produce alphabetic errors as they strove to capture the word's sound. This might be predicted from studies such as those of Dodd which indicated that for some deaf people at least alphabetic knowledge could be recruited in some spelling tasks.

The experiment itself tested 15 deaf school leavers (all with profound deafness from birth and no other handicap) who were about to leave their special schools for the deaf in Hertfordshire and Cambridgeshire, England. They were 16 to 18 years old. Their reading age was assessed by SPAR and GAP test (reading for content and context). Their mean reading age was nine to ten years on these tests. We found 15 hearing children of similar real age and another fifteen nine-to-ten-year-olds to match against our deaf group.

The task they had to do was to spell the name of a presented picture by writing it down. The words corresponding to the seen pictures varied systematically in regularity and frequency. Half the words were of high frequency (more than $76/10^6$) and half were low frequency ($4/10^6$ or less). Within each frequency group words were of three levels of regularity of spelling:

- regular words like *bone, spring;*
- exception words like *love,* where context-specific rules (*glove*) override more general ones: in this case the rule that an -E after the vowel lengthens it (*hove, rove, stove*); and
- strange words: that is words that have idiosyncratic spellings that are unique to that sound and letter pattern (*choir, eye*).

After pre-testing the line drawings we had made to make sure that they were unambiguously named by children at even the youngest age, we showed the pictures on cards to the subjects and asked them to write down the name of the object shown. Subjects were seen one at a time and the pictures were shown in random order. All subjects could do the task properly — that is fewer than 2% of responses were errors of naming or omissions. But they certainly made spelling errors. Table 11.1 shows how these broke down.

As the figures show, regularity and frequency both had very marked effects on spelling accuracy — at all levels and ages. Most interestingly from our point of view was the finding that the deaf resembled neither their age-mates nor their reading-age mates in terms of accuracy, but rather came out in between the two. There was a significant difference in spelling skill

TABLE 11.1 *Mean percentage error in spelling pictures*

Group	High frequency			Low frequency		
	Regular	Exception	Strange	Regular	Exception	Strange
Deaf	2.3	3.0	13.7	7.0	22.2	35.1
9–10 years	8.4	20.9	31.1	23.1	43.5	60.4
16–18 years	0.4	0.8	4.4	3.1	8.0	20.4

between all three groups. So our first conclusion is that *these (normal) deaf children are better spellers than is predicted by their reading age scores.* Now, as we have mentioned, this conclusion has been arrived at before — for instance by Gates & Chase (1927). They thought that good spelling in the deaf reflected relatively better irregular word spelling. But this was not so in our study. The deaf were highly sensitive to spelling regularity. It was *not* the case that their spelling superiority arose through good spelling of irregular words; quite the contrary. They were worst at spelling strange words and pretty bad at exception words. In this pattern they were indistinguishable from the hearing youngsters. Moreover their actual spelling errors confirmed this highly 'alphabetic' pattern. All of their errors were admissible as (lip-read) approximations to the spoken word and a number were very close indeed: **SKWRL** for *squirrel,* **IORN** for *iron,* **SPONCH** for *sponge,* were actual errors produced by these deaf youngsters — they were also seen in hearing children's spellings and are clearly based on how the word is spoken rather than the pattern of its seen letters.

This pattern of results, moreover, is not due simply to a few 'phonologically skilled' deaf students. It held for all of them — even those with unintelligible speech and who were said by their teachers to have 'poor lip-reading'. There is a general and robust spelling pattern in these deaf youngsters: they are much better at spelling than their reading-age-matched cohort and their spelling accuracy is governed by regularity of sound–letter correspondence, just as in hearing people.

Because the deaf are (clearly) better spellers than they are readers (as measured by reading age) it would seem that Frith's and Seymour's models, in which reading and spelling skill need to roughly align at different stages of development, may not hold for the deaf. Waters & Doehring's (1989) study of deaf youngsters who are very similar to our subjects in terms of their language training (oral) and hearing loss (profound), indicated no regularity effects in word recognition. This contrasts sharply with the powerful regularity effects in spelling found here. Together, these contrasts suggest there can be sharp *discontinuities* between reading and spelling in the deaf, while each independently follows a roughly normal developmental progression.

This is a paradoxical conclusion, and much experimental work needs to be done before its worth can be finally judged, but it may not be too offbeam. The spelling of the deaf in this task looks as if it reflects *isolation* of reading from spelling skills. This could have arisen for a number of reasons, but is still important. For instance, let's assume these students had extensive training in spelling by alphabetic means. They certainly are exposed to tiring phonic drills in order to improve their speech and speech awareness. That might be thought to account for their 'alphabetic spelling'. But in hearing children who are exposed to such spelling drills there is an immediate effect on their reading; they become efficient at alphabetic decoding in reading and often improve markedly (see Bryant & Bradley, 1985). These deaf youngsters don't show reading skills commensurate with their spelling achievements.

No, the isolation of an alphabetic stage in deaf spelling which fails to accompany a similar pattern in reading in the deaf suggests we must probe deeper. Perhaps this evidence can link up with the review with which we started this chapter. There we showed that one interpretation of the varied pattern shown by the deaf on tasks of phonological skill may reflect their *strategic* use of such skills, with *automatic* phonological activation being confined to relatively few tasks. These could include reading words aloud (as in Dodd's (1987) study, and also Leybaert's demonstration for naming colours carried on words and homophones of colour words). When the reading task does not demand such phonological activation — for instance, in silent reading and in word recognition — the deaf child, unlike the hearing one, could 'uncouple' the phonological inner-speech apparatus and use a system that relies more on visual properties. This would account for finding no regularity effects in visual word recognition tasks such as lexical decision (Waters & Doehring, 1990). In turn this implies a possible 'uncoupling' of the processes required to master reading and writing, with writing maintaining a somewhat drawn-out alphabetic phase in development, while reading may follow a different course.

Such speculations may be premature, but the facts remain. The deaf *can* use phonology in all sorts of tasks, and in spelling we find that they are extremely 'phonological' and better than one might expect given their reading age. This might be because they can switch phonology on and off in reading, as they appear to do in other tasks (see, for instance, Campbell & Wright, 1990). Their generally poor reading and writing cannot be ascribed directly to a failure 'to recode into a phonological code' (*pace* Rayner & Pollatsek, 1979). A deeper, more intransigent linguistic delay, possibly contingent on a degree of language deprivation in many deaf children, may provide a surer basis for explaining and, possibly, remediating their poor literacy. We are sure, however, that even at the age of 16, the deaf child's 'inner ear' and 'inner speech' are useful and can be recruited for a number of tasks. Spelling seems to be one of them.

Practical Implications

The aim of this chapter has been to describe some aspects of what is known about how deaf people spell words and to describe some experiments that suggest that born-deaf school-leavers can use letter–sound correspondences in their spelling and reading in a very similar way to reading-age-matched controls. This occurs despite every sign that these students have very poor overt speech and often not even very good lip-reading.

The point of this is that, however it occurs, here is another means for enhancing literacy in people who are born deaf and who tend to have to do a lot of catching up in language in order to be effectively integrated in school work.

While individual deaf students vary enormously in their skills and abilities, they are already deprived of many aspects of communication that we take for granted. We should not deprive them of the opportunity to use the alphabetic principle in learning to read and write. They can learn to make use of it in decoding words. This way, they can start to use the written language as a clearer window on to the world; to enhance and develop vocabulary, to improve grammar and to deepen comprehension of language.

Acknowledgements

This work was supported by MRC (UK) project grants to Ruth Campbell and Helen Wright (G8325534N) and to Ruth Campbell and Vivian Burden (G8930119N). We are most grateful to all the school pupils who let us test them and their teachers who permitted and encouraged the work.

Note

1. The alphabetic stage in learning to read and write has been completely sidestepped by R.E., the phonologically dyslexic student. She shows us that the three-stage model of reading and writing acquisition may be usual but is not necessary for mastering English.

Suggestions for further reading

R. Conrad's (1979) *The Deaf School Child* is a classic study of cognitive processes and deafness. A more recent review, which takes a thorough, non-dogmatic and panoptic view of the relation between pre-lingual deafness, cognitive skills and language training is Michael Rodda and Carl Grove's (1987) *Language, Cognition and Deafness*. Usha Goswami and Peter Bryant's (1990) monograph *Phonological Skills and Learning to Read* is a detailed, thorough, lively and partisan account of current debate on the relationship between phonological skills and the acquisition of literacy in normal children.

References

BADDELEY, A., THOMSON, N. and BUCHANAN, M. 1975, Word length and the structure of short-term memory. *Journal of Verbal Learning and Verbal Behavior* 14, 575–89.

BRYANT, P. E. and BRADLEY, L. 1980, Why children sometimes write words which they do not read. In U. FRITH (ed.) *Cognitive Processes in Spelling* (pp. 355–72). London: Academic Press.

—— 1985, *Children's Reading Problems*. Oxford: Basil Blackwell.

BUTTERWORTH, B. L., CAMPBELL, R. and HOWARD, D. 1986, The uses of short-term memory: A case study. *Quarterly Journal of Experimental Psychology* 38A, 705–37.

CAMPBELL, R. and BUTTERWORTH, B. 1985, Phonological dyslexia and dysgraphia in a highly literate subject: A developmental case with associated deficits of phonemic processing and awareness. *Quarterly Journal of Experimental Psychology* 37A, 435–75.

CAMPBELL, R. and WRIGHT, H. 1988, Deafness, spelling and rhyme. *Quarterly Journal of Experimental Psychology* 40A, 771–88.

—— 1990, Deafness and immediate memory for pictures: Dissociations between inner speech and the inner ear? *Journal of Experimental Child Psychology* 50, 259–86.

CONRAD, R. 1964, Acoustic confusions in immediate memory. *British Journal of Psychology* 55, 75–84.

—— 1972, Short-term memory in the deaf: A test for speech coding. *British Journal of Psychology* 67, 173–80.

—— 1979, *The Deaf School Child*. London: Harper and Row.

DODD, B. 1980, The spelling abilities of profoundly deaf children. In U. FRITH (ed.) *Cognitive Processes in Spelling*. London: Academic Press.

—— 1987, Lipreading, phonological coding and deafness. In B. DODD and R. CAMPBELL (eds) *Hearing by Eye: the Psychology of Lipreading* (pp. 177–90). Hove: Lawrence Erlbaum.

DODD, B. and HERMELIN, B. 1977, Phonological coding by the prelinguistically deaf. *Perception & Psychophysics* 21, 413–17.

FRITH, U. 1985, Beneath the surface of surface dyslexia. In K. PATTERSON, J. C. MARSHALL and M. COLTHEART (eds) *Surface Dyslexia*. London: Lawrence Erlbaum.

FURTH, H. 1966, *Thinking Without Language: Psychological Implications of Deafness*. New York: Free Press.

GATES, A. I. and CHASE, E. H. 1927, Methods and theories of learning to spell tested by studies of deaf children. *Journal of Educational Psychology* 17, 289–300.

GOSWAMI, U. and BRYANT, P. E. 1990 *Phonological Skills and Learning to Read*. Hove: Lawrence Erlbaum.

HANSON, V. L. and FOWLER, C. 1987, Phonological coding in word reading: Evidence from deaf and hearing readers. *Memory and Cognition* 15, 199–207.
HITCH, G. 1990, Developmental fractionation of working memory. In G. VALLAR and T. SHALLICE (eds) *Neuropsychology of Short Term Memory* (pp. 221–46). Cambridge: Cambridge University Press.
LEYBAERT, J. 1987, Le traitment du mot ecrit chez l'enfant sourd. D.Phil. thesis, Universite Libre de Bruxelles.
LEYBAERT, J., ALEGRIA, J. and FONCK, E. 1983, Automaticity in word recognition and word naming in the deaf. *Cahiers de Psychologie Cognitive* 3, 255–72.
LEYBAERT, J., ALEGRIA, J. and MORAIS, J. 1982, On automatic reading processes in the deaf. *Cahiers de Psychologie Cognitive* 2, 185–92.
LIBERMAN, I. Y. 1973, Segmentation of the spoken word and reading acquisition. *Bulletin of the Orton Society* 23, 65–77.
PRING, L. 1992, More than meets the eye: Cognitive skills in two young blind girls. In R. CAMPBELL (ed.) *Mental Lives: Case Studies in Cognition* (pp. 24–46). Oxford: Blackwell.
RAYNER, K. and POLLATSEK, A. 1979, *The Psychology of Reading*. Englewood Cliffs, NJ: Prentice-Hall International.
RODDA, M. and GROVE, C. 1987, *Language, Cognition and Deafness*. New Jersey: Erlbaum.
SCHIANO, D. J. and WATKINS, M. J. 1981, Speech-like coding of pictures in short-term memory. *Memory and Cognition* 9, 110–14.
SEYMOUR, P. K. E. and ELDER, L. 1986, Beginning reading without phonology. *Cognitive Neuropsychology* 3, 1–36.
WATERS, G. and DOEHRING, D. G. 1990, The nature and role of phonological information in reading acquisition: Insights from congenitally deaf children who communicate orally. In T. CARR and B. A. LEVY (eds) *Reading and its Development: Component Skills Approaches*. New York: Academic Press.
WATERS, G., SEIDENBERG, M. S. and BRUCK, M. 1984, Children's and adults' use of spelling sound information in three reading tasks. *Memory and Cognition* 12, 293–305.

12 Why Are Some 'Normal' Readers Such Poor Spellers?

VIVIAN BURDEN

Introduction

Most teachers have encountered the able student who appears to be a good reader, but who is an irredeemably 'careless' speller. Exhortations to proofread written work seldom have the desired effect as good readers/poor spellers, or Type B spellers (Frith, 1980), are often unable to detect their own misspellings or to select the correct version from a number of plausible alternatives. Errors commonly occur on unstressed vowels (e.g. **RELEVENT** for **RELEVANT**) or reflect a failure to apply higher-level spelling rules (e.g. **HOPING** may be confused with **HOPPING**).

The Type B spelling disorder is of particular interest both to teachers and to psychologists who study the development of literacy skills. One intriguing aspect of the problem, which particularly concerns remedial teachers, is that it appears to be very difficult to bring about any lasting improvement in spelling accuracy and the disorder usually persists into adulthood.

The apparent dissociation of reading and spelling processes in Type B spellers also challenges psychological theories which propose that the two processes are developmentally interdependent (Frith, 1985; Seymour & MacGregor, 1984). Consistent with this view is the common finding that adolescents and adults of normal intelligence and with no history of physical or neurological impairment, usually show an association between reading and spelling abilities. Good readers are normally good spellers and poor readers are invariably found to be poor spellers.

Other groups have been identified who show a dissociation between reading and spelling processes, but in these cases a physical disability or specific learning difficulty is evident. Campbell, Burden & Wright (Chapter 11 this volume) report that pre-lingually-deaf teenagers are better spellers than would be predicted on the basis of their standardised reading test scores. Despite their profound hearing impairment these deaf students produced phonologically plausible spelling errors (e.g. **SKWRL** for **SQUIRREL**) which indicate that they have developed normal, although severely delayed, phonological coding skills.

Good phonological abilities appear to be necessary for the development of good spelling skills and deficits in phonological processing are often associated with spelling difficulties (Snowling, Stackhouse & Rack, 1986). Phonological dyslexics (or in the case of spelling, dysgraphics) are unable to master the correspondence rules which enable other children to transcode between sound and spelling. This means that in the early primary-school years, unlike their classmates, they are unable to 'sound out' unfamiliar written words or to use sound as a guide to the spelling of simple words (Funnell & Davidson, 1989; Temple, 1986). Their spelling errors typically preserve the visual characteristics of the target word (e.g. **HERAT** for **HEART**) rather than its sound.

Despite this, some phonological dyslexics, given appropriate instruction, manage to improve their reading skills, although their spelling remains very poor. It has been suggested (Snowling, 1987) that the improvement in reading is the outcome of an atypical reading strategy which capitalises on the use of a good visual memory to learn new words in 'Chinese' or 'look and say' fashion, and heavy reliance on context to facilitate word recognition.

Unlike the deaf, Type B spellers have no history of hearing impairment nor, like phonological dyslexics, have they experienced any obvious difficulty in learning to read. Why then are they such atrocious spellers and why are they unable to improve their spelling skills? Two slightly different explanations have been offered, both of which view Type B spelling as a developmental disorder rather than the result of carelessness or lack of motivation.

Uta Frith was the first person to compare systematically the reading and spelling performance of good and poor spellers matched for reading age. Frith found that Type B spellers had little difficulty in using correspondence rules to transcode between sound and spelling (in spelling tasks) and spelling and sound (in reading tasks). However, the results of a series of interesting experiments (Frith, 1979; 1980), which included a letter cancellation task and reading misspelled or partly obliterated text, indicated that her Type A and B adolescent subjects were characterised by different reading strategies. When performing these tasks the good readers/good spellers (Type A) attended to the detailed letter-by-letter structure of the word **they were** decoding, whereas the good readers/poor spellers (Type B) appeared to recognise words on the basis of partial visual cues.

According to Frith this between-group difference in reading style may help to explain the difference in spelling ability. The full cue reading strategy adopted by Type A subjects is likely to provide detailed information to the spelling system about the identity and position of the constituent letters in a word, and thus to result in accurate recall of the correct spelling. On the other hand, the partial cue reading strategy adopted by the Type B subjects will provide incomplete information to the spelling system. Type B spellers will, therefore, be forced to rely upon their knowledge of sound–spelling correspondences to fill the gaps in the spelling sequence; a procedure which is unlikely to result in the correct spelling of the many English words which have an unusual relationship between sound and spelling, e.g. *love*.

Frith (1985) suggests that Type B spelling is a mild developmental disorder which is manifested in the late primary or early secondary grades. She gives a theoretical account of the aetiology of the disorder within the framework of her stage model of literacy development (see Campbell, Burden & Wright, Chapter 11 this volume; Seymour, Chapter 3 this volume). Frith hypothesises that Type B spellers experience a developmental lag during the early orthographic stage when, in the normal course of events, children are becoming 'full cue' readers who are aware of morphological structures and are able to analyse written words into orthographic units.

At this stage of literacy development divergent strategies predominate for reading and spelling. The orthographic principle is applied first to reading and it is not until fully specified, orthographic representations have been established for reading, that they become available for spelling. Any delay at this stage means that Type B individuals will be slower than Type A to adopt an orthographic (full cue) reading strategy and a phonological, or in Frith's terms, alphabetic strategy will persist for spelling. Frith predicts that Type B spellers will eventually become orthographic readers, but that their atypical developmental experience will continue to be evidenced in very inaccurate spelling.

Bruck & Waters (1988; in press) offer a different explanation of the Type B spelling disorder. Like Frith, they compared the performance of Type A and B adolescents who achieved similar scores on standardised reading tests, but who differed in spelling ability. The two groups were asked to complete a number of component reading and spelling tasks. The results indicated that these Type B spellers lacked age-appropriate development of the subword transcoding system. Although the good readers/poor spellers had mastered basic correspondence rules, they had failed to adduce higher-level constraints on the use of certain correspondences (e.g. the use of hard and soft **G** or the role of a final, silent **E** in a monosyllabic word).

The phonological difficulties evidenced by Bruck & Waters' Type B subjects were not restricted to the domain of spelling, but were also detectable in reading performance. Although Type A and Type B students achieved comparable levels of comprehension accuracy, Type B subjects proved to be much slower than Type A and they relied more on context to facilitate 'linguistic guessing'. It would appear that, like some tutored dyslexics, Type B adolescents may be deploying an atypical reading strategy to compensate for inefficient decoding skills.

The two studies discussed above lead to different conclusions about the severity and generality of the Type B disorder. Frith suggests that the poor spelling demonstrated by Type B individuals is the outcome of a mild developmental disorder which has a late onset and results in a failure to develop orthographic spelling skills. She predicts that, in the course of time, Type B individuals will complete full development of the reading system, but still remain very poor spellers.

On the other hand, Bruck & Waters view Type B spelling as the result of a phonological processing deficit which affects both reading and spelling. Subword transcoding difficulties are reflected in poor encoding and decoding skills. Thus, according to Bruck & Waters, poor spelling is the result of an interruption to the normal developmental sequence during Frith's alphabetic stage, with subsequent atypical development of the system as a whole. In effect, according to this hypothesis, Type B spellers are suffering from a mild form of classical developmental dyslexia.

In the absence of crucial longitudinal studies, one way of adjudicating between these positions is to compare the reading and spelling performance of Type A and B adults. If Frith is correct there should be no qualitative or quantitative differences in the way in which Type A and B adults perform the reading tasks. Type B should also prove to be as competent as Type A when confronted with non-word naming and spelling tasks which demand good subword transcoding skills. If the Bruck & Waters position prevails, one would expect to find evidence of a continuing Type B deficit in higher-level alphabetic skills. This should result in obvious between-group differences in the performance of non-word tasks and also in less efficient Type B reading skills.

A Study of Adult Type A and Type B Spellers

Twenty Type A and 20 Type B subjects were selected from the subject panel of the Applied Psychology Unit, Cambridge. All were superior readers as measured by the Nelson Adult Reading Test (Nelson & Willison, 1992) and there was a clear discrepancy between the two groups in spelling accuracy. Group A (Type A spellers) comprised subjects who scored over 80% on a specially devised adult spelling test and Group B (Type B spellers) achieved less than 50% on the same test. All subjects had received some form of tertiary education or professional training.

The first experiments compared the accuracy and speed with which the Type A and Type B subjects named and wrote to dictation words sharing similar structural characteristics. Both the reading and spelling stimuli were divided into three word classes and within each of these word classes items were matched for length (four to seven letters) and for word frequency (high, low).

Regular words (e.g. *chant*) had a common spelling pattern and an unambiguous relationship between sound and spelling. Exception words also had a common spelling pattern, but contained a segment with an unusual relationship between sound and spelling (e.g. *worry*) or spelling and sound (e.g. *gone*). Strange words had both an unusual spelling pattern and an uncommon pronunciation (e.g. *laugh, busy*). In order to interpret the effect of word structure on performance it was assumed that a comparison of regular and exception words would give information about the effects of phonological structure, while a comparison of exception and strange words would yield information about the effects of unusual orthography.

Word naming and spelling tasks

Word naming

Both groups made very few errors when naming high-frequency words (see Table 12.1). For members of Group A, accuracy was negligibly affected by a decrease in the frequency or an increase in the phonological and orthographic irregularity of the target words. The performance of Group B subjects was, however, more sensitive to word structure. Progressively more errors were made on low-frequency words as the mappings between spelling and sound became more unusual and the orthographic sequence less word-like. The Type B subjects were also much slower than Type A, and the response time data reinforced the between-group accuracy differences. All frequency and word class differences were statistically significant.

TABLE 12.1 *Mean percentage correct for naming and spelling words*

	High frequency			Low frequency		
	Regular	Exception	Strange	Regular	Exception	Strange
Naming						
Group A	100.0	99.3	99.3	100.0	96.0	97.5
Group B	98.7	98.0	98.0	98.3	86.9	77.5
Spelling						
Group A	100.0	99.3	98.7	99.2	94.2	90.0
Group B	94.8	83.3	77.4	86.7	64.8	46.7

Word spelling

Overall the Type A subjects achieved high levels of spelling accuracy (Table 12.1), but their performance was significantly affected by the unusual sound-to-spelling mappings contained in low-frequency exception and strange words. Type B proved to be reliably less accurate when spelling than when reading words matched in terms of their structural characteristics. They were significantly less accurate than Type A subjects at all levels of word class and frequency and their spelling accuracy was sensitive to both phonological and orthographic irregularity.

Discussion of reading and spelling performance

As expected, a comparison of Groups A and B results highlighted the disparity between Type B reading and spelling accuracy. In addition to this obvious quantitative difference in reading and spelling abilities, more subtle aspects of the data indicated that Type B adults lacked full development of both reading and spelling systems.

The most obvious difference between the two groups lay in speed of response. Group B subjects were much slower than Group A. This was true even for the correct pronunciation and spelling of familiar words. Another important between-group difference was indicated by the effect of word structure on the latency and accuracy of responses. For Group A adults, reliable differences in the accuracy with which they named and spelled regular, exception and strange words were related to word frequency. High-frequency items showed no associated word class differences. Most errors were in response to low-frequency exception words and low-frequency strange words were given the longest correct response times. This outcome suggests that the Type A adults spelled and pronounced unfamiliar words 'by ear' (i.e. using šubword correspondences), but processed known words 'by eye' (i.e. on the basis of orthographic structure).

Unlike Type A subjects, Type B adults did not show exactly the same pattern of effects for word naming and spelling. Their word-naming performance shared some of the characteristics of skilled adult reading. For instance, Group B subjects named high-frequency words as accurately as Group A and showed no reliable word class effects for these familiar items. However, word frequency exerted a stronger effect on Type B spelling. They found both high- and low-frequency strange and exception words more difficult to spell than regular words. This is a pattern of performance normally associated with novice spellers.

The Type B spellers were also more sensitive to word structure. In both the domains of reading and spelling, low-frequency strange and exception words proved to be more difficult for the Type B adults than for Type A. Since a correct response to these words can only be the outcome of word-specific knowledge, this result suggests that Type B adults have impoverished reading and spelling vocabularies.

Another anomalous finding was that the Type B adults showed an effect of word length on correct naming latencies. Length effects are not normally detected in adult word naming but have been reported for younger children and phonological dyslexics (Seymour, 1987). Taken as a whole these deviations from Group A performance suggest that the Type B adults were operating upon an immature processing substrate for both reading and spelling tasks.

A detailed error analysis of the reading data was also carried out. For Group A there was a predominance of regularisation errors (e.g. *indikt* for **INDICT**). Only 12% of the inaccurate responses produced by the good readers/good spellers were visual errors which resulted from confusing words with a similar spelling pattern (e.g. *rogue* for **ROUGE**). By contrast, over half of the Type B naming errors were visual confusions and less than one-quarter were regularisations.

This qualitative error analysis indicates that Type A and B adults may be, as Frith has suggested is the case for her adolescent subjects, adopting different reading strategies. The regularisation errors typical of Type A adults are likely to have been generated on the basis of a full cue reading

WHY ARE SOME READERS POOR SPELLERS?

strategy, while the visual confusions typical of Type B adults suggest that these words may have been recognised on the basis of partial visual cues.

The error analysis also provided some evidence that Type B adults may have greater difficulty than Type A in using the subword correspondence procedure. A significant proportion of the Type B non-visual naming errors were nonsense words which resulted from errors in mapping spelling to sound, e.g. *gouch* for **GAUGE**. A qualitative analysis of spelling errors also indicated Type B inaccuracies in transcoding between sound and spelling. Although both groups generally used sound as a guide to the spelling of unfamiliar words and produced phonologically plausible misspellings, Type B adults, unlike Type A, made errors in mapping between sound and spelling, e.g. **OBAQUE** for *opaque*.

Non-word naming and spelling tasks

In order to pursue this issue and to investigate the operation of the subword transcoding procedure, the two groups were asked to name and spell non-words (e.g. *ceft, dage*). To permit a comparison between word and non-word tasks the non-word stimuli shared the phonological and orthographic characteristics of the word stimuli.

Non-word spelling

Type B subjects (Table 12.2) proved to be much slower and less accurate than Type A (i.e. they produced fewer phonologically plausible non-word spellings). Their performance was also more disrupted by stimulus length. Unlike the good spellers, their non-word spelling was characterised by lack of consistency in the selection of sound-to-spelling mappings and they were less likely to select the most common mapping. The Type B spellers made significantly more errors than Type A on items which required transcoding across a group of letters in order to apply contextual constraints on spelling, e.g. *dage* was spelled as **DAIG**.

TABLE 12.2 *Mean percentage correct for naming and spelling non-words*

	Spelling	Naming
Group A	91	96
Group B	75	83

Non-word naming

A comparison of Group A and B performance confirmed that for decoding, as for encoding, Type B adults were slower, less accurate and less consistent than Type A. Again the major difference between the two groups lay, not at the level of simple one-to-one mappings between spelling and sound, but at the more advanced alphabetic level where there are orthographic constraints on the use of certain correspondences. This was exemplified by the different error patterns produced by the good and poor spellers. Many of the Type B errors stemmed from a failure to appreciate the role of a final, silent -E in a monosyllabic non-word, e.g. **SPILE** would be pronounced *spill* and **DROD**, *drode*. The Type A subjects made very few errors of this kind. The most common errors made by Group A concerned positional constraints on the use of certain consonants, i.e. a final -CH was sometimes inappropriately rendered as /-k/ as in *Christmas*, a pronunciation never given to terminal -CH in any real word of the language.

Discussion of encoding and decoding performance

When compared with good reader/spellers the Type B adults show a deficit in transcoding at the higher alphabetic level. The development of advanced subword transcoding skills requires close integration of alphabetic and orthographic codes. Type B spellers appear to have been less successful than Type A in abstracting and applying the general principles which govern complex relationships between phonology and orthography. In this respect they resemble the adolescents studied by Bruck & Waters (1988; in press).

A failure to complete Frith's alphabetic stage of development should mean that Type B adults ought to show some of the processing characteristics normally associated with younger children (e.g. Waters, Bruck & Seidenberg, 1985) and, indeed, this appears to be the case. Group B subjects proved to be more sensitive than Group A to the length of the non-word stimulus and there was a marked decrease in accuracy as length increased.

Their performance was also less consistent than that of Group A subjects. They were less likely to use the same spelling pattern to represent the same sound in different non-words. When naming non-words they were less likely to pronounce the same spelling pattern in the same way on subsequent presentations. They were also less likely than the good spellers to use the most common mapping and they produced many idiosyncratic responses such as rendering *vark* as **VARQUE**.

The two groups were also asked to perform a spoonerism task devised by Perin (1983) to compare the ability of Type A and B adolescents to segment and manipulate phonemes. This task requires subjects to transpose the initial phoneme of the first and second name of well-known personalities, e.g. *Phil Collins* would become /kɪl/ /fɒlɪnz/ (*Kill Follins*). Group A (97% accuracy) proved to be better than Group B (88% accuracy) at performing the spoonerism task. Both groups made errors which resulted from segmenting on the basis of a visual image (switching letters) rather than sound (switching phonemes), i.e. *Phil Collins* became /tʃɪl/ /pɒlɪnz/ (*Chill Pollins*). In addition, Type B adults, unlike Type A, made many errors in segmenting and manipulating the initial phonemes. This outcome adds weight to the conclusion that Type B spelling is the outcome of a phonological processing deficit which prevents normal progression through the alphabetic stage. A comparison of the performance of Type B adolescents (Bruck & Waters, in press; Perin, 1983) and adult subjects of this series of experiments suggests that there has been little improvement in phonological skills with increasing age and literacy experience.

Why Are Type B Spellers Unexpectedly Good Readers?

The initial selection tasks rated the Type B adults as being above-average readers and yet the experimental results confirm that they are inefficient decoders. In the face of their persistent decoding difficulties how do these individuals become 'normal' readers. Stanovich (1986) provides a potential explanation. His interactive-compensatory model of reading proposes that if decoding is slow, context can be used to aid word recognition. A poor decoder must, therefore, integrate information from stimulus-based and conceptually-based (e.g. context, general knowledge) sources before words are identified. Since the word recognition of efficient decoders is automatic, they are better able to focus attention on higher level comprehension processes.

Stanovich predicts that the use of a compensatory strategy should result in more error prone performance and slower reading speed. Bruck & Waters report that Type B adolescents were slower, but not reliably less accurate than their Type A peers. It remained to be seen how the adult groups compared on a test of text reading speed and comprehension. I used the Nelson-Denny reading test (Brown, Nelson & Denny, 1972) for this purpose as it provides adult norms in the form of percentile scores. The results placed Type A in the top quartile for comprehension, speed and vocabulary subtests. Group B subjects proved to be less proficient than Group A on all measures. They were characterised by this test as average in terms of comprehension and vocabulary subskills, but as very slow readers. Test norms placed them in the 33rd percentile.

If we compare the adult Type A and B results with those of the adolescents studied by Bruck & Waters it is evident that the developmental trend is for text reading to remain slow and for differences in comprehension to increase with age and complexity of the reading material. This is in accord with the predictions of the interactive-compensatory model.

The results of this series of experiments, therefore, support Bruck and Waters' hypothesis that Type B spelling is indeed a mild form of classical developmental dyslexia. It is the outcome of a phonological disorder which is less pervasive and severe than that experienced by phonological dyslexics. This phonological deficit results in an interruption to the normal developmental sequence during Frith's alphabetic stage, with subsequent compensatory development of the reading system.

Basic transcoding rules are mastered, but higher level alphabetic skills fail to develop. Word identification appears to be based on a partial cue visual strategy which results in the establishment of incomplete and imprecise reading representation. Words which have similar spelling patterns must be distinguished by the associated use of supplementary sources of information, such as spelling–sound correspondence knowledge for context-free word naming and reliance on context for text reading. Oral reading is inaccurate and marked by substitution errors which preserve the meaning of the text, and silent reading is slow. The severe and persistent spelling difficulties which are the hallmark of the Type B individual are merely the most obvious indication of their underlying phonological difficulties and of their atypical development experience.

Practical Implications

There are two main practical questions which this series of experiments helps to answer. The first concerns when and how the Type B speller can first be identified by the classroom teacher. Between the ages of eight and ten years one would expect to find a growing discrepancy between spelling accuracy on one hand and comprehension skill and general language abilities on the other. This should be associated with difficulty or delay in mastering simple subword transcoding skills like 'sounding out' regular words such as *truck* or using sound to guide the spelling of *fish*. This aspect of development is most directly observable in non-word naming and spelling tasks. At this stage the potential Type B speller may also have difficulty in recalling a series of instructions or in playing word games such as 'pig Latin'. Although their comprehension abilities may be good, Type B students may prove to be inaccurate oral readers and their reading speed may be slower than that of classmates who achieve similar levels of comprehension accuracy.

By adolescence the disparity between comprehension accuracy and spelling skill should be much clearer. At this stage spelling errors are likely to reveal difficulties in understanding and applying complex spelling rules. Type B spellers may also be slow to acquire the specialised vocabulary associated with more advanced scientific and mathematical concepts. It is also anticipated that these students will be poor at proofreading their own written work since they may lack fully specified reading representation for words they spell incorrectly (see Funnell, Chapter 5 this volume).

The second applied question concerns remediation. How can the teacher help Type B spellers to improve their spelling skills? Systematic studies of the efficacy of alternative intervention strategies have yet to be carried out, but on the evidence available so far some tentative suggestions can be offered. In the early grades a structured approach to teaching phonics can be used to integrate encoding and decoding skills and overlearning will be required to ensure that subword transcoding routines become fully automated. Explicit instruction and regular practice must be maintained throughout the primary grades as alphabetic skills develop slowly in these children. Type B spellers have particular difficulty in transcoding across groups of letters and in segmenting phonemes. It is, therefore, important to draw their attention to word 'families' (e.g. *light, might, tight*, etc.).

Since Type B spellers have good visual memories, training in a recall-based spelling strategy is likely to be beneficial. This means that the child must be discouraged from copying spellings and encouraged to study the whole word, to register its letter-by-letter sequence, to recall and write the complete spelling and then to check and verify that it is correct. Older Type B spellers should benefit from a morphemic spelling scheme which trains them to recognise the structural units which comprise words and provides rules for combining these. This 'cognitive' approach to improving spelling may mean that accurate spelling is achieved by Type B individuals only at the expense of a great deal of time and energy. Under stressful conditions, such as examinations, their spelling is likely to revert to its unreconstructed state.

Summary

Although poor readers are invariably poor spellers, the converse may not always be true. There are reports of children and adolescents who, despite experiencing severe spelling difficulties, appear to function as normal readers. This chapter has attempted to establish the underlying cause of this specific spelling disorder in adults who are competent readers. It reports the results of a series of experiments which compare the performance of a group of poor spellers/good readers (Type B) with that of a group of good readers/ good spellers (Type A) on a number of component subskills common to both reading and spelling.

It is argued that results support the view that Type B spellers suffer a mild phonological deficit which impedes the development of encoding and decoding skills. Despite their phonological processing difficulties, Type B spellers are able to improve their reading skills by adopting an atypical strategy which capitalises on good visual memory and general language abilities to compensate for weak decoding skills. Spelling, however, remains immature and inaccurate and the underlying phonological deficit is detectable in slow and variable performance of both reading and spelling tasks.

References

BROWN, J. I., NELSON, M. J. and DENNY, E. C. 1976, *The Nelson-Denny Reading Test.* Boston, Mass.: Houghton Mifflin Co.

BRUCK, M. and WATERS, G. S. 1988, An analysis of the spelling errors of children who differ in their reading and spelling skills. *Applied Psycholinguistics* 9, 77–92.

—— in press, An analysis of the component reading and spelling skills of good readers–good spellers, good readers–poor spellers, and poor readers–poor spellers. In T. CARR and B. A. LEVY (eds) *Reading and Its Development: Component Skills Approaches.* New York: Academic Press.

FRITH, U. 1979, Reading by eye and writing by ear. In P. A. KOHLERS, M. WROLSTAD and H. BOUMA (eds) *Processing of Visible Language, 1.* New York: Plenum Press.

—— 1980, Unexpected spelling problems. In U. FRITH (ed.), *Cognitive Processes in Spelling.* London: Academic Press.

—— 1985, Developmental dyslexia. In K. PATTERSON, J. C. MARSHALL and M. COLTHEART (eds) *Surface Dyslexia.* London: Lawrence Erlbaum.

FUNNELL, E. and DAVIDSON, M. 1989, Lexical capture: A developmental disorder of reading and spelling. *Quarterly Journal of Developmental Psychology* 41A, 471–87.

NELSON, H. and WILLISON, J. 1992, *Nelson Adult Reading Test* 2nd edn. Windsor: NFER-Nelson.

PERIN, D. 1983, Phonemic segmentation in spelling. *British Journal of Psychology* 74, 129–44.
SEYMOUR, P. H. K. 1987, Developmental dyslexia: A cognitive experimental analysis. In M. COLTHEART, A. SARTORI and R. JOB (eds) *The Cognitive Neuropsychology of Language*. London: Lawrence Erlbaum.
SEYMOUR, P. H. K. and MACGREGOR, C. J. 1984, Developmental dyslexia: A cognitive experimental analysis of phonological, morphemic and visual impairment. *Cognitive Neuropsychology* 1, 309–39.
SNOWLING, M. J. 1987, *Dyslexia: A Cognitive Developmental Perspective*. Oxford: Basil Blackwell.
SNOWLING, M. J., STACKHOUSE, J. and RACK, J. 1986, Phonological dyslexia and dysgraphia: Developmental aspects. *Cognitive Neuropsychology* 3, 309–39.
STANOVICH, K. E. 1986, Matthew effects in reading: Some consequences of individual differences in the acquisition of literacy. *Reading Research Quarterly* 21, 360–407.
TEMPLE, C. M. 1986, Developmental Dysgraphias. *Quarterly Journal of Experimental Psychology* 38A, 77–110.
WATERS, G. S., BRUCK, M. and SEIDENBERG, M. S. 1985, Do children use similar processes to read and spell words? *Journal of Experimental Child Psychology* 39, 511–30.

Section Five: Educational Practice

Introduction

There are four chapters in this section, although a number of others could well have been included (e.g. Funnell, Chapter 5; Pattison & Collier, Chapter 6). The classification decision was made on the grounds of whether the papers addressed educational practice directly. Peters' chapter argues for a multi-sensory approach. Seymour, Bunce & Evans provide a framework for assessment and training. Nicolson, Pickering & Fawcett report on their use of an interactive computer program to improve dyslexic's spelling. Sterling & Seed explore the potential diagnostic value of different types of error.

Towards Spelling Autonomy (Peters)

Peters' chapter centres around the results of a comprehensive research programme she carried out into the spelling and handwriting of children in the final two years of primary school. The findings most relevant to the teaching of spelling were the visual perception of word form and handwriting. She argues in this chapter for the importance of the visuo-motor aspects of spelling.

Peters argues that English spelling is an example of a stochastic process (i.e. governed by the laws of probability); that the sequences of letters which make up English words are not random strings, but strings with different probabilities of occurrence. Some letter sequences are frequent, others less so. Learning to spell is a process of learning these sequences, partly by becoming aware of the serial probabilities that govern their occurrence. Given this, practice in writing letter sequences, requiring as it does both visual and motor skill, is of crucial importance in improving spelling ability.

A Framework for Orthographic Assessment and Remediation (Seymour, Bunce & Evans)

Seymour, Bunce & Evans argue that assessment and teaching procedures depend on having a model of the spelling lexicon, a goal they have already accomplished for a reading lexicon. This chapter outlines their achievements for the latter, though what they have produced can also be used for spelling.

Theoretically, dual process theory implies that assessment and teaching should focus on both lexical and phonological spelling while Frith's model implies that they should focus on determining the stage an individual has reached and on facilitating movement on to the next stage. Both these views, however, require a general purpose model of the orthographic system and lists of words which can be used for assessment and teaching.

Seymour and his colleagues began with a unidimensional model, which represents the orthographic lexicon as a list of words (used by lexical spelling) and non-words (used by phonological spelling), structured on the basis of dimensions such as frequency and regularity of spelling. From the exhaustive list they produced they selected a representative sample of words and non-words for a research programme (Chapter 14, Appendix 1) involving the monitoring and teaching of individual children. They refer to procedures which can use these lists for assessment and teaching.

The model they prefer is the dual foundation model which assumes that the orthographic lexicon develops on foundation processes consisting of a logographic word store, letter–sound associations and phonological awareness. They have produced lists of words, non-words, letter–sound associations and phonological awareness tests which can be used to assess whether a child has these foundation processes (Chapter 14, Appendix 2A). Moving on to the orthographic store, they argue that it can either be two dimensional (syllables composed of onset and rime structures in combination) or three dimensional (syllables composed of initial consonant, vowel and terminal consonant structures in combination). They prefer the latter. In either case the result is again a structured, exhaustive set of words and non-words in which the orthographic relationships between words and between the orthographic and phonological forms of words are evident. A sample of these (for the 3D model) are produced in Chapter 14, Appendix 2B.

In the next section of the chapter they go into more detail about this 3D orthographic list, which they divide into a core and a series of expansions (with each expansion increasing the complexity of the words and vocabulary size) because they assume orthographic development to occur in stages.

INTRODUCTION: EDUCATIONAL PRACTICE

Thus, for example: the core structure consists of monosyllabic words (regular and irregular) and non-words composed of single consonants, single vowels and consonant digraphs; the first expansion increases complexity by introducing consonant clusters; the second and third expansions increase it further by introducing long vowels; and so on. For each expansion they produce representative lists (Appendices 3, 4, 5, and 6). Appendix 2A is a truncated version of these lists for use in assessment.

In the final section they outline some of the properties that teaching procedures should embody. For example, lists appropriate to the child's level of development should be used; words and non-words should be used to develop different strategies; and colour coding should be used to identify the building blocks of which the words are composed. These procedures are currently being tested. The results to date suggest that the unidimensional model lists are valuable for assessment but less so for instruction. The evidence on Seymour et al.'s 3D model, with its distinction between foundation processes and orthographic development, is, as yet, limited but positive. There is still much work to be done before these lists can be recommended for general use.

Spelling Remediation for Dyslexic Children Using the SelfSpell Programs (Nicolson, Pickering & Fawcett)

Nicolson, Pickering & Fawcett report evaluations of two interactive computer programs whose purpose is to help those with spelling problems. One of the problems in the past has been the fact that interactive programs have required use of the keyboard, a major obstacle for those with literacy problems. New technology, however, allows users to interact with the machine with a device called a 'mouse'. Moving this around on a mat beside the computer produces corresponding movements of a pointer on the screen. Commands are initiated by pressing a button on the mouse when the pointer is poised above the desired command indicator on the screen. If commands are represented by symbols or pictures, the necessity for the ability to read or write is minimised. We also see that playing around with such a system might be fun for children.

In the first study, using adolescent dyslexics, each child wrote two passages to dictation and both these, together with spelling mistakes, were put into the computer. The authors decided to focus their efforts on the poorer spellers and to train them on only eight of the errors they made in one of the passages. Accordingly, in the second phase, for each child they produced bug cards for each of eight selected errors in one passage. On each bug card there are slots for (a) the precise location of the error in the word, and

(b) a rule that would put it right. In the third phase the children worked through each bug card, filling in the slots by locating the error and formulating an appropriate rule. In the final phase they went through the passage fixing the errors using the information on the bug cards. The results of this training when tested on both passages a month later were most encouraging: the children's performance on the bug words improved dramatically. Furthermore, while their performance on the other misspellings in the same passage didn't also improve, their performance on the second passage did improve. Feedback from both parents and children suggested an overall improvement in motivation and attitude.

In the second study with younger dyslexics, they compared this rule-formulating training regime with a procedure (the mastery method) in which the child is presented with each problem word (in context), has to spell it, and is given immediate feedback, which allows the child to type it in correctly before moving on to a new word. Each word is presented from time to time until it has been spelled correctly (first time) on its three previous appearances. The results indicated that both regimes were successful with these younger dyslexics but that the mastery method was slightly more successful. The participants also seemed to prefer this method because of the greater success it produced.

Phonological Spelling in Young Children and some Origins of Phonetically Plausible and Implausible Errors (Sterling & Seed)

Sterling & Seed are concerned with the origins of different types of spelling errors. They distinguish competence errors, which are due to ignorance, from performance errors, which are due to 'carelessness'. Their concern are the former. They argue that spelling errors can be usefully interpreted only within the framework of a model and to this end introduce dual process theory.

According to dual process theory there are two strategies or sets of processes which are used in spelling — the lexical strategy and the phonological strategy. Sterling & Seed cite evidence from phonological dysgraphics and developmental phonological dyslexics showing that in the absence of the phonological strategy the spellings produced are phonetically implausible errors (e.g. **PTEZRL** (*pretzel*), **RTHYTM** (*rhythm*)). They also cite evidence from lexical dysgraphics showing that in the absence of the lexical strategy the spellings produced are phonetically plausible (e.g. **SED** (*said*)). These data suggest that the lexical strategy is responsible for phonetically implausible spellings while the phonological strategy is responsible for phonetically plausible spellings.

Sterling & Seed's research focuses on phonological spelling. They distinguish between two of its components: phonological ability and knowledge of phono–graphic correspondences. They argue that as the phonological complexity of words increases so should the incidence of phonetically implausible errors (plausible errors should not be affected) and that when correspondence complexity increases so should the incidence of phonetically plausible errors (implausible errors should be unaffected).

They tested these hypotheses in three experiments with young children. In the first they compared words which are phonologically complex but have simple correspondences (e.g. **GLAD/SEND**) with words which are phonologically simple but have complex correspondences (**BOOT/READ/NAME**). (The consonant clusters in **GLAD** and **SEND** increase phonological complexity.) They found, as predicted, that the former produced more phonetically implausible errors than the latter but that the latter produced more phonetically plausible errors than the former. In the second experiment they used non-words and compared two groups which differed only in their phonological complexity (**IND** versus **NID**). They found, as predicted, that the phonologically complex non-words (with the cluster) induced more phonetically implausible errors than the phonologically simple non-words, but that phonetically plausible errors were the same. In the third experiment they compared non-words which differed only in the complexity (and ambiguity) of the vowel correspondences (e.g. **BAF** versus **BOOP, DEET** versus **FIKE/GADE**). They found, as predicted, that phonetically plausible errors increased with complexity but that phonetically implausible errors were the same across all groups.

Sterling & Seed conclude with a short discussion of the work that remains to be done before errors can be used as a diagnostic tool. They consider their work to have two practical implications. First they recommend phonological awareness training to combat the difficulties caused by phonologically complex words. Second they argue that non-word spelling errors, even at this early stage in our knowledge, can be used to indicate general strengths and weaknesses of children's phonological spelling ability.

13 Towards Spelling Autonomy

MARGARET L. PETERS

Twenty years ago the spelling and handwriting of a complete age group in one local education authority throughout the two final primary school years was closely monitored (Peters, 1970). Teachers' attitudes, their behaviour, their correction practices and their teaching strategies, in relation to children's spelling progress, were explored and documented. One of the findings most relevant to the teaching of spelling was that the most significant factor was visual perception of word form. Children, including very poor spellers, were found to be able to reproduce, correctly, briefly exposed words that were unknown to them. These children had just not been previously challenged to do any such thing. The second most significant factor was the handwriting. Good and progressing spellers wrote swiftly and legibly. That spelling is primarily a visuo-motor activity was being confirmed in this large-scale research project.

Now this finding, one amongst many others accruing from this research, has been repeatedly put forward in the literature.

Long ago, Schonell (1942) pointed out that the visual, auditory and articulatory elements must be 'firmly cemented in writing', for by writing the attention is focused and helps to bridge the gap between visual and auditory symbols by successive production of the constituent part of the visual form.

Frank Smith (1982) stated 'Children who spell by ear are the worst spellers', and added 'knowledge of phonics is not much help in spelling'. In short, 'Writing' wrote Stubbs (1983) 'is designed to be seen and not heard'.

In the case of grapho–phonemically regular languages, such as Spanish or Finnish, learning to spell by phonics, through phonological access, is reasonable, which is why in learning to read by Initial Teaching Alphabet (i.t.a.) a child learned to spell so easily and wrote so easily *in* i.t.a. From my research at that time into the influence of reading methods on spelling ability, children taught through the medium of i.t.a. presented a sort of non-redundant skeletal structure from which conventional English spelling could be readily developed, provided it was followed up by the learning of generalisable rules of spelling.

The case for visuo-motor learning would be untenable if it were not for the fact that the English orthography is by no means irregular. The orthography consists of a vast number of letter sequences, many of which have varied pronunciations. As in the grammar of a language where there is a stronger possibility of some words occurring next in a sequence than there is of others, so it is with strings of letters. It is an example of what is known as the stochastic process, which is any process governed by the laws of probability. In the case of the language process the expected probability of occurrence of any single element in sequence, from the point of view of the reader or listener, is governed by the immediate context and his or her previous personal experience of similar kinds of context. Now far from being the unsystematic, unpredictable collection of words handed down from a muddled and motley collection of etymological sources, spelling is just another example of this stochastic process. For in spelling we are concerned with letter sequences, not word sequences. Spelling is a kind of grammar for letter sequences that generates permissible combinations *without regard to sound* (Gibson & Levin, 1975). As in word sequences (grammar) there is a scale of probability range from letters that can occur in sequence to those that cannot, i.e. from highly probable to highly improbable and even impossible letter sequences (Peters, 1985).

We must remember, of course, that although this is a kind of grammar for letter sequences *within* a word, the spelling can be affected by grammatical and meaningful constraints, as in the case of homophones, where, for example, the spelling of **MIST** or **MISSED** depends on the context. Indeed Albrow (1972), in describing the English Writing System, saw many of its apparent irregularities as ceasing to be irregular if we accept that there are different conventions in spelling for representing different grammatical and meaningful elements. It is providing repeated practice in writing the most common letter strings in the orthography, strings of three or four letters, such as **PER** in **PERHAPS, PERIOD, WHISPER**, or the **EPH** in **STEPHEN, TELEPHONE, ELEPHANT** or **NEPHEW** that children who have not acquired spelling incidentally are in fact being taught. With hearing-impaired children, it avoids speech-relationships. With dyslexic children it avoids the time-consuming phonological sequencing that so often eludes them, and since letter-string learning facilitates generalisation it avoids the burdensome rule-learning which so frequently dogs the dyslexic child and this has not been found to preclude those dyslexic children with a specifically visual-perceptual deficit. This is the way into what Ehri (1989) calls 'spelling knowledge'. She says that this, as well as phonological awareness, develops when children learn to read and spell an alphabetic orthography.

These assertions are not made lightly or arrogantly. They are the consequences of working from the findings of the research quoted above, which led to the teaching of spelling by visuo-motor means. As McKay, Thompson & Schaub (1978) said in the early days of *Breakthrough to Literacy*, 'the traditional spelling lesson is an *ad hoc* approach to the task of internalisation and one for which lack of awareness of the working of the orthography falls back on random procedures and on rote learning'. As they are made aware of the regularity of the orthography and the redundancy of letter strings, teachers in mainstream classes as well as in special units, have welcomed this knowledge of the working of the orthography, that is of serial probability. It is a means of teaching spelling completely in tune with the demands of Attainment Target 4 (AT4) of the National Curriculum (National Curriculum Council, 1989) which speaks, for example, of the need at Level Two to 'recognise that spelling has patterns', and that children should 'apply their knowledge of those patterns in their attempts to spell a wider range of words', and at Level Three, it speaks of words which have 'common letter patterns'.

Teachers are encouraged to be aware of the function of 'invented spellings' which were, in my 1970 research, termed 'trying out words', there was seen to be some relationship between this activity and spelling progress, but what was more important, it indicated an attitude to autonomy in the children's learning to spell. Early intervention by exposure to and practice in the writing of letter strings, undoubtedly facilitates what is now called 'inventive spelling'.

This chapter describes the work that has ensued from twenty-five-year-old research, research that has been replicated and confirmed in practice in many classrooms and with individual children. In action research the influence of handwriting on spelling has been confirmed by, for example, Cripps (1983). Indeed the importance of speed of writing has forced schools to reconsider the value of joined-up writing from the beginning and this is now demanded by level three in the National Curriculum.

Arising from the research there followed the teaching by visuo-motor means of a host of children who have failed to learn to spell. Many non-reading children learned to spell and in the process of learning to spell they learned to read, for although a child can read a word he or she cannot necessarily spell it, but by being able to spell it he or she can inevitably read it.

Finally, for the 'revising and redrafting of their own writing', as expected by Level Three in AT4 of the National Curriculum, necessary checking is made possible through looking at word structure, that is, through having acquired 'awareness of spelling patterns' and 'spelling generalisation' at Level Two, which comes through the repeated visualising and writing of letter strings, common to our orthography.

It is this that sensitises children to the serial probability of their own orthography. It is this that frees them from one of the many constraints in writing.

References

ALBROW, K. H. 1972, *The English Spelling System: Notes Towards Description.* London: Longman for the Schools Council.
CRIPPS, C. C. 1983, A report of an experiment to see whether young children can be taught to write from memory. *Remedial Education* 18, 1.
EHRI, L. C. 1989, The development of spelling knowledge and its role in reading acquisition and reading disability. *Journal of Learning Disability* 22, 6, 356.
GIBSON, E. J. and LEVIN, H. 1975, *The Psychology of Reading.* Cambridge, Mass.: MIT Press.
MCKAY, D., THOMPSON, B. and SCHAUB, B. 1978, *Breakthrough to Literacy: Teachers' Manual.* London: Longman for the Schools Council.
National Curriculum Council 1989, English Key Stage I. Non-statutory guidance. York: NCC.
PETERS, M. L. 1970, *Success in Spelling.* Cambridge Institute of Education.
—— 1985, *Spelling: Caught or Taught? A New Look.* London: Routledge and Kegan Paul.
SCHONELL, F. J. 1942, *Backwardness in the Basic Subjects.* Edinburgh: Oliver & Boyd.
SMITH, F. 1982, *Writing and the Writer.* London: Heinemann.
STUBBS, M. 1983, The sociolinguistics of the English writing system or why children aren't adults. In M. STUBBS and H. HILLER (eds) *Readings on Language, Schools and the Classrooms.* London: Methuen.

14 A Framework for Orthographic Assessment and Remediation

PHILIP H. K. SEYMOUR, FRANCES BUNCE and
HENRYKA M. EVANS

Introduction

In Chapter 3 of this volume, Seymour reviewed some cognitive theories of spelling processes and their development, and outlined ways in which the ideas might be translated into practical procedures for assessment and teaching. These applications depend on the construction of a model of the orthographic output lexicon (system for storage and generation of spellings). Work directed towards this end is currently in progress in Dundee.

Our previous research was based on a model of the *input* lexicon — the system for recognition of words in reading. This has led to the development of a comprehensive scheme for assessment and instruction which provides a blueprint for an analogous approach in the area of spelling. A primary idea is that instruction is aimed at the building up of a general purpose orthographic framework and that this process involves the establishment of a 'core' which is subsequently expanded and elaborated. An earlier statement of the approach is provided by Seymour (1990). Further details, together with data obtained from two contrasting dyslexic cases, are given by Seymour & Bunce (in press).

Implications of Cognitive Models

Part of the background is provided by descriptions of the cognitive architecture of the orthographic system (Ellis & Young, 1988). Theories of this type appear relevant to instruction primarily in terms of their capacity to identify the modules which might be impaired and in need of remediation. As noted earlier, a standard assumption is that there are four component modules which deal with reading (input) and spelling (output) at lexical and non-lexical levels. The model also hypothesises systems which code information at different levels of abstraction. On the input side, there are peripheral systems for visual analysis and more central systems involved in comprehension (semantic processes) and speech coding (phonological processes). In order to apply the model to education we require: (1) assessment procedures which are capable of determining the status of each module or coding level; and (2) sets of instructions, activities and exercises which collectively form module-specific teaching procedures.

A second class of relevant model is concerned with the stages of development of the orthographic system, e.g. the sequence of logographic, alphabetic and orthographic processing proposed by Frith (1985) and Morton (1989). Educational applications will depend on: (1) the availability of test procedures capable of identifying the developmental level an individual has reached; and (2) instructional procedures which encourage completion of the stage at which 'arrest' has occurred and assist movement forward into the next stage. There is again an assumption that teaching procedures exist which can exert a selective impact on particular classes of process (logographic, alphabetic, or orthographic).

Unidimensional Model of the Orthographic System

We initially approached the task of assessing the availability of an orthographic system by adapting the psycholinguistic approach which has become standard in cognitive neuropsychology. For some workers (e.g. Frith, 1985; Olson *et al.*, 1985), the term 'orthographic' seems to be approximately equivalent to 'lexical' or 'morphemic', involving an equation with the precise and correct spelling of individual words or morphemes. According to this view, the content of the lexicon is defined as a list of items. We will refer to this as a unidimensional model of orthographic organisation, or as a 1D structure.

The unidimensional model represents the lexicon as a list of words. The words vary in terms of linguistic dimensions, including frequency, concreteness of meaning, regularity of spelling-to-sound mapping, length, etc. A goal in assessment is to select sets of items which are representative of these variations. In order to create a procedure for use with primary school children we took Edwards & Gibbon's (1973) lists of *Words Your Children Use* as a word pool. The entire vocabulary was classified in terms of several psycholinguistic dimensions. Following this, we selected items of concrete meaning which varied in frequency (high versus low), length (three to six letters) and regularity/complexity. This latter factor was varied at three levels:

1. *RG — regular.* The pronunciation of the word was predictable given a knowledge of the standard sound values of its individual letters.
2. *RL — rule.* The word contained letter combinations which were generally associated with a consistent pronunciation.
3. *I — irregular.* The word contained one or more single letters or combinations whose pronunciation was non-standard or determined by higher-order (morphological) influences.

Appendix 1 contains versions of these lists which are currently in use. We would normally administer them in the order: RG–RL–I, preferably via a computer, so that reaction times for oral reading can be obtained. The lists are also dictated for spelling.

In the unidimensional model, the lexicon is viewed as a system for recognition of words. Hence, the reading or spelling of unfamiliar items (including non-words) is usually assigned to a secondary translation process, operating on grapheme–phoneme correspondences or larger structures (Patterson & Morton, 1985). As noted by Seymour (Chapter 3 this volume) other views are possible, particularly the suggestion that non-words may be processed in the same system or network as words (Henderson, 1982; Shallice & McCarthy, 1985; Seidenberg & McClelland, 1989). Whichever of these views is sustained, it seems essential that an assessment procedure should include lists of non-words which are approximately equivalent to the word sets in terms of gross dimensions such as length and orthographic content.

We therefore derived sets of non-words, mainly by procedures of exchange of elements, to parallel the RG, RL and I word lists. Current versions of these lists are included in Appendix 1. The lists can be used for oral reading, again preferably with the inclusion of response timing, and for spelling to dictation.

Illustrations of assessments using these word and non-word lists are provided by Seymour (1990), Seymour & Evans (1988), and Seymour & Bunce (in press). Teaching approaches based on the 1D model are described by Coltheart & Byng (1989) and Bryant & Bradley (1985). Our own procedures included some whole word exercises, e.g. selection of words according to overall length and shape.

Dual Foundation Model

In our own work we have used a modification of Frith's (1985) scheme, which is referred to as the 'dual foundation model' (Seymour, 1990; Seymour & Evans, 1992; Seymour & Bunce, in press). This theory places a main emphasis on the development of orthographic structure but assumes that this is assisted by the availability of foundation processes, including: (1) a logographic store of word forms; (2) a set of alphabetic letter–sound associations; and (3) a 'phonological awareness' (PA) of the segmental structure of speech. This framework is represented schematically in Figure 14.1. The model differs from the Frith–Morton scheme in that it allows that logographic and alphabetic processes may develop in parallel rather than in succession and that they may continue to function throughout the period during which the orthographic system is being constructed. A further assumption is that PA contributes both to the development of alphabetic associations and to the provision of a higher order phonological structure which serves as an organising principle for the orthographic framework. It can be noted that the 'dual foundation' model includes two components or subtheories, the first concerned with the foundation processes and the second with the details of orthographic development.

Foundation processes

In our current research we have defined the foundations in terms of performance on a small number of simple tests. The materials have been listed in Appendix 2A.

1. *Logographic.* Direct reading of items from lists of high frequency content words and functors.
2. *Alphabetic.* Sounding of visually presented letters; writing letters in response to their sounds; reading and writing items from a list of simple C–V–C non-words.
3. *Phonological awareness (PA).* Giving rhymes and alliterations; division of words into two parts (onset + rime), three parts (initial consonant, vowel, terminal consonant), or many parts (phonemes).

We have found that the logographic and alphabetic foundations are usually present in children whose reading age (as assessed by the Schonell graded word tests) is above a level of about 6.7 years. In the absence of the foundation, our first move would always be to attempt to establish it, using standard techniques, particularly pairing of letters and words with pictures.

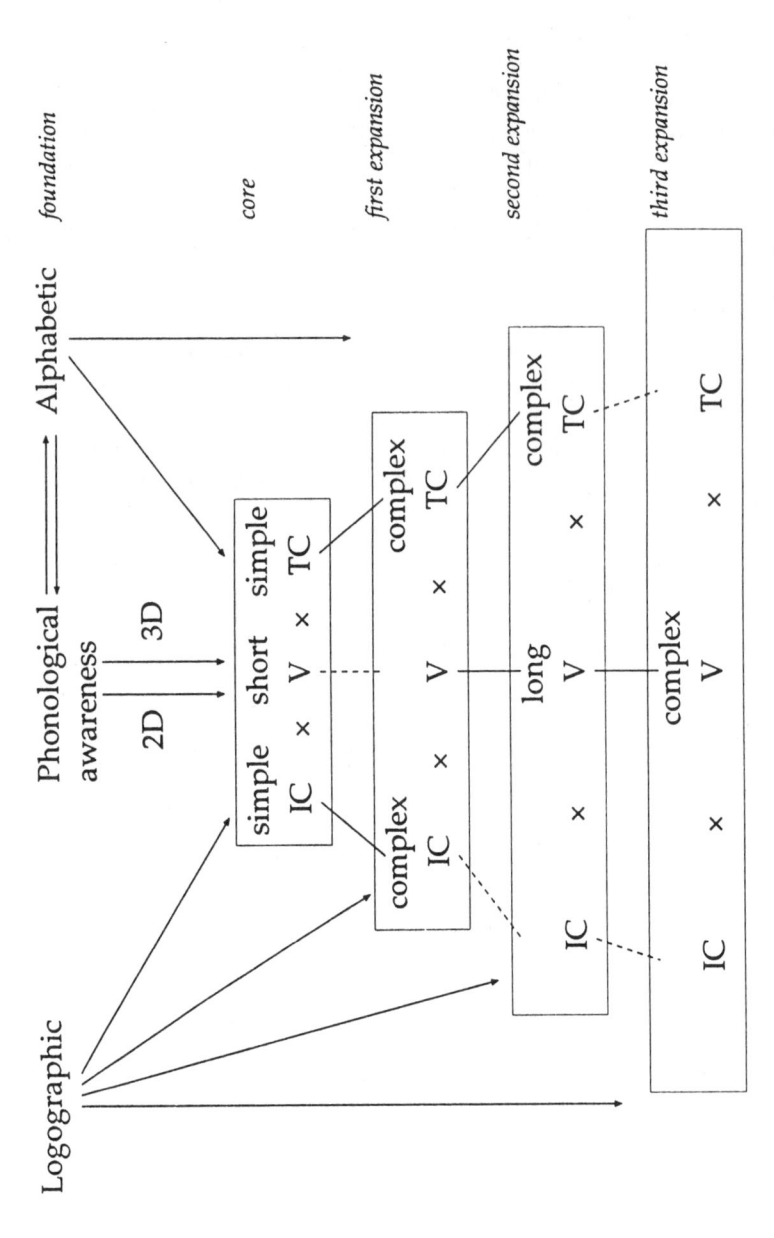

FIGURE 14.1 *Schematic representation of dual foundation model of orthographic development* — Logographic, alphabetic and phonological processes provide the basis for formation of a 'core' lexicon which is progressively expanded (from Seymour, 1990). Solid lines indicate acqusition of new structures.

Orthographic Framework

Our own usage of the term 'orthographic' refers to the spelling patterns used as building blocks for words. An orthographic system is defined by the elements it contains and by the way in which they are organised, both internally and in relation to phonology. We have taken the view that an orthographic lexicon might be seen as a combinatorial structure formed by the multiplication of elements on two or three dimensions. These are referred to as 2D and 3D structures:

- *2D structure*. The elements defining the lexicon consist of a set of x initial consonant (IC) groups (onsets) which combine multiplicatively with the members of a set of y vowel (V) + terminal consonant (TC) groups (rimes) to form xy onset + rime constructions.
- *3D structure*. The elements defining the lexicon consist of a set of x IC groups, y V, and z TC groups. These combine multiplicatively to form a set of xyz IC + V + TC constructions. It will be clear that this analysis refers to a lexicon of *syllables* and that additional considerations are posed in the case of polysyllabic or morphemic forms.

According to the combinatorial view, the goals of remedial instruction are to establish the elements which form the dimensions of the lexicon, to show how they relate to the phonological structure of the syllable, and to assist the placement of real words within the larger orthographic framework. We suggest that this task might involve different structural emphases, corresponding approximately to the 1D, 2D or 3D models outlined above. It is, in theory, possible that one of these emphases is optimal, either in general or for children with a particular pattern of strengths and weaknesses.

Stages of Orthographic Development

An orthographic system is a complex structure which must be built up step by step. The key problems for the design of a method of 'orthographic instruction' are to determine the overall form of the system which is to be built up and to diagnose the stages by which this can be achieved.

In our own work, we initially adopted a 3D combinatorial model, based on the IC × V × TC analysis of the syllable. We identified the principal letter groups which occur in the consonant initial, consonant terminal and medial vowel positions of English monosyllables. (For the purposes of this analysis words containing unstressed second syllables, such as *battle*, were treated as monosyllables.) We started with a set of over 50 ICs, about 20 Vs, and more than 70 TCs. In order to obtain a picture of the content of the lexicon, a computer program was written which allowed the operator to specify a set of ICs, a set of TCs and a single V structure. The program systematically generated the full set of possible IC × TC combinations with the selected vowel and allowed the user to mark each one as a word or nonword. The output from the program consisted of a series of IC × TC matrices, one for each vowel, in which words appeared in their appropriate cells (see Seymour, 1987).

Following examination of the content of the lexicon we proposed a model of orthographic development which is stated in terms of a 'core' structure and a series of elaborations or expansions (see Figure 14.1).

Core structure

The proposals for the 'core' structure were based on criteria of simplicity and consistency. In practice, this means that the core can be viewed as the imposition of a 3D organisation on the simple letter–sound correspondences associated with the alphabetic foundation. Seymour (1990) has listed the suggested IC, V and TC elements. They consist of the single consonants, the single vowels, and some digraphs which correspond to single phonemes (**TH, SH, CH, WH, CK**). The structure contains 24 × 5 × 14 = 1,680 cells of which about 480 contain English words. Given the well-known relationship between frequency and numbers of examples (Oldfield, 1966), it is expected that the majority of the words will be of relatively low frequency. A consequence is that vocabularies containing only words of high frequency may not be well adapted for transmission of the core. It is also true that the structure contains irregular forms, some of very high frequency: **DO, GO, HE, HIS, PUT, WAS, WHAT**, etc., which could work against internalisation of the overall structure if over-emphasised. (*Was* and *what* are, in fact, instances of a 'rule' which converts /æ/ to /ɒ/ following an initial /w/ sound but not before a velar, e.g. *wag, whack.*) Appendix 3 shows the incidence of the core structures and provides information about the distribution of word frequencies and irregularities.

First expansion

Inspection of the matrices suggested that the introduction of consonant clusters constituted a natural first step towards expansion of the core lexicon. In the IC position the clusters are principally combinations of simple elements (**PR, PL; GR, GL; SCR, SPL, SN**, etc.) though there are a few novel structures (**QU, GU**) and irregularities (**KN, GN, WR**). They form the enlarged set of 59 ICs shown in Appendix 4. There is also a set of predictable TC clusters (**MP, FT, NK, NCH**, etc.) plus a few special cases (**NG**) and irregularities (**TCH**). A problem is that some TCs affect the preceding vowel, producing inconsistent pronunciations (cf. the effect of **-LD** in *bald* and *wild*) (Henderson, 1982; Patterson & Morton, 1985). We omitted these TCs from the first expansion. The new set included **SS** (contrast with single **S** in the core) and **K, F**, and **L**. Vowel lengthening was introduced by the inclusion of the **-Y** structures (**AY, EY, OY, UY**), used only with a null TC, and one highly consistent form, **EE**, which combines with the new single consonants. The expansion generated almost 800 additional words (see Appendix 4).

Second expansion

The first expansion creates a system which includes most of the ICs but which leaves the issue of vowel lengthening largely untouched and which also omits a number of complex TCs. Inspection of the matrices suggested that a key to the movement forward into this area was provided by the role of final **-E** in English spelling. The occurrence of **-E** after a single TC typically exerts a lengthening effect on the preceding vowel. The second expansion therefore included the five vowels (**A, E, I, O, U**) modified by final **-E**. The IC set retained the full set of clusters with the addition of one infrequent form (**SCH**). The final **-E** also has effects on the pronunciation of the TCs. These include softening of **C** and **G** (**-CE; -GE, -DGE, -NGE**), obligatory inclusion after **V** (**-VE**), and a large set of possibilities which are created by the addition of **-LE** and **-ER**. These have been listed in Appendix 5. It can be noted that the TCs are related to vowel lengthening by a principle of consonant doubling. In general, the medial vowel is shortened if a double consonant is used (**-PPLE, -TTER**, etc.) but is lengthened before a single consonant (**-BLE, -TLE**, etc.). There are other generalities, such as shortening before **CK**, as in **-CKLE**, and before consonant clusters (**-NDLE, -NKLE**), plus some areas of systematic variability (e.g. **-NGER** has different readings in *finger, ginger* and *singer*). The expanded matrix generates over 1,000 additional words and presents the conditions for vowel lengthening in a moderately systematic form. Appendix 5 contains the details.

Third expansion

The elements not covered by the core and first two expansions consist principally of a large set of orthographically complex vowels (**EA, OU, IGH, AW, OR**, etc.) and the TC structures which were omitted from the first expansion. A new series of matrices was plotted, one for each of the vowels listed in Appendix 6, using the full set of ICs and the core TCs plus the omitted structures. These matrices maximise variability of spelling–sound mapping, partly because of the retroactive effects of the TCs and partly because many of the vowels have multiple pronunciations (**EA** → /iː/, /e/ or /eI/ as in *treat*, *bread* and *break*). The expansion generates almost 1,200 additional words while introducing a complex arbitrary element into the issue of vowel lengthening. See Appendix 6.

The listings of orthographic elements constitute a concrete realisation of the model of orthographic development which is schematised in Figure 14.1. This explicit structure forms the heart of our approach to orthographic instruction and assessment.

Orthographic Lists

The conversion of the orthographic model into an assessment and teaching programme required the derivation of sets of items which were representative of the content of the core and of each of the expansions. Appendix 3 gives the five word lists, each of 28 items, which were derived to represent the core. A comparable set of five lists, each of 51 items, is given in Appendix 4 for the first expansion. In these lists the IC, V and TC elements have an overall incidence which approximates their distribution in the lexicon. The lists also contain high, medium and low-frequency words in similar proportions to the lexicon as a whole. The lists for the second and third expansions contained 67 and 77 items respectively. One example from each set of five is provided in Appendices 5 and 6.

Parallel sets of non-word lists were derived for the four orthographic levels. These consisted of IC + V + TC combinations sampled from the empty cells of the core and expanded lexicons. As far as possible, the non-words were derived by interchanging the IC and V + TC (rime) components of each word list. The effect of this procedure is to produce non-word lists which match the word lists in terms of the distribution of frequencies of orthographic elements found in the word lists. Appendix 3 gives the core non-word lists. The lists match their parent word sets in orthographic content (i.e. Non-word List 1 parallels Word List 1). The full set of non-word lists derived for the first expansion appear in Appendix 4. Examples of lists for the second and third expansions have been included in Appendices 5 and 6.

The sets of words and non-words provide materials for the teaching and assessment of each orthographic level. Thus, Seymour & Bunce (in press) used the items from a single list as teaching materials but applied the full set (for the core and first expansion) to monitor orthographic progress. In making a general assessment it may be convenient to employ the truncated version included in Appendix 2B.

Properties of Teaching Methods

The approach to teaching involves traditional pedagogic techniques, applied one-to-one, but governed by a set of constraints imposed by cognitive theory and by the model of developing orthographic structure. We found it convenient to think in terms of episodes of varying size, distinguishing between:

- an exercise — a specific task in which a circumscribed set of cognitive operations are applied under the guidance of the teacher;
- a session — a meeting with the child involving a variety of exercises; and
- a teaching phase — a series of sessions extending over a number of weeks.

What we attempted to do was to construct exercises which were defined with respect to a number of properties, of which the following were the most important:

- *Orthographic level.* Given availability of the foundation, we would normally expect to start teaching at the core level. This involves work with exercises which use the vocabulary of one (or more) of the core lists (see Appendix 3). The lists are also used to assess progress following a period of teaching and to indicate the point at which the move to the first expansion should be made (indexed by success on the core word and non-word lists). For the cases described by Seymour & Bunce (in press), this move was made after two periods of core teaching, occupying approximately two months each. There then followed three periods directed at the establishment of the first expansion, each of about ten weeks, using materials based on the lists given in Appendix 4.
- *Lexical versus non-lexical focus.* The cognitive architecture (Ellis & Young, 1988) makes a distinction between lexical and non-lexical processes in reading and spelling. We manipulated this aspect by using either a word list or a non-word list as the basis for teaching examples. Thus, in the case of D.K. (Seymour & Bunce, in press), it seemed appropriate to focus the teaching towards the non-lexical systems, since the subject's main difficulty was in non-word reading and spelling.
- *Input versus output focus.* The second major distinction in the cognitive model is between input processes, required for reading, and output processes, involved in spelling and writing. We attempted to manipulate this

aspect by developing some exercises which appeared, prima facie, to emphasise recognition processes, and others which explicitly demanded production of written output.
- *Coding focus.* This aspect concerns the level or depth of processing demanded by an exercise. Some tasks may be limited to visual matching while others may require the consideration of meaning or operations on phonology.
- *Structural emphasis.* This feature concerns the distinction between the unidimensional (1D) model of the lexicon and the combinatorial (2D and 3D) framework models. We used various techniques in an effort to emphasise a particular organisation. One of these was colour coding. Teaching was supported by letter groups printed on separate cards. For 3D, IC = blue, V = red, TC = green. For 2D, onset = blue, TC = green. Pupils also recorded words in a personal dictionary, listing them under IC, V and TC headings for 3D emphasis, and under onset and rime headings for 2D. These features were not used in 1D teaching, where items occurred on single cards, without colour coding, and were listed according to features such as initial letter and length. The exercises were designed to support the structural focus. Thus, in a crossword puzzle problem clues might be stated by reference to IC, V or TC components for 3D, or onset or rime components for 2D.

It is not possible to provide a detailed account of the exercises here. They consisted of commonly used techniques, involving puzzles, incomplete sentences, matching problems, etc., which were intended to provide variety and a degree of challenge. Each exercise was defined in terms of the orthographic level of its materials, whether the items were words or non-words, whether or not written output was required, the coding level involved, and the structural organisation which was emphasised. These features were held constant within each of the sessions making up a teaching phase. The phases were bounded by orthographic assessments (pre- and post-tests). The shift to a new phase was usually accompanied by a change in some aspects of the teaching approach. We use the term 'teaching programme' to refer to a sequence of phases, each characterised by a different combination of properties (see Seymour, 1990; Seymour & Bunce, in press).

Conclusion

The orthographic model has potential as a framework for the planning and evaluation of programmes of remediation. A particular advantage is that assessment and instruction depend on a common theoretical view. The problem is to determine which of the possible models is the most appropriate in an instructional setting.

Modular architecture

The standard cognitive model (e.g. Ellis & Young, 1988; Morton, 1989) identifies lexical systems, containing word (or morpheme) representations, and subsidiary non-lexical (alphabetic) systems. This model is helpful for purposes of general assessment (Seymour, 1990), especially where the aim is to determine the balance of disadvantage in the lexical and non-lexical processes. Vocabulary-based lists of the kind provided in Appendix 1 serve this function by revealing the degree of contrast between familiar and unfamiliar forms (word versus non-word difference) and the difficulties created by non-standard forms (regularity effect).

The two cases, D.K. and R.C., described by Seymour & Bunce (in press) illustrate the value of the method for assessment of contrasting patterns of impairment. However, the implications for instruction are more limited. So far as methods are concerned, the theory suggests the repeated presentation of vocabulary items, perhaps ordered by frequency, to build up the lexical systems, and the rehearsal of letter–sound associations to establish the non-lexical systems. A key suggestion is that instruction might focus on the modules which have been shown, by assessment, to be impaired. Seymour & Bunce attempted to follow this prescription by directing teaching towards the lexical or non-lexical levels of reading or spelling but failed to demonstrate module-specific effects. If this outcome is verified in future studies the applicability of the modular architecture to instruction (but not assessment) will be weakened.

Foundations model

The advantage of the developmental theories is that they offer some guidance regarding the overall sequence of instruction. In the Frith–Morton model this is stated in global terms, mainly by reference to the conditions which lead to a change of dominant strategy. The dual foundation model suggests a structural relation between the early processes and the later development of an orthographic system and also the possibility of different origins of breakdown (visual-logographic or phonological-alphabetic) and hence of contrasting patterns of dyslexia — as exemplified by Seymour & Bunce's cases, D.K. and R.C. The extent to which the foundations must be established before proceeding with orthographic instruction remains to be determined. However, the attempt to establish a core orthographic system in D.K., who initially lacked alphabetic processes in reading or spelling, did result in a period of effortful letter–sound processing, suggesting that Frith (1985) may be correct in her assertion that the alphabetic phase is indispensible and cannot simply be skipped.

Orthographic framework

The main contribution of the framework model is that it provides a detailed specification of the content and sequence of instruction. The preliminary study by Seymour & Bunce suggested that the distinction between core and expanded structures was workable in that both subjects made significant gains which persisted and generalised to new (untaught) items, including non-words. Manipulation of the 2D versus 3D structural contrast did not produce clear effects. Nor were there strong indications that different approaches were required for children with contrasting dyslexic patterns. The course of development differed between the cases, but this seemed to depend more on their underlying characteristics than on the teaching approach adopted. The implication is that orthographic instruction might be constrained by a core-expansion model of the kind described in this chapter, but might otherwise exploit as full and varied a range of pedagogic techniques as possible.

A final point concerns the distinction between reading and spelling. The materials presented in the appendices were derived from an analysis of the *visual forms* which occur in print and their relation to phonology. Strictly, therefore, the model refers to the input lexicon and the establishment of the reading process. There is, none the less, no reason why the materials should not be used for instruction in spelling (Seymour & Bunce, in press). Indeed, in the case of D.K., the instructional programme had more dramatic effects on spelling than on reading. However, it is clear that materials derived from an analysis of the output lexicon, starting from *phonological forms* and their mapping onto orthography, and taking due account of sound–spelling contingency (Seymour, Chapter 3 this volume), would be more directly appropriate for spelling instruction.

Summary

A model of orthographic development has been presented as a framework for assessment and remediation. Given the availability of logographic, alphabetic and phonological foundations, development involves the formation of a core structure of simple elements and its expansion to include consonant clusters and lengthened vowels. Materials for the assessment of the foundations and orthographic levels were included together with some comments on the way the scheme can be used as a framework for the design of remedial interventions.

Appendix 1: Vocabulary-based Lists

Items are presented individually for reading and writing to dictation. Word sets are stratified by frequency (HF > 800, LF < 100 per 5 million), regularity (RG, RL, I) and length (three to six letters).

Word lists

Regular — RG

HF: dog cut yes stop milk help black still until cannot animal bottom
LF: lid van jam bump twin skip crisp frost comic dragon ribbon puppet

HF: ran six sun left next hand spell class stand second across common
LF: cot cub fox moss tank snap prick robin camel carrot packet wicked

Rule-based — RL

HF: car boy air here girl draw reach voice might ground square family
LF: ark zoo owl knee jail dash uncle crown fairy chapel sledge saucer

HF: say saw sea blue take tree stood short house winter strong letter
LF: fie bee toy wrap kite curl bunch lorry purse switch fright prince

Irregular — I

HF: who has own kind door does ready world often colour enough always
LF: ivy tow ski oven soup bomb apron flood glove cousin diesel castle

HF: any two use warm want once money music learn school should answer
LF: mow sew guy bush worm calf angel sword yacht autumn brooch monkey

Non-word lists

Regular — RG

rad cag dex bis vot jun skup stin himp molp belk twip blist frack ucrel crill rimic stosp pattom rinnot drofal coppet anicon bebbon

lan sig yut fon pib cux lund nass hoxt mank tift snep spack clell stass prand remel cobin simmot ucress sackon cacked pecund worret

Rule-based — RL

arl zoy foo sar owk aib kere jorl knue graw daip hish crean intle fawch moiry rairt vight semily faupel chicer squape grodge slound

soy ree zay jie vea taw blee turp grue wrop kide gake stoce shurd horry booce lorch punse witter strang lenter frince pritch swight

Irregular — I

ipy sni spo fas yow owb koes ovep noor gind vour somb teald aprit trood aften worby flove colsel enstle amough diesin cousel alnour

cew kuy aby zow dwo ude wamp talf walp worg dush onge musey swird vacht yorel angic mearn emswer schoon brould lonkey trooch aidumn

Two alternative forms of each list are given.

Appendix 2: Dual Foundation Model

A. Foundations

a. Logographic foundation
(direct reading of early content and functor words)

Content: look home call green father high come read run back ball ship man make like mother good fast three end
Functor: too get all out did on got at an down him my it am but had up soon where there

b. Alphabetic foundation
(giving sounds of letters and writing letters in response to sounds)

Consonants: b c d f g h j k l m n p qu r s t v w x y z ch th sh wh
Vowels: a e i o u

ORTHOGRAPHIC ASSESSMENT AND REMEDIATION

Lengthened vowels and complex forms (ee oo ar or er ou ow ai y oi au aw augh ea ew ir ur oa ay ey ie igh oy) may be included but are not strictly part of the foundation.

Non-words (read and write simple non-words)
nos cug fem pid tas wex keb vut yit zad rop hon
cax fot nin peb hig jas sug bup gam lud mip dob

c. Phonological awareness (PA)
(synthesising words from segments, dividing words into segments)

Synthesis: Repeat back item presented: (1) as a whole, (2) as two parts (onset/rime), (3) as three parts (IC–V–TC) or (4) as sequence of phonemes.
Analysis: Respond to item by giving : (1) a rhyme, (2) an alliteration, (3) two parts (scored for onset/rime division), (4) three parts (scored for IC–V–TC division), or (5) many parts (scored for phonemes).

Word lists
1. green town thief screen blunt sent lip wash stem kind
2. book scratch pack kite moist dress sharp fluff red twist
3. post check grab clench map leak press list squirt mouse
4. skirt spell squirm shave snug match hop point fence noise
5. girl ship chain strength mud comb pound crisp crab plum

Non-word lists
1. woth dief pleem jown fent blund steb lep screet gind
2. pook flig chack doist twesp stratch yite gress rud sarp
3. priss deak grem mip sprirt shist vost chouse sheck clelch
4. thave hap sneb gence splirm moint datch coise drell skest
5. craff shane bip mog pousk spum lirl vomb squength crirt

(The lists may be used interchangeably with the different tasks.)

B. Orthographic structure

Orthographic levels lists (truncated version):

a. Core

Words: check fish sat put us bed Bob leg mud hat Jim son shock cash whip Ruth vex gag dam tho kid nip tan ye
Non-words: vo re ip hus lon tud feg yed gat kex jip san nid cag bam dat chut sish whob shim meck bock puth thash

b. First expansion

Words: thing French speech drink glass slept clay squint scrimp throng sprung kneel grasp flask scalp breed twang croft stump blunt plank weed prep wry
Non-words: twy glay flink plept frint climp stoft brask scump slank screp crunt drass prasp wralp kning weech grung theed bleel spench sprong squang threed

c. Second expansion

Words: matter space wonder quite whose love splutter strangle skelter swindle wrestle crinkle stumble shiver trifle ledger offer bathe tuber ample scope theme dune sage
Non-words: ope wune tove iver spose stite dathe muber quage treme splace bonder lelter lindle crifle sumble wroffer scutter shangle whestle swedger thinkle skample stratter

d. Third expansion

Words: night could great smooth chief walk farm poor ears shrewd squirm broach strain thrown snore stork moist guilt scold gnaw herb slur gall bind
Non-words: filt pown nalk mief ooth graw bork hain starm chind snold gight scewd guirm gnerb shrur woach coist smoor slould strall squeat brears throre

Appendix 3: Core Orthographic Structure

Component elements

a. Initial consonants

P(7) B(7.5) T(5.6) D(5.6) C(4.4) K(2.1) G(4.4); CH(2.9) J(3.8); F(4) V(0.1) TH(2.5) S(5.8) Z(0.1) SH(2.9); M(5.8) N(4); H(6.5) L(5.6) R(6.1) W(3.5) WH(2.5) Y(2.3) #(3.5).

b. Vowels

A(27.1) E(14.4) I(20.5) O(20.9) U(17.1).

c. Terminal consonants

P(9.6) B(7.3) T(13.1) D(9.4) CK(10.4) X(3.1) G(9.6); CH(1.3) F(0.5) TH(3.1) S(2.9) SH(5.4); M(6.9) N(12.5); #(4.8).

(Values refer to incidence in words as per cent of all occurrences = blank.)

Lexical content of the core matrix

TABLE 14.1 *The incidence of words in the matrix, their distribution across frequency classes, and the proportion of irregular items (pronunciation of one or more elements differs from the main trend in the matrix)*

		Frequency High >5,500	Medium	Low <100	Total
Words	N	44	139	296	479
	%	9	29	62	100
Irregular	N	25	13	20	58
	%	57	9	7	12

Core word and non-word lists

a. Word lists

HF: his* we* that* go* a can
MF: path* Jack bad men top yes six sum
LF: dish nag rush shop wad* loch* chub pit Ben deck Mum rug lit tub

HF: has* she* than* to* I* with*
MF: God rich lot big sun yet map Tom
LF: duck jab fix push* wan* chat nap cub bus Dick hid rim pin sash

HF: as* he* them* no* in which
MF: met gas fun set cut dog box rock
LF: wash* van shed Dad lath Pam bib beg sick tip lap rub pot hash

HF: is* me* then* do* of* what*
MF: gun led Sam much both* ran hot job
LF: pack keg wax neck pap chum mesh hut sad log tap rat tin dab

HF: was* be* this* so* if the*
MF: pick hit cat such let red ten Dan
LF: fog zip mix whom* gash nib bun hath bag rod lock dip Tim mob

b. Non-word lists

dis re yat co U lan sath gack tad chen dop hes bix pum bish pag sush thop wap roch mab jit shen teck wum nug dit mub nas E yan cho ji bith dod lich ot hig thun cet fap wom huck pab shix tush wab gat dap mun mus bick tid sim rin pash

das ve bem po min cich et ras lun tet dut rog gox bock thash han ped nad wath bam hib seg ick fip whap lub sot shash

sis che en ko bot whaf un med nam ruch toth san mot wob dack deg gax meck hap lum tesh lut rad pog thap jat hin bab

waf ge bis o ris de hick thit dat nuch ret ced sen zan sog bip hix whon tash lib fum tath mag lod bock thip mim pob

Appendix 4: First Expansion

Component elements

a. Initial consonants

P(3) PL(2) PR(2) B(3) BL(2) BR(2) T(2) TR(3) TW(1) D(3) DR(2) DW(0) C(1) K(1) CL(4) CR(3) QU(1) G(1) GU(<1) GL(1) GR(3); CH(1) J(<1); F(1) FL(4) FR(2) V(<1) TH(1) THR(1) S(2) SP(2) SPL(<1) SPR(<1) ST(4) STR(2) SC(1) SK(1) SCR(1) SQU(<1) SM(<1) SN(<1) SL(4) SW(3) SH(<1) SHR(<1); M(2) N(<1) KN(1) GN(<1); H(3) L(3) R(3) W(2) WH(<1) WR(1) Y(<1) #(2)

b. Vowels

A(23.7) E(10.2) I(18.8) O(11.3) U(15.1) EE(12.8) AY(3.4) EY(1) OY(1) UY(<1) Y(2.3)

c. Terminal consonants

P(5) SP(1) MP(5) LP(1) B(3) T(5) PT(<1) FT(3) NT(6) K(1) CK(4) SK(2) NK(7) X(<1) G(3); CH(<1) TCH(5) NCH(3); F(<1) TH(1) S(1) SS(5) SH(3); M(4) N(3) NG(7); L(1) #(3)

ORTHOGRAPHIC ASSESSMENT AND REMEDIATION

Lexical content of first expansion

TABLE 14.2 *Distribution of words and irregular forms across frequency ranges*

		Frequency			
		High >1,000	Medium	Low <100	Total
Words	N	42	169	575	786
	%	5	22	73	100
Irregular	N	7	16	49	72
	%	17	9	9	9

Word and non-word lists for the first expansion

a. Word lists

HF: play stop two*
MF: inch bring sheep key* swam beef stress grass* lamp trunk rang stick
LF: gong Jess shrunk spleen thresh clump bleed dank flint scrub spit clamp fry truss grog sled bang monk* gnat wasp* whisk smack squid crutch sleet seep tint font wretch craft* drunk sweep flit prick pump hatch

HF: front* they* song
MF: bay sweet trap watch* strip bee guess brass* crash deep dress wrong
LF: quack kneel cask* Scot sprint snub teen trim slit gang lump crag ramp gross* prod glut hump bled spy screech kink etch skimp cheep clunk stud flinch graft* mint pluck slink swank fleck patch stunt

HF: day keep try
MF: sketch queen cloth sprang sung block speed buy thank creek sleep witch fresh
LF: vent glee cuss scent* chimp greed Ross tramp mask* strap flick slob clang swum cramp pang boss drat flux knit ass snack swot stint tuft scrunch limp plug writ pint* stunk bred grip hitch prank

HF: boy see why*
MF: gay steel cross loss step ask* plus king meet tank print
LF: yelp jeep shred splint thrush cluck deem weft slab scratch trench crimp blink spud trump grant* wring drip hiss shank twin smog squat* swamp* peep fleet fuss grid strung clomp batch slang swatch* flock frock brink rant

HF: went think need

MF: catch toy seek match bunch dry lay swept spring screen string

LF: quit fee gloss amp snap creep greet brig dusk trot plop hint pant clod spat flip rink frump swab* knack kiss scum skunk chess cleft creed trash flung slump wrack stink stamp grunt bless prong slack botch

b. Non-word lists

floy swo rinch gneep squam scress wamp lang hong pess thrunk sleen shresh flump cleed jank plint strub crit slamp ky stuss wrog cled mang smonk trop tring ey deef frass crunk swick stat basp shisk spack twid grutch spleet geep sint tont pretch braft grunk beep blit drick whump fatch

mont bong skay steet grap satch sprip cree clack gueel pask quot scub scrint een frim glit flang kump trag hamp tross drod blut tump gred chey cess dass prash feep bress knong swy streech crink letch stimp theep wunk clud slinch wraft bint sluck flink pling snank sweck ratch spunt

ay teep swuy chank treek cleep mitch gresh hent wree duss quent thimp treed poss dramp wask sprap scrick flob glang blum pramp cang voss crat gry snetch speen floth strang kung plock sceep slux stit rass skack stot swint buft slunch bimp clug frit fint lunk kned crip sitch brank

doy sply yay sheel tross foss swep belp meep sted rint shrush bluck keem seft clab statch scrench trimp plink smud drump crant gring crip whiss gee hask flus bing leet pank brint strank swin spog wrat twamp eep cleet wuss frid thrung slomp jatch flang squatch slock prock grink tant

fent cheed datch loy eek natch tunch clit ree closs samp skap greep dreet crig pusk crot spop kint bant flod strat blip bink prump quab knink bry cay trept hing steen scring scack wiss stum snunk thess sleft spreed grash plung glump swack swink wramp trunt sless flong frack motch

Note: For ease of administration each list is sub-divided into two.

Appendix 5: Second Expansion

Component elements

a. Initial consonants

P(4) PL(<1) PR(2) B(4) BL(1) BR(1) T(5) TR(2) TW(<1) D(4) DR(<1) C(4) K(<1) CL(1) CR(2) QU(<1) G(2) GU(<1) GL(<1) GR(2); CH(1)

ORTHOGRAPHIC ASSESSMENT AND REMEDIATION

J(2); F(3) PH(<1) FL(<1) FR(<1) V(<1) TH(<1) THR(<1) S(3) SP(2) SPL(<1) SPR(<1) ST(2) STR(1) SC(1) SK(<1) SCH(<1) SCR(<1) SQU(<1) SM(<1) SN(<1) SL(1) SW(<1) Z(<1) SH(2) SHR(<1); M(4) N(3) KN(<1) GN(<1); H(4) L(4) W(3) WH(1) WR(<1) R(5) Y(<1) #(4)

b. Vowels

A(32) E(8) I(28) O(18) U(14)

c. Terminal consonants

PE(3) PLE(<1) PPLE(<1) PER(<1) PPER(1) SPER(<1) MPLE(<1) MPER(<1); BE(1) BLE(<1) BBLE(2) BER(<1) BBER(<1) MBLE(2) MBER(1); TE(5) TLE(<1) TTLE(2) TER(<1) TTER(4) FTER(<1) STE(<1) STER(2) NTER(<1) LTER(<1); DE(4) DLE(<1) DDLE(2) DER(<1) DDER(<1) NDLE(<1) NDER(2) LDER(<1); KE(4) CLE(0) CKLE(2) KER(<1) CKER(<1) SKER(<1) NKLE(<1) NKER(<1); GUE(<1) GLE(<1) GGLE(1) GGER(<1) NGLE(1) NGER(1); CHE(<1) CHER(<1) TCHER(<1); GE(<1) DGE(<1) GER(<1) DGER(<1) NGE(<1); FE(<1) FLE(<1) FFLE(1) FER(<1) FFER(<1) LFER(<1); VE(4) VER(2); THE(<1) THER(2); SE(2) CE(3) SLE(<1) STLE(1) SER(<1) CER(<1) SSER(<1); ZE(1) ZZLE(1); SHER(<1); ME(3) MLE(0) MER(<1) MMER(<1); NE(5) NLE(0) NER(<1) NNER(<1); LE(4) LER(<1) LLER(<1)

Lexical content of second expansion

TABLE 14.3 *Distribution of words and irregular forms across frequency ranges*

		Frequency			
		High >1,000	Medium	Low <100	Total
Words	N	59	186	788	1,033
	%	6	18	76	100
Irregular	N	22	27	69	118
	%	37	15	9	11

Word and non-word list for second expansion

a. Word list

HF: give* after*
MF: drove Steve snake plane middle guide
LF: sake cute pope tote jute lute elder chafe stale shame teller coffer dapper rumble jitter ponder blubber shudder whimper scatter cluster vase* laser* writhe* spruce* thistle*

HF: summer done*
MF: pile flame globe slide waste cover*
LF: rude nape hake tile bide spine bridle fondle hanker kettle fickle meddle totter dabble bangle prosper cripple cracker squiggle Roger* grace* triple* waffle* ginger* lather*

b. Non-word list

tive wafter mide nane meve tove chake giddle hafe ruce dake lale eller clute stame plope drote blute telder jubber cudder poffer donder ruster sprute trimper grapper snatter shumble shase flaser whithe wristle guitter

lummer brone wame tobe spile fover thide vaste sude dace bape bine jile pide iggle glake rosper condle fanker keddle cotter labble sangle slipple stettle craffle crickle piple gidle proger hather scacker squinger

Appendix 6: Third Expansion

Component structures

a. Initial consonants

P(5) PL(<1) PR(<1) B(6) BL(2) BR(2) T(4) TR(1) TW(<1) D(3) DR(1) DW(1) C(4) K(<1) CL(1) CR(2) QU(<1) G(3) GU(<1) GH(<1) GL(1) GR(2); CH(2) J(2); F(4) FL(1) FR(1) V(1) TH(<1) THR(<1) S(4) SP(2) SPL(<1) SPR(<1) ST(2) STR(<1) SC(1) SK(<1) SCH(<1) SCR(<1) SQU(<1) SM(<1) SN(<1) SL(1) SW(1) Z(<1) SH(3) SHR(<1); M(4) N(2) KN(<1) GN(<1); H(5) L(5) W(4) WH(<1) WR(<1) R(3) Y(1) #(4)

b. Vowels

A(4) AI(6) AR(6) AW(3); E(5) EA(10) EW(3) ER(2) EAR(4) EER(2) ERE(<1); I(6) IE(4) IGH(2) IR(3); O(3) OA(4) OI(2) OU(5) OO(8) OW(5) OR(4) ORE(2) OOR(<1); U(2) UR(3)

c. Terminal consonants

P(3) B(<1) T(10) ST(6) NT(1) LT(3) D(7) ND(4) LD(2) K(5) LK(1) X(<1) G(<1); CH(3) TCH(<1); F(2) LF(<1) TH(2) S(5) SH(<1); M(4) LM(<1) N(9); L(7) LL(7) #(16)

Lexical content of third expansion

TABLE 14.4 *Distribution of words and irregular forms across frequency ranges*

		Frequency High >1,000	Medium	Low <100	Total
Words	N	122	319	745	1,186
	%	10	27	63	100
Irregular	N	43	78	131	252
	%	35	24	18	21

Word and non-word lists for third expansion

a. Word list

HF: felt how* talk* heart*
MF: law film fight chain cream bow* tear* cook* ghost* quiet* flood*
LF: void self mead brew lurk coop maid gloat snarl mount joust spawn trait spill roast skull whirl steal germ* poll* coup* blown* sweat* sighs*

HF: her shall past* would*
MF: ore park east deer birth north stream lies* wool* tears*
LF: urn boor kilt plea fend gull dart lark bail pend shrew aitch yield* thorn brood shawl groan scorch starch woof* rind* sown* droll* chores*

b. Non-word list

telt malk ghow seart hilm ight glaw shain fow wook bost biet cear plood wheam oid melf herm surk swoat sparl stirl snawn drait strill loast ount yead goop fown leat moup scew caid foll soust blighs stull sheal ger wast lould thall trore ceer vool wark nies kirth deast borth shream flears pilt lail bart rark rurn dend croor broan horch paitch sparch ea skew toof pown gend pind jull broll grood tores chorn chawl quield

* Irregular words

Acknowledgement

The work described in this chapter was supported by a grant from the Medical Research Council of the UK.

References

BRYANT, P. and BRADLEY, L. 1985, *Children's Reading Problems*. Oxford: Basil Blackwell.
COLTHEART, M. and BYNG, S. 1989, A treatment for surface dyslexia. In X. SERON and G. DELOCHE (eds) *Cognitive Approaches in Neuropsychological Rehabilitation*. London: Lawrence Erlbaum.
EDWARDS, R. P. A. and GIBBON, V. 1973, *Words Your Children Use*. London: Burke Books.
ELLIS, A. W. and YOUNG, A. W. 1988, *Human Cognitive Neuropsychology*. London: Lawrence Erlbaum.
FRITH, U. 1985, Beneath the surface of developmental dyslexia. In K. E. PATTERSON, J. C. MARSHALL and M. COLTHEART (eds) *Surface Dyslexia: Neuropsychological and Cognitive Studies of Phonological Reading*. London: Lawrence Erlbaum.
HENDERSON, L. 1982, *Orthography and Word Recognition in Reading*. London: Academic Press.
MORTON, J. 1989, An information-processing account of reading acquisition. In A. M. GALABURDA (ed.) *From Reading to Neurons*. Cambridge, Mass.: MIT Press.
OLDFIELD, R. C. 1966, Things, words and the brain. *Quarterly Journal of Experimental Psychology* 18, 3–16.
OLSON, R. K., KLEIGL, R., DAVIDSON, B. J. and FOLTZ, G. 1985, Individual and developmental differences in reading disability. In G. E. MCKINNON and T. G. WALLER (eds) *Reading Research: Advances in Theory and Practice*, Vol. 4. Orlando, FL: Academic Press.
PATTERSON, K. E. and MORTON, J. 1985, From orthography to phonology: An attempt at an old interpretation. In K. E. PATTERSON, J. C. MARSHALL and M. COLTHEART (eds) *Surface Dyslexia: Neuropsychological and Cognitive Studies of Phonological Reading*. London: Lawrence Erlbaum.
SEIDENBERG, M. S. and MCCLELLAND, J. L. 1989, A distributed developmental model of word recognition and naming. *Psychological Review* 96, 523–68.

SEYMOUR, P. H. K. 1987, Developmental dyslexia: A cognitive experimental analysis in M. COLTHEART, G. SARTORI and R. JOB (eds) *The Cognitive Neuropsychology of Language*. London: Lawrence Erlbaum.
—— 1990, Developmental dyslexia. In M. W. EYSENCK (ed.) *Cognitive Psychology: An International Review*. Chichester: Wiley.
SEYMOUR, P. H. K. and BUNCE, F. in press, Application of cognitive models to remediation in cases of developmental dyslexia. In G. HUMPHREYS and J. RIDDOCH (eds) *Cognitive Neuropsychology and Cognitive Rehabilitation*. London: Lawrence Erlbaum.
SEYMOUR, P. H. K. and EVANS, H. M. 1988, Developmental arrest at the logographic stage: Impaired literacy functions in Klinefelter's XXXY syndrome. *Journal of Research in Reading* 11, 133–51.
—— 1992, Beginning reading without semantics: A cognitive study of hyperlexia. *Cognitive Neuropsychology* 9, 89–122.
SHALLICE, T. and MCCARTHY, R. 1985, Phonological reading: From patterns of impairment to possible procedures. In K. E. PATTERSON, J. C. MARSHALL and M. COLTHEART (eds) *Surface Dyslexia: Neuropsychological and Cognitive Studies of Phonological Reading*. London: Lawrence Erlbaum.

15 Spelling Remediation for Dyslexic Children using the SelfSpell Programs

RODERICK I. NICOLSON, SUSAN PICKERING
and ANGELA J. FAWCETT

Introduction: Computers and Dyslexia

Developmental dyslexia is characterised by severe problems in reading for children who otherwise appear to be of average or above average intelligence. Interestingly, however, most dyslexic children suffer from even more severe problems in spelling than in reading. Frith (1985) has suggested that dyslexic children have particular problems in mastering the 'alphabetic' stage of reading and spelling, in which the correspondences between letters and their sounds are exploited both for decoding printed words (reading) and for analysing spoken words into their written equivalents (writing). Seymour's chapter in this book (Chapter 3) provides a valuable overview of Frith's model and the research issues it has raised. The focus of this chapter is an applied one: namely how can we help dyslexic children to spell better? Two studies will be presented, first a demonstration that new technology can be married to good pedagogy to provide a supportive environment (Self-Spell) for adolescent dyslexic children, and second a further investigation of the efficacy of the approach with younger dyslexic children who have made little or no progress with spelling. First it is necessary to provide some background on the technological developments exploited by the SelfSpell program.

The SelfSpell Environment

The early generations of computer hardware had very limited capability for interacting with the user: the user was required to input commands by typing on the keyboard in response to written questions displayed on the computer. Although dedicated programmers made valiant efforts to circumvent these limitations, the fact remained that dyslexic children, with their poor reading and spelling skills, were at a particular disadvantage with such systems. Educational technology has taken a major step forward with the introduction of a new generation of affordable but very powerful micros such as the Apple Macintosh. In particular, the availability of hypermedia and multimedia environments which allow the smooth integration of text, graphics and synthesised or digitised speech, together with capability for interaction using 'point and click' rather than keyboard text entry, promise a solution to the problems for dyslexic children noted above. The SelfSpell environment represents an initial attempt to use these new developments.

We designed the SelfSpell program in an effort to remedy established problems of computer-based presentation for dyslexic children (Thomson, 1984). Our design requirements were that the program should be effective at remedying dyslexic children's most serious difficulties — in particular, spelling problems. Just as important, since motivation contributes crucially to a program's success (e.g. Malone, 1981) it should be fun to use. It should give immediate feedback — thus offering no opportunity for persistent errors; it should rely on active learning — with the user involved the whole time making active decisions; and it should support a range of forms of learning, including mastery learning. Support available should include synthesised speech to supplement text displays and self-selection of materials — using the user's own passages, own spellings and own spelling rules. Furthermore, parental support should be encouraged, both for authoring materials and for checking progress.

In order to meet this specification, we developed the program within the Apple HyperCard™ environment, using a 1 Mbyte Macintosh Plus micro (see Figure 15.1 for an illustration of the introduction stack). The intention was that the child should be able to use the system unaided much of the time, but with initial support from a parent or teacher. Use of this SelfSpell prototype fell into four distinct phases: first the parent/teacher read an interesting passage slowly to the child, repeating words as necessary, and the child wrote down the words as best he/she could (see Figure 15.2a for a partial transcript). Next the parent/teacher typed the child's version of the passage into the computer, and identified all the 'bugs', making a bug card for each (see Figures 15.2b and 15.2c). **Next the child went through the**

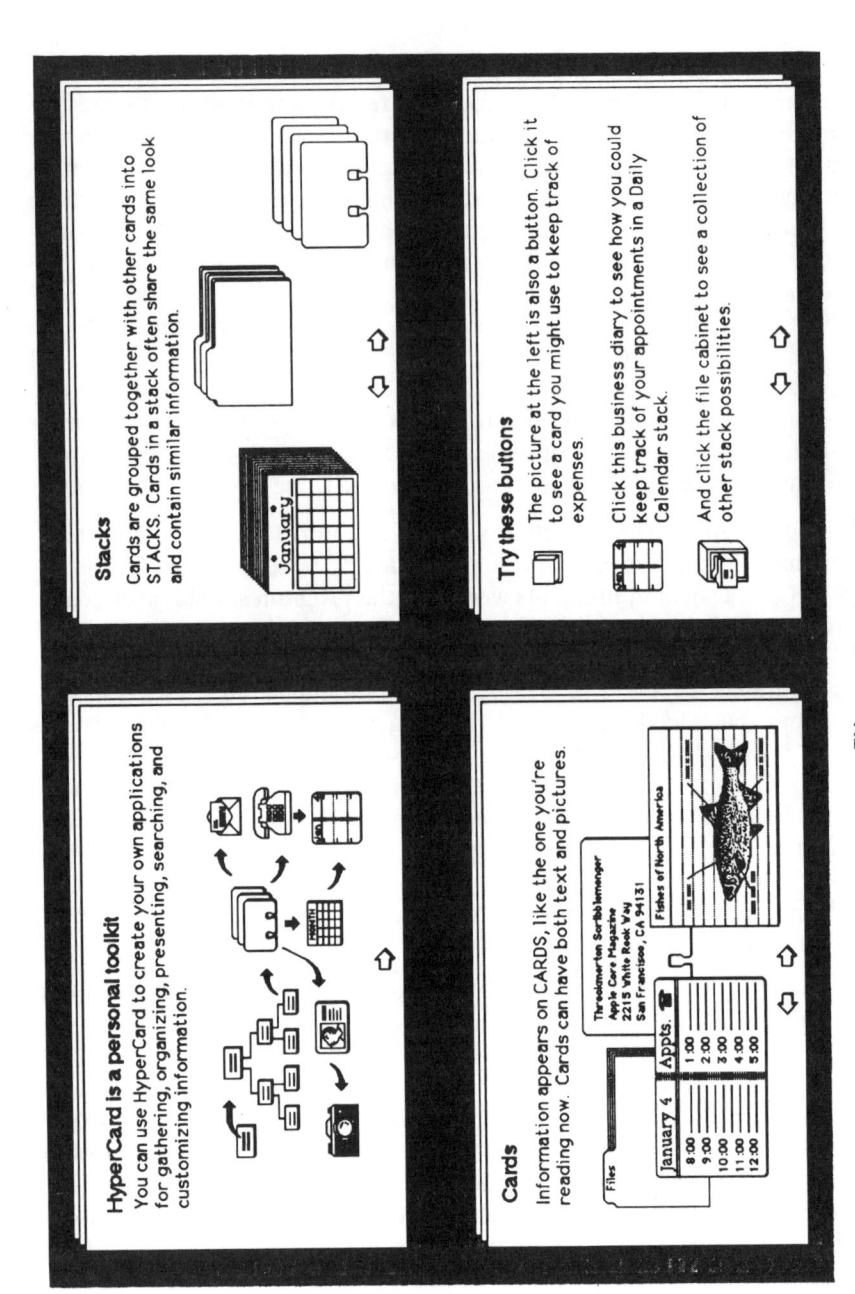

FIGURE 15.1 *Four cards from the HyperCard^{TM} introduction stack*

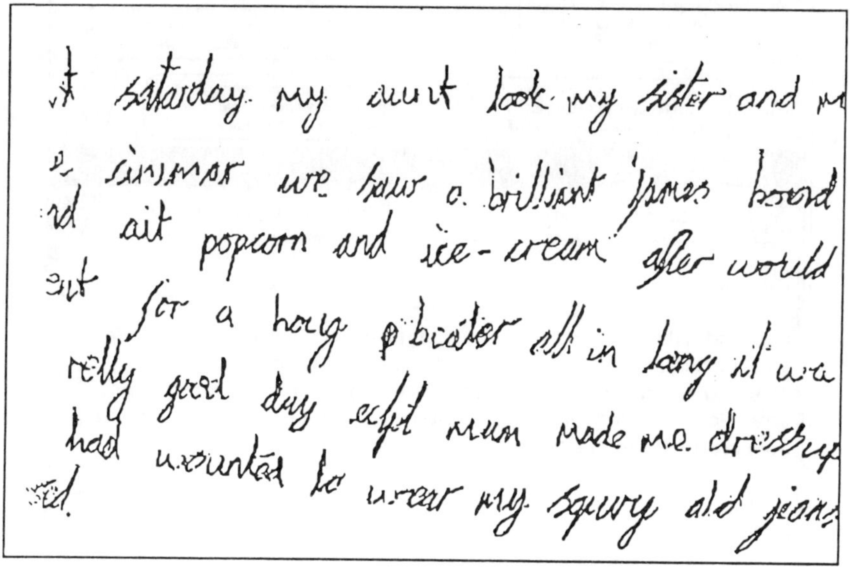

SPELLING REMEDIATION USING SELFSPELL

FIGURE 15.2a *A handwritten transcript*

passage (helped by the parent/teacher) identifying all the bugs, and for each one thinking up a rule to help them spell it right the next time (in Figure 15.2c, the child has typed in the rule 'U R Saturday' to help him remember the **UR** in the middle). In the final phase the child went through the passage fixing all the bugs, without human help but with support from the program which could either give a hint, a rule or 'speak' the correct spelling for a bug (see Figures 15.2e, 15.2f and 15.2g — the latter demonstrates the use of scoring to help with motivation). In this version of the program, rule help (e.g. 'U R Saturday' in Figure 15.2f) was not 'spoken' using synthesised speech, though in subsequent versions spoken help was available if required (via pressing a 'speak' button). All the responses were monitored automatically thus allowing easy record keeping. A novel feature of the program was that all the buttons were programmed to 'say' their name if the user 'hovered' over them with the mouse pointer, and furthermore there was a 'speak' button which used speech synthesis to 'pronounce' any words highlighted. Figure 15.2g shows the screen once the 'bug' had been corrected.

PSYCHOLOGY, SPELLING AND EDUCATION

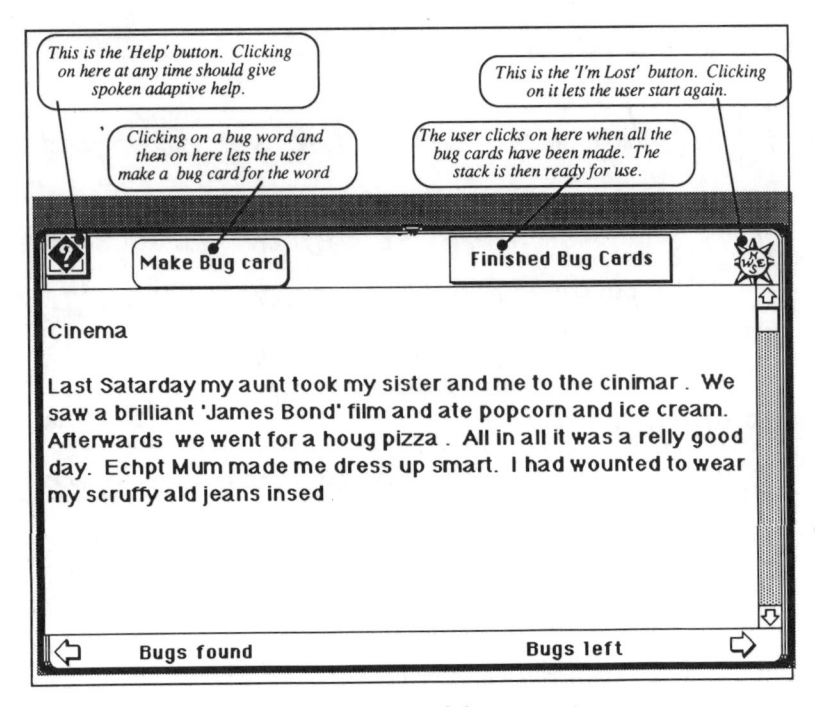

> This is the 'Help' button. Clicking on here at any time should give spoken adaptive help.

> This is the 'I'm Lost' button. Clicking on it lets the user start again.

> Clicking on a bug word and then on here lets the user make a bug card for the word

> The user clicks on here when all the bug cards have been made. The stack is then ready for use.

Make Bug card   **Finished Bug Cards**

Cinema

Last Saturday my aunt took my sister and me to the cinimar. We saw a brilliant 'James Bond' film and ate popcorn and ice cream. Afterwards we went for a houg pizza. All in all it was a relly good day. Echpt Mum made me dress up smart. I had wounted to wear my scruffy ald jeans insed

Bugs found   **Bugs left**

FIGURE 15.2b *The computer version of the transcript*

SPELLING BUGS

Correct Spelling: Saturday

Wrong Spelling: Satarday

> This button returns the user to the passage

Hint: The middle vowel is wrong here

Rule: u r saturday

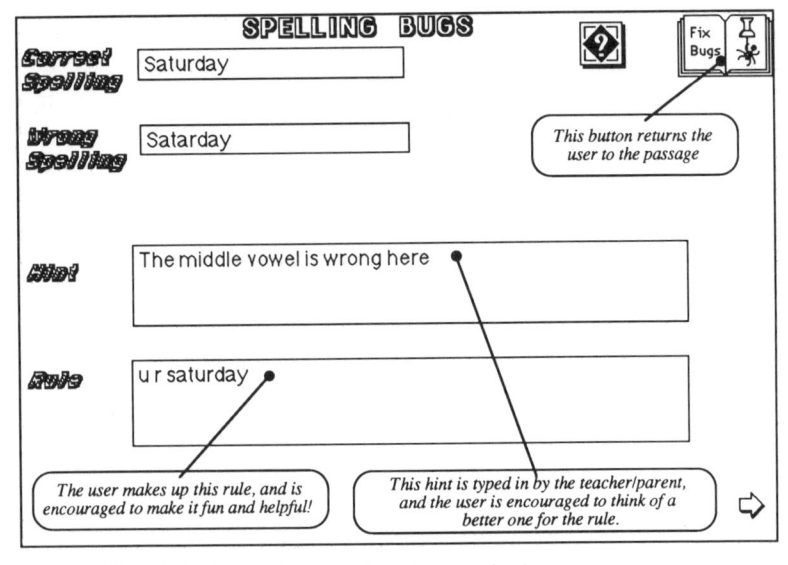

> The user makes up this rule, and is encouraged to make it fun and helpful!

> This hint is typed in by the teacher/parent, and the user is encouraged to think of a better one for the rule.

FIGURE 15.2c *Making a bug card for 'Satarday'*

SPELLING REMEDIATION USING SELFSPELL

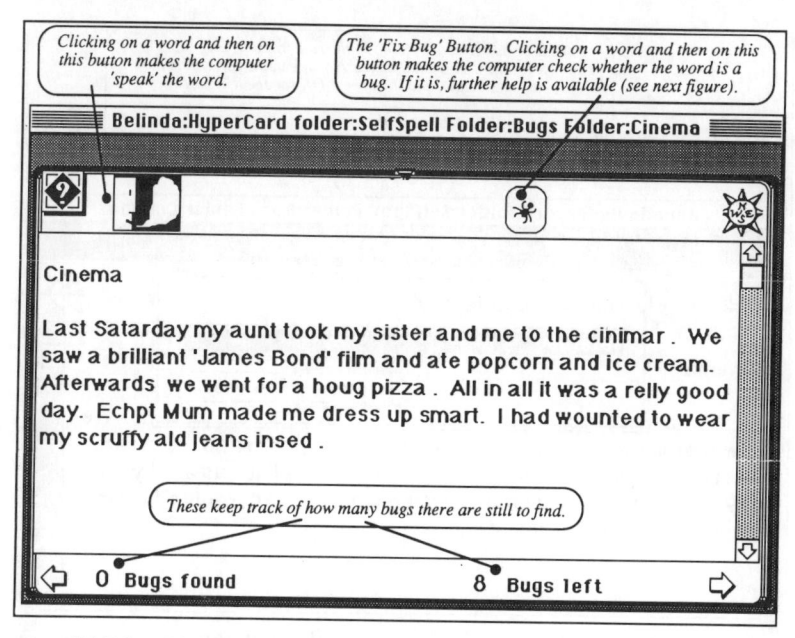

255

Clicking on a word and then on this button makes the computer 'speak' the word.

The 'Fix Bug' Button. Clicking on a word and then on this button makes the computer check whether the word is a bug. If it is, further help is available (see next figure).

Belinda:HyperCard folder:SelfSpell Folder:Bugs Folder:Cinema

Cinema

Last Satarday my aunt took my sister and me to the cinimar. We saw a brilliant 'James Bond' film and ate popcorn and ice cream. Afterwards we went for a houg pizza. All in all it was a relly good day. Echpt Mum made me dress up smart. I had wounted to wear my scruffy ald jeans insed.

These keep track of how many bugs there are still to find.

0 Bugs found   8 Bugs left

FIGURE 15.2d *Child's view of the support environment (click on a bug)*

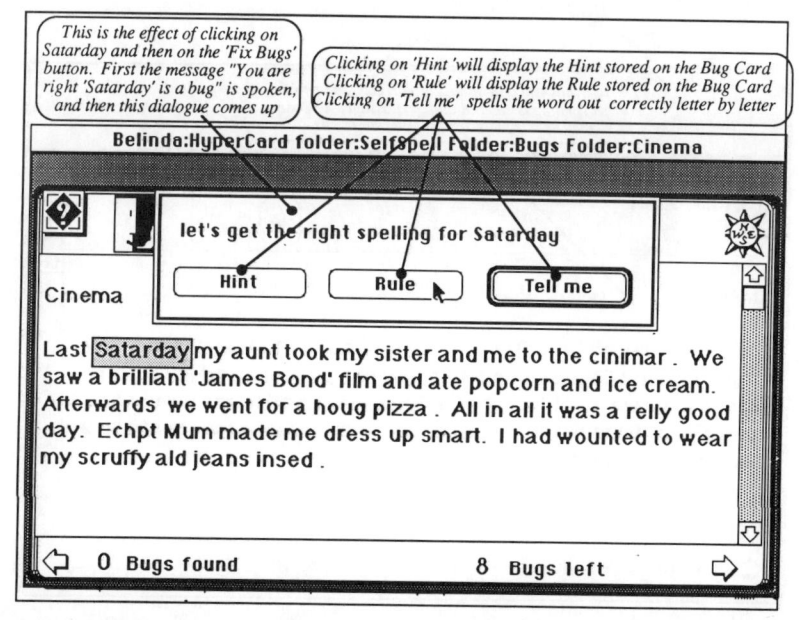

This is the effect of clicking on Satarday and then on the 'Fix Bugs' button. First the message "You are right 'Saturday' is a bug" is spoken, and then this dialogue comes up

*Clicking on 'Hint' will display the Hint stored on the Bug Card
Clicking on 'Rule' will display the Rule stored on the Bug Card
Clicking on 'Tell me' spells the word out correctly letter by letter*

Belinda:HyperCard folder:SelfSpell Folder:Bugs Folder:Cinema

let's get the right spelling for Satarday

    Hint   Rule   Tell me

Cinema

Last Satarday my aunt took my sister and me to the cinimar. We saw a brilliant 'James Bond' film and ate popcorn and ice cream. Afterwards we went for a houg pizza. All in all it was a relly good day. Echpt Mum made me dress up smart. I had wounted to wear my scruffy ald jeans insed.

0 Bugs found   8 Bugs left

FIGURE 15.2e *After selecting Satarday, then clicking on the 'bug' button*

256   PSYCHOLOGY, SPELLING AND EDUCATION

> The user has selected 'Rule', so the rule from the Bug Card is displayed. The user should then try to type in the correct spelling into the box below, and then press OK (or the RETURN key).
>
> If the new spelling is correct, the program says well done, changes the spelling in the passage, and updates the score counters.
> If not it says 'Bad luck' and changes nothing.

Belinda:HyperCard folder:SelfSpell folder:Bugs Folder:Cinema

Rule: u r saturday

Satarday

OK   Cancel

Cinema

Last Satar[   ]r. We saw a brilliant 'James Bond' film and ate popcorn and ice cream. Afterwards we went for a houg pizza. All in all it was a relly good day. Echpt Mum made me dress up smart. I had wounted to wear my scruffy ald jeans insed.

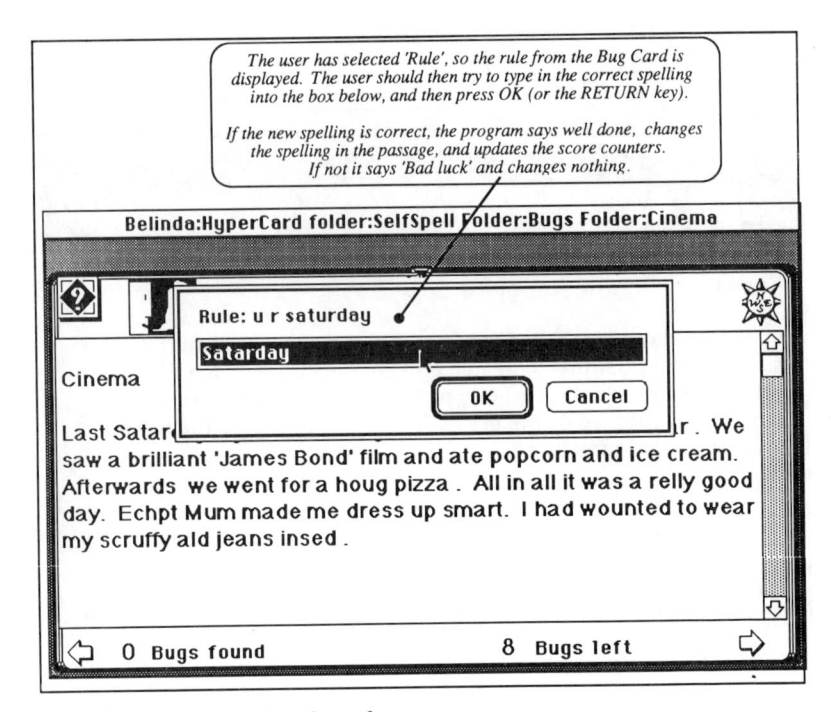

0 Bugs found   8 Bugs left

FIGURE 15.2f   *Going for the rule*

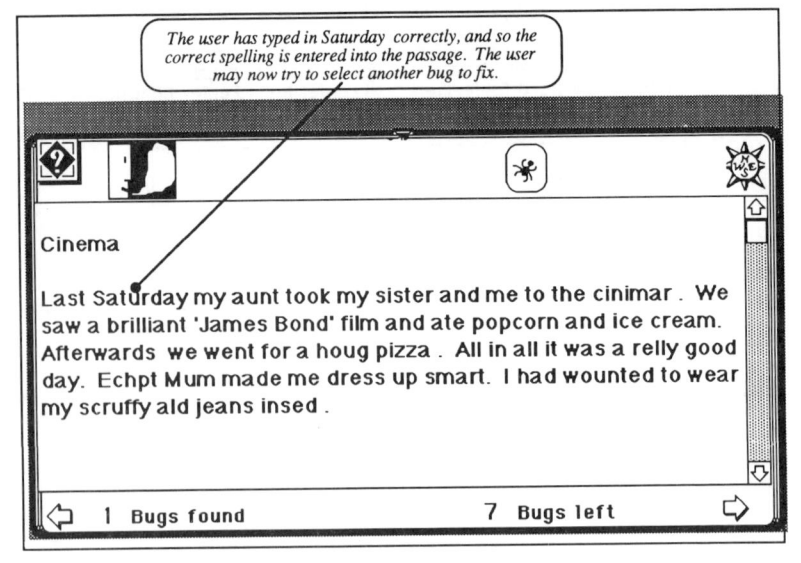

> The user has typed in Saturday correctly, and so the correct spelling is entered into the passage. The user may now try to select another bug to fix.

Cinema

Last Saturday my aunt took my sister and me to the cinimar. We saw a brilliant 'James Bond' film and ate popcorn and ice cream. Afterwards we went for a houg pizza. All in all it was a relly good day. Echpt Mum made me dress up smart. I had wounted to wear my scruffy ald jeans insed.

1 Bugs found   7 Bugs left

FIGURE 15.2g   *The result of entering 'Saturday'*

Evaluation Study 1: Use of SelfSpell with Adolescent Dyslexic Children

Informal observations of a few dyslexic children interacting with the program convinced us that it was on the right lines, with the users showing considerable enthusiasm in the use of the program and good improvement in the spellings targeted by it. It was, however, important to undertake a formal evaluation with a good range of dyslexic users, in order to identify whether all the children showed benefits from use of the program, and whether such benefits tranferred to the everyday world of pencil and paper work. The study is described in detail in Nicolson, Pickering & Fawcett (1991), and an overall summary is given here.

TABLE 15.1 *Reading and spelling ages for the participants*

Participant	Chronological age	Reading age	Spelling age
P.S.	12.9	7.2	6.0
M.N.	13.4	6.7	6.0
R.T.	12.5	7.7	7.0
G.F.	14.3	10.2	8.8
J.H.	14.4	10.1	8.0
S.P.	13.9	9.0	7.0
D.K.	14.3	9.3	8.0
S.G.	13.5	9.0	7.0
J.A.	14.0	13.9	13.0
N.L.	14.2	12.8	10.9
J.B.	13.6	13.5	10.5
P.R.	13.8	12.9	12.0
J.N.	13.4	11.5	9.8
R.F.	13.9	11.3	6.3
M.H.	14.3	12.6	9.0
Mean	13.76	10.51	8.62

Participants

The evaluation study was undertaken using a panel of 23 dyslexic children (mean age 13.4). None of them was familiar with use of the Apple

Macintosh. An indication of the reading and spelling problems of the 15 children who completed all stages of the test is given in Table 15.1, which shows their age-normed performance before the study described here. It should be noted that all the children had been diagnosed as dyslexic several years previously (using the standard criterion of an 18-month or more deficit in reading age over chronological age; together with normal or above normal IQ and no primary emotional or neurological problems), and it can be seen that by the time of the study several of the children were technically 'remediated' in terms of reading age (i.e. their reading age was within 18 months of their chronological age). None the less, even for the 'remediated' children the spelling performance was very poor.

Experimental method

Six interesting passages of about 50 words were constructed, with two passages at 8, 10 and 13 years reading age respectively, using the modified Fogg index (see Lewis & Paine, 1985). For each child the experimenter determined the reading age, and selected the appropriate passage for dictation. The experimenter read the passage aloud with expression, reading a short section at a time, and the child was told to write the words down as carefully as possible, saying them aloud as they wrote them.

Next the child's dictation was typed into HyperCard by the experimenter and bug cards created for each error. Children making less than eight errors were omitted, and for children making more than eight errors, their passage was adjusted to have exactly eight errors. Each child then went through three sessions of the program. Session one was used primarily to familiarise the child with the program and to invent rules for each of the bugs. In session two the experimenter guided the child through the program, encouraging him or her to identify and fix all the bugs, and in session three the child attempted to fix all the bugs with minimal help from the experimenter. Sessions took place one week apart. Parents were often present during the session, but they were not directly involved.

Finally, in order to evaluate the effectiveness of the computer program, the original dictation was repeated one month after session three. Immediately after completing the passage the child was asked to circle any words that he or she thought were probably spelled wrongly, and, if they thought they could now spell it correctly, to write down the correct spelling. This task was an informal method of checking whether, even if the child could not spell all the words correctly, he or she did at least know which ones were probably wrong. The child's written passage was then scored for errors. A spoken structured interview was conducted for each child and a questionnaire administered to those parents who had been present during the experimental sessions.

Results of the evaluation

Seven participants made less than eight errors on the dictation and one was unavailable for further testing, and so the following results are based on the remaining 15 children. The mean time spent on the three sessions was 65, 24 and 18 minutes respectively, reflecting the initial need to make bug cards, followed by the relatively speedy subsequent completion of the passage. After just three sessions on SelfSpell, the children were able to identify 80% of the bugs; to fix 70% of them immediately and to recall 50% of their rules (see Figure 15.3).

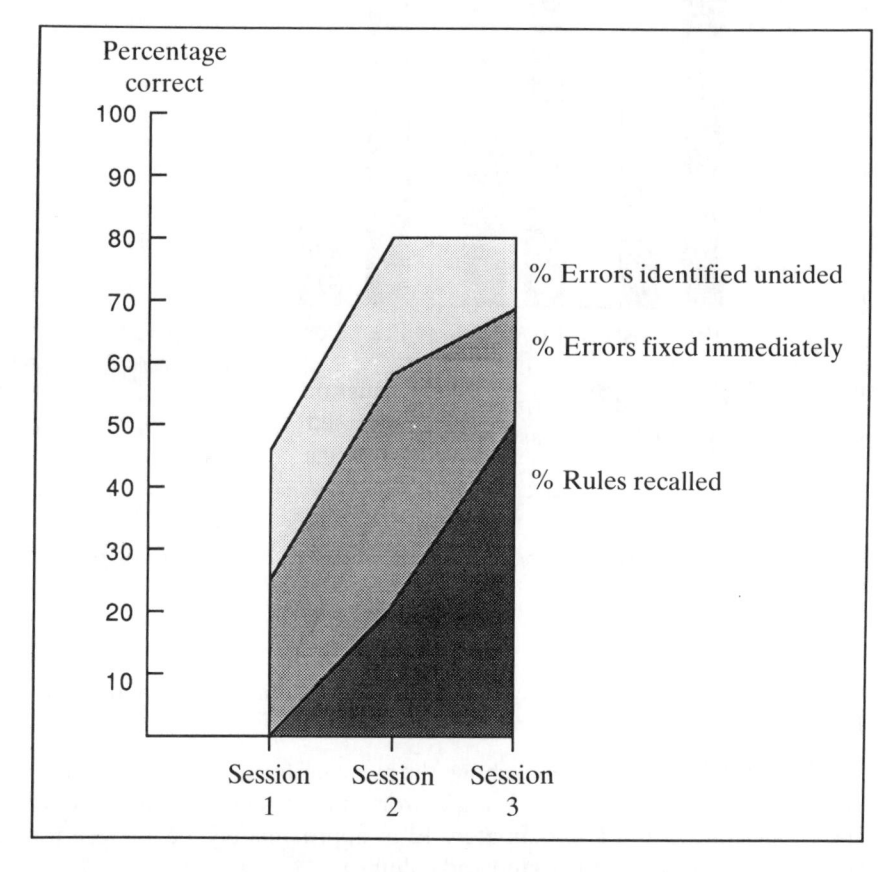

FIGURE 15.3 *Performance on the computer*

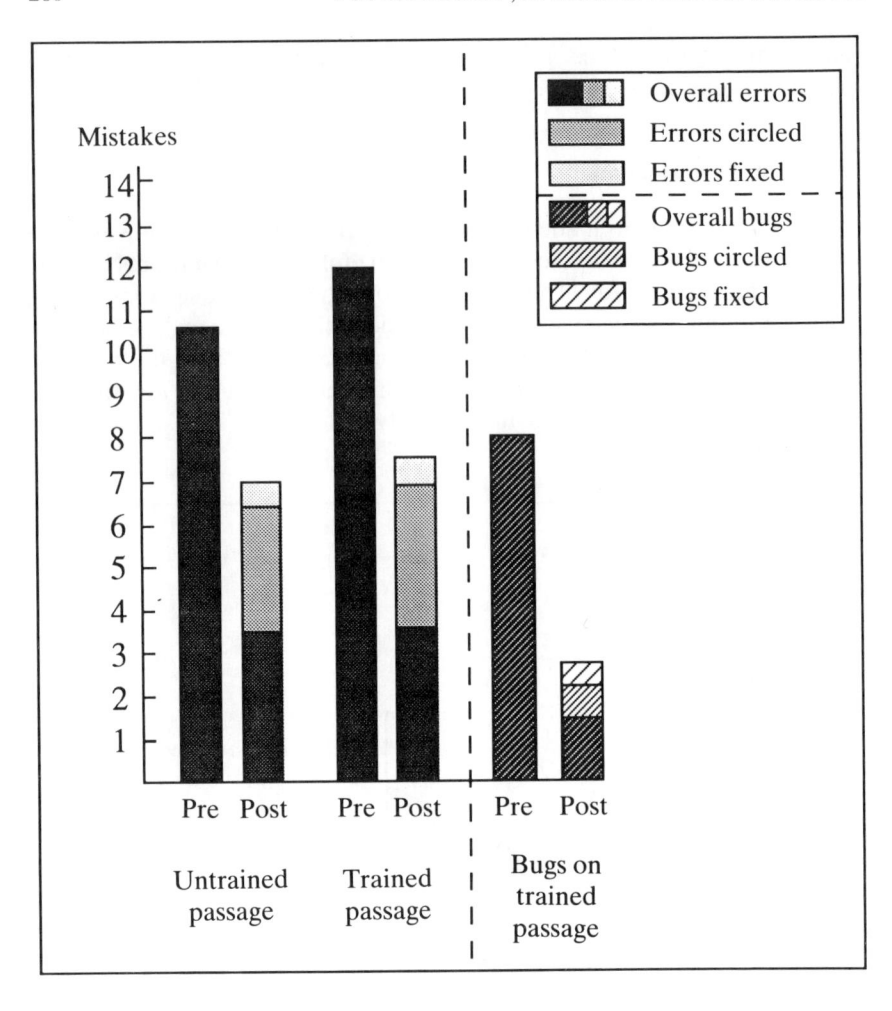

FIGURE 15.4 *Analysis of dictation errors at pre-test and post-test for the dyslexic children*

The dictation performance before and after training is shown in Figure 15.4.

The middle pair of columns shows the mean performance on the trained passage. It can be seen that the *overall* errors after training were reduced by about one-third, from approximately 12 to approximately 7.5 (ignore for now the subdivisions of the right hand column).

The rightmost pair of columns shows the performance on the bugs targeted (only eight errors were targeted as bugs for each child). Again ignoring the subdivisions of the right-hand column, there was clearly a larger improvement on the eight bugs targeted for each child, since the errors after training were reduced by about two-thirds (a reduction from 8 to approximately 2.5 errors), compared with the one-third reduction reported above. Indeed, the improvement overall (the middle pair of columns) is accounted for entirely by the improved performance on the bugged words (the rightmost pair of columns). The number of errors on untargeted words did not decrease.

The two columns on the left-hand side show the performance on a matched passage which was tested at pre-test and post-test but not shown in between. It may be seen that there was a performance improvement also on this untrained passage, again about one-third reduction in total errors, from approximately 10.5 to approximately 7 (ignore again the subdivisions of the right-hand column). The reason for this improvement is unclear. We would like to think it shows the generalised effects of the increased attention to detail resulting from the improved motivation reported by the participants (see below), but this is speculation at this stage. All these improvements in performance were highly statistically significant.

The top two subdivisions within the right-hand column of each pair indicate the number of errors that the participants circled after completing their post-test dictations, indicating that they thought they might be wrong. In both the untrained and trained passage about one half of the errors were circled (reductions from approximately 7 to about 3.5 in both cases), and of these only a very small proportion were fixed (the topmost subdivision). This indicates that the participants were aware that their spellings were probably wrong for about half their misspellings but that they were, in general, not very successful at correcting them. On the bugs, again about one half were circled but they were more successful in fixing them because about one half were fixed.

All 15 children and eight of their parents completed the questionnaires. Improved motivation and attitude were reported by 75% of the parents, and all the children and parents reported that it was fun to use SelfSpell. Comments were uniformly favourable. A selection includes:

'She seems to be more aware of spelling mistakes and wants to put them right.'
'He has a new strategy for remembering correct spellings.'
'He has been checking through his spellings more carefully.'
'He is more aware of spelling errors and seems to be enjoying reading more.'

'He seems to have grasped the spelling side and seems to have gained confidence.'
'N. has had lessons on a one-to-one basis, but has improved more from this method of teaching.'
'Of all the methods that have been used this is the most successful.'
'The computer talking makes it better and helps them remember what they have written.'

Discussion

It seems clear that the SelfSpell program was successful in its major objectives. It was fun to do, the participants enjoyed and valued it, as did their parents. It was effective even after one month in its narrow objective of improving the spellings of the targeted bugs. In addition, there are also encouraging signs that it aided the children's confidence in that, first, 75% of the parents said they had noticed an improvement in attitude and in confidence, and second, in the delayed dictation test significant improvements were shown even on the untrained passage.

Evaluation Study 2: Use of SelfSpell with Younger Dyslexic Children

Study one demonstrated clearly that SelfSpell was valuable for adolescent dyslexic children, but it left two questions unresolved; namely whether it would be equally effective for younger dyslexic children whose spelling age was much lower; and whether the use of self-generated rules and a passage-based format were uniquely effective, or whether mastery learning techniques could also prove valuable. This second study investigated both possibilities. The study is described more fully in Fawcett, Nicolson & Morris (1991).

Participants

The participants in this study were seven dyslexic children aged 10–13 years (mean 11.7) diagnosed as dyslexic between the ages of seven and ten, on the same exclusionary criteria as the older panel. Their age normed performance in reading and spelling before the study reported here is shown in Table 15.2.

SPELLING REMEDIATION USING SELFSPELL

TABLE 15.2 *Reading and spelling ages for the participants*

Participant	Chronological age	Reading age	Spelling age
C.J.	11.6	8.9	6.0
C.E.	10.0	7.0	5.0
I.T.	12.2	9.5	9.0
M.C.	11.5	8.3	9.0
M.Cr.	13.2	9.8	7.0
R.H.	12.8	8.0	6.0
T.A.	10.8	8.3	6.0
Mean	11.7	8.5	6.9

It may be seen that the children in this study had made little or no progress in spelling, with a mean deficit between spelling and chronological age of 4.8 years. Attempts to remediate their spelling performance should therefore provide a stringent test of the efficacy of the spelling program.

Method

In addition to the rule-based approach outlined above a more directive, mastery learning approach is also available under SelfSpell in a program called Spellmaster. In this approach a list of words may be typed in (together with their homophone under speech synthesis, and an appropriate context description), and each word is then presented individually from time to time until it has been learned. Immediate feedback is used at all times, and the correct spelling is displayed immediately following any error. The spellings are introduced cumulatively, first with four spellings, then three more when the first four are learned, and so on.

In order to compare the rule-based, undirected approach with the directive mastery learning approach, we decided to test the learning of 20 spellings, with ten learned using the rule-based approach and a matched set of ten learned using the mastery approach.

Three training sessions, each lasting 20 minutes, were run for each set of ten words for each child. A pencil and paper pre-test on performance was administered by the parents before training began, and an exactly equivalent post-test was administered by the parents one week after the last training session. By contrast with the previous experiment, the spellings were selected by each child's parents as particularly important to him or her, and so the spellings selected were not matched to the spelling age of the child. Consequently, some of the words selected represented a considerable challenge. An example of the spellings made in the second session for one of the participants is given in Table 15.3. *Farrant* was a word of family significance, and the first four words had been mastered in the first session. It may be seen that, in effect, the program requires the user to spell all the words correctly at least three times consecutively, and usually more in that even 'learned' spellings are re-tested from time to time.

TABLE 15.3   *Results from spelling mastery*

CJ Session 2
17/2/91, 12:38 pm
Score = 42 out of 53

Word	Spellings on session 2	Pre-test	Post-test
evidence	evidence, evidence, evidence, evidence	evdans	evidence
farrant	farrant, farrant, farrant, farrant	farant	farrant
orange	orange, orange, orange, orange	oreg	orange
crayon	crayon, crayon, crayon, crayon	craneon	crayon
hospital	hosptil, hosptial, hospital, hopital, hospital, hospital, hospital, hospital, hospital	hosptal	hospital
picture	picher, piture, picture, picture, picture, picture, picture	picher	picture
sense	sense, sence, sense, sense, sense	sencs	sense
reason	resant, reason, reason, reason	resan	reason
kettle	ketal, kettle, kettle, kettle, kettle, kettle	kettal	kettle
perfect	perfcket, perfaket, perfect, perfect, perfect, perfect	pefeckt	perfect

Results

The results for each child are given in Table 15.4. It may be seen that the children scored few marks on the pre-tests, but that both approaches led to excellent learning, as evidenced by the high scores on the post-test. An analysis of variance confirmed that both methods led to highly significant learning, but that when one analyses the proportion of the words that were misspelled in the pre-test that were correctly spelled in the post-test, the mastery approach was significantly more effective overall.

As in the previous experiment, an informal questionnaire established that all the children had enjoyed both the SelfSpell and Spellmaster programs. However, while they found the SelfSpell program great fun, 75% preferred the Spellmaster program for the success it engendered.

Analysis of the errors on the rule-based words suggested that, although in most cases the children had correctly remembered their rules, for the more complex words the rule alone was insufficient, and they misspelled some other portion of the word. It seems likely that if the words had been more appropriate for the spelling age of the children involved, the rule-based system would also have been extremely effective.

TABLE 15.4 *Individual results for pre- and post-tests*

Participant	Rule-Based Pre	Rule-Based Post	Mastery Pre	Mastery Post
C.J.	1	7	0	10
C.E.	0	6	0	6
I.T.	3	7	3	10
M.C.	0	10	1	10
M.Cr.	1	3	5	8
R.H.	4	6	2	7
T.A.	1	6	1	9
Mean	1.4	6.4	1.7	8.6

Conclusions

It is worthwhile here to consider the theoretical issues underlying the acquisition of spelling in the dyslexic child. Frith (1985) has argued that dyslexic children tend to get locked into the initial, 'logographic' stage for reading, in which performance is based on whole-word recognition, and are unable to make the transition to the phonologically mediated alphabetic stage. This causes severe problems for spelling, which is predominantly a retrieval process and cannot be sustained by the visual route alone. Spelling performance for the younger dyslexics breaks down in the segmentation process, or for the more competent older dyslexics at the stage of phoneme–grapheme translation.

It is therefore particularly encouraging, from both a theoretical and applied perspective, to note that all the children in this study seemed able to use the alphabetic principle when given the appropriate support. Clearly, given sufficient practice and motivation to succeed, even the most intractable spelling problems can be ameliorated to some extent. It appears, therefore, that the learning processes are largely intact, and that with appropriate support the spelling problem could diminish over time. An interesting parallel can be drawn between these results and those of Bradley (e.g. 1988) who demonstrated that early support in phonological processing led to very much better subsequent acquisition of reading. Given early intervention, it seems likely that the initial problems can be substantially alleviated, leading to relatively normal acquisition of spelling skills.

In conclusion, we have argued that the Apple HyperCard multimedia environment has the potential to provide outstanding support for dyslexic children, using the immediacy and reinforcing effect of computer presentation with digitised or synthesised speech available to avoid reliance on textual presentation. The SelfSpell program proved both fun and effective for all our dyslexic children, including even those with a spelling age of well under ten years. Both mastery and rule-based techniques proved very effective. We are sure it would prove fun and effective for non-dyslexic children also. We believe that the new developments in educational technology, added to the decreasing cost of such powerful systems, make the development of this type of multimedia environment a practical, affordable and very desirable target for the whole educational system.

Summary

This chapter has described the SelfSpell HyperCard environment for dyslexic children which helps them to learn to spell their problem words. Synthesised speech is used to augment the written text and different levels of help are available at all times. Two versions are available: (1) SelfSpell, where the children are encouraged to enter rules to help them remember how to spell each word, and (2) Spellmaster, where a mastery learning technique is used. Evaluations of the effectiveness of the software indicated substantial improvements with either version in the spelling and motivation of two groups of dyslexic children.

References

BRADLEY, L. 1988, Making connections in learning to read and to spell. *Applied Cognitive Psychology* 2, 3–18.
FAWCETT, A. J., NICOLSON, R. I. and MORRIS, S. 1991, Spelling remediation for dyslexic children: A comparison of rule based and mastery techniques. LRG 7/91 University of Sheffield, Department of Psychology.
FRITH, U. 1985, Beneath the surface of developmental dyslexia. In K. E. PATTERSON, J. C. MARSHALL and M. COLTHEART (eds) *Surface Dyslexia*. London: Lawrence Erlbaum.
LEWIS, R. and PAINE, N. 1985, How to communicate with the learner. *Open Learning Guide 6*. London: CET.
MALONE, T. W. 1981, Towards a theory of intrinsically motivating instruction. *Cognitive Science* 4, 333–69.
NICOLSON, R. I., PICKERING, S. and FAWCETT, A. J. 1991, Open learning for dyslexic children using HyperCard™. *Computers and Education* 16, 2, 203–9.
THOMSON, M. E. 1984, *Developmental Dyslexia: Its Nature, Assessment and remediation*. London: Edward Arnold.

16 Phonological Spelling in Young Children and some Origins of Phonetically Plausible and Implausible Errors

CHRIS STERLING and JULIE SEED

Introduction

Spelling errors are a clear and convenient indicator of spelling ability. However, while the *quantity* of errors made provides valuable information about spelling ability it should be regarded as a gross measure because it fails to take into account the fact that spelling is a complex skill and that errors may have different origins. For example, they may be performance errors, which are due to a temporary lapse, or competence errors which stem from uncertainty or ignorance (Sterling, 1982). To determine the origins of an error we need to know the circumstances under which it was made, the nature of the target and *type* of error it is.

This chapter is concerned with competence errors (analyses of performance errors are to be found in papers by Hotopf, 1980; Sterling, 1982; and Ellis, 1982). To probe the relative strengths and weaknesses of a speller's ability we need to classify and analyse the errors they make. The problem is one of identifying the relationships between error type and origin. Only when this is done can we produce spelling tests which are reliably diagnostic.

To make headway we need a model of how spellings are produced. This provides a framework which gives us an understanding of why, and the conditions under which, different types of error occur. Such a model is 'dual process theory' (see Ellis, 1984; Seymour, Chapter 3 this volume). This holds that there are two strategies or sets of processes which can be used to spell a word: (1) the lexical strategy, and (2) the phonological strategy.

Lexical spelling

The lexical strategy uses spellings stored in (orthographic) memory. If a *known* word has to be spelled this mental representation of the spelling is retrieved from memory and written down. For an accurate spelling both the identity and order of the letters have to be stored in memory (Funnell, Chapter 5 this volume). It follows that the accuracy of a spelling will depend on how well the word is known. How can we tell when lexical spelling has been used?

Lexical spelling is deduced when the speller produces *correct* spellings of irregular words (e.g. **SAID, COLONEL**). The argument is that because irregular words *can't* be spelled correctly using phono–graphic correspondences the speller *must* have been using word-specific (lexical) information. By the same token we can tell when the lexical strategy has not been used because the speller can't spell irregular words correctly. This leaves the question of how we can tell when a lexical strategy has been used but has failed. This can be deduced when the spelling produced has letters which have been added, omitted and transposed in a way which renders the string produced an implausible (e.g. unpronounceable) spelling of the sound structure of the target, i.e. a phonetically implausible error. Evidence for this comes from acquired phonological dysgraphia, a condition in which the phonological strategy has been lost (through disease, injury, etc.). These people have to use the lexical strategy and frequently produce errors such as **PTEZRL** (*pretzel*) and **KINFE** (*knife*) (Roeltgen, Sevush & Heilman, 1983).

According to Frith (1985) lexical spelling is the first strategy used, though in a primitive version called logographic spelling. Beginning spellers represent spellings in much the same way as they remember pictures — perhaps partially, with only some distinctive components being remembered. Evidence for logographic spelling comes from Seymour (Chapter 3 this volume), who reports young children who can spell their names in the absence of being able to spell phonologically, which suggests use of logographic spelling. Unfortunately, distinguishing failures of logographic spelling from random scribblings is currently not possible. Information about failures in the use of a more sophisticated lexical strategy also come from people who fail to develop a phonological strategy and who have to use lexical spelling. When these people (developmental phonological dyslexics) misspell a word they frequently produce phonetically implausible errors such as **RTHYTM** (*rhythm*) (Campbell & Butterworth, 1985). See also Burden's work (Chapter 12 this volume) for the errors of Type B spellers, who are mildly dyslexic. Note that 'normals' also sometimes make such errors when spelling difficult words.

Phonological spelling

The second strategy is phonological. The speller uses the sound of the word, segmenting it into its component phonemes, and a knowledge of phono–graphic (sound–spelling) correspondences to produce a spelling. How do we know when phonological spelling has been used? Target words which are known, regular and *correctly* spelled (e.g. **DOG**) are no help because both strategies are capable of doing this. We can, however, deduce phonological spelling when an error is made, as long as this error preserves the sound structure of the target (e.g. **DAWG** for *dog*). Irregular words are particularly exploitable in this respect because phonological spelling will regularise the spelling of the word, producing errors which are phonetically plausible (e.g. **SED** for *said*). Evidence that phonological spelling is responsible for such errors comes from people with a condition called 'acquired lexical dysgraphia', who, because of disease or injury, have lost the lexical strategy and can therefore use only phonological spelling (Beauvois & Dérouesné, 1981). Phonological spelling can also be deduced when non-words are spelled, either correctly or phonetically plausibly, because they have no lexical representation and so have to be spelled phonologically. (A non-word is defined as a letter string that could be an English word but happens not to be, e.g. *gluft*.)

According to Frith (1985), phonological spelling is a product of the alphabetic stage of development, a stage in which the child masters the alphabetic principle and the rules that govern sound–spelling relationships. According to Ehri (1986), spellings in this stage are first semi-phonetic and then phonetic. Briefly, semi-phonetic spellings are usually found in pre-school and kindergarten children and are characterised by a number of features: only some phonemes are spelled, with a progression from singleton sounds (**S**, *dress*), through boundary sounds (**BK**, *back*) to medial sounds (**TST**, *test*); vowels tend to be omitted (**WTR**, *water*); the child uses letter names (**PKN**, *picking*; **LFT**, *elephant*) or the sounds *in* letter names (**HKN**, *chicken*; **JRN**, *dragon*) to spell phonemes; and random letters might be used to make up the word to an appropriate length (**FLME**, *feet*). In general the phonetic stage is characterised by the representation of most, if not all the sounds in the word, exceptions being the nasals in clusters (**BOPE**, *bumpy*) and vocalic elements in unstressed syllabic consonants (**CHIKN**, *chicken*). Vowels are now spelled, with short vowel spellings being learned before long vowel spellings, for which they still tend to use letter names (**BOT**, *boat*; **PAT**, *pate*), and morphemes are spelt the way they sound (**DREST**, *dressed*; **CAPEEN**, *camping*).

Error classification

We see from these examples that there is a potential classification problem because some spellings (e.g. **S** (*dress*), **WTR** (*water*)) could easily be attributed to the lexical (logographic) strategy. See Pattison & Collier (Chapter 6 this volume) for a discussion of multiple classification. To minimise the classification problem in this paper we require phonetically plausible spellings to preserve the consonant–vowel structure of the sound of the word (sounds can't be added, omitted or transposed), to spell consonant sounds correctly or plausibly (**K** or **C** for /k/), and to spell vowel sounds with vowel letters.

The Components of Phonological Spelling

This chapter is concerned only with phonological spelling. Frith (1980) argues, and there is evidence from lexical dysgraphics studied by Shallice (1981) and Roeltgen, Sevush & Heilman (1983), that there are two components to phonological spelling: a phonological component and a correspondence knowledge component. We shall argue that each of these components is potentially responsible for a different kind of error.

The phonological component

The first major component of phonological spelling has to do with phonological ability. To spell the sounds in a word the speller has first to identify them. He or she has to hold the word in short-term memory, segment it into its component phonemes, hold these in short-term memory without losing any or confusing their order, and then spell them. It seems reasonable to assume that if the component *sounds* are not separated and identified accurately, or sounds are added, lost or transposed then the *sound* structure of the word will be mutilated. When this inaccurate string of sounds is converted to graphemes the spelling will be phonetially implausible because it will not have preserved the sound structure of the target.

We have decided to home in on the processes involved in producing separated phonemes in readiness for conversion to graphemes. There are two hypotheses why this might fail to occur. First, the child's phonological awareness may not be sufficiently developed. He or she may not have sufficient awareness of the phonemes of English and the fact that words are composed of strings of phonemes to identify the number, identity and order of phonemes in a given word. Indeed, according to Trieman (1985) awareness of phonemic structure is an acquisition which comes at the end of a developmental sequence: the child is initially only aware of syllables, then sub-syllabic units called the *onset* and *rime,* and only finally phonemes. The second hypothesis is that while the child's awareness of the phonemes in a word may be sound he or she may not have developed the phonological skills necessary to break it up into these phonemes; the child may know that the word consists of phonemes and what these phonemes are, but may not be able to separate them from each other.

These two explanations are currently indistinguishable. Fortunately this confounding is not important for the present work because in both hypotheses the problem lies in the phonology — poor awareness of sounds *or* poor ability to segment sounds — not in correspondence knowledge (see below). In both hypotheses the prediction is that the spelling of a phonologically problematic word will probably misrepresent its sound structure. A class of words known to be phonologically problematic are words with consonant clusters (Trieman, 1985): children have problems separating and identifying the phonemes in clusters like /**cl**/- and -/**nd**/. Furthermore, there is evidence that they induce large numbers of spelling errors (Trieman, 1985; Groff, 1986), a common error being the omission of the inner consonant (i.e. a phonetically implausible error), producing, for example, **GAD** for *glad*. While this supports our thesis that phonologically problematic words induce phonetically implausible errors, what has not been shown is that their incidence in words with consonant clusters is greater than in words without consonant clusters *or* that other errors in the spelling of these two types of words are the same.

Correspondence knowledge

The second component has to do with a child's knowledge of the phoneme–grapheme correspondences of English. Although English orthography is full of ambiguities and idiosyncrasies it is, nevertheless, a substantially alphabetic system. Some relationships are simple in that a phoneme maps onto a single grapheme (/b/ → B). Others are more complex, with a phoneme mapping on to two graphemes /ʃ/ → SH). Sometimes the relationship is ambiguous but rule governed (double the L at the end of monosyllabic words with a short vowel, e.g. FULL, BELL, etc.) but sometimes it is arbitrarily ambiguous (/eI/ → AI, A_E). We assume that correspondences will be differentially difficult to learn, depending on whether the sound is spelled with a single letter or double letter, whether it has more than one major alternative spelling, and so on.

What kinds of errors can we expect from poor correspondence knowledge? The 'stage' that concerns us is when the child has mastered the basic correspondences (e.g. /b/ → B; /f/ → F), but has yet to master the complex and ambiguous correspondences so prevalent in English. A poor knowledge of these is likely to produce phonetically plausible but incorrect spellings (e.g. KAT, *cat*; CKAT, *cat*). Vowel spellings are likely to prove particularly fertile sources of error, firstly because about 45 vowel sounds are spelt using letters drawn from a pool of about eight (A, E, I, O, U, W, Y, R), and secondly because of the numerous ambiguities, which are sometimes principled (/eI/) is spelt -AY only at the ends of monosyllabic words) but often not (MAID/MADE). In two of the experiments to be reported we shall be using words which vary in the complexity and ambiguity of their vowel correspondences (e.g. /æ/ → A; /u:/ → OO; /i:/ → EE or EA). This should produce corresponding variations in the numbers of errors produced. As to the type of error, if we assume that the child is sufficiently advanced to spell consonant sounds with consonant letters and vowel sounds with vowel letters then as complexity and ambiguity of correspondence increase the number of phonetically plausible errors (e.g. RUM, *room*) should also increase. The number of phonetically implausible errors should remain unchanged.

Measures of Error Incidence

The incidence of correct, phonetically plausible and phonetically implausible spellings are not independent. To minimise this (we can't eliminate it) we shall be using the following measures:

- The proportion of all spellings that are phonetically implausible:
  PI = (phonetically implausible)/(all spellings)
- The number of phonetically plausible spellings as a proportion of correct plus phonetically plausible spellings:
  PP = (phonetically plausible)/(correct + phonetically plausible).

Experiment One: Tying Errors to Origins

We have argued that phonologically problematic words induce phonetically implausible errors while words with difficult correspondences produce phonetically plausible errors. To test this we need to look at the errors produced when children are asked (1) to spell phonologically complex words compared with phonologically simple words, and (2) to spell words which have complex/ambiguous correspondences compared with words which have simple/unambiguous correspondences. Greater phonological complexity should increase the number of phonetically implausible errors while greater correspondence complexity should increase the number of phonetically plausible errors. Accordingly, we shall be comparing the spellings of words such as *glad* and *send* — phonologically complex (because of the cluster) with simple correspondences — with words such as *boot, read* and *name* — phonologically simple(r) (no cluster) with complex and (sometimes) ambiguous vowel correspondences (**EE** and **AI** are valid alternative spellings of /i:/ and /eI/).

We tested 47 children from third year infants of an inner city school in London. Average age 7:3 years. They were given two kinds of words to spell, all taken from the Schonell (1932) book of spellings: 20 words such as **GLAD** (ten words) and **SEND** (ten words) and 30 words such as **BOOT** (ten words), **READ** (ten words) and **NAME** (ten words). The test was administered by the teacher in four sessions and the words were presented in random order to the whole class.

The results were as predicted.

Table 16.1A presents the incidence of the different types of spelling for the two types of words. We see that while the number of correct spellings was the same the type of incorrect spelling produced was a function of the type of word being spelt. **DUST/GLAD** words induced few phonetically plausible but many phonetically implausible errors, while **BOOT/READ/NAME** words induced many phonetically plausible errors but few phonetically implausible errors.

In the statistical analysis we used, for reasons explained, the measures PP (phonetically plausible) and PI (phonetically implausible). To allow for the fact that differences in the familiarity of the words might be responsible for the results, we compared the two groups using a multiple regression analysis with word frequency as the first and word type as the second factor. The **GLAD/SEND** group produced a *greater value of PI* than the **BOOT/READ/NAME** group ($t = 15.93$; $p < 0.001$), but a *smaller value of PP* ($t = 5.93$; $p < 0.001$). See Table 16.1B. This was over and above the effects

TABLE 16.1 Results of experiment 1

	DUST/GLAD	BOOT/READ/NAME
A. Incidence of different types of spelling for the two types of word expressed as percentages — presented for information		
Correct	56%	55%
Phonetically plausible	9%	33%
Phonetically implausible	35%	12%
B. Values of PP and PI for the two types of word — used in statistical analysis		
Phonetically plausible	0.14	0.38
Phonetically implausible	0.35	0.12

of word frequency, which also had a significant effect, with PI and PP (i.e. both kinds of error) increasing as word frequency decreased ($t = 2.03$; $p < 0.05$ for PI and $t = 3.06$; $p < 0.01$ for PP).

While consistent with our hypotheses, there are several problems with this experiment. Firstly, we used real words, which means that the children may have used a lexical strategy. Secondly, the words differed not only in terms of the presence of a cluster, but the phonologically complex words also had more phonemes (four) than the phonologically simple words (three) — so the differences could have been due to this. Accordingly, we went on to do two more experiments, one looking only at the effects of phonological complexity and the second looking only at the effects of complexity of correspondence.

Experiment Two: The Effects of Phonological Complexity

In this experiment we used two groups of non-words, with each word in one group being matched with a word in the other. The members of each pair were composed of the same phonemes/graphemes and differed only in the presence or absence of a cluster (e.g. **IND** versus **NID**). Using non-words ensures that the child uses phonological spelling because the lexical strategy is not available, and using groups matched in every way except for the consonant cluster ensures that obtained differences cannot be attributed to other factors. The group with the cluster should produce more phonetically implausible errors than the group without, but the number of phonetically plausible errors should be the same.

Thirty-two children from third year infants (average age 6:10 years) of an inner city school in Newcastle Upon Tyne were tested on two kinds of non-word: nine three-phoneme non-words with a cluster and one-to-one phoneme–grapheme correspondences, e.g. **IND** and nine matched non-words without a cluster, e.g. **NID**. The children were told that they were going to be asked to spell words which they hadn't heard before by using the sound of the word: that they were to 'sound it out' and then spell each sound as best they could. They were tested in small equal-ability groups to facilitate administration. There were no problems.

The results were as predicted.

Table 16.2A presents the incidence of the different types of spelling for the two types of words. We can see that while the number of PP spellings was the same for both word types the number of PI spellings was greater for the phonologically complex words.

In the statistical analysis, when PI scores for the two groups were compared, PI for the phonologically complex words (**IND**) was significantly greater than for the phonologically simple(r) words (**NID**) ($t = 2.82; df = 32; p < 0.01$). There was no difference between the groups on PP scores ($t = 0.4; df = 23$). See Table 16.2B.

TABLE 16.2 *Results of experiment 2*

	IND	NID
A. Incidence of different spellings for the two types of word expressed as a percentage — for information		
Correct	55%	62%
Phonetically plausible	4%	5%
Phonetically implausible	41%	33%
B. Values of PP and PI for the two types of word — used in statistical analysis		
Phonetically plausible	0.08	0.09
Phonetically implausible	0.22	0.12

The results of this experiment show quite clearly that the presence of a consonant cluster in a non-word produces an increase in PI errors while leaving the incidence of PP errors unchanged. The increase cannot be attributed to a differential difficulty of phoneme–grapheme correspondences.

Experiment Three: Effects of Differential Knowledge of Phoneme–Grapheme Correspondences

In this experiment we again used matched groups of non-words. There were three sets, consisting of non-words with the same degree of phonological complexity and composed of the same consonant sounds (e.g. roughly the same number of /b/ phonemes in each group), although the words couldn't be matched as precisely as in experiment two. The first group consisted of non-words like **BAF** (vowel sound spelled with one letter); the second of non-words like **BOOP** and **DEET** (vowel spelled with a doubled letter). The third group consisted of words such as **FIKE** and **GADE** (vowel being spelt using the silent E rule). The first group should produce the least amount of phonetically plausible spellings, the second group the next most and the third group the most. The number of phonetically implausible spellings should stay the same across groups. Note that words from the **DEET** and **GADE** groups have an alternative major spelling (e.g. **DEAT** and **GAID**) so we can also test for the effects of ambiguity of correspondence.

We tested the same subjects as in experiment two, with the same instructions and in the same groups. There were no problems.

The results were as predicted.

From Table 16.3A we see that the incidence of PI errors was the same across all word types, but that the incidence of PP errors increased from **BAF**, through **BOOP/DEET** to **FIKE/GADE**. There is also a slight inflation of phonetically plausible spellings of **DEET**, relative to **BOOP**, due to the presence of the alternative **DEAT** spellings.

In the statistical analysis we need to allow for the ambiguity of correspondence of the /iː/ and /eI/ sounds in **DEET** and **GADE**. Accordingly we used a regression analysis with (1) correspondence complexity, and (2) ambiguity of correspondence as factors. There was no significant effect of correspondence complexity on PI ($t = 1.04; p > 0.25$) but it did have the predicted significant effect on PP ($t = 26.34; p < 0.001$). Similarly, ambiguity of correspondence had no significant effect on PI ($t = 0.09; p > 0.9$) but did have a significant effect on PP ($t = 2.12; p < 0.05$), with PP increasing when the vowel had a major alternative correspondence.

TABLE 16.3 *Results of experiment 3*

	BAF	BOOP	DEET	FIKE	GADE
A. Incidence of types of spelling for the different vowel correspondences expressed as a percentage — presented for information					
Correct	64%	45%	35%	8%	11%
Phonetically plausible	6%	24%	33%	58%	56%
Phonetically implausible	30%	31%	32%	34%	33%
B. Values of PP and PI for the different vowel correspondences — used in statistical analysis					
Phonetically plausible	0.08	0.35	0.48	0.88	0.88
Phonetically implausible	0.30	0.31	0.32	0.34	0.33

The results show quite clearly that the error rate increased as the complexity of the vowel correspondence increased *but only in terms of phonetically plausible errors*. This was over and above the effect of ambiguity of correspondence which also increased these errors. The numbers of phonetically implausible errors remained the same in all conditions. The differences cannot be attributed to phonological complexity.

Conclusions

We have shown that spelling errors can be tied to particular origins. We found that phonetically implausible errors, traditionally associated with the lexical strategy, increased with an increase in phonological complexity. This result cannot be attributed to either the interfering effects of a lexical strategy or to differences in correspondence knowledge. However, we would note that phonetically implausible errors can be used only as a diagnostic for phonological problems when *non-words* are being spelled. We also found that phonetically plausible errors increased with an increase in the correspondence complexity (and, separately, ambiguity of correspondence) of the vowel spellings. These differences cannot be attributed to differences in phonological complexity and are consistent with the data on acquired lexical dysgraphics obtained by Beauvois & Déruoesné (1981).

While these experiments are promising there is still a long way to go. Phonological spelling is a complex skill with a number of components which remain to be investigated. For example, we have not been able to disentangle the effects of poor phonological awareness from those of poor segmentation ability. Neither have we disentangled the many factors that determine how difficult a phoneme–grapheme correspondence is to learn — factors such as when and how they are taught, and whether they are high- or low-continengency spellings (Barry & Seymour, 1988 — see the Introduction to this volume). Nevertheless, these shortcomings don't detract from our general thesis that a child's phonology and knowledge of phoneme–grapheme correspondences are sources of different kinds of error.

More generally, we suspect that at least one other component of phonological spelling, short-term memory, is responsible for large numbers of errors in these early stages of development. Consider that the child is being required, simultaneously, to hold the sound of the word in short-term memory, break it up into its components, hold the identity and order of these components as they are identified; and retrieve the spelling of each sound. This is a highly demanding task which, we suspect, also induces phonetically implausible errors. However, this is an hypothesis which remains to be tested. Another major area in dire need of research attention is the relationship between lexical spelling and error type. We need to know, for example, the relationship between how well a word is known and the errors produced when it is spelled.

Practical Implications

There are two major implications of our work. First there is a need for phonological awareness training. The majority of children we tested were considered average or good spellers, presumed to be adept at the basic skill of separating and identifying the component sounds of all words. This presumption has been shown to be unwarranted. The fact that phonological awareness has been shown by Bryant and his colleagues (see Bryant & Bradley (1985) for coverage of their work) to underpin the development of literacy suggests that phonological awareness training will go some considerable way to reducing the problems posed by phonologically complex words. We therefore suggest that programmes aimed at developing spelling ability include exercises in making judgements of rhyme and alliteration, segmenting words into their components and manipulating phonemes. For example, asking the child to identify the word left when the first sound of *glad* is omitted — see the concluding chapter of this volume.

Second, that non-word spelling is a potentially valuable diagnostic which can be used to get some indication of the child's grasp of phonological spelling. While there is some way to go before non-word spelling ability can be used as a precise diagnostic we can make a useful generalisation: that children who can spell non-words correctly or phonetically plausibly are more advanced in their grasp of phonological spelling than children who can't even begin to spell them or who make phonetically implausible errors. Furthermore, that the latter group are likely to be having problems with the phonological component of phonological spelling. Seymour and his colleagues are currently developing tests and training programmes using non-words (see Chapters 3 and 14 this volume).

Summary

This paper is concerned with phonological spelling. It argues that we can profitably distinguish between a phonological component of phonological spelling (e.g. segmenting a word into its component sounds) and knowledge of the relationships between sound and spelling (e.g. phoneme–grapheme correspondences) because each of these is associated with a different kind of error. There are basically two kinds of error: (1) those which preserve the sound structure of the target word and are hence phonetically plausible versions of it (e.g. **LAYT** for *late*) and (2) those which do not preserve the sound structure of the target and are hence phonetically implausible versions of it (e.g. **GADL** or **GAD** for *glad*). The results of three experiments using real and invented words were reported. These support the hypotheses that phonologically complex words increase the incidence of phonetically implausible, but not phonetically plausible, errors, and that words with complex correspondences increase the incidence of phonetically plausible, but not phonetically implausible, errors. The implications for educational practice were discussed.

References

BARRY, C. and SEYMOUR, P. H. K. 1988, Lexical priming and sound-to-spelling contingency effects in non-word spelling. *Quarterly Journal of Experimental Psychology* 40A, 5–40.

BEAUVOIS, M. F. and DÉROUESNÉ, J. 1981, Lexical or orthographic agraphia. *Brain* 104, 21–49.

BRYANT, P. and BRADLEY, L. 1985, *Children's Reading Problems*. Oxford: Basil Blackwell.

CAMPBELL, R. and BUTTERWORTH, B. 1985, Phonological dyslexia and dysgraphia in a highly literate subject: A developmental case with associated deficits of phonemic processing and awareness. *Quarterly Journal of Experimental Psychology* 37A, 435–75.

EHRI, L. C. 1986, Sources of difficulty in learning to spell and read. In M. WOLRAICH and D. K. ROUTH (eds) *Advances in Developmental and Behavioural Paediatrics* Volume 7 (pp. 121–95). London: J. Kingsley.

ELLIS, A. 1982, Slips of the pen. *Visible Language* 13, 265–82.

—— 1984, *Reading, Writing and Dyslexia*. London: Lawrence Erlbaum.

FRITH, U. 1980, Unexpected spelling problems. In U. FRITH (ed.) *Cognitive Processes in Spelling*. London: Academic Press.

—— 1985, Beneath the surface of developmental dyslexia. In K. PATTERSON, J. C. MARSHALL and M. COLTHEART (eds) *Surface Dyslexia*. London: Lawrence Erlbaum.

GROFF, P. 1986, The spelling difficulty of consonant letter clusters. *Educational Research* 28, 2, 139–41.

HOTOPF, N. 1980, Slips of the pen. In U. FRITH (ed.) *Cognitive Processes in Spelling*. London. Academic Press.

ROELTGEN, D. P., SEVUSH, S. and HEILMAN, K. M. 1983, Phonological agraphia: Writing by the lexical semantic route. *Neurology* 33, 755–65.

SCHONELL, F. J. 1932, *The Essential Spelling List*. London: Macmillan.

SHALLICE, T. 1981, Phonological agraphia and the lexical route in writing. *Brain* 104, 413–29.

STERLING, C. M. 1982, Spelling errors in context. *British Journal of Psychology* 74, 353–64.

TRIEMAN, R. 1985, Phonemic analysis, spelling, and reading. In T. H. CARR (ed.) *The Development of Reading Skills,* New Directions for Child Development, no. 27. San Francisco: Josey-Bass.

Conclusions

CHRIS STERLING

The papers presented at the Psychology, Spelling and Education conference held at Newcastle Polytechnic dealt with a range of topics. However, particular issues have recurred and the purpose of this chapter is to identify and comment on these issues.

English Orthography

We begin with the problems presented by English orthography. Upward (Chapter 1) argued that English orthography is a serious obstacle to literacy and should be simplified. In contrast Veltman (Chapter 2) argued that English orthography is a workable system because it represents not just phonemic but also lexical, morphemic and phonetic information. These chapters raise *general* issues.

The evidence that English orthography represents several types of linguistic information is often convincing. Less convincing is the argument (*not* supported by Veltman) that it is therefore 'near-optimal' because this is difficult to square with the fact that it causes many problems for its users. To be convincing the 'optimality' school have to show that English orthography is psychologically better than a regular script. While this is unlikely to be generally true, it might well be partially so. For example, spelling morphemes (e.g. the past tense morpheme) consistently (e.g. with an **-ED**), regardless of variations in pronunciation, might well confer an advantage on users. If this were experimentally demonstrated it would suggest one way in which the script could be regularised, but this would be morphemic rather than phonetic (e.g. changing the spelling of **SAID** to **SAYED**, and so on). The point is that regularisation does not necessarily mean phonetic regularisation.

CONCLUSIONS

While there is clearly dissatisfaction with the current orthography it is by no means clear that educators, politicians and the public are sufficiently dissatisfied to embrace any of the alternatives on offer (if only because of their conservatism). To achieve their goal the more radical reformers (*not* Upward) need to do two things. Firstly, they need to propose a principled system sufficiently exhaustive and detailed to survive detailed analysis and experimentation by linguists, psychologists and educators. The proposed system must emerge as clearly better than traditional orthography. Secondly, they need to present a detailed account of the practicalities of reform. They need to be able to answer, in detail, questions about the timetable of reform, the changes it will require in the educational system, the readability and fate of publications in the current orthography and, of course, the cost.

Until these various issues are resolved the simplest way to proceed is pragmatically. Firstly, there are some sources of confusion we might have to learn to live with. For example, while we would clearly prefer to be without homophones and the problems they cause, the fact is that we have them and, given this, it is probably a good idea to retain the different spellings. Secondly, when there are principled arguments for either particular reforms or retaining particular aspects of the current system these must be empirically evaluated before decisions are made. Finally there are some areas where there is room for immediate reform. For example, there are large numbers of uncontentiously idiosyncratic words (e.g. **YACHT**, **COUGH**) which could quite easily be spelt phonetically without causing too much inconvenience.

Phonological Spelling

Most chapters focused on the phonological aspects of spelling. A good reason for thinking this preoccupation to be more than just another swing of the educational pendulum documented by Ellis & Cataldo (Chapter 7) is the fact that it is well embedded in experimental evidence.

There is a lot of evidence, documented by Goswami & Bryant (1990), which links phonological awareness to literacy. There is less evidence showing the direction of relationships involved. Ellis & Cataldo provided strong evidence, based on longitudinal data, that phonological awareness has a *causal* role in the development of spelling and that it is explicit phonological awareness that is required for spelling to develop. Implicit awareness is not sufficient beyond the early stages of development. Their paper showed that as explicit awareness increases, the nature of the child's spelling changes appropriately. Thus whilst one would expect any theory of spelling development to predict a decrease in the overall number of errors, only a theory that couches spelling ability in terms of phono–graphic expertise which develops out of phonological awareness would predict an increase in the proportion of phonetic and semi-phonetic errors. This is what they found. Such an important finding clearly has practical implications and we shall return to these later.

The chapter by Campbell, Burden & Wright (Chapter 11) was concerned with phonological spelling in the born-deaf. Like Campbell's other work on priming (Campbell, 1983) it is an important paper whose implications are, as yet, unclear. It forces us to re-examine our ideas on what constitutes a phono–graphic system and how such a system might develop. They found that all the born-deaf spellers tested showed evidence of a phonological spelling strategy. What these results indicate is that it is possible to develop a phono–graphic system very similar to that posesssed by hearing subjects (of the same reading age) without a *conventionally acquired* knowledge of phonology, i.e. through the processes of unimpaired hearing and speaking. Furthermore, it seems that a number of the born-deaf children didn't even possess particularly good lip-reading skills, which would certainly have gone a long way to providing an explanation. As Campbell *et al.* point out, their data suggest that teachers of the deaf should not give up on the idea that their deaf pupils are capable of acquiring a phono–graphic system, even if it is a relatively primitive one.

A number of chapters threw light on various aspects of phonological spelling. Evidence was produced as to when children begin using phonological spelling. Huxford, Terrell & Bradley (Chapter 9) suggest at about age four, Ellis & Cataldo (Chapter 7) at between four and five years, and Goulandris (Chapter 8) at about 5.5 years. The precise age will, of course depend on other factors such as teaching method, underlying ability (precocious or backward) and social class. In a different vein, Goulandris provided evidence to suggest that non-word spelling ability in young children predicts reading and spelling ability a year later. On yet another theme Taylor & Martlew (Chapter 10) and Sterling & Seed (Chapter 16) looked at the components of phonological spelling. Taylor & Martlew focused firstly on the phonology of the process, suggesting that some of their children's errors were the product of a failure to discriminate between vowel sounds, and secondly on the child's knowledge of phoneme–grapheme correspondences, providing support for Barry & Seymour's (1988) thesis that sound–spelling contingency predicts the correspondences that will be produced. Sterling & Seed's chapter took an analytical look at phonological spelling, arguing that it is a multi-component skill. They distinguished between the phonological processes of phonological spelling (e.g. segmentation) and correspondence

CONCLUSIONS

knowledge, and suggested that an immaturity in each of these aspects produces characteristically different errors.

Most of these chapters' research used non-word spelling as the experimental task. The results show that non-word spelling has the potential to indicate when phonological spelling begins, to predict future literacy and to diagnose weaknesses in the child's grasp of the strategy. Before its potential can be realised, however, particularly as a precise diagnostic tool, there is a *general* problem which has to be resolved.

One aspect of this is the obvious problem of how we can be sure that an error is indeed the product of phonological spelling. To some extent this reduces to the problem of defining criteria for identifying phonetic and semiphonetic errors which produce good inter-user reliability. Most investigators deal with this satisfactorily. The residual problem, however, is one of validating the connection between error type and putative source. This requires independent evidence of the source ability and demonstration of a contingent relationship between the source problem and error type. For example, to claim that misspellings of consonant clusters have specifically phonological origins it really needs to be shown that if a child has a phonological problem with clusters then he or she will produce particular kinds of error (e.g. consonant deletion), if the child hasn't a problem he or she won't. In this respect, while Sterling & Seed (and Trieman, 1985) go a considerable way to establishing the connection, they don't go far enough.

Another aspect of the general problem was identified by Pattison & Collier (Chapter 6) who argued that there is a danger that we become so preoccupied with phonological spelling that we neglect other explanations of our results. This applies particularly to spelling real words. They remind us that phonetically plausible errors are also often classifiable as visually plausible errors, a point that is rarely considered. Thus classifying **HKN** (*chicken*) and **LFT** (*elephant*) as semi-phonetic rather than lexical is, in the absence of other evidence, plausible but unjustified. They also argue that we probably get the results we do, and attribute so much of children's spelling to phonological processes, at least partly because the experimental conditions *promote* the use of phonological spelling. They showed, for example, that if the mode of presentation of to-be-spelled words is changed from oral to visual the use of phonological spelling decreases. Pattison & Collier's point is well taken, for the majority of chapters in this volume and in the literature neglect lexical spelling. Given the difficulties caused by the irregularities of English spelling this neglect is difficult to justify.

The Relationship Between Reading and Spelling

Another issue which cropped up in a number of chapters was the relationship between reading and spelling. Huxford *et al.* found a consistent difference between the ability to read non-words and the ability to spell them, with the latter being consistently superior to the former, from the point when explicit awareness was just beginning (they could identify only the first sound in the word) to the point when the children could identify all the sounds in the word and use a decoding strategy for reading test words.

Stronger support for the idea that spelling is the pacemaker for reading in the alphabetic stage came from Ellis & Cataldo (Chapter 7). They showed that spelling ability underpins the development of reading ability in the first year of school, during which time it acts as mediator for explicit phonological awareness. That is, explicit awareness governs the development of spelling ability which, in turn governs the development of reading ability. Spelling ability only ceases to govern reading ability when explicit awareness takes over direct government. This finding suggests that spelling practice, particularly with non-words, will help the development of reading and that this will occur because (phonological) spelling promotes a change in reading strategy from logographic to alphabetic.

Campbell *et al.* produced data which challenged Frith's assertion that reading and spelling are closely coupled, with only the identity of the pacemaker changing as each stage is encountered. They found that deaf spelling, relative to controls, was generally more advanced than deaf reading and that deaf spelling had a phonological component. This latter finding contrasts with evidence about deaf reading from other sources which indicate that deaf reading is generally, but not always, non-phonological. They argued that these findings, together, indicate that deaf reading and spelling, far from being closely coupled, develop along largely different paths, with spelling being phonological and reading being predominantly 'visual'. This is consistent with Bryant & Bradley's (1985) more general views on reading and spelling development. They argue that different strategies are initially used for reading (visual or global) and spelling (phonological) and that development is (partly) a process of learning to apply each strategy to both skills, i.e. to read phonologically and spell 'visually'. Thus they found (Bryant & Bradley, 1980) that beginning readers/spellers read visually and spelt phonologically but showed the potential for strategic flexibility in that they could, when pushed, read phonologically. Bryant & Bradley (1985) argue that backward readers/spellers fail to develop strategic flexibility. They found (Bryant & Bradley, 1980) that the number of words that could be spelled but not read and read but not spelled was greater for backward readers/spellers than for reading age controls. Now it might be that the deaf are like backward readers/spellers in that they fail to develop strategic flexibility. If so (and this needs to be confirmed) then one focus of remediation should be the promotion of flexibility. They must be encouraged to use both strategies (phonological and 'visual') for both skills (reading and spelling) appropriately.

Whereas other chapters were concerned with the relationship between the phonological *processes* underlying reading and spelling, Funnell (Chapter 5) focused on how they led to different amounts/kinds of spelling information being stored in memory. Using a proofreading task she showed that the information acquired when words were learned through reading was sufficient to detect correct spellings, but was not sufficient to detect misspellings, which could be detected only if the word could be correctly spelled. Funnell argued that the information acquired through reading is partial, consisting probably only of letter *identity* information, while that acquired through spelling a word is full, probably including letter *order* information. The implications of Funnell's chapter are clear. First, it confirms the intuition that the spelling information acquired through spelling is more comprehensive than that acquired through reading. Second it implies that we shouldn't expect a child to be able to detect a misspelling simply because he or she has the word stored in his or her *reading* vocabulary.

Theory

It is clear that Frith's (1985) is a highly influential theory. For some papers it provided a conceptual framework within which experiments were designed (e.g. Goulandris, Chapter 8) while for others it provided a specific hypothesis to test (e.g. Burden, Chapter 12).

Attention generally focused on Frith's alphabetic stage of development (e.g. Sterling & Seed, Chapter 16). Goulandris, however, tackled the important issue of the developmental relationship between phonological and lexical spelling. She looked at the degree to which the ability to apply the alphabetic principle predicts later literacy and argued that the acquisitions of the alphabetic stage provide a framework for the acquisition of word-specific knowledge. This proposed connection between the alphabetic and orthographic stages is pertinent to the more general issue of whether the units which become active during the orthographic stage (e.g. spelling patterns, morphemic strings such as **-ED**) develop (partly) out of phonological units acquired during the alphabetic stage (e.g. consonant clusters, syllables, morphemic units). Although neither Morton (1989) nor Frith (1985) are very clear about the development of orthographic units, the proposal is consistent with what they have to say, because to argue that orthographic units *develop* partly from phonological units is not to deny that they eventually function as abstract, non-phonological units. Indeed it is difficult to see why the mechanisms responsible for development of the orthographic stage should be impervious to the huge body of phono–graphic knowledge built up during the alphabetic stage.

Frith's theory also provides explanations for a number of developmental disorders of literacy. Her argument is that disorders occur when a child locks into a given stage of development, after which normal development is not possible. Burden's chapter addressed the performance of Type B spellers, whose problem (poor spelling and allegedly good reading) is explained by Frith in terms of the differential developmental of reading and spelling ability, with spelling following reading into the orthographic stage but never progressing beyond the weak orthographic stage. Burden's careful probing of their reading ability revealed that Type B spellers are not good readers and are, in fact, mildly dyslexic. Apart from providing a more parsimonious explanation of the Type B phenomenon, Burden's paper also reveals spelling to be a more sensitive indicator of abnormality than reading because while Type B spellers' phonological deficit is not evident in their reading unless tested very carefully, it is immediately evident in their spelling. This is probably because poor reading can be obscured by the use of compensatory strategies in a way that poor spelling can't be.

What contribution then do the papers reported here make to an evaluation of Frith's theory? First, although Goswami & Bryant's (1990) charge that there is no evidence for logographic spelling is blunted by Seymour's evidence (that pre-alphabetic children can spell some words), there is currently insufficient evidence to support the idea of a logographic *stage* of spelling development, principally because the notion of a stage suggests systematic and extensive behaviour of a particular kind. Turning to the alphabetic stage, the evidence reported here indicates quite clearly that phonological spelling is a reality and that phonological spelling precedes and promotes phonological reading, i.e. spelling is the pacemaker for reading. This latter finding seems to contradict Campbell *et al.*'s data (and Bryant & Bradley's (1985) argument) which suggest that reading and spelling are not *necessarily* coupled (in the way Frith (1985) suggests). The two positions are not, however, incompatible if we allow that phonological spelling promotes phonological reading by alerting the child to the fact that the priciples of the strategy they use for spelling can also be applied to reading.

While Frith's is a theory of development, dual process theory is a model of performance. It is clear from the chapter by Barry (Chapter 4) and the review by Seymour (Chapter 3) that dual process theory is under pressure. Part of this pressure comes from the notion of sound–spelling contingency, which blurs the distinction between regular and irregular words, one of the foundations of dual process theory (the other is the word/non-word distinction). The pressure comes principally, however, from the phenomenon of spelling by analogy (priming), in which prior exposure to a real word influences the spelling of a non-word, something which should not occur if the two sets of processes are separate and independent. Barry argues that priming phenomena can be dealt with by asssuming that the two sets of processes, although independent, interact. Thus the prior occurrence of a real word primes the sound–spelling contingency in that word so that when a non-word with the same sound has to be spelt the correspondence that has been primed has its probability of production incremented. The model is thus modified, but essentially intact. On the other hand, Seymour is clearly more generally dissatisfied with the model and prefers to replace it with one in which there is one set of processes (the literagraphic lexicon — a single process theory) which is subject to at least two influences, one lexical and one to do with sound–spelling correspondences. As Seymour pointed out, it is too early to decide between modified versions of the theory and various alternatives.

Now, even though Morton (1989) has linked Frith's model with dual process theory, showing how the developmental sequence can lead to the two sets of independent processes assumed by dual process theory the fact that the latter has to be modified or even abandoned does not really affect Frith. Seymour argues that a modification to Frith's theory, which would assume that the orthographic stage develops on phonological foundations laid in the alphabetic stage (I would argue that it already does so), permits compatibility with the literagraphic lexicon, his version of single process theory. This, of course, can deal with the priming data. In short, decisions about Frith's model need only be made on the basis of direct evidence, not on the basis of the current status of dual process theory.

Educational Practice

It is a source of regret that only a very few papers specifically about the teaching of spelling were submitted to the conference. Nevertheless, we can draw a few useful generalisations from those that were submitted, bearing in mind the danger that we may apply what seem to be good ideas before they have been properly evaluated.

Phonological awareness has been a recurrent theme, and a number of papers concluded by advocating the training of phonological awareness skills. This is consistent with the excellent discussions of the effects of awareness training provided by Bryant & Bradley (1985) and Goswami & Bryant (1990). It seems generally agreed that children like playing word games, especially those involving rhyme, and the consensus is that they should be encouraged to play as many of these as possible as early as possible. While helpful this suggestion doesn't go far enough because this kind of informal approach is likely to be less potent than a structured programme. The key to developing a structured programme is probably the implicit/explicit dimension. What is needed is a scaling of awareness tasks, with different word games being identified with the level of awareness they require, so that the child's level of awareness can first be determined, and then systematically trained. Intuitively, it seems likely that judging rhyme requires less awareness than identifying embedded sounds and that this requires less awareness than segmenting into phonemes, which in turn, requires less than transposing phonemes. Until such a (validated) classification of awareness tasks is produced phonological awareness training will tend to have the diffuse qualities of a shotgun rather than the focused potency of a rifle.

Some of the papers also promoted 'phonics' training, an idea which has a long history in education. For a well-written discussion of the rationale, efficacy and procedures of phonics teaching, see Bryant & Bradley (1985). For the purposes of this volume a few generalisations, drawn partly from their text, will suffice. One of the problems with phonics programmes is that they vary quite considerably, and this, together with the fact that it is very difficult to evaluate phonics programmes properly because of practical difficulties (see Bryant & Bradley, 1985), means that we don't have cast iron evidence that they work. Nevertheless, the evidence (a good example is Gittelman & Feingold, 1983) does indicate that they are effective. All phonics programmes seem to have two essential components, promoting the ability to identify the phonemes in a word and promoting the learning of the relationships between phonemes and graphemes. The first of these components is clearly related to phonological awareness training, and this raises the question of whether a phonics programme is better than the comparable phonological awareness programme. The evidence (Bradley & Bryant, 1985) indicates that it is, and that the reason for this lies in the requirement that sounds be linked to letters. This, of course, does not mean that phonics programmes should replace awareness programmes but that the sound–letter connection is an important one that has to be introduced when the child's awareness is sufficiently advanced to be receptive to it. To promote the development of both phonological skills and phono–graphic relationships Bradley & Bryant (1985) devised a simple programme in which the child is encouraged to realise that words like **PIG, BIG, DIG, FIG** etc. have a common sound (/**Ig**/) and common letters (**-IG**), from which it can be deduced that /**Ig**/ = [**IG**].

A task related closely to phonics training is non-word spelling. Non-words, constructed according to the rules of English phonology, are presented to the child who is then required to spell them. While there are a number of problems which have to be solved, particularly before it can be used as a precise diagnostic tool, it is a task which calls on all the components of phonological spelling and so can be used as a general indicator of a child's ability (see Sterling & Seed, Chapter 16 this volume). Its use can therefore be empirically justified. For example, given that phonological processing ability is strongly associated with developmental dyslexia (Snowling, Stackhouse & Rack, 1986) and given that phonological spelling requires phonological processing ability, it follows that non-word spelling can serve as a preliminary diagnostic for severe disorders of literacy. Also if we assume that non-word spelling is related to non-word reading then we can justify its use on the grounds that Bryant & Impey (1986) found non-word reading ability to be the best differentiator of dyslexics from reading age controls. In general, non-word spelling ability is best regarded as an easily administered screening task, to be followed up with tests of phonological awareness and correspondence knowledge. Assuming that a structured assessment programme is better than an unstructured one, its value would be particularly enhanced if based on the classification system being devised by Seymour (reported in Chapter 3 in this volume).

Non-word spelling may also have value as part of a training programme (but see Goulandris' chapter (Chapter 8) for arguments against this), again because it exercises all the components of phonological spelling, e.g. segmentation, correspondence knowledge. Furthermore the evidence indicates that practising spelling will improve not just spelling ability but also reading ability (Ellis & Cataldo, Chapter 7). What is clear from our earlier discussion is that a carefully structured programme is likely to be more effective than an unstructured programme. Such a programme is Seymour's (devised for reading, but the principles stand). While it is likely to be some time before the results can be evaluated, the work he and his colleagues report provides an excellent model of the form that training programmes might take. The demands made on the child are never excessive and the task seemingly always within their capabilities. In addition, the words they are asked to spell are presented not in a haphazard way but systematically so that there is a layered increase in complexity with relationships between types of words always being maximally evident. Unfortunately it may be some time before their programme is validated and available in user-friendly form for spelling.

While the majority of chapters recommended a variety of interventions that promote the development of phonological awareness and phono–graphic knowledge there was one that did not. Peters' chapter (Chapter 13) instead focused on the idea that spelling should be taught by concentrating on its visuo-motor aspects (a fuller account of her views are to be found in Peters, 1985). The first part of her thesis was that letter sequences have various probabilities of occurrence and that sequences such as **PER** or **EPH**, though often idiosyncratic when tied to the sounds they spell, form coherent units by virtue of their frequency of occurrence. The second part of her argument is that these letter sequences are quintessentially *visual,* because writing is a visual medium, and *motor,* because writing is also a motor act. Consequently children become good spellers by concentrating on the visual aspects of spelling and by (simultaneously) practising the writing of these sequences until they become unified motor acts. Spelling **THE** is a good example of such a motor act: it occurs so often that the speller eventually learns to write it automatically, with scarcely a thought for the component letters involved. Whilst stressing the importance of visuo-motor aspects of spelling Peters does not discount the importance of the phonological component (personal communication). She sees phonological ability as an essential precursor; as a necessary, but not sufficient condition for good spelling. Phonological awareness, she suggests, can be seen as signalling the need for intervening with visuo-motor teaching.

Peters' ideas come from the tradition of multi-sensory methods which are based on the assumption that reading and, particularly, spelling are best learned by co-ordinating the different sensory experiences involved in performing them. Consider, for example, the spelling of **CAT**, which consists of three letters, each of which is associated with a sound and has a name, a visual shape, a tactile shape, and a motor shape. When combined these components become associated with the sound of the word, with its visual appearance and with the motor movements required to spell it. Learning to spell **CAT** is therefore best achieved by co-ordinating the sensory experiences of each of the components and of the sequence as a whole. A fuller discussion of the theory, a teaching programme and a history of multi-sensory methods is to be found in Bryant & Bradley (1985).

The implications of Funnell's (Chapter 5) work are as simple as they are important. She has shown that asking a child to proofread his or her own work is likely to be only partially successful because while the child will be capable of identifying errors due to 'carelessness' he or she will not be able to identify misspellings which are the product of his/her ignorance of the spelling. The child has to know how to spell the word if he or she is to be capable of detecting misspellings of it. A corollary of Funnell's work is the find-

CONCLUSIONS

ing that learning a word so that it becomes part of the reading vocabulary will not help with knowing its spelling. Reading practice will not help the child's spelling very much. Spelling practice is required.

Finally, it is clear that edcucational practice is becoming increasingly computer oriented. Interactive systems, in which the child communicates with the computer, provide the child with guidance but also allows him or her to be actively involved in the learning process. It is the next best thing to individual attention from a teacher. Nicolson, Pickering & Fawcett showed (Chapter 15) that it is possible to produce a package which has both educational value and which is fun to use. The latter point is particularly important for backward readers who, one suspects, find their problem both embarrassing and a source of frustration. Any system that allows them to work on their area of difficulty in their own time and without the social stigma of constant attention from the teacher is to be welcomed. With respect to the educational value of such programs, it is clear that both versions of the program are effective and that they can be used in tandem: a rule-based version of such a program is ideal for learning spelling generalisations (as well as idiosyncrasies) while a mastery version can be used to complement this by practising on words of a similar type. Particularly enouraging is the fact that the effects of learning generalised and improved spelling on words that hadn't been targeted.

In summary, we can list the generalisations that have emerged from this volume:

1. Phonological awareness training promotes good spelling — use word games that involve rhyming judgements, breaking the *sounds* of words up in various ways, and adding, omitting or transposing phonemes.
2. Phonics training promotes good spelling (e.g. see 'Improving phonological skills', in Bryant & Bradley, 1985).
3. Non-word spelling practice promotes good spelling, preferably as part of a systematic programme such as that being devised by Seymour (but see Goulandris, this volume).
4. Multi-sensory methods promote good spelling (e.g. see 'Simultaneous oral spelling', in Bryant & Bradley, 1985).
5. Proofreading is of dubious value if its purpose is for the child to detect misspellings of words he or she can't spell.
6. Spelling practice, as opposed to reading practice, promotes good spelling.
7. Interactive computer programs such as SelfSpell are effective in enhancing both performance and motivation.

Finally, it is a source of regret that we have not been able to say more about the learning and teaching of non-phonological spelling. Given the problems caused by the *irregularities* of English spelling this is an unjustifiable neglect on the part of most researchers in the psychology of spelling.

References

BARRY, C. and SEYMOUR, P. H. K. 1988, Lexical priming and sound-to-spelling contingency effects in non-word spelling. *Quarterly Journal of Experimental Psychology* 40A, 5–40.

BRADLEY, L. and BRYANT, P. E. 1985, *Rhyme and Reason in Reading and Spelling* (International Academy for Research in Learning Difficulties Monograph Series, No. 1). Ann Arbor: The University of Michigan Press.

BRYANT, P. E. and BRADLEY, L. 1980, Why children sometimes write words which they do not read. In U. FRITH (ed.) *Cognitive Processes in Spelling*. London: Academic Press.

—— 1985, *Children's Reading Problems*. Oxford: Basil Blackwell.

BRYANT, P. E. and IMPEY, L. 1986, The similarities between normal children and dyslexic adults and children. *Cognition* 24, 121–37.

CAMPBELL, R. 1983, Writing nonwords to dictation. *Brain & Language* 19, 153–78.

FRITH, U. 1985, Beneath the surface of developmental dyslexia. In K. PATTERSON, J. C. MARSHALL and M. COLTHEART (eds) *Surface Dyslexia*. London: Lawrence Erlbaum.

GITTELMAN, R. and FEINGOLD, I. 1983, Children with reading disorders — I: Efficacy of reading remediation. *Journal of Child Psychology and Psychiatry* 24, 167–92.

GOSWAMI, U. 1988, Children's use of analogy in learning to spell. *British Journal of Developmental Psychology* 6, 21–33.

GOSWAMI, U. and BRYANT, P. E. 1990, *Phonological Skills and Learning to Read*. London: Lawrence Erlbaum.

MARSH, G., FRIEDMAN, M. P., WELCH, V. and DESEBERG, P. 1980, The development of strategies in spelling. In U. FRITH (ed.) *Cognitive Processes in Spelling*. London: Academic Press.

MORTON, J. 1989, An information processing account of reading acquisition. In A. M. GALABURDA (ed.) *From Reading to Neurons*. Cambridge, Mass.: MIT Press.

PETERS, M. L. 1985, *Spelling: Caught or Taught? A New Look*. London: Routledge and Kegan Paul.

READ, C. 1986, *Children's Creative Spelling*. London: Routledge and Kegan Paul.

SNOWLING, M. J., STACKHOUSE, J. and RACK, J. 1986, Phonological dyslexia and dysgraphia – a developmental analysis. *Cognitive Neuropsychology* 3, 309–39.

TREIMAN, R. 1985, Phonemic analysis, spelling, and reading. In T. H. CARR (ed.) *The Development of Reading Skills*. New Directions for Child Development, no. 27. San Francisco: Josey-Bass.

Index

Alphabet, augmented 23
Alphabetic spelling 55, 56, 144-7, 154-5
  (see also Assembled spelling;
  Phonological spelling)
— in the deaf 182, 185-6, 193, 195
— and later literacy 118
— practical implications of 156
— in very young children 117
Alphabetic stage of development 7
Alphabetic strategy (see Alphabetic
  spelling)
Analytical focus 35, 37
Anecdotal accounts 26
Assembled route (see Assembled
  spelling)
Assembled spelling 71 (see also Phonological spelling; Alphabetic spelling)
— Barry & Seymour model 76
— relationship to lexical spelling 76, 84
Assessing spelling 64, 65, 66, 227 (see
  also Measuring spelling)
Assessment, word lists for 44

Bullock Report 25, 26

Careful pronunciation 36
Comparative literacy studies 18
Compatibility 27
Correct spelling detection 46, 47, 87,
  89-97 (see also Proof reading)
Cox committee 19, 20
Cut Spelling 26, 27

Database for test materials 237-248
Damage to children's intellect 25
Deaf spelling 101, 181, 182, 190, 194-197
Deep orthography 78
Developmental phonological dyslexia
  189, 201
Digraphs 23, 39
Double consonant rule 30, 39-41
Dual foundation model database 239-248

Dual process theory 58, 59, 218 (see
  also Dual route theory)
Dual route theory 4, 5, 43, 45, 50, 51,
  71-74, 144, 145, 269-71, 288- 289
Dysgraphia 51, 52
— acquired 5, 72
— acquired lexical 51, 270-1
— acquired phonological 72, 269
Dyslexia 10-11, 51

Elitism 36
English orthography 1-3, 52, 168, 169,
  221, 282-283
— analytical focus of 35, 36, 37
— lexical nature of 2
— modernisation of 15
— multiple analytical focus of 16
— and phonetic features 37-39
— regularity of 3
English spelling 18, 19 (see also English orthography)
Error classification 273
Evolution of spelling 27
Examination candidates 20

Fonotypy 21, 22
Frith's theory 6-7, 55-56, 192, 195, 250,
  266, 287-289

Geminate 40
Grammar 32, 34
Grapheme 31, 37
Graphology 33
Graphotactic rules 16, 17, 30, 36, 39-42

History of English teaching 18
Homonym 31
Homophone 35
HyperCard 250-67

Iconic 40, 42
Inconsistencies, irregularities 19, 20
Initial Teaching Alphabet 15, 21-26
Interactive computer software, in education 293

Invented spellings 118, 146, 147, 160-161, 170
— practical implications of 119, 165

Kingman Report 19

Learning new spellings 117, 144-146
Letter naming 135
Levels of language 32, 33, 34
Lexeme 40
Lexical priming 59, 60
— in Italian and Welsh 45, 46
— of nonwords
   in English 75-78, 82-84
   in Italian 79, 80
   in Welsh 81, 82
Lexical route 5, 71, 78, 144 (see also Lexical spelling)
Lexical spelling 59, 269-70 (see also Lexical route)
Lexicon 32, 37
Linguistic level 31
LISREL 126
Literacy First, Spelling Second 21, 22
Literagraphic lexicon 56, 57
Logographic
— stage of development 6
— strategy 52, 55, 56
Longitudinal study 147-54, 161-164
— of spelling errors 128-33
— of spelling, phonological awareness and reading 124-8
Look-and-say 136-7

Measuring spelling ability 48, 102, 103, 104, 106, 108-111 (see also Assessing spelling)
Misspelling detection 87, 292 (see also Proof reading)
— and Frith's theory 88, 96-97
— by a good reader-good speller 89-92
— by a poor reader-poor speller 92-94
— of familiar and unfamiliar words 94
— and reading and spelling knowledge 46, 47, 94-97
Models of spelling 61, 62
Morpheme 31, 37
Morpho-lexical 41
Morphology 32
Morphophonemic scripts 53
Multiple spellings 54

Naming, effects of regularity and frequency on Type A and Type B spellers 204-7
National Curriculum 20, 101, 102, 159, 222, 223
New alphabet 27
New spelling 22
Non-phonetic spelling errors 150, 152
Nonword
— naming 208
— reading 162-3
— spelling 151-3, 162-3, 207, 275-278
   assessing 291
   diagnostic tool 219, 280
   training 291

Ormulum 39
Orthographic
— lists 216, 217, 232
— representations 145
— stage of development 7-8
— strategy 55, 56
Orthographical competence 35, 36
Orthographic lexicon
— dual foundation model 216, 227, 228
— models of 225, 235-236
— unidimensional model of 216, 225, 226
Orthographies
— analytical focus of 35
— as analyses of language 31
— principle underlying 30, 31, 33
— as representations of language levels 16, 31, 32
— shallow 79

Phoneme 31, 37
Phoneme-grapheme correspondences 1, 2
Phonemic analysis 21, 36, 37
Phonetic features 16, 17, 30, 32, 36, 37, 42
— alveolar 37
— approximant 37
— consonant 37, 39-41
— fricative 37, 39
— lax 37, 39
— lip-rounding 38
— lip-spreading 38
— nasal 38
— palatalisation 38-9

INDEX 297

— plosive 38
— stress 41
— tense 37, 39
— voiced 37
— vowel 37, 39, 41
Phonetic judgements 170, 176
Phonetic spelling errors 150, 152, 275, 276, 278, 279
Phonics 19, 21
— training 135-8, 290
Phonographic writing systems 31, 52
Phonological awareness 8-9, 125-126, 272
— development of 120, 121
— as function of development and phoneme position 132-3
— and literacy 283, 284
— and reading and spelling 115, 116
— relationship to reading and spelling 122, 123, 127-8, 133-4, 138
— training 136, 138, 219, 279, 290
Phonological complexity 275-7
Phonological route (see Phonological spelling)
Phonological skills
— in the deaf 181, 186-188, 196
— in reading and spelling 100, 101
— verbal memory, reading and spelling 186
Phonological spelling 4, 169-170, 270-1, 284 (see also Alphabetic spelling; Assembled spelling)
— components and spelling errors 219
— correspondence knowledge component 272-3, 277-8
— and the deaf 284
— development of 119, 120, 175-178
— and error classification 285
— methodological issues 48
— phonological component of 271-2
— relationship with phonological reading 119, 161-5
— teaching of 178-9
Phonology 33
Private spelling 35
Proof reading 46-47, 87-98 (see also Correct spelling detection; Misspelling detection)
Prosodic 33, 37

Real word spelling 274-5

Received pronunciation (RP) 36
Relationship between reading and spelling 200, 201

Scripts
— alphabetic 31
— charactery 35
— featural 33, 37
— syllabic 33
SelfSpell 250-67
Semantics 32, 33, 37
Semology 39
Shorthand 21
Simplified Spelling Society 22, 23, 26
Sound-spelling contingency 3, 60, 61
Sound-spelling knowledge, role in learning new spellings 144-6
— and development of the alphabetic principle 123
— effects of regularity and frequency on Type A and Type B spellers 204-7
— regular and irregular words 148, 149, 150
— relationship to phonological awareness and reading 123, 127-8, 133-4, 138
— relationship to reading 9, 57, 192, 196-7, 286, 287
— stages of 129
— as a visuo-motor activity 215, 220-223
Spelling by analogy 5-6
Spelling consonant clusters 275-7
Spelling development, models 43, 44
Spelling errors
— analysis of 104-106, 111
— changes 116
— classification of 48, 130, 131
— as function of development 132
— origins 218, 219, 268, 278-279
— orthographic scoring 107
— phonological scoring 107
— regularisation 206
— transcoding 207, 208
— visual scoring 107, 206
Spelling patterns 215, 229
Spelling problems
— dyslexia 10-11
— generally backward readers 10
— physical origins 9

Spelling reform 27, 28, 30, 36
Standard English orthography (SEO) 30ff
Standard pronounciation 27
Sub-lexical route 144 (see also Assembled spelling)
Synthesised speech 250-1

Teaching dyslexics using SelfSpell 217-218, 251, 252, 257-265
Teaching spelling 44, 66, 67, 157, 217, 221
— characteristics of procedures 217
— interactive software 251, 253
— properties of exercises 223-4
— via regularised spelling systems 15, 21-23

Test materials, foundation processes 238, 239
Transcription 33
Type A spellers 201, 202
Type B spellers 87, 88, 182-184, 200-203, 208-211

Unidimensional model database 237, 238

Verbal memory, in the deaf 188
Visuo-motor spelling, training 292
Vowel correspondence knowledge, adults versus children 120, 173-175

Wording 32, 33, 37
Writing systems 52, 53